Fodor's

E X P L O R I N G

AUSTRALIA

FODOR'S TRAVEL PUBLICATIONS, INC.

NEW YORK • TORONTO • LONDON • SYDNEY • AUCKLAND

Copyright © 1996 by The Automobile Association.
Maps copyright © 1996 by The Automobile Association.

All rights reserved under International and Pan-American Copyright conventions. Distributed by Random House, Inc., New York. No maps, illustrations, or other portions of this book may be reproduced in any form without written permission from the publishers.

Published in the United States by Fodor's Travel Publications, Inc.
Published in the United Kingdom by AA Publishing.

Fodor's and Fodor's Exploring Guides are registered trademarks of Fodor's Travel Publications, Inc.

ISBN 0-679-03003-4
Second Edition

Fodor's Exploring Australia

Author: **Michael Ivory**
Series Adviser: **Ingrid Morgan**
Joint Series Editor: **Susi Bailey**
Revisions Editor: **Donna Dailey**
Cartography: **The Automobile Association**
Cover Design: **Louise Fili, Fabrizio La Rocca**
Front Cover Silhouette: **M. Berge/Photographers/ Aspen**

Special Sales

MANUFACTURED IN ITALY
10 9 8 7 6 5 4 3 2

After studying modern languages at Oxford, Michael Ivory became certified as a landscape architect and town planner and is now a freelance lecturer and travel writer. His books include *Essential Hungary*, *Essential Czech Republic*, and parts of *Exploring Germany* and *Exploring France*.

Sydney Harbour Bridge and Opera House

How to use this book

This book is divided into five main sections:

❏ Section 1: *Australia Is*
Discusses aspects of life and living today, from landscape to culture.

❏ Section 2: *Australia Was*
Places the country in its historical context and explores those past events whose influences are felt to this day.

❏ Section 3: *A to Z Section*
Breaks down the country into regional chapters, and covers places to visit, including walks and drives. Within this section fall the Focus-on articles, which consider a variety of subjects in greater detail.

❏ Section 4: *Travel Facts*
Contains the strictly practical information vital for a successful trip.

❏ Section 5
Hotels and Restaurants
Lists recommended establishments throughout Australia, giving a brief summary of their attractions.

How to use the star rating
Most of the places described in this book have been given a separate rating:

▶▶▶ **Do not miss**

▶▶ **Highly recommended**

▶ **Worth seeing**

Not essential to see

Map references
To make each particular location easier to find, every main entry in this book has a map reference to the right of its name. This comprises a number, followed by a letter, followed by another number, such as 176B3. The first number (176) refers to the page on which the map can be found, the letter (B) and the second number (3) pinpoint the square in which the main entry is located. The maps on the inside front cover and inside back cover are referred to as IFC and IBC respectively.

Contents

*Above: Palm Valley, Finke Gorge
National Park
Left: Yachts moored in Hobart*

Quick reference

This quick-reference guide highlights the features of the book you will use most often: the maps; the introductory features; the Focus-on articles; the walks and the drives.

Bright flowers of the bottle brush

My Australia

by Michele Field

Michele Field
Michele Field has been a consultant to the Australia Council, the literary editor of *The Sydney Morning Herald*, a radio broadcaster for the Australian Broadcasting Commission, and a teacher. At the moment she writes a column in *The Australian* newspaper and freelances for many publications in Australia and abroad.

8

Australia is like a movie starlet who always looks lovely in her pictures and has never experienced the wars and strikes that have "scarred" the faces of other nations. It is years before newcomers to the country discard the two-dimensional, ad-man's idea of incessant golden sunsets, rosy dawns and sloping surf. When they do finally concede that Australia has its own share of bad taste, bald men and soggy salads, they finally belong.

My Australia is the city life. The "bush" needs special equipment to conquer, it needs a "what will be, will be" attitude to cope with the rural supermarkets, and it requires a cavalier attitude towards time and distance. Most Australians are fonder of beaches and cities (the cities are built close to the best beaches) than of Australia's dry plains.

What I love about Australia is that it is skin deep. It laughs easily, follows fashions, and gives its schoolchildren a respect for the present instead of the past. When my daughter was about ten she tried to explain to her teacher that she was a "born pessimist." He made it quite clear that as she was born in Australia she *couldn't* be a pessimist. Thank God she believed him.

My Australia

by Brian Matthews

Brian Matthews
Brian Matthews is a university professor and award-winning writer of biography, fiction and popular culture essays. At present, he is head of The Menzies Centre for Australian Studies at the University of London. In December 1995 he will return to Australia where he teaches at Flinders University and has his home in the Mount Lofty Ranges.

The endlessly unraveling vastness of it; the shy, understated beauty of this most ancient wilderness; the huge, dramatic spaces beneath a dispassionate brush-stroke of blazing blue; the featureless ridges, each one rippling in the silent desert heat. This is the Australia that tested, reduced and often defeated the explorers; the Australia through which the Aborigines moved safely and with impassive confidence along invisible song lines; the landscape that now delights and awes the more intrepid traveler; and that white Australians, regardless of whether they've ever seen it or not, know and fear as their imagination's home.

I too carry that vision in my head. But it is the backdrop to "my Australia" which is a necessarily smaller, more personal place. *That* country—the one that sustains and haunts me—is a place real and in the present, yet colored and populated fleetingly by the past. It is in the smoky light of a Melbourne winter evening and the polyglot voices of the inner suburbs where I grew up; it is in the easygoing tolerance of the sports-mad crowds; and it is in the great sweep of impossibly golden beaches. It is the Australia in whose scattered settlements one still hears the taciturn, nasal rhythms of the world's most ironic accent unselfconsciously exploited by the most deadpan of humorists.

Partly an Australia of the imagination, perhaps, but still quite real enough to rediscover, to go back to always...

AUSTRALIA IS

Landscape

Australia occupies a lonely place on the globe. Apart from the frozen Antarctic, it is the only continent to lie wholly within the southern hemisphere; though Papua New Guinea is only just over the horizon on the far side of the shallow Timor Sea, the Asian mainland at Singapore is nearly 1,865 miles distant, and New Zealand is more than 1,240 miles across the Tasman Sea.

Girded by nearly 23,000 miles of coastline, the "island continent" has a simple threefold structure.

The Western Plateau Almost two-thirds of the land surface belongs to the Western Plateau, a vast and arid tableland covering most of Western Australia, South Australia, the Northern Territory and part of Queensland. Mostly flat and low-lying, it is interrupted by spectacular individual features like Ayers Rock

Mount Warning National Park, New South Wales

and the Olgas, by rocky strongholds like the Kimberley and Arnhem Land, and by rugged ridges like those of the MacDonnell, Flinders and Hamersley Ranges.

The plateau is an ancient land whose fertility was leached away by rains that fell millions of years ago, leaving arid wastes with evocative names like the Nullarbor Plain or Sturt's Stony Desert. Similarly, winds that ceased to blow long ago left achingly repetitive patterns of sand dunes. Except in the tropics, rainfall is not only minimal but also irregular; none may fall for years, then sudden downpours will fill the normally vacant river beds, only to peter out in the great salt lakes.

Much of the area is uninhabited or very thinly settled, with a population measured in hundreds of square miles per person. Only to the west of the Darling Ranges, on the relatively fertile coastal plains around the great city of Perth, are there extensive farmlands and a network of settlements linked by roads and railroads. Elsewhere, settlements exist in isolation as ports, mining towns and staging posts along an interminable highway, or, increasingly, as centers for Outback tourism.

The Great Dividing Range Running down the whole of Australia's eastern coastline from Cape York in the far north to the hills and highlands of New South Wales and Victoria in the south, the Great Dividing Range leaps Bass Strait to reappear in the mountains of Tasmania. It is here that the continent's highest peaks are found: Mount Kosciusko in New South Wales (7,316 feet), Mount

Bogong in Victoria (6,516 feet) and Mount Ossa (5,305 feet) in Tasmania.

However, much of the area is not made up of mountains but instead of high plateaus, from which rivers run eastward across the coastal plain. The bulk of the country's population lives here, clustering for the most part in the metropolitan areas around the great coastal state capitals of Sydney (New South Wales), Melbourne (Victoria), Adelaide (South Australia) and Brisbane (Queensland). Rural settlement is quite dense in the valleys between the uplands and all along the fertile strip extending into the tropics along the Queensland coast. The only inland city of any size is Canberra, the artificially implanted federal capital.

Central Eastern Lowlands Between these two great geographical divisions run the Central Eastern Lowlands, sloping down gradually from the east towards the interior. A series of broad basins succeed one another, from the southern rim of the Gulf of Carpentaria through Queensland's Channel Country to the area drained by the country's greatest river system, the Murray/ Darling/Murrumbidgee. Here in the Outback, grazing animals outnumber people by a factor of several hundred to one, and rural life depends as much on unreliable rainfall as on the state of world markets. Mineral wealth has created a small number of towns like Broken Hill and Mount Isa, linked by interminably long roads and railroads to the coast.

South Australian opals

❏ In view of its size, the world's driest continent after Antarctica has a surprisingly small range of climates. The highest rainfall is in the tropical or subtropical north, where temperatures stay high all year round (84°F in summer and 75°F in winter). Unlike the north, where the rain falls during the summer, temperate southern Australia experiences its highest rainfall in winter and spring, and there is more variation in average temperatures (75°F in summer to 50°F in winter when snow falls on the higher peaks). Much of the interior is arid, with little rain (none at all in some years), and temperatures here soar to scorching heights—a maximum of 127½°F was recorded at Cloncurry in Queensland in 1889—although nights can be cold. ❏

11

The uniqueness of Australia's plants and animals is the result of the continent's 40 million years of isolation from the rest of the world. Over this long period, both fauna and flora evolved in response to local conditions quite independently of developments elsewhere, resulting in the array of strange creatures and plants that so surprised and delighted Joseph Banks as he accompanied Captain Cook aboard the *Endeavour* in 1770. Despite subsequent development that had little regard for environmental side effects, Australia was quick to create national parks, some 2,000 of which await today's visitor.

12

Forests The richest habitat in Australia is that of the rain forest. Tropical rain forest is best seen in northern Queensland (see page 222), but also lies in parts of the northern coastlands in the Northern Territory and Western Australia where rainfall is sufficient. Temperate rain forest, of equal fascination and beauty, spreads over much of the wild country of southwestern Tasmania. This is the domain of the **southern beech** and of one of the longest-lived trees on earth, the **Huon pine**.

Great forests still cloak some of the less accessible areas of the southeast and southwest, but all of Australia's woodland has suffered grievously at the hands of the timbercutters. The majority of the country's trees are variations on the theme of **eucalyptus** (also referred to as eucalypts and gum trees); they include some of the tallest trees on earth, like the mountain ash of the Victorian coastal forests or the karri of southwestern Western Australia.

Scrubland and desert Away from the coast, the pioneers found impenetrable **mallee** (a dense scrub of low-growing eucalyptus) or more open, park-like woodland. Most of these original plant communities have been cleared for grazing land, while native grasses and herbs have given way to exotic, high-yielding varieties. The desert is perhaps the most intriguing

The rainbow lorikeet

of all Australian ecosystems, where **saltbush, spinifex** and the occasional **desert oak** provide shelter for creatures like scorpions and spiders, themselves food for snakes, lizards and **goannas**. The seeds of many small plants lie in wait for the sparse rain, flowering spectacularly when thus nourished.

From pouches to platypuses Of all the marsupials that inhabit the island continent, the macropods—**kangaroos** and **wallabies**—seem to need little introduction, having long been

familiar as one of the country's best-known emblems. But there's a whole world of roos and wallabies out there; in addition to the red kangaroo (reaching over 6 feet), there are some 50 other varieties, ranging from the equally large Forester kangaroos to the quokkas (mistaken for rats by early explorers) and brush-tailed bettongs. Kangaroos live in most parts of the country, even occasionally on the fringe of towns.

After the kangaroo, it is the endearing **koala** that every visitor wants to see and, if possible, hug. Koalas spend most of their time asleep and the rest chewing on the leaves of certain eucalypts. The population is recovering after being hunted for its fur, but it is still subject to disease and loss of habitat. As a result, you're more likely to see them in one of the country's excellent wildlife parks than in the wild alongside of **wombats**, burrowing marsupials, and **possums**, some of which are able to glide from tree to tree thanks to their flight membrane.

Another creature that you are more likely to see in an artificial environment is the **platypus**. This shy, egg-laying mammal with its soft

The kangaroo—one of Australia's best-known marsupials

bill was thought to be a hoax when a specimen was first sent to Britain for examination. The spiny anteater, or **echidna**, is less timid, being well defended by its ability to burrow below ground or present an attacker with its array of sharp spines.

National parks Australia declared its first national park (**Royal National Park**) as early as 1879. Today more than 2,000 such areas are protected and managed in order to conserve their natural beauty, protect their wildlife, and make them accessible to visitors. The outstanding quality and global importance of the country's natural heritage has also been recognized by the designation of no fewer than nine World Heritage Areas. Visitors to national parks will generally find a high standard of management in evidence, with good information services and lots of walking trails created to encourage people to explore the landscape. Always seek the advice of wardens and rangers if you are at all unfamiliar with local conditions.

It's quite possible you'll meet a stereo-typical Australian male while Down Under. You've probably imagined him already: tall, sunburned, probably blond and blue-eyed, short on words but long on ability to sink the stubbies (get drunk) with his mates, unhurried, an enemy of pretentiousness, and unreconstructed in his male chauvinism. The stereotype exists, of course, but today's Australians are much less easy to categorize.

Early immigrants The country's population is far more diverse than it was in the not-too-distant past. A few non-British found their way here in the early days of the colony, among them a solitary Austro-Hungarian transported for stealing a length of Nottingham lace. But the convicts were overwhelmingly Anglo-Celtic—in other words, English, Scottish, Welsh and Irish (their jailers were mostly English). And indeed, until quite recently, Australia stayed more British than Britain, admitting fewer immigrants

The archetypal old-timer

❏ An old cartoon shows hopeful British immigrants disembarking beneath a quayside banner bearing the cryptic message: "Welcome Pommie Bastards!" Among the derogatory terms for non-Australians, the one describing the British is the most venerable and, surprisingly, the most obscure in origin. The name has a variety of explanations, none of them really convincing. Could Pom really come from "Prisoner of Motherland"? or "pomegranate" (which, like Poms, turn red in the sun)? ❏

of non-British stock than did the mother country.

The 19th- and early 20th-century non-British immigrants to Australia were very conspicuous and were often resented, although the pious and hardworking Germans who helped settle South Australia fitted in well enough. Gold rushes brought in thousands of Chinese, who were treated with extreme prejudice, and South Sea Islanders known as Kanakas worked the sugar plantations of Queensland, until they were sent back home in order to preserve "white jobs."

War refugees Until World War II, the flow of British immigrants was sufficient to satisfy Australian needs. But the postwar boom demanded more workers than Britain could supply, and the country opened its gates to a Europe crowded with "reffos"

(refugees) and displaced persons. Without asking too many questions of the "what did you do in the war?" variety, Australia accepted hundreds of thousands of immigrants from northern and central Europe, the Netherlands, Germany, Scandinavia, Czechoslovakia and the Baltic states.

When this source began to dry up, the emphasis changed to southern Europe, and the next wave of "New Australians" consisted of Italians, Greeks, Maltese, Croats and Serbs. A tacit "White Australia" policy was followed; non-Europeans were rarely admitted, excluded sometimes by means of the infamous dictation test that allowed an immigration officer to give the would-be immigrant a test in a language of his (the immigration officer's) choice. An undesirable applicant of Chinese origin could thus have been examined on his knowledge of Gaelic, and, not surprisingly, fail.

A multi-cultural society A continuing though fluctuating demand for labor, coupled with an increasing awareness of Australia's geopolitical position on the fringe of Asia, made a continuation of this policy unsustain-

Greek deli in Melbourne

able—a fact instantly verifiable on the streets of any of the state capitals, where plenty of faces belonging to recent Cambodian, Vietnamese, Filipino and other Asian immigrants may be seen.

Australia is now definitely multicultural, a concept promoted with vigor in the media and elsewhere, and one that has brought far-reaching changes to the way Australians live, not least in what they eat. The Anglo-Celtic roasts and puddings can still be had, but are now supplemented by a bewildering array of other cuisines. Total assimilation has been abandoned in favor of preserving immigrant cultures; one T.V. channel (S.B.S.) even specializes in programs in a variety of different languages. For a country that pursued a policy of racial purity for much of its life and that still has a rich repertoire of seemingly abusive (but actually fairly harmless) terms for anyone who isn't a "fair dinkum" Aussie, to have accomplished such a transition in so short a space of time without serious social repercussions is a remarkable achievement.

"No worries" seems to sum up much of the average Australian's attitude to life. Work doesn't play the central role here that it does in some societies around the Pacific Rim or even in Europe. Life is to be made the most of, preferably out in the open, enjoying food and drink, watching sports with passionate intensity, or swimming, surfing, bushwalking, and simply lazing around in the great outdoors of the "best country in the world."

Celebrating at the Melbourne Cup

Once a source of shame, the founding period of convicts is now looked back on with pride, and can be seen as a positive factor contributing to the way Australians are today. Australian "mateship" has its roots in shared oppression and in the importance of comrades in making a life in a harsh and empty land. The land posed a tough physical challenge, in which the conventional qualities of "manliness" were directly related to success or even survival. Work was originally performed under duress and for someone else, after which you were free to lead your own life. Authority was exercised by prison wardens and governors, and consequently resented, but there was no old ruling class or complicated code of manners. Strangers were seldom seen, but if they needed help they could be sure of getting it.

Everyone is equal So Australia has long been a land where people feel themselves to be basically equal and as good as the next person. Money and the making of it are admired, but this does not mean that the monied become beings apart. There is an openness about social contacts that is surprising to many visitors. When Australians say "How are you?" there's a good chance that they actually mean it, and will enjoy hearing your answer (especially if you reveal to them how much you like their country). If you expect to be deferred to, you could be in for an unpleasant surprise; Australians don't like pretension, least of all the British variety, and will prickle if they detect it.

The outdoor life Given the character of the country, with its space, climate, the grandeur of its natural landscapes and the fact that the vast majority of the population lives close to a beach, it's hardly surprising that people seem obsessed with outdoor life and sport. Everyone loves a "barbie" (a barbecue) and a session on the beach, whether sunbathing or surfing. Though the great days of lifesaving clubs and parades may be over, the life of the beach certainly isn't; surfing is indeed a way of life for quite a number of people.

Gambling is also a national passion, taking place indoors in front of endless ranks of "pokies," at the casino or outdoors at the racetrack. On the

Lifeguard at Bondi Beach

❑ Even though women got the vote in Australia at an early date, Australia was always a man's country. The male-female ratio among the transportees brought by the First Fleet was hardly a balanced one, and the scenes that took place when the first cargo of women was discharged were said to be "indescribable." "Sheilas" (women) were kept in their place longer here than in most other countries, both at home and behind the bar, where they filled the glasses while the men on the other side got on with the serious business of drinking. Big changes came during World War II, however, and then later with the growth of feminism, one of the key works of which, *The Female Eunuch*, was by the Australian writer Germaine Greer. ❑

17

first Tuesday in November life stops across the nation for the big horse race, the Melbourne Cup.

Sport Most Australians have a favorite sport, to watch if not to play. A passion for cricket is shared with other members of the British Commonwealth, and has been made less stuffy by innovations like one-day matches, floodlighting and the wearing of colored clothing instead of the traditional white. Rugby Union exists and Rugby League is played in N.S.W. and Queensland. The really big football game, however, and certainly in its Melbourne stronghold, is that known as Australian Rules. It originated on the goldfields, a crude version of Gaelic football played by prospectors taking time off from the diggings, and has been described as "a kind of organized mayhem remarkable for its lack of obvious rules." Up to 120,000 spectators gather to watch the grand final at the M.C.G. (Melbourne Cricket Ground) every September.

The year 2000, however, is set to place Australia on the world's sporting map, when Sydney plays host to the XXVII Olympiad.

Australian culture goes back far longer than the 200 years of white settlement, and visitors will be fascinated by the evidence of 40,000 years of uninterrupted civilization in the dot and x-ray style rock- and cave-paintings, and in the haunting stories of the creation legends of the Aboriginal Dreamtime.

The "cultural cringe" that once caused Australians to defer to the supposed superiority of the artistic and intellectual life of Europe has vanished. Australians today have a high regard for culture and talent, and pride in the international success of Australian artists and writers. Most Aussies cannot resist a good performance, and visitors who are aware of this and who let themselves go a bit are bound to get a warm welcome.

Literature and films Drama has developed from such elegies for lost youth as Ray Lawlor's *Summer of the Seventeenth Doll* to the plays of David Williamson, exploring many aspects of Australian life including politics, business, crime, retirement and "mateship." His *Emerald City* is a must for anyone who wants to understand modern Sydney.

In literature, Judith Wright and Gwen Harwood are poets of world stature, weaving together the per-

Tongue-in-cheek Crocodile Dundee

sonal and the public, and capturing the elusive character of the Australian environment. Patrick White's *Voss* and *The Tree of Man* evoke the spirit of the land, while the younger generation of writers such as Thomas Keneally, David Malouf and Peter Carey explores more universal problems of the human condition. Films have also moved from the tongue-in-cheek stereotypes of *Crocodile Dundee* to the more sensitive social commentary of Baz Luhrmann's *Strictly Ballroom,* Gillian Armstrong's *The Last Days of Chez Nous* and Fred Schepisi's *A Cry in the Dark.*

Painters Marvelous light and scenery have contributed to a tradition of outstanding painting. The early dreamy landscapes of McCubbin and the Heidelberg School, lending the Australian scenery a European beauty, gave way to the more distinctively Australian works of painters like Sidney Nolan with his series of pictures depicting the fatal defiance of Ned Kelly. Arthur Boyd's and Brett Whiteley's enlargements of their own dreams and obsessions sometimes achieve a vast scale, and Fred Williams' wonderful evocations of the arid Australian landscape rival the originality of Aboriginal art.

Music Australia also has much to offer musically. The golden voice of Joan Carden makes her a worthy successor to Dame Nellie Melba and Dame Joan Sutherland ("La Stupenda"). Each state capital boasts an Australian Broadcasting Commission symphony orchestra of world standard, with internationally recognized conductors and

19

The Sidney Nolan painting Dog and Duck Hotel

Yunupingu. The country is also a hotbed of good jazz (James Morrison), folk (Kev Carmody), and country and western (John Williamson), all competing for listeners.

The media In contrast, most Australian newspapers and T.V. channels are owned by three media moguls—Murdoch, Packer and Black. Their content is dominated by personality trivia, sports, sentimental "bushwhacker" pap and investigations into the private lives of public figures, often making the Australian press as sensationalist as any in the world.

The Australian Broadcasting Commission's radio and television programs, on the other hand, gain many international awards for quality and interest, particularly in the fields of science, environment and religion. Especially outstanding is the current-affairs weekly *Four Corners*, which for nearly 20 years has exposed big business and government scandals that have been ignored by the commercial media.

repertoires including music by contemporary Australian composers such as Colin Brumby, John Antill and Peter Sculthorpe. Aboriginal music is increasingly entering the mainstream of the country's culture, and the growing international reputation of Yothu Yindi, the Aboriginal rock band, was recognized by the 1992 "Australian of the Year" award given to its lead singer, Mandawuy

The six states that came together on the first day of the 20th century to create the nation of Australia had all developed outwards from the isolated footholds of their port-of-entry capital cities, with very different characteristics and cultures. The evolution of a national consciousness has been slow, and states still maintain vigorous political and economic competition with each other and with the Federal Government.

Since 1940 Commonwealth control of tax revenues and appointment of Supreme Court judges has guaranteed the Federal Government victory in most disputes. This included the 1983 prohibition of damming of the World Heritage-listed Franklin River in Tasmania (where British botanist David Bellamy joined young Australian protesters in front of the bulldozers) and the 1990 exclusion of logging from the unique tropical rainforests of northern Queensland. In these matters, the Commonwealth Government has been influenced by a Green movement that commands a disciplined voting block—generally estimated at between eight percent and 15 percent of the electorate.

The political parties In other policies, there is now little difference between the traditional party of organized labor, the Australian Labor Party (A.L.P.), which won an unprecedented fifth term of office in 1993, and the Liberal Party (representing the urban middle classes and employers) and their coalition partners, the National Party (the traditional voice of rural interests). Current politics focus on personalities—the aggressive populist opportunism of Prime Minister Keating against the more self-righteous and conservative style of Liberal leader John Howard.

Republicanism has become an unlikely major issue, with increasing support for Labor's anti-monarchical campaign, which the Liberals' traditionalist loyalties oblige them to oppose. Similarly, the A.L.P. is more energetic in advocating trading and cultural links with Southeast Asia. Since the early 1970s, both parties have abandoned the "White Australia" policy and welcome the immigration of wealthy Asian business people, although quotas for political refugees, particularly Vietnamese boat people, are progressively being restricted.

Economic development There is little genuine debate about alternative economic policies. The "Lucky Country" cannot now find enough markets for its wool, wheat, beef or mineral exports to pay for its insatiable appetite for expensive imports. The tariffs that previously protected small local industries from being swamped by European and Asian manufacturers have been drastically cut in the interests of economic rationalism, unemployment is approaching nine percent and the overseas debt increases each year. Governments hope that growth in international tourism will help save the economy.

There is now bipartisan political agreement on the need to develop manufactured goods for export, though current government policy of reducing tariff barriers has had the opposite result and has caused massive unemployment. However, about the need to integrate better with the economies of the demographic and economic giants of Southeast Asia and the Pacific Rim—Australia's closest neighbors—there can be no argument.

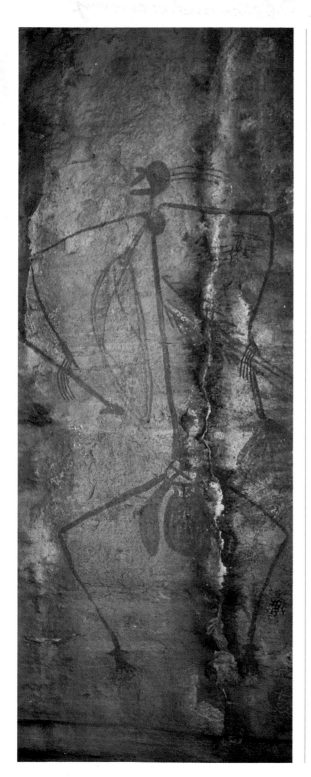

AUSTRALIA WAS

In some parts of the globe vigorous land-shaping processes are obviously hard at work. Ice and snow attack alpine peaks, glaciers grind through valleys, torrents and waterfalls erode, while elsewhere geysers boil and lava pours from beneath the earth. In contrast, Australia is a quiet continent, much of whose active geological history ended long ago.

Ancient tectonics Some 50 million years ago Australia was part of Gondwanaland, the great southern supercontinent that slowly split into the separate fragments we know today as Antarctica, South America, Africa and India, as well as Australia and New Zealand. But its geological evolution goes back much further than this time of continental drift; Precambrian rocks more than 600 million years old are exposed over much of the continent, among them the ancient iron ore deposits of the Pilbara in Western Australia. Subsequently, much of the heart of the continent was periodically submerged beneath the sea, leaving deposits of sands, shells and grits, or the limestone of the Nullarbor Plain. Great coral reefs were also formed, which, when uplifted, became the basis of the extensive cave systems

The Great Dividing Range

of New South Wales and Queensland, or the great bastion that today guards the southern rim of the Kimberley. The Great Artesian Basin came into being at this time too, its pumped waters still supporting life in much of the Outback.

More recent changes About 2 million years ago, what is now the arid Red Centre of the continent enjoyed a far higher rainfall and carried a rich vegetation of tropical forest, traces of which can still be seen in the palms and other plants that have found a refuge in the gorges penetrating the area's harsh ranges. In the east, the Great Dividing Range was thrown up as the result of convulsive earth movements; its southern, alpine area, together with the Tasmanian highlands, is the only part of the continent to have been subjected to glaciation in the last Ice Age (10,000 years ago). As the ice

melted, the sea level rose, creating a wonderful natural harbor for the future city of Sydney. At the same time, the land bridges with Tasmania and New Guinea were cut. Later still (some 5,000 years ago), an outburst of volcanic activity covered the plains of southwestern Victoria with lava, leaving a legacy of cones and crater lakes and of deep fertile soil.

Right: Tessellated sidewalk on the Tasman Peninsula
Below: Australia in 1848—note the dearth of information on the unexplored interior of the continent

23

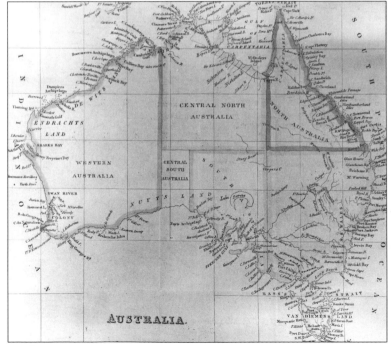

European explorers and educated early settlers tended to romanticize the black people they encountered on the shores of the unknown continent. Aborigines were seen by some as typifying the "Noble Savage" dreamed up by the imaginative powers of 18th-century thinkers; an endlessly fascinating subject for artists and draftsmen, the first Australians were sometimes depicted in the heroic poses of ancient Greek statuary.

Victims of the white man The Aborigines failed to correspond to the European stereotypes; in what now seems an entirely appropriate response, albeit one doomed to failure, some groups put up a vigorous resistance to the encroachment of white settlement on the lands that had formed the basis of their lives since time immemorial. Others fell

Aboriginal people take great pride in their culture and traditions

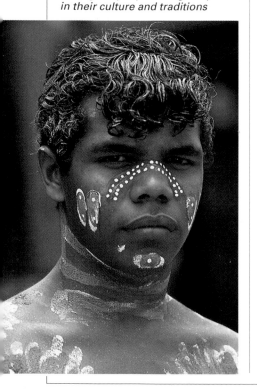

easy victim to the diseases and vices of their conquerors. Only a few decades after the arrival of the First Fleet, the Aborigines of the Sydney region had been decimated by drink and influenza, and before the 19th century had run its course, the Tasmanians had disappeared altogether. For much of this century Aborigines have been seen as unreliable farm hands, "welfare bludgers," or, huddled on a few remaining reserves, as ripe material for conversion to Christianity.

It is only in relatively recent times that white Australians have begun to appreciate the richness and subtlety of the life that their appropriation of the continent all but destroyed, but which sustained the first Australians in material and spiritual harmony with the Australian environment for at least 40,000 years.

Dreamtime Aboriginals inhabited the land in a way remote from European concepts of ownership and property. They believed not only that the landscape had been created by ancestral beings during the Dreamtime, but that these very ancestors were incorporated in landscape features. The land itself was part of the spiritual realm of the whole of creation, in which all creatures, animals as well as men and the dead as well as the living, had their being. The landscape was therefore venerated by individuals, large family groups or clans, with certain places—"sacred sites"—having a particularly intense meaning.

A deep understanding of the spiritual significance of the land was

passed on by highly refined and diversified traditions of song and dance. Never codified in writing, many of these oral traditions tragically have been lost. Ritual gatherings, sometimes known as *corroborees*, took up large amounts of time, with men and women often having rigorously separate ceremonies. Visual arts, like cave- or wall-paintings, or designs executed on the ground had a ceremonial or storytelling role, and were ephemeral or subject to periodic renewal.

Lifestyle Virtually all Aboriginal groups were nomads, living a Stone-Age lifestyle of hunting, gathering and fishing based on seasonal availability of game, seeds and fruits. Controlled burning of the bush took place in order to encourage regrowth and thus attract animals to the area. Material belongings were kept to an absolute minimum: baskets and nets, digging sticks, shelters of brushwood, weapons of carved wood and sharpened bone, canoes of bark and boomerangs. Clothes were minimal, except in the colder, wetter areas of the southeast, where skins and furs were worn.

Each clan had its own distinct territory, defined orally by song rather

Aboriginal rangers are happy to share their knowledge of the land

than marked out on the ground. For another group to cross such an invisible but nevertheless definite boundary might have involved complex negotiation. The whole of Australia can now be mapped in terms of these traditional territories, but at the time of European settlement no such map existed except in the hearts of its inhabitants. This allowed legalistic Europeans to appropriate the land with a more or less clear conscience.

❑ Some 200 Aboriginal languages existed, related to one another but not necessarily mutually intelligible. Most people were multilingual, speaking perhaps five or six tongues. The language of the Aborigines around the future site of Sydney was, of course, unknown to Europeans, and the cry of "*Warra! Warra!*" they were greeted with was not understood. Even if it had been, would they have taken any notice? "*Warra! Warra!*" means "Go away!" ❑

The first people to explore Australia were the ancestors of today's Aborigines, who may have crossed the still intact land-bridge linking the continent to New Guinea more than 40,000 years ago. Living at first along the coasts and in other areas where food was easily obtainable, they eventually spread all over the country, learning to live even in those regions where survival seemed all but impossible to later explorers.

Portuguese and Dutch explorers

The European discovery of the island continent began in a tentative, almost accidental way in the 16th century, as Portuguese mariners looked for routes to the eastern Spice Islands. But the first definite landfall was made in 1606 by the Dutch ship *Duyfken* ("Little Dove") sailing out of the Dutch colony of Batavia (now Jakarta). Her captain, Willem Jansz, was unimpressed by what he saw of the desolate western coast of Cape York and its "wild, cruel black savages."

A little later, Dutch skippers on their way to Java found that they could cut weeks off their journey by making use of the Roaring Forties until they made a northward turn well short of the coast of western Australia. Some sailed straight on, like Dirk Hartog in 1616 (who left an inscribed pewter plate nailed to a post on the island that bears his name), and Frederik de Houtman, who landed on the Houtman Abrolhos islands in 1619.

Under the command of a captain whose name is unrecorded, the *Leeuwin* ("Lioness") sighted the southwestern tip of the continent in 1622. Subsequently, more systematic attempts were made by the Dutch East India Company to survey the coastline. The most famous of them was the voyage of Abel Tasman in 1642–3 in the *Heemskerck* and *Zeehaan*; put ashore on Tasmania's Blackman Bay, his pilot heard voices coming from the bush, but the natives failed to show themselves. Tasman had the flag run up, and named the island after the Governor

W. R. Stott's painting shows William Dampier being attacked by Aborigines when he landed in 1699

of the Dutch East Indies, Van Diemen, a name only changed to honor the actual discoverer in 1855.

In the course of a second voyage, Tasman failed (as had all his predecessors) to find the gap between New Guinea and Australia, subsequently called the Torres Strait, but mapped 1,865 miles of the north coast instead. By this time, the coast had been explored by Dutchmen from the tip of Cape York around Western Australia to the archipelago in the Great Australian Bight. Although the Dutch did not take the continent under their control, they did name it—New Holland.

The British arrive The first Englishman to set foot on the shores of New Holland was the adventurer William Dampier, who landed twice on its northwestern coast, first in 1688, then again in 1699. It was Captain Cook, however, who not only found the unknown east coast, but sailed the length of it and identified the spot where British settlement was to take place. He completed his mission in spite of the fact that his ship the *Endeavour* ran aground on the Barrier Reef (see page 214). The name he gave to the land he claimed for the British Crown was New South Wales.

Even after British settlement had been well and truly established around Sydney Harbour (by Captain Phillip in 1788), many uncertainties remained as to whether the three known fragments added up to a continent. Part of the answer was provided by two truly intrepid men, George Bass and Matthew Flinders, who by 1798 had proposed the existence of a channel between the mainland and Van Diemen's Land, now named Bass Strait.

Aboard the *Investigator*, Flinders went on to explore the south coast with great thoroughness, meeting the French survey ship *Geographe* in what came to be known as Encounter Bay. The master of the *Geographe*, Nicolas Baudin, behaved

Early settlers—Captain Phillip arriving at Sydney Cove in 1788

impeccably, though Flinders, not unnaturally, was suspicious of the intentions of a servant of France, a country with which Britain had recently been at war. A lack of comparable wariness was Flinders' later undoing; having sailed around Australia in 1802–3, he was arrested by the Governor of French Mauritius on his way back to England, unaware that war had broken out again. Held for six years by the French, he returned to England a prematurely aged 40-year-old, barely able to complete his *A Voyage to Terra Australis* before dying in 1814.

❑ Non-Europeans also made contact with Australia. Chinese junks seem to have sailed as far south as Australia's northern coast, possibly as early as the 15th century, and there were exchanges between the Aborigines and the warlike inhabitants of New Guinea. From about 1700 onward, fishermen from Macassar in the Celebes frequented the north coast in search of trepang (sea-cucumbers), an activity that only ended quite recently. ❑

The map of Australia is scattered with surnames attached to natural features or to settlements, honoring governors or similar worthies. But there are others like Sturt's Stony Desert, which are memorials to a different kind of fame—that earned by the inland explorers, a breed of men who set out with varying degrees of success to explore the new country's unmeasured interior.

Straightforward curiosity may have impelled some adventures into the interior, but another factor was the hunger for land as the colony grew and needed to be fed. In addition, industrial England had developed an insatiable appetite for wool, which the merino crossbreeds so successfully developed by John Macarthur could satisfy if only enough pastures could be found. For many years, the Blue Mountains seemed to bar the way from Sydney to the interior, but in 1813 this obstacle was overcome by William Lawson, William Charles Wentworth and Gregory Blaxland. Governor Macquarie had a road built across the mountains in record time, and settlers rushed into the rich grazing lands beyond.

Sturt's journey For many years the puzzle of what became of the rivers flowing westward from the moun-

Many lost their lives in the exploration of Australia's interior

tains perplexed authorities and explorers alike. Did they perhaps feed a great inland sea? A partial answer—no!—was given in 1829–30, when Charles Sturt hauled a whaling boat over the hills and sailed down the Murrumbidgee to its confluence with the Murray. From there he continued downstream to wide Lake Alexandrina and the river mouth, which had thus far been concealed from maritime explorers behind a sand bar. Sturt's return, rowing upstream against a swelling current, was an epic of endurance, and one that nearly ended in disaster as food for his party ran out and their strength ebbed.

❑ Not all those who braved the unknown were of British descent. In 1839–40 a Polish adventurer, self-styled "Count" Paul Strzelecki, underwent hardships almost equal to those suffered by Sturt as he traversed the uplands to which he gave the name Gippsland, and from which he was only extracted by the skills of his Aboriginal guide. An impetuous and quarrelsome Prussian, Ludwig Leichhardt, was less lucky, though in 1844 his first journey succeeded in covering an amazing 2,983 miles from Brisbane to Arnhem Land. An even more ambitious foray that was intended to carry him right across the center from Sydney to Perth failed. Leichhardt and his companions simply disappeared into the void. ❑

Above: Burke and Wills leave Melbourne in August 1860

Burke's expedition Another great failure, but a fully documented one, was the expedition that set out from Melbourne in 1860 under the impatient leadership of Robert O'Hara Burke. This did reach its objective, the mangrove swamps of the Gulf of Carpentaria, but when the party returned to base camp at Cooper Creek, they found it had been abandoned a mere seven hours previously by their support group. Both Burke and his deputy Wills perished, though another man, John King, was fed roots and fish by the Aborigines and survived to tell the tale.

Before successfully crossing Australia's center, Stuart had reached Alice Springs

Eyre and Stuart The names of highways spanning the great emptiness of the center and the west commemorate the epic treks undertaken by two explorers whose persistence has an almost legendary quality. In 1840–1, with the loyal support of his Aboriginal guide Wylie, Edward Eyre reached Albany, having crossed the waterless desert across the top of the Great Australian Bight. In 1862, John McDouall Stuart, almost blind and with hair turned white, finally reached the coast near what was to become Darwin. His previous attempts to cross the center from south to north had been frustrated by spinifex, scurvy and native hostility, though he had planted the Union Jack on a hilltop near Alice Springs. His return to Adelaide, where he was mobbed by the ladies of the city, was made partly on a stretcher.

In the first half of the 19th century Australia developed at a steady but unspectacular pace. Free settlers soon outnumbered convicts, and each colony won its right to a separate existence from New South Wales. But it was the discovery of gold that transformed the country, drawing in a mass of enterprising folk who helped lay the foundation of Australia's essentially urban civilization.

Gold fever The news of early gold finds was suppressed by the authorities, who were fearful of the disruption that such an announcement might cause. But there was no stopping Edward Hargraves, a veteran of the Californian gold rush of 1849, who struck gold near Bathurst in N.S.W. in February 1851.

The rush began, draining the cities of population and making Melbourne so fearful for its prosperity that city officials offered a prize to whoever found gold within a certain distance of the city. One James Esmond obliged, and his find at Clunes in July 1851 was followed by others at Castlemaine, Bendigo and Ballarat.

Prospectors in the mid-19th century

Melbourne was emptied of able-bodied men and ships stood crewless in the harbor as sailors hurried inland to make their fortune.

Life in the goldfields was raw enough, although there was nothing like the violence that had cropped up around the North American finds. Many of the prospectors longed for nothing more than solid respectability, founding farms and businesses after striking lucky, or returning to seek their fortune among the seemingly limitless opportunities offered by "Marvellous Melbourne."

More rebellious spirits made their stand at the Eureka stockade (see page 110), and even though this grass-roots revolt failed, their gesture helped create a new democratic atmosphere in which representative government was to thrive. Victoria's population rose in 10 years from less than 100,000 to more than half a million, and the whole country received an injection of energy that carried it through a boom lasting until the 1890s.

Fortune-seekers Prospectors came from all over the world, but mainly arrived from Britain. The largest minority were the Chinese, many of whom disembarked in South Australia and walked overland to the Victorian goldfields rather than pay the £10 landing tax at Melbourne. They were much resented for their willingness to work hard, for keeping to themselves, and for their sheer numbers. At the time of the Palmer River gold rush in the 1870s in North Queensland, Chinese diggers formed a majority of men in the state.

From boom town to ghost town In Victoria, the rip-roaring days were soon over. By the late 1850s, most of the gold available on the surface or by shallow diggings had been worked out. Individual miners could not afford the equipment needed for the excavation and maintenance of deeper mines, and the initiative passed from the self-sufficient pioneer to companies able to raise the necessary capital. Ballarat ceased being a muddy chaos and turned itself into the most respectable of Victorian cities.

In the second half of the 19th century gold strikes were made all over Australia, many of them ephemeral and leaving a legacy of strangely poignant ghost towns. The last great rush was to the Eastern Goldfields of Coolgardie and Kalgoorlie/Boulder in Western Australia in 1892–3. This gave a similar boost to the languid economy of the colony, and transformed Perth into a real city. Large-scale operations continue in this area today, based on vast open-cast pits worked by huge machines, a method that is in total contrast to the primitive hand tools and hard manual labor of the prospectors of early days.

Sovereign Hill at Ballarat in Victoria is a re-creation of gold-rush days

❏ Highway robbery had been practiced in the colony for as long as highways had existed, and increased in appeal as the wealth created by the gold rush was moved around. Australia's bushrangers were adept at "bailing up," their dash and daring sometimes giving them legendary status among a population none too enamored of the law. The most notorious of them all, and a symbol of Australian defiance and sheer cussedness, was of course Edward "Ned" Kelly, son of an Irish ex-convict. After a series of exploits, which included holding up whole towns, the Kelly gang was cornered in June 1880 at Glenrowan, a small town in northeastern Victoria. The wounded Kelly emerged wearing his famous homemade suit of armor, but was shot in the legs, brought to trial and hanged in Melbourne on November 11, 1880. ❏

The Australian landscapes that the early European settlers first cast eyes upon lacked the ordered character of the scenes they had left behind. Much of the European effort in Australia was to impose a rational and productive discipline on this unfamiliar and seemingly chaotic scene, sometimes at a cost that only now is being calculated in terms of destruction of habitat and loss of beauty.

In Europe, the conversion of the forest into farmland began in neolithic times and took some 5,000 years to complete. In the wooded southeastern and western areas of Australia, the same process was virtually complete after a single century. The replacement of the bush by productive fields was one motive, but in many areas the timber itself was highly valuable and logging quickly developed into a major industry.

The removal of the native forest or its replacement by exotic tree species like radiata pines continued into the 20th century, but a partial halt has now been called, and no visitor should miss seeing such glories of the Australian landscape as the tropical rainforest of Queensland, its temperate equivalent in the southeast and in Tasmania, the blue gums that have given their name to the Blue Mountains, or the splendid karri forests of Western Australia.

The farmers move in Once the bush had been cleared, squatters and sheep farmers parceled out their land, erecting fences, planting European trees to give the place a more homey look, and building themselves homesteads with whatever degree of architectural elaboration they could afford. Australian country properties range from elegant stone mansions to tin shacks of decidedly temporary appearance.

This attempt to impose order often faltered in the face of the capricious nature of the land. Rainless years ruined many a farmer who had tried to push the frontier of agriculture too far inland, and Australia has as many

forgotten farmsteads as it has ghost towns abandoned by prospectors when mineral wealth ran out.

As settlement advanced, native animals retreated, displaced in many cases by flocks of sheep grazing on the imported grass species sown by farmers. Often shot as pests, kangaroos and other animals sometimes profited by the irrigation of otherwise arid landscapes, and became a greater nuisance than ever.

Conflicts of interest The effect of the other changes was to convert a seemingly formless scene into one that made economic and visual sense to the Europeans, and that could be controlled and managed. It also meant that the landscape became uninhabitable by the Aborigines in any traditional way. Such basic differences of viewpoint probably contributed more than anything else to conflict between settlers and natives, a conflict in which the latter were the inevitable losers.

❑ Rabbits were imported as game to Victoria in the 1850s. Within a few years, the population exploded, and rabbits advanced at the rate of 60 miles a year, destroying much of the native herbage for ever. Supposedly rabbit-proof fences were built, one running 1,240 miles across a large part of Western Australia. But the rabbits found ways round them, and were only defeated when myxomatosis was introduced in the 1950s. ❑

How to tackle Australia

Many visitors to Australia will already have a good idea of what they want to do once there. For those whose plans are less definite, however, the first thing to remember about Australia is that it is a continent. Planning a holiday here is like visiting Europe or the United States; you could get an overall idea of the country in one trip, but you need several months and quite a lot of money (though not as much as elsewhere) if you want to get to know it really well.

How far?
Before you head off into the Outback in your rental car or camper-van, contemplate the distances involved. Remember that Cairns is 1,582 miles from Sydney, Alice Springs is 1,644 miles distant, Darwin 2,484 miles and Perth a staggering 3,791 miles from Sydney—no short hop!

The extended visit An absolute minimum for an extended trip that takes in all major sights would be three months. In this time it would be feasible to visit all the states, including Tasmania, and cover most of the three-star attractions of this guide, especially if you were able to do most of your traveling—and some of your sightseeing —by plane. If you have more time, so much the better; you could then stay in some places and absorb their atmosphere in a relaxed way rather than just hitting the principal sights. Now that it is feasible to drive right around the continent on paved roads, many retired Australians are discovering the pleasures of getting to know their own country in a leisurely way, usually by driving an R.V. or camper-van.

The shorter trip Most visitors to Australia will only have limited time at their disposal, and choices will have to be made. As well as seeing something of city life, if you want to enjoy what Australia has to offer you will need to get

Camper-vans are ideal for exploring the country

out into the country, drive along the unsurfaced roads of the Outback, leave your car behind and walk through the bush or along the beach, wander around an old gold-rush township, sit at the bar of an Outback pub, or let yourself be persuaded that diving and snorkeling are not just for the experts.

Australians are exceptionally good at inviting you to join in; you can take part in all kinds of activities, from riding a camel in the desert to digging for witchetty grubs in the company of an Aboriginal ranger. Not only are there probably more museums per head than anywhere else in the world (from the impeccably professional to the endearingly amateur), but all kinds of industries and enterprises open their gates to visitors. Wineries without tastings are unheard of, fruit and animal farms make you welcome and there is plenty of accommodation on country properties with the chance to take part in rural activities.

Planning an itinerary Within the confines imposed by a conventional vacation of a few weeks, setting definite limits on what you can reasonably undertake is very important. Though vast, nearly all the Australian states are dominated by their capital city, each with its own character and wealth of attractions. This is where colonial life began and where its traces are thickest on the ground. Wild landscapes start just beyond the suburbs; no big city lies out of sight of the hills or mountains of a national park. One solution therefore would be to choose one city or town as a base and then make excursions, some involving overnight stays in order to appreciate the extraordinary contrasts between city and rural life that are such a feature of Australia. An overland trip by rental car, train, bus or organized tour beginning at one point and taking your time to reach another is a good way of getting the feel of the country; your round-trip airline ticket from abroad can usually be arranged to accommodate this. It would be a pity to miss the Outback, but remember that you don't have to go all the way out and back overland; if time is short, you can fly to one of the many bases for Outback tours and start from there.

Australia now has a well-developed and very varied tourist infrastructure, mostly staffed by people who will go out of their way to be helpful, particularly if you are prepared to treat them as human beings and not just dispensers of information. Apart from accommodations and restaurants to suit all pockets, there are also many travel operators standing by to take you on tours. It is, however, always worth while checking that the tours offered are exactly what you want; the ingredients of a package may have been put together to suit the operator's convenience rather than yours. But if you want to go somewhere really badly, you're bound to find an Australian who will help you get there!

Drivers: beware of camels!

Australian islands
Far out in the Pacific, Lord Howe Island (435 miles northeast of Sydney) and Norfolk Island (another 620 miles farther on) don't feature in the itineraries of most visitors to Australia, though both are favorites with Australians in search of something different. Some 15 square miles in size, Norfolk was a prison island where unrepentant offenders from Sydney were sent to suffer under a notoriously brutal regime, and the remains of convict-era buildings give it something of the atmosphere of Tasmania. The climate is subtropical and as well as rainforest, there are stands of the famous Norfolk pines and rolling pasturelands. Lord Howe Island is less than half the size of Norfolk Island and is dominated by mountain peaks, with unique vegetation and birdlife that have led to its designation as a World Heritage Area. There are hardly any cars, and when not snorkeling you will have to get around by bike.

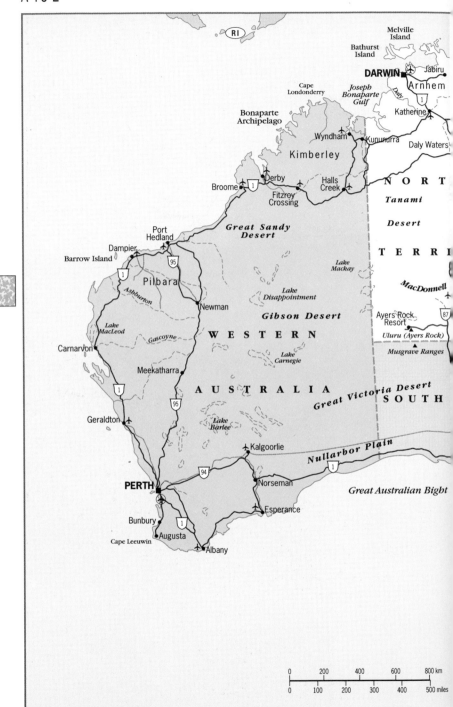

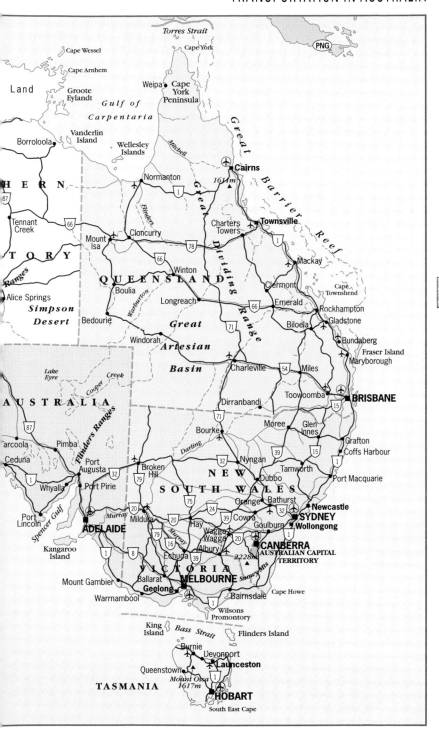

37

Torres Strait
Cape Wessel
Cape Arnhem
Cape York
PNG
Land
Groote
Eylandt
Weipa
Cape
York
Peninsula
Gulf of
Carpentaria
Vanderlin
Island
Borroloola
Wellesley
Islands
Mitchell
Normanton
Cairns
1611m
HERN
87
Tennant
Creek
66
Cloncurry
Mount
Isa
78
Charters
Towers
Townsville
1
Great Barrier Reef
TORY
Flinders
66
Winton
Mackay
Ranges
QUEENSLAND
Boulia
Clermont
Cape
Townshend
Alice Springs
Longreach
Emerald
Rockhampton
Simpson
Desert
Bedourie
Warburton
71
Biloela
Gladstone
Great
Windorah
Bundaberg
Artesian
Fraser Island
Maryborough
AUSTRALIA
Lake
Eyre
Cooper Creek
Basin
Charleville
54
Miles
Dirranbandi
Toowoomba
BRISBANE
15
87
Bourke
71
Moree
Glen
Innes
arcoola
Pimba
Darling
Grafton
Coffs Harbour
Ceduna
Flinders Ranges
Port
Augusta
79
32
Broken
Hill
32
Nyngan
39
15
Tamworth
Whyalla
Port Pirie
NEW
75
Dubbo
Port Macquarie
SOUTH WALES
Orange
Bathurst
Port
Lincoln
Spencer Gulf
20
Murray
Mildura
20
Hay
24
39
Cowra
Goulburn
32
Newcastle
SYDNEY
Wollongong
ADELAIDE
Murray
Wagga
Wagga
20
1
Kangaroo
Island
1
8
79
16
Echuca
Albury
CANBERRA
AUSTRALIAN CAPITAL
TERRITORY
39
2228m
Mount Gambier
VICTORIA
Ballarat
MELBOURNE
Snowy Mts
Warrnambool
Geelong
Bairnsdale
Cape Howe
1
Wilsons
Promontory
King
Island
Bass Strait
Flinders Island
Burnie
Devonport
Launceston
Queenstown
Mount Ossa
1617m
TASMANIA
1
HOBART
South East Cape

Dawes Point

Pier One

Sydney Harbour Bridge

Bennelong Point

DAWES POINT

Millers Point

The Earth Exchange

E

Garrison Church (Holy Trinity)

The Rocks Heritage & Information Centre

Overseas Passenger Terminal

Sydney Opera House

Government House

MILLERS POINT

ARGYLE PLACE

Argyle Centre

Cadman's Cottage

Sydney Cove

Observatory Hill & Sydney Observatory

Museum of Contemporary Art

Ferry Terminal

THE ROCKS

Circular Quay Station

CAHILL EXPRESSWAY

Conservatorium of Music

D

National Trust Centre SH Ervin Art Gallery

Customs House

MACQUARIE PLACE

BRIDGE STREET

GROSVENOR STREET

Museum of Sydney

Australia Square

Wynyard Station

State Library of NSW

State Parliament House

38

GEORGE STREET

PITT ST

PHILLIP ST

MACQUARIE STREET

Darling

Harbour

Jones Bay

WESTERN DISTRIBUTOR

ERSKINE STREET

CLARENCE STREET

YORK STREET

MLC Centre

GPO

Martin Place Station

Martin Place

Sydney Hospital

Sydney Mint Museum

Pyrmont Bay

KING STREET

St James Church

Hyde Park Barracks

C

National Maritime Museum

Strand Arcade

Centrepoint Sydney Tower

QUEENS SQUARE

PYRMONT

Sydney Aquarium

YORK ST

MARKET STREET

St James Station

Pyrmont Bridge

ELIZABETH STREET

Hyde Park

HARRIS STREET

PYRMONT STREET

Monorail

Harbourside Festival Market Place

Queen Victoria Building

State Theatre

Great Synagogue

DRUITT STREET

PARK STREET

B

Harris Street Motor Museum

Sydney Convention Centre

Sydney Town Hall

Town Hall Station

Museum Station

DARLING HARBOUR

DAY STREET

St Andrews Cathedral

BATHURST STREET

GEORGE STREET

Sydney Exhibition Centre

Tumbalong Park

Chinese Garden

Monorail

Liverpool Street

Anzac Memorial

BRIDGE ROAD

Wentworth Park

PIER STREET

HARBOUR ST

DIXON ST

GOULBURN STREET

ELIZABETH STREET

WENTWORTH AVENUE

GOULBURN ST

WATTLE STREET

WILLIAM HENRY STREET

Sydney Entertainment Centre

Chinatown

CAMPBELL

Powerhouse Museum

Paddy's Markets

HAY STREET

SURRY HILLS

A

WENTWORTH PARK RD

HARRIS STREET

MARY ANN STREET

HAYMARKET

GEORGE STREET

RAWSON PLACE

Belmore Park

ALBION

Harbourside and History Walk

EDDY AVE

Central Railway Station

City Centre and Darling Harbour Walk

ULTIMO

FOVEAUX ST

1

2

3

0 — 500 m
0 — 500 yards

Fort Denison

Port Jackson

Garden Island

Mrs Macquarie's Point

Mrs Macquarie's Chair

Farm Cove

Woolloomooloo Bay

Andrew "Boy" Charlton Pool

Royal Botanic Gardens

The Domain

POTTS POINT

Fleet Base

National Herbarium

Elizabeth Bay

The

Art Gallery of New South Wales

COWPER WHARF ROAD

LINCOLN CRESCENT

Domain

Elizabeth Bay House

Beare Park

MACLEAY STREET

ELIZABETH BAY

GREENKNOWE AVENUE

St Mary's Cathedral

WOOLLOOMOOLOO

VICTORIA STREET

Fitzroy Gdns

ROSLYN GARDENS

PALMER STREET

KINGS CROSS

Kings Cross Station

DARLINGHURST ROAD

WARD AVENUE

Rushcutters Bay Park

WARATAH STREET

STREET

Australian Museum

KINGS CROSS ROAD

BAYSWATER ROAD

RUSHCUTTERS BAY

WILLIAM ST

CRAIGEND STREET

EAST SYDNEY

CROWN

BOURKE STREET

MC LACHLAN AVENUE

AVENUE

DARLINGHURST

VICTORIA STREET

STREET

NEILD

OXFORD STREET

STREET

BOUNDARY STREET

BROWN ST

STREET

TAYLOR SQUARE

GLENMORE ROAD

STREET

PADDINGTON

FLINDERS STREET

SOUTH DOWLING STREET

OXFORD STREET

Juniper Hall

CROWN STREET

BOURKE STREET

STREET

Victoria Barracks

Paddington Town Hall

4

5

40

Sydney Curling seductively around its sparkling harbor, Sydney has a superb setting that makes you forget its wretched beginnings. One of the world's great cities, with nearly a quarter of the population of the continent in its metropolitan area, it seems still in the first flush of youth—enthusiastic, welcoming, vibrant, and open to growth and change. Two of its landmarks, the Harbour Bridge and Opera House, became instant icons the day they were completed. Seen from across the water, the recent transformation of the city center adds a further element of drama and excitement, while all around the 150 miles of harbor foreshore, waterfront suburbs of dream homes mingle with the remains of wild bushland.

Sydney, then, is beautiful, almost extravagantly so. There is also a fair measure of what has been called "the Australian ugliness." The skyscrapers make no attempt to harmonize with their immediate surroundings; close up, much of the city center appears chaotic. Beyond the often charming Victorian suburbs sprawls an almost horizonless sea of red-roofed bungalow suburbs. But the monotony of this urban sprawl is compensated for by magnificent natural surroundings: the heaths and forests of **Ku-ring-gai Chase** and **Royal National Park**, the high wall of the **Blue Mountains** and the string of beaches along many miles of Pacific coastline. One's enjoyment is enhanced by a climate that, despite a fair amount of rain, gives hot summers and bright winter days.

Early days In January 1788, a favorable climate played no part in Captain Phillip's choice of Port Jackson as a landing place for his motley cargo of convicts. It was simply that the area around today's Circular Quay seemed more promising than the bleak expanses around Botany Bay

where the First Fleet had originally anchored. And so the flag was run up. The name given to the landing place, Sydney Cove (after the British Home Secretary of the time), was soon transferred to the not very orderly settlement that grew up around its shore.

As the colony became more firmly established, free settlers moved in, and the population of the city increased sharply when gold was found to the west of the Blue Mountains in the 1850s. Handsome villas were built in the outskirts, while in the later years of the 19th century middle- and working-class suburbs like Balmain and Paddington unrolled their streets of humble cottages and superior terraces over the countryside nearby, leaving areas like The Rocks to a life of drink, vice and violence. By the time the population of the city had reached the million mark in the late 1920s, Sydney was a confident, swaggering sort of place, where a strong trade union movement helped insure one of the highest living standards in the world for its members.

Up to date World War II brought the city into abrupt contact with a wider world, which came even closer in the postwar period, when Sydney became the recipient of waves of New Australians, first from devastated Europe and later from all over the world. Once resolutely Anglo-Celtic, it is now a thoroughly multicultural city.

Sydney is a great tourist destination: its charms are not hidden away, but put boldly on display; its history is readily accessible; and it has all the museums, galleries, stores and entertainment that you would expect in a metropolis.

For some, Sydney is "the best address on earth"

Penetrating the defenses
Sydney's first fortification, on Observatory Hill, was built to protect the colony's Establishment against a possible convict uprising; later, it was potential foreign invaders who became the worry, and by the mid-19th century virtually every promontory had been fortified. In World War II, despite a boom across the harbor's mouth, a Japanese midget submarine crept up as far as Garden Island. Here it launched its torpedoes at the cruiser U.S.S. *Chicago*; they missed. Depth-charges dealt with the brave and ingenious submariners; their vessel was recovered and is on display in the National Maritime Museum.

41

Pink Water Taxi
AFFORDABLE CONVENIENCE
24 HOUR SERVICE
PITTWATER, HAWKESBURY RIVER & COWAN CREEK
Pho
018

Lovely homes

Not all Sydney's early houses were as unassuming as Cadman's Cottage, though the first Government House (see page 45) was damp and suffered from inexplicable smells. The aspirations of successful citizens were expressed in such delightful dwellings as Elizabeth Bay House, a splendid classical mansion in white stucco that turns its back on its sleazy neighbors in adjacent Kings Cross. Further to the east is another highly desirable residence, Vaucluse House, whose battlements and verandas were added for the explorer William Charles Wentworth in the 1830s.

The Australian Museum houses ethnographic displays from all over the world

▶▶▶ Art Gallery of New South Wales   39C4
Art Gallery Road

This dignified classical sandstone edifice was opened in 1887 and expanded several times over the years, most recently and lavishly to mark the 1988 Bicentennial. Its generous interior houses what can fairly be described as the country's greatest art collection, even though the national collection is now at Canberra. It covers the evolution of Australian art up to the present day, and has major sections on Aboriginal (in the exciting new Yiribana Gallery), Asian, American and European art; the collection of British 20th-century painting is outstanding. In addition the gallery hosts world-class visiting exhibitions. But it is the painters of Australia and their response to the people and places of the strange new land who most fascinate; they are all here, from John Glover's Tasmanian landscapes to Grace Cossington Smith's metamorphosis of the Harbour Bridge and Sidney Nolan's interpretation of the Ned Kelly saga.

▶▶▶ Australian Museum   38B3
Corner of College Street and William Street

Australia's largest natural history museum is a lively place, expanded and altered in recent years so that its Victorian architecture almost becomes part of the intriguing displays on earth history, animals, insects and birds, and the life of the sea. Human rituals of the present as well as of the past are presented in a challenging way, as is the evolution of Aboriginal culture over tens of thousands of years. There are also sections on Indonesia, Papua New Guinea and the Pacific, as well as the "Planet of Minerals," featuring Australia's extraordinary mineral wealth. There are stuffed animals but they are always shown in context rather than as lifeless specimens, and there are plenty of "hands-on" exhibits.

▶ Cadman's Cottage   38E3
George Street

This modest two-story Georgian house has the distinction of being the city's oldest surviving building. It was erected in 1816, getting its name from the pardoned convict John Cadman who lived in it from 1827 to 1845. A lintel carries the initials G.R. for England's King George III in immaculately carved lettering. Cadman's home once faced directly onto the beach, but now stands some 55 yards inland and houses an information center of the National Parks and Wildlife Service.

▶ Chinatown   38B2

Immigrants from China first arrived as part of the gold rush and took up residence in The Rocks or around Botany Bay. Sydney's Chinese citizens are now scattered around the suburbs, but the city's Chinese heart beats strongest along Dixon Street, behind whose ornamental gateways is an array of exotic shops, food centers, and restaurants. A few steps away is the **Chinese Garden▶▶**, part of the redevelopment of Darling Harbour. Laid out by landscape architects from Sydney's sister city of Guangzhou in southern China, the gardens are a calm retreat of sensitively designed planting, lakes, bridges and waterfalls, with a tea house overlooking a lily pond.

Sydney Cove, the First Fleet's landing site

▶▶▶ Circular Quay   38D3

Sydney's "chief people-watching site" (Jan Morris) is also one of the city's most historic places, since it was here at Sydney Cove that the First Fleet dropped anchor on January 26, 1788. It is still the epicenter of daily life, with a continuous stream of people pouring between railroad station, taxis, buses and the busy ferries that bustle in and out of the quays. Trains and traffic roar by overhead, ignored by those with time enough on their hands to bend an ear to the entertainers on the broad promenade. Landward are the cliff-like buildings of the city center, while toward the water are alluring and ever-changing glimpses of the Harbour Bridge and Opera House.

▶▶▶ Darling Harbour   38D1

The deep inlet on the western side of the city center was called Cockle Bay by the early colonists. Like so many docklands of its kind around the world, it eventually lost its commercial functions but is now enjoying a vigorous new lease on life as a tourist center, with major exhibition and entertainment facilities.

The Harbour is an exciting place, an extraordinary medley of old and new, defined to the east by glittering office towers, with expanses of water and pavement framing some of the city's most stimulating new buildings. The parkland at the southern end seems none the worse for its overhead expressways, while the whole area is linked to the center of Sydney by a controversial monorail that glides over Pyrmont Bridge, the oldest swing bridge of its kind in the world.

For details on attractions in the area other than the National Maritime Museum (covered on page 45), see the adjacent panel.

Darling Harbour attractions
Apart from the Pumphouse Brewery Tavern and the splendid Sydney Aquarium there are sports facilities, an amusement park, outdoor entertainments, cruises on the harbor, the 200 shops, boutiques and bazaars of the Harbourside complex, a major convention center and the Sydney Exhibition Centre, which hosts events like the Motor Show. The Harris Street Motor Museum, and the vast Saturday and Sunday Paddy's Market are just a step away.

43

Unknown soldier
The Anzac Memorial in Hyde Park was designed by the Sydney architect Bruce Dellit "to give an impression, not of the glory of war, but of its tragedy and horror." It is a masterpiece of its kind. The external sculptures depicting the different branches of the services (including nursing) are by British-born Rayner Hoff. Inside, the dramatic central figure of the dead soldier can only be observed properly by bowing one's head. The vault above is pierced by 120,000 stars, each one representing a World War I volunteer.

Observatory Hill and Sydney Observatory
With commanding views over the harbor, Millers Point was the site of a citadel, a windmill, and then an observatory. The latter survives, established in 1858 to survey the hitherto unknown southern skies, and functioned until 1982. With its time-ball tower and domes, the observatory building has now been renovated as a museum of astronomy with plenty of intriguing hands-on features.

▶▶ The Domain 39D4

The Domain extends inland from Mrs. Macquarie's Point to the large green space fringed by fig trees that serves as one of the city center's most important parks. This is where orators challenge their audiences along the lines of London's Speaker's Corner, where joggers jog and office workers eat their sandwiches. Open-air opera and classical music concerts are also held here, particularly during the January Festival of Sydney. The Domain has, however, suffered from the incursions of the Cahill Expressway, the Eastern Suburbs Railway and the construction of an underground parking garage.

▶ Garrison Church 38E2
Millers Point

Hacked through the central ridge of The Rocks area, **Argyle Cut** was one of the colony's early engineering feats. It leads to **Argyle Place**, frequently described as Sydney's sole village green, though not many village greens benefit from such close proximity to a multiple-lane expressway (the Harbour Bridge approach). Nevertheless, it is a pleasant enough place, lined with attractive mid-19th-century cottages. Holy Trinity Church, near the entrance to the Cut, was given the name Garrison Church because of its use by the redcoats manning Dawes Point Battery. Built from the stone quarried from the Cut, its squat appearance isn't helped by its lack of a spire, but it has a spacious interior and some of the city's finest stained-glass windows.

▶ Hyde Park 38C3

Like its London namesake, this fine park once marked the very edge of town, but today has become one of those central city oases where people retreat from the heat, fumes and noise of the street. Its avenue of majestic Morton Bay fig trees is particularly fine, and there is a splendid imitation-baroque fountain, but the park's centerpiece is undoubtedly the **Anzac Memorial**▶▶ (see panel). This is a solemn but sumptuous essay in art deco and forms the focal point of the Anzac Day march.

▶▶ Hyde Park Barracks 38C3
Queens Square

This splendid three-story edifice with pediment and pilasters is one of the city's finest classical buildings. Standing in dignified seclusion behind its grand gates, it was designed on Governor Macquarie's orders by the brilliant Francis Greenway, whose architectural skills transformed Sydney. It provided accommodations for up to 1,000 convicts, who until then had had to find their own lodgings. It is now a museum of social history, with excellent displays on the early history of the colony and the lifestyle led by its former inmates.

▶▶ Museum of Contemporary Art 38D3
Circular Quay

The rather forbidding-looking brown sandstone building facing Circular Quay used to be the offices of the Maritime Services Board. Designed at the very end of the art deco period, it is an incongruous setting for the country's major collection of contemporary art.

► ► **Museum of Sydney**   *38D3*

Corner of Bridge and Phillip streets
Sydney's newest museum, on the site of the first (1788) Government House, is an exciting addition to the city's attractions. The house was demolished in 1846, but excavations have revealed the foundations, part of which can be viewed through the paving. Using state-of-the-art technology such as computer displays and a vast video wall, the museum takes you on a journey of discovery—from the story of the local Aborigines to the relatively sophisticated Sydney of the 1850s.

► ► ► **National Maritime Museum**   *38C1*
Darling Harbour
Looking more like a ship of the future than anything so conventional as a museum, this extraordinary structure houses an equally extraordinary array of objects that tell the story of the island continent's intimate relationship with the seas surrounding it.

There are many real vessels in the museum's huge and strangely shaped interior, from Aboriginal canoes to high-tech yachts, but the emphasis is as much on people as on things. There are displays on explorers, convicts, settlers, refugees and other immigrants, on whalers and wharfies who made their living from the sea, on swimmers and surfers who simply enjoyed it, and on maritime "neighbors" like the Americans and Japanese. Tied up at the dock outside are more boats, including the *Tu Do* which arrived in Darwin in 1977 overloaded with Vietnamese boat people, and the destroyer H.M.A.S. *Vampire*.

The Observatory, a colonial building constructed from the local sandstone

Playground of the Pacific
This was the name originally given to Bondi Beach, and the early days of Australia's exuberant beach culture are celebrated with gusto in the National Maritime Museum. Within living memory, the sands were scoured by eagle-eyed inspectors who insured that no male swimmer went topless, but what emerges from the posters, photos and videos here is the sheer joy young Australians have always had in stripping down and letting sea and sun work on their bodies. A somber note is struck by recalling Black Sunday, February 6, 1938, when what was described as an avalanche of waves took five lives in spite of the efforts of 60 lifesavers.

45

One of the great privileges of life in Sydney is excellent access to the beaches of the Harbour and the Pacific Ocean. Astonishing as it might seem, but until the early years of this century swimming was prohibited by law during daylight hours; until finally, the flamboyant editor of a Manly newspaper strolled fully clad into the surf in the middle of the day, defying the prosecution that, in fact, was never made.

Check before you swim
Few big cities are entirely free of water pollution problems, and some of Sydney's beaches occasionally suffer contamination by sewage. Measures are taken to remedy the situation, and conditions can be checked locally.

The Harbour beaches
These hardly compare with those on the ocean, but there are plenty of good spots for picnicking and sunbathing. On the south shore are Vaucluse, Nielsen Park and Parsley Bay; the north shore has beaches around Manly, as well as Mosman's Obelisk and Balmoral.

To the north, **Manly** is the city's shore resort *par excellence*, "seven miles from Sydney, but a thousand miles from care." Lined with shops, take-out stands, cafés and pubs, a broad concourse called the Corso channels you from the ferry landing to the curving sandy beach with its double line of Norfolk pines facing the ocean. It was here, in 1915, that the art of surfing was born in Australia, and a big surf competition is held here every year. Manly has many other attractions, including a waterside amusement park and the Oceanarium.

World-famous **Bondi**, to the south, has an even more magnificent beach, stretching between two headlands, though its setting of cafés, pubs and apartment buildings has a tacky look about it. Bondi is suburban and popular, once connected to the center by a famous tramway whose cars would make the final descent to the beach at breakneck speed, giving rise to the expression "to go like a Bondi tram."

Eighteen other beaches, equally fine if less famous, stretch north from Manly up the Warringah Peninsula to delightful Palm Beach. Some, like Narrabeen, are urban in character, while others, like Freshwater and Whale beaches, are still largely undeveloped. Similarly, a string of beaches runs south from Bondi, ending at 6-mile-long Cronulla, the only beach accessible by suburban train.

Every visitor should take in famous Bondi Beach

► **Parliament House**   38C3
Macquarie Street
Like the Mint, the home of the New South Wales legislature was once part of the "Rum" Hospital built in 1816. The Legislative Council Chamber is a prefabricated iron structure, originally sent out from England to serve as a goldfields church. Parliament House is open to the public, even when in session.

►►► **Powerhouse Museum**   38A2
Harris Street, Ultimo
The cavernous boiler halls and other generous interior spaces of the old power station and tram depot on the edge of Darling Harbour are now home to the vast collections of Sydney's Museum of Applied Arts and Sciences. The array of objects in what is Australia's largest museum is quite astonishing. The decorative arts are strongly represented, as is social history, with stimulating displays on the life of the local Aborigines, women's work, brewing and drinking. There are many hands-on features as well as audiovisual presentations, sound effects and holograms.

►► **Queen Victoria Building**   38C2
George Street
This many-domed late-Victorian shopping gallery occupying an entire city block was completed in 1898; in recent years a thorough renovation has restored it to its former glory. With its many levels, stained glass and mosaics, it is a cathedral to conspicuous consumption.

►►► **The Rocks**   38D2
Named after the sandstone ridge ending in Dawes Point, this is the site of Australia's first European settlement. For many years, it had a reputation as a place of brawling, hard drinking, whoring and villainy of all kinds, but this murky past does no harm whatsoever to The Rocks' present status as a tourist mecca (see panel). In fact, the area has long since been tamed, first by wholesale demolition of many of its unsanitary dwellings after the outbreak of bubonic plague in 1900, and then by another swath of destruction preceding construction of the Harbour Bridge.

►►► **Royal Botanic Gardens**   39D4
These luxuriantly planted 74–acre gardens are the perfect counterpoint to the high-rise buildings and bustle of the city center. They benefit enormously from their proximity to the harbor, looking onto the long curving promenade of Farm Cove, which is set between twin promontories, one crowned by the Opera House and the other by Mrs. Macquarie's Point. Once the site of the first government farm, the gardens contain a visitor center, the National Herbarium (with more than a million plant specimens), a new fernery under a slatted steel dome, and the extraordinary shapes of the Pyramid and Arc greenhouses, which shelter tropical plants from many countries.

►►► **Sydney Harbour Bridge**   38E3
Not just a symbol of Sydney but of Australia itself, the Harbour Bridge leaps in a great arch between its granite pylons to span the narrows between Dawes Point and

The highly entertaining Powerhouse Museum is one of the best places for kids to visit

The Rocks today
The area is now a place to wander at leisure and savor the almost medieval atmosphere—quite absent elsewhere in Australia. You may wish to start your visit at the informative Rocks Heritage and Information Centre in George Street. The Earth Exchange is a fascinating and innovative museum of energy, geology and mining, while the attractively redesigned waterside is definitely a place to linger.

Milsons Point to the north. Opened in 1932 and carrying eight traffic lanes and a double-track railroad, its broad deck is the widest in the world and rises 440 feet above water level.

A footway leads across the bridge (access is via Cumberland Street in The Rocks), giving stupendous views, and you can climb the southeastern pylon to a small museum and an observation platform.

▶▶ Sydney Mint Museum   38C3
Queens Square

Sydney's oldest public building, like the N.S.W. parliament, originally formed part of the "Rum" hospital, built between 1811 and 1816 free of charge in exchange for a monopoly on the import of rum. In its varied career, it has housed the Colonial Mint and is now a museum concentrating on gold objects, and how the discovery of gold changed Australia.

▶▶▶ Sydney Opera House   38E3

Once the site of a ramshackle tram terminus, since 1973 Bennelong Point has been crowned by this spectacular building, which is the inspired and outstanding creation of Danish architect Joern Utzon, born in 1918 and educated at the Royal Danish Academy. The complex curving shapes of the exterior have been compared to billowing sails, shells, or the hoods of nuns' habits, and are covered in over a million Swedish ceramic tiles. The interior houses not just the auditorium of the opera, but a concert hall, a conventional theater and a cinema, plus restaurants, bars, gift shops and a library. Outside are steps of superhuman scale and a promenade around the point.

De Groot's dark deed
The opening of the Harbour Bridge on March 19, 1932, was the excuse for the biggest carnival Sydney had yet known, attended by one million people. As the crowds waited for the Labor Premier of N.S.W., Jack Lang, to cut the tape, a uniformed horseman darted forward and slashed the tape with his sword. Irishman Francis de Groot couldn't bear the thought of a socialist politician getting all this glory.

A drama of an opera
In spite of the brilliance of its design, the Sydney Opera House is not an ideal building for opera, with acoustics inferior to those of Melbourne's Arts Centre. A local joke has it that Australia has the world's best opera house, the outside in Sydney, the inside in Melbourne.

48

The Sydney Harbour Bridge, completed in 1932

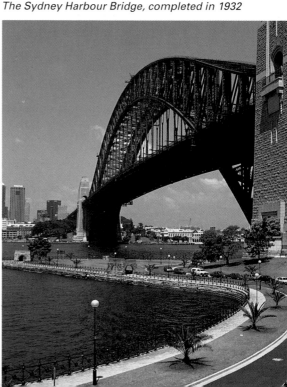

Walk Harborside and history

See map on pages 38–9.

This 3-mile walk gives magnificent harborside views, leads through the splendid botanical gardens, and then returns to Circular Quay past many fine early buildings.

The landward approach to the **Opera House** may lack some of the drama of the waterside approach but is still impressive, made part of the way underneath a canopy, then up gigantically scaled flights of steps. The fine trees of the **Royal Botanic Gardens** and Government House sweep down to the footpath leading around Farm Cove to the promontory of Mrs. Macquarie's Point, a deservedly popular harborside viewpoint. Do not miss the Botanic Gardens Tropical Centre with its "Arc" and "Pyramid" greenhouses.

The bridge leading to the **Art Gallery of New South Wales** spanning the Cahill Expressway allows some stunning views over the city and eastern suburbs. Macquarie Street leads northward, bounded to the west by mostly modern structures, and to the east by an unparalleled sequence of fine historic buildings. Bridge Street penetrates westward, modern buildings vying with old, including the Museum of Sydney. Macquarie Place makes a green interlude before the 1885 Customs House and the quayside.

49

Walk Sydney city center and Darling Harbour

See map on pages 38–9.

A walk through tightly built-up streets to revitalized Darling Harbour and back through the calm and dignity of Hyde Park.

From Martin Place Station, walk to Martin Place, Strand Arcade and Pitt Street Mall, pedestrian-friendly in their different ways. As you cross Pyrmont Bridge look up to see the controversial monorail and back to enjoy the city skyline.

An amazing array of new and varied facilities clusters around **Darling Harbour**. A rest in the **Chinese Garden** could precede the final leg of this walk: across Dixon Street leading to **Chinatown**, then up into **Hyde Park**, with its splendid avenues of fig trees and the imposing **Anzac Memorial**.

The attractive Chinese Garden was designed by landscape architects from China

Accommodations

A tremendous variety of accommodation is available in the Sydney area, though the city is not renowned for being cheap. Hotels range from first-rate to modest, and there are also serviced apartments, motels, backpackers' lodges, campsites, and bed and breakfast accommodation. An important factor is location; it's a good idea to have the *Sydney Transport Map* to hand before making your choice, since there are places that are extremely remote unless you have a car, and others whose distance from the sights is compensated for by good public transportation links. Advance reservation is advisable for peak periods like Christmas and January.

Hotels The city center has an excellent range of first-class hotels, as do a number of inner suburbs like Manly, Kings Cross and North Sydney. Whatever your price bracket, Manly is worth considering for its vacation atmosphere and its link to the center—by conventional ferry in 30 minutes or in about half that time by JetCat. The heart of town also has medium-priced and budget hotels, with a particular concentration around the Central Railway Station; Kings Cross also has a variety of such places, many of them in streets of relative tranquility.

Budget Kings Cross is a backpacker's paradise, with many lodges in Victoria Street. The scene here is in constant flux, so it is wise to check at the time whether a particular establishment is for you. Demand is often heavy, and it might be a good idea to start your tour of inspection early in the day. There is another cluster of accommodation at Bondi—an intriguing temporary address! The emphasis here is on affordable lodgings, with plenty of places offering rooms with cooking facilities. Bed and breakfast establishments are scattered all over the city. Details are obtainable from a number of agencies (see also Hotels and Restaurants on pages 268–81), and again, accessibility is a key factor. Camping sites, not surprisingly, are a long way out of the city.

Manly ferry
If you opt to stay at Manly, not only will you be able to enjoy the seaside atmosphere, but you will also be able to take the best ferry ride in the city. The trip takes 30 minutes from Sydney and passes close to North Head and South Head.

Luxury epitomized—one of the city's best hotels

the Regent SYDNEY

Food and drink

Brasseries and bistros are deservedly popular

Eating out Even more so than in the rest of Australia, eating in Sydney has been revolutionized in recent years, largely because of the huge influx of immigrants. *The Sydney Morning Herald's Good Food Guide* has no less than 50 categories of cooking in its index, beginning with African and ending with Vietnamese. In spite of recession, new restaurants continue to open, ingredients are good and chefs are increasingly skilled. Prices are extremely reasonable, particularly in pubs. Gourmet restaurants often offer a fixed-price lunchtime menu at a considerable saving over their evening prices. Prices are kept even lower because of the Bring Your Own (booze) or B.Y.O. phenomenon. Remember that a small corkage charge may be made. The highest prices are charged for restaurants that offer something extra, like a harborside setting or a panorama from the top of a high building.

Ethnic restaurants These are scattered all over the city, though there are concentrations in particular neighborhoods that have been settled by different nationalities. Thus **Greek** restaurants cluster around Elizabeth and Liverpool Streets, **Chinese** restaurants are found in Chinatown, **Italian** in Leichhardt and Newtown, and **Vietnamese** in the southwestern suburb of Cabramatta. Restaurants of many different kinds keep each other company in certain parts of town, along Oxford Street and on Stanley and Crown Streets in East Sydney, or to the west of the center, along Glebe Point Road, in King Street, Newtown, or Darling Street, Balmain. The eating establishments at Double Bay are as kosher as their designer boutiques, while Manly has an array of cafés, "chippers," take-out places and more conventional restaurants to match its vacation atmosphere.

Drink There is no shortage of places to drink in Sydney. The basic "hotel" or pub is still much in evidence, while other pubs have been renovated and offer a more varied experience, which might well extend to food and entertainment. Further up the scale of sophistication are the many hotel and cocktail bars; the famous **Marble Bar** of Adams' Hotel has found a new home at the Hilton.

Exclusive eating
Given Sydney's extensive shoreline, there are plenty of expensive restaurants with harborside settings, from The Rocks to Watsons Bay near South Head. The most stunning view is from the two restaurants on top of Sydney Tower.

Refreshments
Sydney has plenty of cafés featuring excellent Italian-style coffee. The tourist may be pleasantly surprised at the quality of food and refreshments available at the various museums and galleries.

51

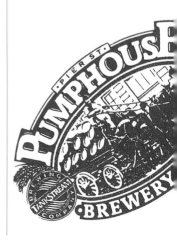

Shopping

Queen Victoria Building, a shopping wonderland

Sydney's C.B.D. (Central Business District) has all the temptations a shopper might reasonably expect in the center of a metropolitan city. There are department stores like **David Jones** and elegant 19th-century galleries like the **Strand Arcade**, or its modern equivalent, the shopping complex inserted into the lower floors of an office block. With its 200 boutiques and cafés on several levels, the immaculately restored **Queen Victoria Building** (see page 47) is a visitor attraction in its own right.

Souvenir hunting In places where tourists congregate like The Rocks or Darling Harbour, souvenirs are plentiful. Faced with the problem of what to bring home from Australia in addition to the inevitable stuffed koala or kangaroo (often made in Taiwan), you might consider a stylish Akubra hat or tough outdoor clothing to go with it, like a bush shirt or an oilskin coat. Sheepskin products, opals, or surfing gear are other possibilities. Australians are great readers, and bookshops are well-stocked with a good range of Australiana, albeit quite expensive, while newsagents (newsstands) sell an almost incredible range of periodicals catering to every possible taste.

First-rate maps are difficult to come by in Australia; a visit to the **Travel Bookshop** (Bridge Street) could be helpful here. Aboriginal artifacts of varying quality—paintings, carvings, boomerangs, didgeridoos (a large wooden trumpet) and fabrics—are widely available, better bought from a specialty store than from a souvenir stall. The best souvenir shops are probably those run by the main museums and galleries; the **Australian Museum**'s platypus actually looks like the real thing!

Markets Outside the center, the shopping streets of the more colorful suburbs such as Paddington and Balmain are good places to browse for something special, while Sydney's markets offer a memorable shopping experience. Usually held on a Saturday, they take place in Balmain, Glebe, Manly, and in Paddington. The famous **Paddy's Market** is not what it was, but the vast and lively fish market at Pyrmont is a daily spectacle well worth watching.

52

Browsers Welcome

Nightlife

Sydneysiders' main evening activity is probably eating and drinking, which can be combined with an enormous range of entertainments, from opera to jazz, from discos to drag acts—everything you would expect to find in a city of this size with a population whose main aim in life seems to be to enjoy itself.

Concerts and theater With several auditoriums, the **Opera House** is also a major site for classical concerts, ballet and drama. Classical music can also be heard at the **Town Hall** and, performed by student musicians, at the **Conservatorium of Music**. Some 20 theaters offer a choice of musicals, mainstream or alternative plays in a variety of locations, some—like the **Wharf Theatre** (near The Rocks) or **Ensemble Theatre** (on the north shore)—in an attractive waterside setting. The exciting **Sydney Dance Company** and the **Aboriginal and Islander Dance Theatre** appear at various locations.

Film City center movie theaters show the latest blockbusters, and there are a number of houses specializing in second runs and foreign films in Paddington (Academy Twin) as well as in the center (the two Dendy cinemas, Mandolin). The **State Theatre**, with its extravagant décor, is the home of the city's June Film Festival.

Music The Sydney jazz scene has a lot going for it, with numerous venues; the **Richmond Riverboat** provides daytime and evening jazz cruises. Rock is also well represented, with mammoth concerts held in the **Entertainment Centre** and a legion of other performers in pubs and clubs. Discos, cabarets and nightclubs abound, catering to all tastes and pockets. There are probably more gays in Sydney than in the rest of Australia put together, with the bars, clubs and pubs of Oxford Street as the main focus of the gay scene.

Information
The wealth of distractions available in this exhilarating city can be found in the Friday edition of *The Sydney Morning Herald*, while various giveaway publications also provide comprehensive entertainment listings. A good way of sampling Sydney's nightlife is to take one of the several guided tours available, although these can be tourist traps.

The American-style Studebaker's Bar, Kings Cross

Practical points

Tourist information The following offices will provide all the help you need: **New South Wales Travel Centre**, 19 Castlereagh Street (tel: 231 4444); **Sydney Visitors' Information Centre**, Martin Place (tel: 235 2424); **Transport Infoline** (tel: 13 1500) for all metropolitan bus, rail and ferry inquiries.

Getting around Probably the best way of familiarizing yourself with the layout of the city and its main sights is to take a guided tour bus, most of which pick up and drop off at central hotels. The bright red **Sydney Explorer** trundles around a 30-mile circuit of the principal attractions, allowing you to get on and off at will for a set fare.

Buses run a comprehensive scheduled service in the city center and suburbs, and with patience it's possible to get almost anywhere. They connect with ferries and trains at Circular Quay and with trains at Wynyard and Central Stations. A shuttle bus links The Rocks with Darling Harbour, while the Airport Express runs from Circular Quay and a few stops in the center as well as from Potts Point, Kings Cross, and Oxford Street.

Ferries travel at frequent intervals between Circular Quay and a number of destinations like Manly and Taronga Zoo on the north shore, or Balmain, Hunters Hill and Meadowbank upriver. There are also daily ferries east to Double Bay, Rose Bay, and Watsons Bay.

Double-decker electrified trains run on an extensive network of suburban lines as well as on a City Circle linking a number of stations in the C.B.D. like Town Hall, Central Station and Circular Quay. There's a useful spur from Central Station and Town Hall to Kings Cross and Bondi Junction (continue by bus to the beach). The line to North Sydney includes a trip over the Harbour Bridge. A novelty is the overhead **monorail,** which runs between the southwestern part of the city center and Darling Harbour.

The city's novel transportation system, the monorail

The SydneyPass

This combined ticket gives unlimited bus (including Airport Express and Sydney Explorer) and ferry travel for three, five or seven days, and is a bargain well worth thinking about.

Taxis are numerous, and can be hailed on the street, picked up at a cab dispatch line or ordered by telephone. Don't get worried if the driver has to consult his street directory!

54

Sydney Harbour

The glorious stretch of water running inland from the twin heads *is* Sydney, the reason for the city's existence, the source of its distinct identity and special glamor. What Captain Cook named Port Jackson and Captain Phillip called "the finest harbour in the world" is still alive with freighters, ferries and pleasure craft.

Twin symbols of Sydney—and Australia

One of the world's largest harbors Sydney Harbour has a complex outline of inlets, tributary rivers, bays, coves and promontories, so that a good proportion of the city's residents has some sight of the water from where they live, though competition is fierce and prices astronomical for dwellings enjoying what are considered to be the best views. Not that the entire 150 miles of shoreline are built up; much of it, like the headlands near its mouth, has been preserved as national park land. Added interest is given by an array of islands, including Fort Denison, where the skeletons of the executed once swung, and Goat Island with its shipyards west of the Harbour Bridge.

How to explore To board your rich friend's luxury ocean yacht, then take all day to cruise past the sights in total comfort would be an offer not to be refused. Water taxis would do the same kind of job, albeit expensively, while realistic alternatives include a variety of commercial cruises. But perhaps the most authentic way is the one enjoyed by the city's inhabitants as a matter of course; now that the tramcar has vanished from the streets, the ferry is the city's only archetypal means of conveyance.

An assortment of vessels plies between any number of points, of which the multiple piers of Circular Quay form the hub. In a matter of minutes you can slip across the water in the shadow of the Harbour Bridge to Kirribilli or chug upstream in the afternoon with uniformed schoolchildren returning to their pleasant suburban homes on the promontory of Hunters Hill.

A stroll around The Rocks
The Museum of Contemporary Art contrasts with Cadman's Cottage of 1816 and the other old buildings above it in well-restored George Street, where the visitor center dispenses useful information. Old and new come together around Campbells Cove, while Dawes Point Park, crouching at the feet of the Harbour Bridge, was the first fortified position in Australia. The way back is via the high-level Gloucester Walk and Argyle Street.

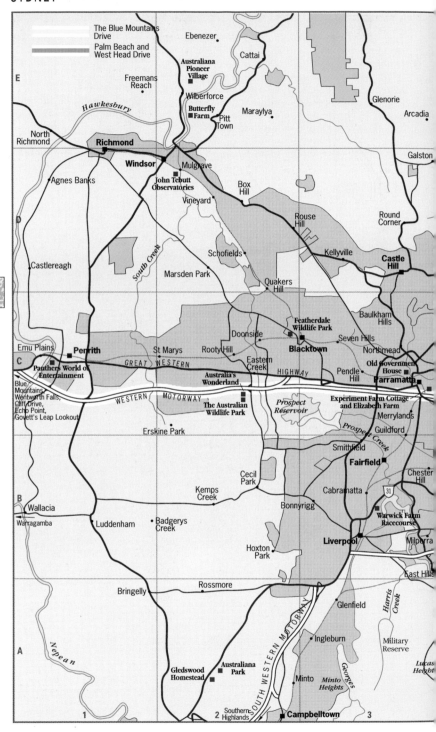

The Blue Mountains Drive

Palm Beach and West Head Drive

Ebenezer

Cattai

E

Australiana Pioneer Village

Freemans Reach

Wilberforce

Glenorie

Hawkesbury

Butterfly Farm

Maraylya

Arcadia

Pitt Town

North Richmond

Richmond

Windsor

Mulgrave

Galston

Windsor

Box Hill

Round Corner

John Tebutt Observatories

Agnes Banks

Vineyard

D

Rouse Hill

South Creek

Schofields

Kellyville

Castle Hill

Castlereagh

Marsden Park

Quakers Hill

Baulkham Hills

Featherdale Wildlife Park

Seven Hills

Doonside

Northmead

Emu Plains

Penrith

St Marys

Rooty Hill

Blacktown

Old government House

C

Panthers World of Entertainment

GREAT WESTERN

Eastern Creek

HIGHWAY

Pendle Hill

Parramatta

Blue Mountains, Wentworth Falls, Cliff Drive, Echo Point, Govett's Leap Lookout

Australia's Wonderland

WESTERN MOTORWAY

Experiment Farm Cottage and Elizabeth Farm

The Australian Wildlife Park

Prospect Reservoir

Merrylands

Prospect Creek

Guildford

Erskine Park

Smithfield

Cecil Park

Fairfield

Chester Hill

Kemps Creek

Cabramatta

31

B

Wallacia

Bonnyrigg

Warwick Farm Racecourse

Warragamba

Luddenham

Badgerys Creek

Liverpool

Milperra

Hoxton Park

East Hills

Bringelly

Rossmore

Glenfield

Harris Creek

Nepean

Ingleburn

Military Reserve

A

Georges

Lucas Height

Gledswood Homestead

Australiana Park

Minto

Minto Heights

Southern Highlands

SOUTH WESTERN MOTORWAY

Campbelltown

1

2

3

Brisbane Water
National Park,
Old Sydney Town
Broken Bay
West Head
Palm Beach
Whale Beach
South Head
Berowra
Waters
Cowan Creek
Ku-ring-gai
Chase
National
Park
Avalon
Church
Point
Newport Beach
Bungan Head
Akuna
Bay
Hornsby
Heights
Mona Vale
Turimetta Head
Waratah
Park
Bobbin
Head
Terrey
Hills
Ku-ring-gai
Wildflower Garden
Narrabeen
Collaroy
Narrabeen
Lagoon
Long Reef Point
Hornsby
St
Ives
Garigal
National
Park
Belrose
Oxford
Falls
Turramurra
Frenchs
Forest
Dee Why
Tennant
Hills
Lane Cove
National Park
Gordon
Killara
Middle Harbour
Beacon
Hill
Koala
Park
Epping
Macquarie
University
Chatswood
Willoughby
Cremorne
Manly
Oceanarium
Balgowlah
Manly
North Head
Sydney Harbour
National Park
Carlingford
Eastwood
West
Ryde
Crows Nest
Wayerton
Mosman
Taronga
Zoo
South Head
Watsons Bay
Dundas
Ryde
Vienna
Cottage
Greenwich
Hunter's Hill
Neutral
Bay
Milsons Pt
Pt Jackson
Vaucluse
Vaucluse House
Rosehill
Racecourse
Parramatta
Hall of
Champions &
Homebush
Bay Olympic
Park
Drummoyne
Sydney Maritime
Museum and
Lego Centre
SYDNEY
Balmain
Kings Cross
Kirribilli
Sydney Harbour
Bridge
Elizabeth Bay
Rose Bay
Lidcombe
Leichhardt
Darlinghurst
Glebe
Paddington
Double Bay
Bellevue Hill
Strathfield
Burwood
University of
Sydney
Central
Station
Redfern
Bondi
Junction
Bondi
Bronte
Tamarama
Bay
Regents
Park
Enfield
Erskineville
Centennial
Park
Coogee
Bankstown
Lakemba
Sydenham
Canterbury
Sydney
Airport
Kingsford
Maroubra
Blue Gum
Farm
Riverwood
Rockdale
Hurstville
Brighton-le-
Sands
Botany
Banksmeadow
Malabar
La Perouse
Monuments
Penshurst
Beverley
Park
La Perouse
Bare Island
Fort
Cape Banks
Picnic
Point
Lugarno
Sans Souci
Botany
Bay
Captain Cook's
Landing Place
Georges
Como
Bridge
Captain Cook
Bridge
Kurnell
Kurnell
Peninsula
Botany Bay
National Park
Potter Point
Como
Jannali
Sylvania
Menai
Woronora
Sutherland
Gymea
Caringbah
Bate Bay
Loftus
Sydney
Tramway
Museum
EG Waterhouse
National Camellia
Garden
Cronulla
Engadine
Audley
Port Hacking
Port Hacking
Point
Heathcote
NP
Heathcote
Royal National Park

0   5   10 km
0   5 miles

57

Drive The Blue Mountains

The famous Three Sisters pillars

See map on pages 56–57.

The truly spectacular cliffs, canyons and forests of the Blue Mountains can be sampled in a day trip.

The exit from Sydney via Route 40 gives good views of the upper harbor from the Gladesville Bridge. The route joins the Western Motorway near Parramatta and crosses the plain past Penrith to begin the climb up into the mountains, running parallel to the railroad. Several places of interest are marked by signs off the freeway; these are described below.

Wentworth Falls are probably the grandest waterfalls in the region. Pretty little Leura marks the start of the **Cliff Drive,** which skirts the 984-foot drop into the valley below. **Echo Point** is, deservedly, the most famous viewpoint in the mountains. Not far from the visitor center, viewing platforms offer panoramas over cliffs, eucalyptus forest and the Three Sisters sandstone columns. There are designated walks from here, or you can ride the Scenic Railway or Scenic Skyway further along the Cliff Drive.

Stops can be made at Katoomba, "capital" of the Blue Mountains, and northeast of Blackheath at the Blue Mountains Heritage Centre. **Govett's Leap Lookout** offers amazing views of the canyon. Parramatta and the Homebush Bay Olympic Site (the main venue for the Sydney 2000 Olympics), which you can tour.

Return on the Western Motorway.

Drive Palm Beach and West Head

A drive from Sydney to the splendid northern beaches and headlands. *See map on pages 56–57.*

Beyond the Harbour Bridge, Route 14 (Military Road) leads northeastward, crossing Middle Harbour by the Spit Bridge. A detour can be made to Manly (better visited by ferry from Circular Quay), or continue northward past the fine beaches of Long Reef, Collaroy, Narrabeen and Whale.

The road narrows and winds, rises and descends past desirable homes and vacation retreats as it approaches **Palm Beach**. To the west are fine views over the calm waters of the Pittwater inlet, a contrast to the crashing surf of the ocean beach to the east. On its headland to the north, the **Barrenjoey Lighthouse** beckons. Return to Mona Vale and follow the road around the southern end of Pittwater, turning right through the trees and wildflowers of the **Ku-ring-gai Chase National Park** to **West Head.** The head offers a completely different but equally spectacular view over Pittwater and Broken Bay.

Return via Mona Vale Road (Route 3) and the Pacific Highway.

There is a great deal to see and do in the various historic inner suburbs of the city; these are covered below.

Sydneysiders seem proud of the red-light district of **Kings Cross►►**, which has its fair share of hookers, strip joints, and adult bookshops. But there are also lots of places to eat and drink and plenty of shops for the local community. A stroll along Darlinghurst Road between Kings Cross and Fitzroy Gardens with its El Alamein Fountain is sure to entertain at most times of day or night.

Bourgeois in its origins, then proletarian and now gentrified, **Paddington►►**, or "Paddo," has had a checkered career as it has passed in and out of favor. Its glory is its delicious row houses with their fine ironwork and their subtle adaptation to the contours of the slopes falling northward to the harbor. Built between the 1860s and 1890s, most of them have been carefully restored by sensitive owners. Also here are **Juniper Hall** (1824), the **post office** (1885), and **Paddington Town Hall** (1891). Laid out to mark Sydney's 100th birthday, **Centennial Park** supports a varied birdlife as well as a whole range of outdoor activities.

The population of **Balmain►** used to work in its shipyards, but its delightful terraces and little detached weatherboard cottages have been colonized by a middle-class population with Paddington-style aspirations, but not the means to realize them. It too has a richly varied shopping street.

Detached from the common folk on its pleasantly wooded peninsula, **Hunters Hill►** is a tranquil place of expensive, fine stone houses and humbler cottages. Many of the former were built in French style in the 1850s, while one of the 19th-century tradesmen's abodes, **Vienna Cottage**, has been restored by the National Trust and houses a local museum.

Eastern suburbs
Sydney's eastern suburbs are nothing if not monied, and at Double Bay it shows, with plenty of designer labels and a discreet lack of price tags in its exclusive shops. There are lots of pleasant cafés too, where the shoppers can be seen relaxing after making their difficult choices.

59

See how the other half lives in exclusive Hunters Hill

Excursions

Easy-to-reach sights from Sydney are covered alphabetically on these two pages.

Broad **Botany Bay►** (7 miles south of the center) where Captain Cook's *Endeavour* dropped anchor on April 28, 1770, was given its name in recognition of the array of Antipodean plants collected here by Joseph Banks. Oil installations and industry now dominate the scene, but to commemorate Cook's historic landing on the Kurnell Peninsula, the national park contains an obelisk, a visitor center and a museum. At the northern edge of the bay, La Perouse, named after the commander of the French expedition that arrived just after the First Fleet, is the site of Sydney's principal Aboriginal settlement.

With splendid coastal and river scenery, **Brisbane Water National Park►** (47 miles north) resembles Kuring-gai Chase, its sandstone foundation supporting the same spectacular range of flowers and wildlife. There are woodlands of eucalyptus and pockets of rain forest, and Aboriginal carvings can be viewed at the Bulgandry site.

Ku-ring-gai Chase National Park►► (19 miles north of Sydney) remains in its wild state thanks to its designation as a national park as far back as 1894. The rugged sandstone plateau of which it consists is deeply incised by the deep sheltered waterways running inland from the Hawkesbury River. From West Head there are spectacular views across Broken Bay and the broad expanse of Pittwater. The Kuringgai (Guringai) Aborigines who once lived here traced many carvings in the sandstone. There is a useful visitor center at Bobbin Head, with displays on the area's varied animal and bird populations.

A short train ride away from today's glittering metropolis is the meticulously researched reconstruction of **Old Sydney Town►►** (stop at Gosford Station), showing what life might have been like as the city struggled to establish itself. Among buildings that faithfully re-create the atmosphere of the pre-1810 period, convincing-looking characters in authentic costume ply their trades, fight duels, or endure the barbaric punishments prescribed by harsh judges and sadistic floggers.

At the very tip of the Warringah peninsula, 25 miles north of the city center, is the exclusive residential area of **Palm Beach►►**. To the east, the ocean surf crashes on the beach, and to the west the tranquil surface of the beautiful **Pittwater** inlet is a paradise for boat lovers and windsurfers. A lighthouse crowns the Barrenjoey headland, offering a terrific view over Broken Bay and inland up the drowned valley of the Hawkesbury River. Founded only a matter of months after Sydney itself because of the fertility of the surrounding area, **Parramatta►►** might have become the colony's capital. Now the focal point of the sprawling western

Up the Hawkesbury

The fertile soil along the upper reaches of the easily navigable Hawkesbury River led to the area around Richmond and Windsor being settled within a few years of the arrival of the First Fleet. The winding lower river is best explored in a leisurely way by cruiser or houseboat; a unique experience is to board the mail boat at Brooklyn and accompany the postman as he delivers letters, packages and much more to isolated little places along the tranquil river.

The loss of La Perouse

Jean-François de Galaup, Comte de La Perouse, had brushed with the British before his meeting in Botany Bay with Captain Phillip. He was taken prisoner after the battle of Quiberon Bay in 1759 and later fought in the American wars. His ships *Astrolabe* and *Boussole* had reached Australia after a long search for the elusive North West Passage. On quitting Botany Bay La Perouse disappeared for ever, though wreckage assumed to be that of his ships was discovered off the New Hebrides in 1826.

Captain Cook's landing place memorial

Experiment Farm Cottage, Parramatta

suburbs 15 miles from the city center, it has been much redeveloped, but many traces remain of early days, including some of the nation's very first buildings.

Beyond the mock-Tudor gatehouse to Parramatta Park stands Australia's most venerable public edifice, **Old Government House**, which was built in 1799 though much expanded early in the 19th century. For many years the official Vice-Regal residence, it contains early Australian furniture. **Elizabeth Farm** in Alice Street is even older, begun in 1793 by the agricultural pioneers John and Elizabeth Macarthur. Its veranda is the prototype of countless others that adorn dwellings all over Australia. It too has been refurnished in the style of that period, as has the interior of **Experiment Farm Cottage** in Ruse Street. The land on which this house stands belonged to one of the few convicts with any farming experience; in 1789, James Ruse was the first man in Australia to sow a crop of wheat successfully.

Australia's first national park, proclaimed as early as 1879, the **Royal National Park►►** consists mostly of a rugged sandstone plateau with a varied vegetation of heathland (a brilliant show of wildflowers in spring), fine forests of blue gum and patches of rain forest. Eaten into by the sea, it has a coastline of spectacular cliffs interspersed with sandy coves. About 22 miles from Sydney and accessible by rail as well as by road, it has long been a favorite of serious bushwalkers, and is now a popular place for weekend outings of all kinds.

The splendid **Taronga Zoo►►** benefits from its superb site on a rocky peninsula almost directly opposite the city center and is worth visiting for the view alone, particularly if you take the cable-car ride (ferry from Circular Quay). Taronga doesn't limit itself to native animals, but it is the Australian fauna that most visitors will want to see. Here, the country's biggest collection has them all.

The road to Parramatta
A road was built from Sydney to Parramatta as early as 1794, but for years it was easier to bring people and goods up the river than along the highway. Partly superseded by an expressway, today's Parramatta Road is neither lovely nor efficient, though a trip along it reveals a cross section of Australian suburbia. In spite of interminable traffic signals and shabby shopping centers, there remains something indefinably romantic about it, a whiff of the days when it alone pointed to the interior of the unknown continent.

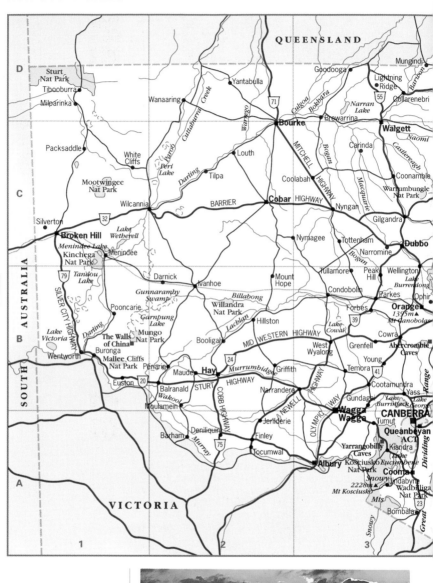

QUEENSLAND

D
Sturt
Nat Park
Tibooburra
Milparinka
Goodooga
Mungindi
Lightning
Ridge
55
Collarenebri
Yantabulla
Wanaaring
Narran
Lake
Walgett
Packsaddle
Bourke
Brewarrina
Naomi
White
Cliffs
Louth
Carinda
Coonamble
Warrumbungle
Nat Park
C
Peri
Lake
Tilpa
Coolabah
Mootwingee
Nat Park
Wilcannia
BARRIER
Cobar
HIGHWAY
Nyngan
Gilgandra
Silverton
Lake
Wetherell
Nymagee
Tottenham
Dubbo
Broken Hill
Menindee Lake
Menindee
Narromine
Wellington
Lake
Burrendong
Kinchega
Nat Park
Darnick
Ivanhoe
Mount
Hope
Tullamore
Peak
Hill
Parkes
Ophir
Tandou
Lake
Billabong
Condobolin
Orange
1395m
Mt Canobolas
Gunnaramby
Swamp
Willandra
Nat Park
Forbes
39
Pooncarie
Hillston
Lake
Cowal
Cowra
Garnpung
Lake
Lake
Victoria
The Walls
of China
Mungo
Nat Park
Booligal
MID WESTERN HIGHWAY
West
Wyalong
Grenfell
Abercrombie
Caves
Wentworth
Buronga
Mallee Cliffs
Nat Park
Penarie
Maude
Hay
24
Murrumbidgee
Griffith
Young
Tembora
41
B
SILVER CITY HIGHWAY
Darling
Euston
20
Balranald
Wakool
STURT
COBB HIGHWAY
HIGHWAY
Narrandera
Gundagai
Cootamundra
Yass
Lake
George
Lake
Burrinjuck
Moulamein
Jerilderie
NEWELL HIGHWAY
OLYMPIC WAY
Wagga
Wagga
CANBERRA
ACT
Queanbeyan
Tumut
Barham
Deniliquin
75
Finley
Tocumwal
Albury
Yarrangobilly
Caves
Kosciusko
Nat Park
Kiandra
Lake
Eucumbene
Cooma
A
VICTORIA
2228m
Mt Kosciusko
Snowy
Jindabyne
Wadbaliga
Nat Park
23
Bombala
Snowy Mts
Great Dividing Range

SOUTH AUSTRALIA

62

1 2 3

*Sunset on Black
Mountain, Canberra*

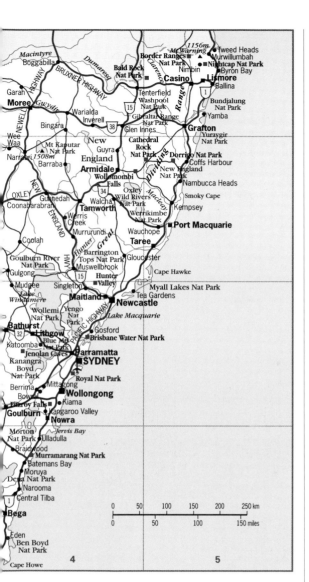

New South Wales This state *was* Australia in the early days of European settlement, and today it is still the country's most populous, as well as having the country's greatest city, Sydney, as its capital. If time is short, tourists are sometimes advised to concentrate on this state alone; and it is true that a vacation spent entirely within New South Wales' far-flung borders can be very rewarding, regardless of whether the visitor comes in search of urban pleasures or the delights of wild nature.

The Coastal Lowlands The "Premier State" can be divided into four regions, between them encompassing much that is typical of the country as a whole. Most of the population lives in the Coastal Lowlands, a fertile strip of country of varying width running some 870 miles from Victoria

NEW SOUTH WALES

What's in a name?
Between 1768 when he set out for Tahiti, and 1779 when he was hacked to pieces on a Hawaiian beach, Captain Cook probably named more places than anyone else in history. Some recall people (Port Jackson), some are a lively evocation of events (Cape Tribulation), some characterize a quirk of topography (Mount Dromedary in Tasmania has two humps). Inspiration seems to have failed him when confronted with the task of finding a suitable name for the whole of the eastern coast of Australia, even given the supposed resemblance of part of it to the coastline of southern Wales. But perhaps New South Wales, as a name, is one up on such masterpieces of inventiveness as South Australia.

to Queensland. Apart from glamorous Sydney, the region is home to the industrial cities of **Newcastle** and **Wollongong**, as well as a glorious chain of little ports and shore settlements like Ulladulla (directly east of Canberra). White Australia's history began here, when Captain Cook's charts led the First Fleet to Botany Bay, and where, after a shaky start, the process of colonization gradually got under way with the founding of townships and the clearing of the bush for farmland.

The area has also been the focus of much of the country's modern history, its industrial heartland and stronghold of the Labor movement that has played an often decisive role in Australian government and politics. It is here that the foundation was laid for Australian beach culture, as love of the sun, surf and sheer physical well-being overcame the remnants of Victorian prudery in the early decades of this century—a process that owed not a little to the incomparable beaches, which are still the state's main tourist attraction.

The Great Dividing Range Providing a constant backdrop to the coast, with its hills, peaks and tablelands also running the length of the state; in places the Great Dividing Range drops almost directly into the sea, elsewhere withdrawing to a distant but always visible horizon. The area formed a puzzling and frustrating barrier in the early years of the colony, until 1813 when the spectacular **Blue Mountains** were successfully crossed.

The highlands are as wonderfully varied as the coast: to the south, in the **Snowy Mountains**, they include the country's highest peaks and most extensive snowfields; to the north lies the high-level plateau of **New England**, named after the old country for its misty coolness and vivid green. In places, as in the **Southern Highlands**, the ranges are interspersed with broad plains that were converted early on into attractive farmland. Here there is a wealth of old buildings in town and country, as well as a 965-square-mile tract carved out of the state to form the Australian Capital Territory (A.C.T.), the site of the nation's capital, Canberra. Most of the rivers of southeastern Australia have their source in the uplands, with their relatively abundant rain and snowfall. Some, like the Hawkesbury and Hunter, are quite short, running east to the Pacific; others, much longer, form part of the huge Murray/Darling system, flowing slowly westward.

The Western Slopes Beyond the mountains and tablelands, the Western Slopes fall gradually towards the interior. Opened for settlement once the way across the Blue Mountains had been established, the area today consists mostly of unspectacular wheat and wool country. To the south, in the Riverina, the waters of the Murray and Murrumbidgee have been used to create huge irrigated areas that now support a variety of crops.

The Western Plains This area stretches to the borders with South Australia and Queensland. It is the New South Wales Outback, with vastly more sheep than people. Here the unfortunate township of **Bourke** has given its name ("back of Bourke") to utter remoteness, the Outback beyond the Outback. In the harsh landscape, the city of **Broken Hill** has grown up based on the world's richest lode of silver, lead and zinc; it is a place that attracts many visitors for its sheer strangeness.

65

Exciting Canberra, a modern planned city

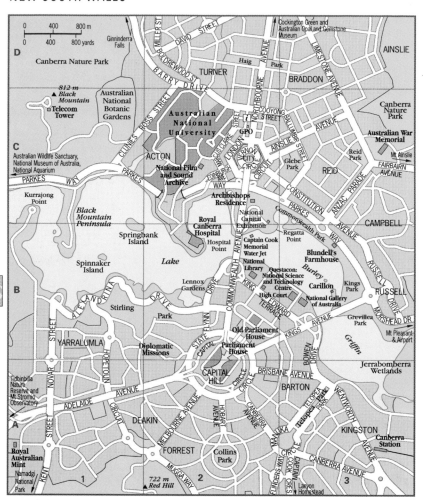

The home of foreign embassies

Canberra

Framed by glorious mountain scenery, Australia's capital comprises the prestigious buildings housing the nation's central institutions, all in a setting of broad boulevards and cozy neighborhoods. As well as being the country's only major inland city, Canberra is unique in having been planned in every detail from its very beginnings.

At the time of Federation, in 1901, the bitter dispute between Sydney and Melbourne about which should become the country's capital was finally resolved by choosing neither. Instead, the new Constitution stipulated that a site should be found in New South Wales, no closer than 100 miles to Sydney. After much debate the present location was chosen, and in 1911 some 965 square miles of land south of the Goulburn Plains became the Australian Capital Territory. Over 130 hopefuls took part in the international competition for the design of the new city, the American landscape architect Walter Burley Griffin emerging as winner.

Griffin had never seen Canberra when he drew up his plans for a new city thousands of miles from his Chicago base, but his experience enabled him to interpret maps and diagrams, and to appreciate the potential of the chosen location. His design is very much of his period, a combination of great vistas framing noble buildings, and self-contained residential neighborhoods.

The target population for the country's capital was 25,000, but Canberra's growth was painfully slow and this total was only reached in the years following World War II. Growth took off in the 1960s, and today the city is home to around 300,000 people. The majority of its workforce has always consisted of public employees, not necessarily a sound basis for a satisfactory social balance. In its infancy and adolescence, the city was seen as a place of exile, populated by bored civil servants longing for the fleshpots of Sydney or Melbourne. Nor is its contemporary image among Australians a particularly happy one; many think of it as a privileged place of parasitic politicians and cosseted bureaucrats.

The city of Canberra has been described with some truth as a collection of suburbs in search of a city, but what it lacks in urbanity it more than makes up for with convenience (there are no traffic jams!), easy access to superb countryside and sheer spacious beauty. It certainly is nothing like any other city in Australia and is well worth visiting for that reason alone, with an array of splendid modern buildings in the immaculately landscaped setting planned for them in the early years of the nation's foundation.

The extraordinary new Parliament House (built in 1988) is rich in national symbolism

The 266-foot flagpole on top of Capital Hill

A capital museum
The National Museum of Australia is still in the early stages of development. Its ambitious plans are presented in a visitor center on Lady Denman Drive, Yarralumla, and some exhibitions are now being held in Old Parliament House.

The Australian-American Museum is at Russell Hill

▶▶ **Australian National Botanic Gardens**   *66C1*

These attractive gardens on the lower slopes of Black Mountain present a wonderful range of native Australian plants—some 6,000 species in all. A network of paths leads through a series of contrasting environments, each with its fully labeled array of trees, shrubs and other plants. This is one of the very best places to appreciate Australia's unique flora.

▶▶▶ **Australian War Memorial**   *66C3*

Limestone Avenue, Campbell

Flanked by massive stone pylons, the dome of the War Memorial stares somberly from the lower slopes of Mount Ainslie down Anzac Parade towards Capital Hill on the far shore of Lake Burley Griffin. With its great courtyard containing the Roll of Honour and the Eternal Flame, it was officially opened in 1941.

It is not just a great monument, but a world-class museum that attempts to make some sense of the senselessness of war. Beyond the carefully crafted symbolism of the exterior are extensive galleries and displays evoking the many conflicts in which the country has been involved, from the Maori Wars of the 1860s to 1970s Vietnam. As well as the hardware of war, like guns and airplanes, there are superb paintings, photographs, huge dioramas, film and sound recordings, and documents and papers. This is not a museum to be visited casually or in a hurry.

▶▶ **Diplomatic Missions**   *66B2*

One of the most fascinating tours in Canberra is to the suburb of Yarralumla. Here many foreign countries built their embassies, free from any of the constraints of fitting into a long-established city. National self-expression takes a variety of forms: America occupies the most space, Greece has classical columns, Papua New Guinea has an exuberantly gabled longhouse and Indonesia has a Balinese temple.

▶▶ **Lake Burley Griffin**   *66B2*

Burley Griffin included a beautiful lake in his visionary plan for the new city, but it was not until 1964 that the great body of water bearing his name finally came into being, with an area of more than 2¾ square miles and a highly varied shoreline 22 miles long. A number of islands enliven the scene, which is further enhanced by lakeside landscaping, as in the recently completed and award-winning **Commonwealth Park**. The **Captain Cook Memorial Water Jet** reaches a spectacular 460 feet in calm weather.

Dating from 1860, **Blundell's Farmhouse** near the lakeshore is one of the few old buildings in Canberra. Rising over the weeping willows on Aspen Island are the crisp white concrete shafts of the **Carillon**, a gift from Britain to mark Canberra's 50th anniversary in 1963. Its 53 bells play Australian melodies as well as a medley of tunes from the old country. Designed to be the focal point of this extraordinary city, the lake makes a splendid setting for many of its most prominent buildings, and is well worth exploring aboard one of the cruise vessels.

The Botanic Gardens are well worth a visit

▶ **National Aquarium and Australian**   *66C1*
Wildlife Sanctuary

Lady Denman Drive, Yarralumla

In a fine setting by Scrivener Dam, the aquarium is a reminder that Australia owes much to the sea, whose myriad creatures can be observed here in a spectacular walk-through environment. The sanctuary features koalas, kangaroos and much more.

▶▶ **National Capital Exhibition**   *66C2*

Regatta Point Commonwealth Park

Boasting "the best view of the national capital," this is a good place for appreciating the meticulous and sometimes controversial planning of the new city.

▶ **National Film and Sound Archive**   *66C2*

McCoy Circuit, Acton

Australia was an early leader in the development of the motion picture, and this new center presents an intriguing selection from the nation's contribution to the delights of the silver screen. Radio and T.V. are also represented.

▶▶▶ **National Gallery of Australia**   *66B3*

Parkes Place

The national art collections are housed in an imposing structure of sandblasted concrete. Its neighbors on the banks of Lake Burley Griffin are also of national significance, like the glass and concrete cube of the High Court. The National Gallery has an excellent array of Australian art, beginning

Capital views

Canberra's ring of uplands provides splendid viewpoints over the carefully planned city in its superb setting. The spike of Telecom Tower sticks up from the top of Black Mountain (2,664 feet), giving panoramic vistas from its viewing galleries. Mount Ainslie (2,762 feet), rising through bushland behind the War Memorial, has equally spectacular views, as does Red Hill, 1¼ miles south of the Parliament.

Parliament House is a popular tourist sight

Capital coinage
As well as a gallery enabling visitors to see the country's money being made, the Royal Australian Mint has a public coining press where you can mint your own coins or tokens.

Capital punishment
Justice has moved on in Australia since the early days when the jail was sometimes the most prominent building in town. But modern Australians are second only to Americans in their fondness for litigation, and any number of interesting cases end up in the imposing High Court, with its lofty Great Hall and exhibition explaining the workings of the country's legal system.

with Aboriginal artifacts and ending with canvases on which the paint seems hardly dry.

There is much else besides, displayed to advantage in well-lit and highly varied spaces, including a good selection of European and American art—particularly of the 20th century —as well as works from Asia and the Pacific. Sculpture benefits from the attractive setting of the Sculpture Garden, which also serves as a venue for outdoor events.

▶ **National Library of Australia** *66B2*
Parkes Place
As well as several million books, this rather severe neoclassical building houses other unique collections relating to the history and evolution of Australia. The interior is adorned with fine tapestries and stained glass.

▶▶▶ **Parliament House** *66B2*
Capital Hill
The truly spectacular structure of Parliament House was completed in time for Australia's Bicentenary in 1988. As well as housing the House of Representatives and the Senate, it has become a major visitor attraction in its own right, rich in artworks and national symbolism. Over three million cubic feet of soil was removed from the top of Capital Hill to make way for the new building, then replaced to form its green roof. This superb viewpoint over the city is topped by a 266-foot flagstaff of stainless steel flying what must be the biggest flag in the world. Below is a complex of beautifully designed internal spaces, adorned with the creations of Australian artists like Arthur Boyd, whose gloriously colorful tapestry graces the far wall of the Great Hall. The 48 marble columns of the foyer recall the country's eucalyptus trees, whose cool green color appears again in the chamber of the House of Representatives, intended perhaps to calm the often inflamed tempers of its occupants.

▶ **Questacon** *66B2*
King Edward Terrace
The recently completed National Science and Technology Centre in its exciting modern building has more than 170 hands-on displays in six different galleries.

By air A comprehensive network of international and domestic air services operates from Sydney's Kingsford Smith Airport, 7 miles south of the city center on Botany Bay. The separate domestic and international terminals are linked by bus and taxi, and the frequent Airport Express bus takes 30 minutes to the city center or Kings Cross (20 minutes to Central Railway Station). There are flights to the N.S.W. Outback and many coastal resorts, to Cooma (for the Snowy Mountains) and to Canberra.

By bus The network of long-distance bus services is a far-flung one, although schedules can be inconvenient in the case of remote townships. On the main routes there is likely to be a choice of operator and times. Organized bus tours are very popular, and many places can be visited in this way from Sydney. Most major towns have a well-developed network of local bus services.

By rail Of all the Australian states, N.S.W. has kept the most widespread rail network, and of those towns that have lost their train service, many are connected to a rail-head by express buses (XPCs) operated by the State Rail Authority. Multiple-unit express trains (XPTs) ply between many major towns (Canberra, Tamworth, Dubbo). Luxurious interstate trains run to Brisbane and Melbourne. Broken Hill is visited by the *Indian Pacific* on its way to and from Western Australia, and has its own link to Sydney, the *Silver City Comet*. The Greater Sydney region is particularly well served by frequent CityRail services, which extend as far as Newcastle and Dungog in the north, the Blue Mountains in the west, Goulburn and the Southern Highlands, and Nowra on the south coast.

By car Driving is not recommended in the Sydney area. Here, public transportation and the occasional taxi should get you anywhere you are likely to want to go. However, many remote parts of the state are only accessible if you have your own vehicle.

Renting a 4WD makes sense if you plan to go off road

A long way by car
New South Wales is comprehensively crisscrossed by a web of named highways, very helpful in planning an itinerary, though they tend to be of variable quality. Driving the Pacific Highway north along the coast can get tedious, and many prefer the inland New England Highway.

71

One of the old buildings in the pleasant town of Bathurst

72

▶▶ Armidale   *63C4*

Unofficial capital of the cool uplands of New England in the northeast of the state, Armidale is the nearest thing Australia has to a university city, with a number of higher education colleges and several private schools as well as the University of New England in its parkland campus. A couple of cathedrals, plus a number of venerable public buildings and delightful old houses further enhance the refined atmosphere. The modern **New England Regional Art Museum▶** has a reputation as the best provincial collection of Australian art, and there is a good Folk Museum housed in a building dating from 1863.

Armidale makes a good base for exploring this part of New England (whose Scottish settlers tried and failed to make the name New Caledonia stick); within easy reach are a number of spectacular waterfalls, including the highest in Australia, **Wollomombi Falls▶** in the Oxley Wild Rivers National Park.

▶ Batemans Bay   *63A4*

This fishing port and popular tourist resort on the estuary of the Clyde River is conveniently situated for the citizens of Canberra, only 93 miles away over the mountains. There are fine oysters and lobsters, and a penguin colony on Tollgate Island.

▶▶ Bathurst   *63B4*

At the end of the Great Western Highway from Sydney, Bathurst was founded by Governor Macquarie in 1815, making it the country's oldest inland town. It was the point of departure for many expeditions farther into the interior, and in 1851 it was the scene of Australia's first gold rush. Those days are recreated in the open-air museum called Bathurst Gold Diggings, and the town itself is full of interest. The scenic drive around Mount Panorama forms part of what is considered to be Australia's finest motor-racing circuit.

▶▶▶ Blue Mountains National Park   *63B4*

Sheer cliffs dropping into deep canyons and glorious eucalyptus forests make up some of the most spectacular landscapes to be seen in Australia. The grandeur of the natural scene is all the more impressive because of the proximity of the manicured residential and retirement areas clustered along the main road and railroad from Sydney, 90 minutes away.

The Blue Mountains are not really mountains, but a vast sandstone tableland, deeply incised by watercourses like the Nepean and Cox's rivers. Their color is real, however, as a vaporous emanation from the leaves of the eucalypts hangs in the air as a blue haze. Since the early part of this century the mountains have attracted serious bushwalkers as well as sightseers, and they offer all kinds of pleasures today, from antiques hunting in sophisticated little townships, to real escape into wild country for those who are prepared to abandon their cars. The following main sights could just about be seen in the course of a day trip from Sydney, but it would be far better to stay at least a couple of days.

A good place to start is at the excellent **Heritage Centre▶** 1¼ miles to the east of the main highway at

The way to the west
Just visible from the area around Sydney, the dark escarpment of the Blue Mountains rises abruptly some 1,968 feet from the valley floor, blocking the way westward to the early colonists. Some convict escapees were convinced that China lay just beyond the mountains as they headed toward what they hoped would be freedom. The puzzle of how to cross the mountains, by keeping to the ridges rather than to the valleys, was solved by Blaxland, Lawson and Wentworth in 1813, and within two years Governor Macquarie had a road built by convict labor on the alignment still followed by the modern road and railroad. This marked a great leap forward in the development of the colony, promising an opening up of the immense potential of the still unknown interior.

73

The scenery becomes dramatic near the sandstone cliffs around Katoomba in the Blue Mountains

Blackheath. A short distance away is one of the most spectacular lookouts in the whole National Park, **Govett's Leap**▶▶, with breathtaking views of the Grose Valley and Bridal Veil Falls. A panoramic walk leads along the clifftop to various other vantage points, while a steep track descends into the superb forest of blue gums far below. The other great viewpoint in the park is **Echo Point**▶▶ just to the south of **Katoomba**, the "capital" of the municipality known as City of the Blue Mountains. Here there is another visitor center whose glass wall looks straight out into the treetops, while projecting platforms give giddy views of the famous sandstone pillars of **The Three Sisters**. A number of popular walks fringe the clifftop or descend into the valley. Just to the west are two exciting forms of tourist transportation, the Skyway, a cable car dangling over the abyss, and the Scenic Railway, a modernized inclined plane dropping steeply into the valley bottom.

To the east are the famous **Wentworth Falls**▶▶, the highest in the area with a drop of 886 feet, and at Faulconbridge the **Norman Lindsay Gallery and Museum**▶ commemorates this well-known artist. Westward are the truly spectacular **Jenolan Caves**▶▶ and the charming late-Victorian guesthouse associated with them, while one of the country's great feats of railroad engineering, the **Zig Zag Railway**▶ (see panel) can be enjoyed near Lithgow.

The great Zig Zag
In 1866, the engineers building the railroad line to the west were confronted with the problem of how to lower it from the top of the Blue Mountains down the sheer cliff face into Lithgow. Their solution, on a par with the great feats of railroad engineering in the Swiss Alps, was to construct a line in the form of a letter Z down the cliff face, with reversing stations at two points. This worked well enough for many years, but was eventually replaced by the present main line, which takes a long way round but eliminates the need for reversing. The Zig Zag has now been restored as a tourist railroad, an impressive spectacle as powerful veterans of the steam age haul their coaches up the steep slope to the accompaniment of much noise and smoke.

Wentworth Falls lookout in the Blue Mountains

With its long coastline, mountains and extensive Outback, New South Wales has wonderful examples of many of the continent's characteristic natural landscapes.

In the far west On the fringes of Australia's Red Centre and well over 600 miles from Sydney are two superb arid wildernesses. In **Sturt National Park** summer temperatures can reach 122°F for days on end; grassy plains alternate with claypans and pebbly desert from which rise flat-topped mesas (rocky tableland). In the extreme west are the ruddy sand dunes of the Strzelecki Desert. **Kinchega National Park** has vast plains of red sand as well as the strange saucer-shaped overflow lakes of the Darling River. Both areas are home to emus and the large red kangaroo.

Not just parks
The N.S.W. National Parks and Wildlife Service manages a number of sites whose interest is primarily human, rather than natural. These include places like Mootwingee Historic Site, with its wealth of mysterious Aboriginal relics, and sites of significance in the early European settlement of the country like Captain Cook's Landing Place at Botany Bay. Sydney's oldest dwelling, Cadman's Cottage, is a National Parks and Wildlife Service shop and resource center, a useful source of information for planning your ventures into N.S.W.'s rich heritage.

To the east The land gradually rises through the western slopes of the Great Dividing Range to the range itself, the backbone of the state. On the border with Victoria is one of the world's great national parks, centered on Australia's highest peak, **Mount Kosciusko**, after which the park itself is named. Glacial lakes, wild heathlands, alpine flowers and glorious forests of snow gums make a superb setting for summer hiking, while the area becomes the nation's winter playground for many months of the year. The forested highlands that extend from near Newcastle through New England to the Queensland border have a rich vegetation that includes much undisturbed rainforest; here 16 separate parks and reserves have been grouped together to form one of Australia's World Heritage Areas, the **Australian East Coast Temperate and Subtropical Rainforest Parks.** Old volcanoes give rise to dramatic landforms here and at **Warrumbungle National Park** farther inland, a weird world of rocky crags and natural skyscrapers. **Bald Rock National Park** is another extraordinary landform, a great granite dome rising 656 feet out of the bush.

Mount Kosciusko: good walking country

►   **Bourke**   62C2

This Outback town 497 miles northwest of Sydney seems utterly remote. It is the center of a vast and semi-arid area supporting large numbers of sheep and cattle as well as some crops on land irrigated with water from the Darling River. Originating in a wooden stockade built in 1835 against Aboriginal attack, Bourke has a number of buildings dating from the latter part of the 19th century. Its main attraction, however, lies in its very remoteness and as a base for penetrating further into the New South Wales Outback.

►►   **Broken Hill**   62C1

Founded on a 4¼-mile lode of silver, lead and zinc, the richest of its kind in the world, the unique "Silver City" faces an uncertain future as rationalization takes place against a background of low world prices for its products.

Thanks to the water piped in from its recreational reservoir at Lake Menindee 68 miles away, Broken Hill is a surprisingly green and leafy spot in what is one of the world's harshest environments: bitterly cold in winter, intolerably hot in summer, with a negligible rainfall that is only a tiny fraction of the evaporation rate. Nearly dead from thirst, the explorer Sturt gave the hump-backed ridge its name in 1844, but it was not until the 1880s that a German-born boundary rider, Charles Rasp, founded the Broken Hill Proprietary Company (see panel), which exploited the underground wealth in uneasy partnership with the workforce for many years. A great strike of 1919 ended in a historic compromise; the companies were insured their profits and the workers granted conditions far in advance of the time, like a 35-hour week. A confederation of labor unions effectively ran the town, not always on what today would be regarded as progressive lines. Broken Hill has always been a long way from the government in Sydney, and its ties are closer to South Australia, with smelters at Port Pirie, union beaches at Adelaide and clocks that keep South Australian time.

Continued on page 78.

Broken Hill Proprietary
B.H.P., as it is universally known, had its roots in Charles Rasp's discovery in 1883 of the immensely rich silver, lead and zinc lode at Broken Hill. It is now Australia's largest company, having long since diversified out of exploiting the mineral wealth of Broken Hill into iron and coal, gas and oil, and steel-making. Its profits are taken by many as an index of the prosperity of the country as a whole.

75

Captain Cook

Born the son of a farm laborer at Marston in Yorkshire in 1728, James Cook became the greatest explorer of his age. He was educated at the expense of his father's generous-minded employer, then learned seamanship aboard a Whitby collier. In 1755 he joined the Royal Navy, where he refined his navigational and other skills in the course of the Seven Years War. His charts of the St. Lawrence River helped Wolfe in the conquest of Quebec. But the achievement for which Lieutenant (as he then was) Cook is best remembered is his masterly voyage of exploration along the wholly unknown east coast of Australia in 1770.

Ahead of his time
Cook was well in advance of his time in seeing beyond the sometimes incomprehensible behavior and apparent material poverty of the Aborigines to the deeper harmony of their lives. He wrote: "In reality they are far more happy than we Europeans, being wholly (*sic*) unacquainted not only with the superfluous but the necessary Conveniences so much sought after in Europe, they are happy in not knowing the use of them. They live in a Tranquillity which is not disturbed by the Inequality of Condition: the Earth and sea of their own accord furnishes them with all things necessary for life."

As Cook had documented an eclipse of the sun off the coast of Newfoundland, he was a natural choice when the Royal Society wished for an accurate observation to be made from Tahiti of the transit of Venus across the face of the sun. Accompanying him on this mission aboard the barque *Endeavour* was an astronomer, Charles Green, together with two eminent botanists, Daniel Solander and Joseph Banks, still a young man of 25.

East coast sighting On July 3, 1769, the transit of Venus was duly observed and Cook opened the sealed orders given him by the Admiralty. These instructed him to investigate the existence or otherwise of a great southern continent and to survey and take possession of New Zealand. Having completed a thorough exploration of the New Zealand coast, Cook decided to return via the hypothetical "East Coast of New Holland." This was sighted on April 19, 1770, when Cape Everard (originally called Cape Hicks in honor of Cook's sharp-eyed second in command) came into view.

1770: Cook takes possession of N.S.W. for Britain...

CAPTAIN COOK'S LANDING PLACE

Sailing northward along the coast, Cook found a convenient harbor to drop anchor and investigate local conditions. The crew feasted on fresh fish, and the delighted botanists discovered an extraordinary array of plants, birds and animals previously unknown to science. In deference to their serious purpose, Cook altered his original name for the anchorage, Stingray Harbour, to Botany Bay.

Grounded on the Barrier Reef Further north, Cook noted in passing the existence of what seemed to be a fine natural harbor and named it Port Jackson. The wonderful setting for the future city of Sydney had to await full discovery until the arrival of the First Fleet 18 years later. Feeling his way into "the labyrinth of coral islands, shoals, rocks and lee shores" of the Barrier Reef, even Cook with his superb seamanship couldn't fend off a grounding, and the *Endeavour* struck a reef.

Although it floated off, thanks to all kinds of impedimenta being jettisoned (a cannon is now in the National Library in Canberra), the barque needed repairs and was beached for a month near today's Cooktown at the base of Cape York. Once more the scientists had a field day, making their first acquaintance with kangaroos and turtles. When the *Endeavour* was seaworthy again, Cook sailed north to the tip of the cape where, on Possession Island, he hoisted the flag and formally declared the whole of eastern Australia to be British, giving it the unremarkable name of New South Wales.

The end of the road Promoted to captain, Cook went on in 1772–5 to become the first to sail within the Antarctic Circle, finally putting paid to the idea of the great southern continent. In the course of an attempt in 1779 to find the elusive northern passage between the Atlantic and Pacific, he landed on Hawaii. As he was mediating in his usual calm and dignified way in a relatively trivial dispute with the islanders, one of his men stupidly discharged his firearm; enraged, the islanders fell upon Cook, who had turned his back on them to restore order, and he collapsed beneath blows from clubs and daggers.

Banks the botanist
Australia's 73 species of *Banksia* commemorate the rich young scientist who sailed with Cook and who has been described as "the father of Australian botany." On the voyage out he listed 230 plant species at Madeira, 316 at Rio, 104 at Tierra del Fuego and 400 in New Zealand. Later, Banks was president of the Royal Society for 32 years, continuing to take an interest in all things Australian.

...having made his mark in Botany Bay

Guess what grows at this Coffs Harbour plantation!

Continued from page 75.

Protected from dust storms by extensive tree belts, Broken Hill is laid out on a grid of streets with names like Chloride, Mica, and Cobalt. The excellent Tourist Information Centre is close to the old Sulphide Street Station, now a mineral and train museum. The Gladstone Mining Museum has interesting exhibits, but it's more exciting to go down a former mine, like Delprat's Mine or Day Dream Mine. The town is also the base for the **Royal Flying Doctor Service** and the **School of the Air**, both of which are open to the public. The strange environment of the city and its surroundings seems to have acted as a stimulant to a number of artists, and there are several galleries, of which the best known is that run by Pro Hart.

► **Byron Bay** 63D5

Cape Byron is the easternmost point of the Australian mainland, capped with a powerful lighthouse. Byron Bay itself, with wonderful beaches and a gloriously scenic hinterland of forests and mountains, has been a focal point of alternative lifestyles since the late 1960s. The beaches to either side of the headland vary in character, from secluded coves to great stretches of sand. Surfing is well established; the first lifesaving club was founded here as early as 1907.

► **Cobar** 62C2

This copper-mining town on the fringe of the Outback straddles the Barrier Highway on its way west to Broken Hill. Founded in the early 1870s as a typical mining city of tents and huts, it soon reached its peak population of some 10,000. That time has left a legacy of buildings like the Great Western Hotel with its extraordinarily long veranda and the mining company's office, which is now the Pastoral, Mining and Technological Museum. After a long decline, the place prospered again in the 1960s.

Silver screen Silverton
About 16 miles west of Broken Hill is the ghost town of Silverton, whose population moved to the bigger town when mining became unprofitable here in the late 1880s. With its restored buildings seeming to typify the spirit of the Outback, it has taken on a new lease of life as a stage set for a number of films, including *A Town Like Alice* and one in the *Mad Max* series.

Our banana's the biggest
The improbably oversized fruit known as the Big Banana dominates the scene on the Pacific Highway just to the north of Coffs Harbour. Made of concrete rather than peel and fruit, it marks the entrance to a banana plantation that welcomes visitors. Here you can see bananas growing, eat bananas in every imaginable form, buy banana-shaped souvenirs, and find out everything you always wanted to know about bananas but never dared to ask.

► **Cockington Green, A.C.T.** ⋃⋃D⋂

The original Cockington in the southwest of England, a picture-postcard village with thatched cottages, a pub, a forge and other assorted items of rusticity, is reproduced here on the outskirts of Canberra in miniature form. There are also scaled-down versions of Stonehenge and other quaint features of the country Australians used to refer to as "home."

►► **Coffs Harbour** 63C5

Roughly halfway between Sydney and Brisbane, this old timber port is famous for its beaches and banana plantations (see panel opposite). A string of fine beaches runs northward from the town's Park Beach, some with good surf. There is rafting on nearby rivers, while manmade attractions for vacationers include the Pet Porpoise Pool, with seals, penguins and sharks as well as amiable porpoises. The harbor is protected by a headland to the south, and by Muttonbird Island (reached by the old timber jetty) where there really are muttonbirds. The town center, with its Historical Museum and Bicentennial Botanical Garden, is some distance inland. It is a popular place for craftsmen and handicraft shops.

► **Dubbo** 62C3

At the junction of the Newell and Mitchell Highways, Dubbo is the flourishing center for a large part of N.S.W.'s Central West area. First settled in the 1840s, it became a stopping point for those in search of "better land, farther out." Overlanders driving their cattle southward to the markets of S.A. and Victoria used to cross the Macquarie River near here. There are a number of fine old buildings in the town center, among them the 1876 bank, which now houses a good local museum and the jail, complete with gallows. But most visitors come here for the **Western Plains Zoo►**, the biggest of its kind in the country, with animals from all over the world roaming its parkland.

► **Eden** 63A4

The last place of any size on the N.S.W. coast before the border with Victoria, this little port and resort began life as a whaling station, recalled in the **Killer Whale Museum►**. On Twofold Bay are the remains of Boydtown, begun around the 1840s by the English entrepreneur Benjamin Boyd and vaingloriously intended to rival Sydney as the colony's capital. More recently, Eden has been the focus of the battle to save Australia's forests from the woodchip industry.

► **Forbes** 62B3

Almost deserted after the gold rush of the 1860s, this western town survived as the center for a rich agricultural area. Some fine late 19th-century buildings like the imposing Town Hall still grace the wide streets. Just outside town is a recreated settlement of pioneer days, **Lachlan Vintage Village►**, where you can pan for gold or watch sheep being shorn. The bushranger Ben Hall met his end in Forbes in 1865, an event recalled in some detail in the old music hall that houses the town's museum.

Whale and chips
The first whaling station on the Australian mainland was established at Eden in 1818, and whaling continued to be based here until the 1930s. A revival of Eden's economy took place in the late 1960s with the building of the Harris Daishowa mill, designed to turn the forests of the area (some of the finest in the state) into woodchips for the Japanese paper industry. The project aroused the ire of the growing Australian conservation movement, whose members saw in it the export of part of the country's irreplaceable natural heritage. The other side of the story is presented in the chipmill's visitor center.

79

These days, whale-watching is popular at Twofold Bay

Watering the wilderness
The explorer John Oxley reckoned no white man would ever want to take up residence in the "barren and desolate" country he glimpsed from Mount Binya in 1817. But in the early 1900s, the N.S.W. government, enthused by private successes with irrigation experiments, built the Burrinjuck Dam and encouraged settlement in the Murrumbidgee Irrigation area. Many settlers were out-of-work miners from Broken Hill; later, returned servicemen and Italian immigrants with important agricultural skills moved in, and in spite of many disappointments and technical difficulties, the area produces crops of fruit (including grapes), vegetables, cotton and rice. Together with similar projects in the region, a total of 2,317 square miles of near desert has been made to bloom.

All of the 30 or so wineries in the Hunter Valley welcome visitors; most are around Cessnock and Pokolbin

▶ **Glen Innes**   *63D4*

This high-altitude town in northern N.S.W. is at the center of a prosperous farming area, once named the "Land of the Beardies" after two pioneers. The region is well known for the sapphires and other gemstones that are extracted commercially (amateur fossicking or searching is also possible). The town center has several well-cared-for late 19th-century buildings; the old hospital houses the **Land of the Beardies History House Museum▶**, one of the most interesting of its kind in Australia.

▶ **Goulburn**   *63B4*

The second oldest inland town in Australia straddles the Hume Highway some 125 miles southwest of Sydney and is the focal point of the well-tended farmlands all around, whose specialty is proclaimed by another one of those Australian "big ones"; 50 feet high, the Big Merino guards the town's western approach. Goulburn is a "real" city, with two cathedrals, a long main street and a number of imposing 19th-century buildings. On the edge of town is Riversdale, a coaching inn dating from the late 1830s, authentically restored and furnished.

▶ **Grafton**   *63D5*

Center of the Clarence River district, Grafton was "green" before its time. The town council initiated a policy of tree-planting as early as the 1860s, and today's citizens are benefiting from the many jacarandas and other flowering species that grace its broad streets. The bend of the Clarence was only bridged in 1932, when the present double-decker structure was built. Grafton is a good base for tours, with several national parks within easy reach.

▶ **Griffith**   *62B2*

Designed by Walter Burley Griffin, the architect responsible for the planning of Canberra, this model township was built to act as the main urban center for the

Murrumbidgee Irrigation Area. Its conception on the drawing board can be seen in its radial street pattern and in the decorative use of irrigation water in its gardens.

▶ Gundagai   62B3

The name of this township along the Hume Highway is derived from an Aboriginal word meaning "up-river"; in spite of warnings from the local Aborigines, the first settlers built their houses on the floodplain of the Murrumbidgee, and were duly swept away when the river broke its banks in 1852, causing the country's worst-ever flood disaster. The Murrumbidgee is crossed here by the longest wooden viaduct in Australia.

▶▶ Hunter Valley   63C4

The broad valley of the Hunter River, which ends in the sea at Newcastle, has contrasting landscapes created by mines and wines. The coalfield has been exploited for a century and a half, and has been the making of the city of Newcastle. The vineyards were first planted here in the 1830s and, after periods of decline, are flourishing once more. A day trip or, better still, one lasting a couple of days is a favorite outing for Sydneysiders, not least because of the excellent food offered in the area.

The landscape of the Hunter is one of its attractions, in its framework of wooded hills running down from the Brokenback Range to the southwest of the valley. Grapevines benefit from the rich soil, which has its origin in the outpourings of ancient volcanoes. The wineries range from family-sized concerns to large-scale commercial enterprises. Australia's oldest wine-press is on display at the **Golden Grape Estate**. The Wyndham and Rothbury Estates are well worth visiting, while Hungerford Hill has a complex of attractions including restaurants, playgrounds, shops and carriage rides. Other wineries are situated in the Upper Hunter Valley, some 56 miles farther on.

The dog sat on the tuckerbox

The teamsters traveling along the rough roads of early Australia were inevitably accompanied by various breeds of dog, one of which seems to have committed an unspeakable act while sitting on his master's tuckerbox by the side of the road. This and other deeds were recorded in the crude ballads of the time, refined somewhat in a version by the poet Jack Moses, and commemorated in a sculpture just outside Gundagai. This is the work of one Frank Rusconi, who was also responsible for the amazing model cathedral of marble on show in the Tourist Information Centre.

81

This part of the Great Dividing Range is the roof of Australia, much of it a highland plateau from which rise a number of peaks more than 6,500 feet high. Parts of it make up the country's most popular winter sports area, with several well-equipped ski resorts. But the mountains are glorious in summer too; a carpet of alpine wildflowers is unrolled as the snow retreats and there are superb paths and trails offering some of the most exhilarating hiking in Australia.

The Snowy Mountains Scheme

This was a visionary project to make the rivers in the mountains work for their living. Well-muscled (and well-paid) immigrants did most of the work, which aimed at altering the course of rivers to irrigate the parched agricultural areas farther west and generate hydroelectric power in the process. Many dams were built, of which the largest, at Lake Eucumbene, holds back more water than is contained in Sydney Harbour. There are 50 miles of aqueducts, 93 miles of tunnels and seven power stations, the latter providing a good proportion of the electricity consumed in southeast Australia. Some of the impressive installations (like Murray No.1 on the Alpine Way, or Tumut 2 north of Cabramurra) are open to the public.

The region is popular with winter sports enthusiasts

History The mountains attracted graziers (sheep raisers) from early on and a few determined bushwalkers between the two world wars, but it was only after the start of the Snowy Mountains Scheme in the late 1940s, when roads were driven through the wilderness and many other facilities created, that the area became accessible and visitors were able to come here in large numbers. Aboriginal interest in the mountains was more recent than in many parts of Australia, dating only from the end of the last Ice Age some 10,000 years ago. This is one of the few Australian landscapes with glacial lakes, cirques and moraines, all the result of the action of the ice sheets that were absent elsewhere in the country.

A popular starting point for exploring the mountains is the town of **Cooma** at the junction of the Monaro and Snowy Mountains highways. It was from here that the Snowy Mountains Authority oversaw what was to become one of the greatest 20th-century engineering projects in the world. Two tourist offices provide all conceivable kinds of information about the mountains and the great project that so transformed them: the visitor's information center in town and the Snowy Mountains' Authority Information Centre on the Canberra road.

The resort town of **Jindabyne** on its lake provides plenty of accommodations for winter sports enthusiasts heading for the snowfields farther west. The National Parks Service has a useful visitor center at Sawpit Creek

on the way up to some of the skiing areas in the heart of the mountains. These include **Smiggin Holes**, **Perisher Valley**, and **Mount Blue Cow**, the latter reached by the underground railroad known as the Ski Tube. At the end of the road is Charlotte Pass, with superb views of the mountain peaks. This is the starting point for a number of wonderful walks, including the Summit Walk to the top of **Mount Kosciusko**, at 7,310 feet the highest peak in Australia.

Jindabyne is also the terminus of the **Alpine Way**, the splendid scenic highway that leads to the 5,190-foot pass at Dead Horse Gap. From here the (partly unmade) road descends into the valley of the Murray River and on to Khancoban. This is the starting point for a fair-weather highway leading to **Mount Selwyn**, a winter sports resort on the north side of the peaks, and to the remains of the old gold-mining township of Kiandra. Farther north still are **Yarrangobilly Caves**; of the 60 caves so far discovered, four are open to the public.

Cenotaph at Cooma
People of 60 different nationalities flocked to the Snowy Mountains to work on the scheme, which took from 1949 to 1972 to complete. They frequently lived in conditions that recalled the tent cities of the gold-rush era. Their labor and sacrifice is commemorated in Cooma by the flags that fly in Centennial Park and by the memorial recording the names of the 121 men who died in the course of the great project.

83

Murray No. 1 hydroelectric power station

A souvenir of your visit to Kangaroo Valley

► Kangaroo Valley 63B4

This is a delightful old settlement tucked away in an upland valley on the beautiful scenic road leading inland from Nowra, 62 miles south of Sydney. Apart from being the starting point for bushwalks, its main attraction is the **Pioneer Farm Museum**, a faithful reconstruction of a dairy farm of the 19th century.

► Kiama 63B4

The most famous feature of this pleasantly situated little port and resort on the "Kiama Coast" south of Wollongong is the **Blowhole**, through which rough seas send a 197-foot spout high into the air. With its rocky headlands and fine beaches, Kiama has long been popular with visitors. To the west is **Minnamurra►**, with rain-forest and 164-foot waterfalls.

►►► Kosciusko National Park 62A3

See pages 74 and 83.

►► Lanyon Homestead A.C.T. 66A3

This fine building on the Murrumbidgee River near Canberra was built in 1859 and added to around the turn of the century. Now in the care of the National Trust, both buildings and gardens have been restored with care. There is a gallery housing a collection of the works of Sidney Nolan, one of the best places to get to know this idiosyncratic Australian artist.

►► Lightning Ridge 62D3

Just off the Castlereagh Highway before it quits N.S.W. for Queensland, this far northwestern township is famed for its black opals, mined here since 1902, in recent years by machine rather than by hand. Amateur fossickers (searchers for gold) are welcome, provided they don't trespass on professionals' rights, and there are many old mines to visit and demonstrations of cutting to watch, as well as artesian baths to relax in.

►► Mootwingee National Park 62C1

Beyond Broken Hill, in N.S.W.'s farthest northwest, are the rugged sandstone ranges of this remote national park,

Black is beautiful

The Lightning Ridge black opals are not quite unique, but this is the only place in the world where this unusual stone occurs in quantity. It has been described as combining "the iridescence of the dewdrop with the colour of the rainbow, set in the blackness of night." Its allure is certainly enough to maintain interest in its extraction. The biggest stone ever found was given the name "Queen of the Earth."

which is nevertheless accessible on gravel roads. Arid sandy plains and pebble deserts contrast with pools and watercourses fringed with river red gums and other lush vegetation. Aborigines occupied the area for countless years, leaving a wealth of rock paintings and engravings.

▶▶ **Mount Warning National Park** *63D5*

This 3,796-foot peak is the plug of an ancient volcano, given its name by Captain Cook to mark the reefs off Point Danger, on which the *Endeavour* almost came to grief. It is the first place on the Australian mainland to receive the rays of the rising sun, and the view from the top is well worth the 2,460-foot climb from the parking lot and visitor center. The steep but well-made path rises through splendid woodlands that change from subtropical rainforest to temperate rainforest and finally to open bush.

▶▶ **Myall Lakes National Park** *63B4*

These tranquil lakes (37 miles north of Newcastle), separated from the Pacific Ocean by windswept sand dunes, are best reached from the township of Tea Gardens by boat up the Myall River. There is little development along the shores of the lakes, though the fishing village of Seal Rocks on the coast at the eastern end of the park is popular with visitors, who come here to get away from it all.

▶ **Nambucca Heads** *63C5*

Subtropical crops now grow here (31 miles south of Coffs Harbour) where the cedar forests were cleared last century, making this an attractive and popular resort with fantastic views from various lookout points, of which Yarrahapini is the most spectacular. You can take tours inland to the rugged ridges and deep forested valleys of the New England and Dorrigo national parks.

Myall Lakes flora and fauna
The Myall Lakes make up the largest such lake system in the state, and are fringed by splendid forest, which includes rain forest species like cabbage palms. The lakes are also famous for the shrimp that breed in them. Waterbirds abound, as well as sea eaglos, and the area is rich in other wildlife, too.

Swim or surf from the beach at Nambucca Heads

Attractive Lake Macquarie, near Newcastle

Australian country
Far inland from Port Macquarie, halfway between Sydney and Brisbane on the New England Highway, is the town of Tamworth. This sizeable place claims fame as the capital of Australian country music. An annual festival, held in January, draws thousands of fans to hundreds of performances; other attractions are the Gallery of Stars (waxworks), and the Hands of Fame Corner Stone (handprints). More enduring stars can be contemplated at the Pyramid Planetarium to the north of town, where the solar system is reproduced in miniature.

► **Newcastle**   63B4

Dominated by the B.H.P. steelworks, industrial Newcastle is the largest city in Australia not to be the capital of a state. It began as the convict colony of a convict colony, but its later fortunes were founded on the abundant coal reserves of the Hunter Valley; Newcastle coal constituted the country's first export.

But there's much more to Newcastle than trade and industry. The Foreshore Park, Queen's Wharf and Customs House Plaza make a fine setting for festive occasions. **Fort Scratchley►** is one of the few such places in Australia to have fired its guns in anger—at a Japanese submarine in 1942. The old stronghold gives a good panorama over the city in its setting, and houses the **Maritime Museum** and **Military Museum**. The city center has some imposing 19th-century buildings and more museums and galleries. The "Bogey Hole" on the city beach below beautiful King Edward Park was built as a saltwater bath in convict days. To the south of the city is the country's largest saltwater lake, popular **Lake Macquarie►**, offering all kinds of watersports.

► **Nimbin**   63D5

Set among the natural splendors of northern N.S.W., Nimbin developed from the early 1970s as a center for alternative lifestyles. Today, its crafts shops and cafés attract the curious as well. It is on the way to **Nightcap National Park►►**, whose 2,953-foot peaks form part of the outer walls of the huge extinct volcano of which Mount Warning is the core. The park, with its glorious rain forest and diverse wildlife, is now part of N.S.W.'s World Heritage Area protecting the temperate and subtropical forests of the north.

▶ **Nowra** *63B4*

Nowra is located just upstream from the mouth of the Shoalhaven River. It is an extremely popular tourist resort, largely because of the beaches that extend north and south along the coast, one of them (Hyams Beach on Jervis Bay) boasting the whitest sand in the world.

▶ **Orange** *62B3*

Lava flows from the extinct volcano of Mount Canobolas —the highest point between the Great Dividing Range and the Indian Ocean—have broken down over the milleniums into fertile soils that today support great tracts of orchards growing apples, pears, cherries—but no oranges! The town of Orange has prospered from the fertility of its surroundings and is a busy but pleasant place, leafy with parks and trees. The first goldfield to be exploited in Australia was at nearby **Ophir**, where two prospectors made a sizable strike in 1851. You can try your luck at searching for gold today in attractive surroundings along Summer Hill Creek.

▶ **Port Macquarie** *63C5*

At the mouth of the Hastings River, Port Macquarie has turned from trade and commerce to tourism and retirement with considerable success. **St. Thomas' Church** is a reminder of these early days; one of the very first churches to be built in Australia (1824), it has box pews and a view from its tower. The **Hastings District Historical Museum**▶ has exceptionally good displays on the evolution of the town and its hinterland, and nature is on show at **Sea Acres Rainforest Centre**▶ with a long boardwalk through the rain forest. A series of good beaches stretches southward from the town.

▶▶ **Southern Highlands** *56A2*

Easily accessible by train and by the Hume Highway, this is one of the great rural playgrounds of Sydneysiders. The district was opened up early in the colony's history, in the 1820s, and much of it has a pleasant air of maturity, with lush landscapes recalling those of Tasmania. Recreational facilities cater to every possible desire of the city weekender.

 Among the towns in the area, Bowral is a leafy place with a number of fine old buildings along its main street. **Berrima**▶▶ is even more interesting; founded in the 1830s, it still has many sandstone buildings dating from that period, though the inns have dwindled in number from the original 13. The Surveyor General Inn is one of those that claim to be the oldest licensed premises in the country. Popular **Bundanoon** acts as the gateway to the Morton National Park, a starting point for energetic bushwalks or casual strolls up Glow Worm Glen.

▶▶ **Tidbinbilla A.C.T.** *66A1*

There are two important visitor attractions at Tidbinbilla, 25 miles southwest of Canberra. The **Tidbinbilla Tracking Station**▶ is a combined U.S./Australian deep-space tracking station; it is open to the public, with multimedia displays and model spacecraft. Back on earth, **Tidbinbilla Nature Reserve**▶ is a vast tract of countryside with bushwalks and an array of Australian wildlife.

Morton National Park
This high sandstone plateau into which rivers have cut deep gorges is one of the great attractions of the Southern Highlands. Waterfalls pour into the depths from high cliffs, as at Fitzroy Falls, where there is a visitor center. Scenic highways connect the area to the coast (one of them goes via Kangaroo Valley), making an interesting round trip from Sydney possible.

Morton National Park is popular with Sydneysiders

The list of Australian creatures able to cause you harm, in some cases of a fatal kind, is an impressive one. Do bear in mind, however, that you are much more likely to come to grief at the hands of a local driver or suffer heatstroke than you are to fall victim to any of the following.

Marine hazards Of the 85 species of **sharks** around the coast of Australia, only some are man-eaters. Attacks are rare, and the average number of fatalities per year is just one person. The highest risk occurs in summer when the water temperature is in excess of 72°F, and during this time it might be advisable to swim only from one of the many beaches protected by systems of netting. More dangerous are **saltwater crocodiles** (salties—see page 183), and on no account should you swim (or stand close to the water's edge) in areas frequented by these formidable creatures. Their numbers are also on the increase, since they have been given the status of protected species.

Box jellyfish breed in river estuaries and infest the coastal waters of Queensland and the N.T. from October to May. Practically invisible, they deliver a sting that can be fatal. The advice is to stay out of the sea at this time! Some of the beautiful corals are also unpleasantly poisonous, as is the crown-of-thorns starfish that is attacking the Barrier Reef. Much worse, however, is the **stonefish**, which looks like a rock as its name suggests; wear shoes when walking on a reef, and avoid messing around in rockpools. There are also sea snakes, which become active at the same time as the box jellies.

Terrestrial hazards **Snakes** also inhabit the land, and there are some 170 species, the venomous ones outnumbering the harmless. Rangers and bush folk are fond of detailing their degree of poisonousness in terms of the number of mice a bite could kill; this can get into the hundreds of thousands, and is quite enough to knock you off. However, even the most lethal of snakes—like the taipan, tiger snake, death adder or brown snake—will get out of your way if it possibly can.

Spiders and insects
Spiders can reach an alarming size, and their bite can be unpleasant. In the case of two species, the redback (or black widow) and funnel-web, avoid them at all costs or make sure you are near a hospital if you are bitten. The funnel-web, unlike most of its kind, is aggressive and rears up for the attack. It's also a Sydneysider, so don't think you are safe in that city. Insects abound in Australia, but flies, mosquitoes, wasps, ants and even scorpions are more of a nuisance than a real hazard.

Steer clear of the deadly taipan

Akubra hats are made in Kempsey, near Wauchope

▶ **Wauchope**   63C5

Among the forests of the Hastings River district, Wauchope has long been a center of the logging industry, a fact made much of in **Timbertown▶▶**. This ambitious re-creation of a late 19th-century pioneer settlement has a whole range of buildings (shops, houses, church and sawmill), demonstrations of all the activities associated with logging and processing, as well as rides around the area aboard a cart or a steam train.

    Kempsey▶, 16 miles north of Wauchope, is home to the world-famous Akubra hat.

▶ **West Wyalong**   62B3

In the harsh countryside at the junction of the Mid-Western and Newell highways, West Wyalong was N.S.W.'s busiest goldfield at the turn of the century. Now the center for an extensive wheat-growing area, it also produces and exports that quintessential Australian fluid, eucalyptus oil. However, visitors may be more interested in the model of a gold mine in the District Museum.

▶ **White Cliffs**   62C1

This old opal-mining settlement more than 620 miles northwest of Sydney is a place to experience life in the Australian Outback. A small, highly individual population of opal miners lives here, some of them underground, thereby avoiding the need for air-conditioning in the sometimes intolerable climate. There are plenty of opportunities to see opals in their various states, as well as a real oddity, the opalized skeleton of a plesiosaur.

Wollongong   63B4

The life of New South Wales' third largest city is based on heavy industry and there are few conventional tourist attractions. But, as always in Australia, you are never far away from natural beauty, and the rugged Illawarra Coast has wonderful beaches while inland there are splendid hills and forests. There are fantastic views from the **Illawarra State Recreation Area▶** with its peaks of Mount Kiera and Mount Kembla.

Wagga Wagga or Wogga Wogga?
More famous for its name (pronounced Wogga) than for its tourist amenities, Wagga (150 miles south of West Wyalong) is a fair-sized town that has profited from its location on the Murrumbidgee River and Sydney–Melbourne railroad line to become the thriving center of N.S.W.'s Riverina district.

Map of Victoria showing major towns, highways, national parks and geographic features including Melbourne, Geelong, Ballarat, Bendigo, Mildura, Swan Hill, Shepparton, Wangaratta, and the surrounding regions of New South Wales and South Australia. Labeled features include Lake Victoria, Murray River, Sturt Highway, Ouyen Highway, Western Highway, Calder Highway, Murray Valley Highway, Hume Highway, Princes Hwy, Grampians Nat Park, Little Desert National Park, Wyperfeld Nat Park, Big Desert, Otway Ranges, Port Phillip Bay, Bass Strait, and many others.

SUNRAYSIA
100% NATURAL
GRAPE JUICE
MADE FROM AUSTRALIA'S FINEST GRAPES
FOR THE FRUIT JUICE GOURMET
250ml / 8.5 FL. OZ.
PRODUCT OF AUSTRALIA
BEST BEFORE PACK
0 8370

The Dandenong Ranges harbor a rich profusion of native flora

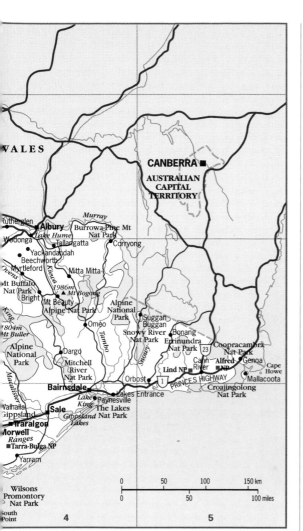

Victoria The Garden State is the smallest of Australia's mainland states. However, it is comparatively densely populated and highly industrialized, with something like a quarter of the country's inhabitants living on what only amounts to 3 percent of its land surface, a good proportion of which is agriculturally productive. Out of the state's total of 4½ million people, just over 3 million live in the metropolitan area of Melbourne, whose area of more than 2,300 square miles makes it one of the largest cities in the world.

Beyond the metropolis, Victorians live in a variety of settlements, many of them of considerable charm and historic interest. There are delightful little ports and well-established resorts along the 745-mile coastline, a multitude of places founded in the mid-19th-century rush for gold such as charming Yackandandah, old river ports along the Murray and prosperous agricultural centers quietly getting on with their own lives.

The state's landscapes are diverse; with varied and spectacular coastal scenery, high mountains and extensive forested uplands, rich farmlands and near desert, Victoria has been described as a microcosm of Australia, though true Outback lies beyond its border. Agriculture takes many forms. The rolling hills of Gippsland feed dairy cattle, sheep graze on the vast pastures of the plains stretching to the west, and fruit grows in profusion along the Goulburn River and by the Murray too, thanks to irrigation works carried out on a huge scale at the turn of the century.

For the tourist, the presence of such variety in close proximity to the state capital makes a stay particularly rewarding; few places are more than half a day's comfortable drive from Melbourne.

As it was Victoria belonged to the second, or even third phase of European colonization of the new continent. The coast had been sighted from aboard the *Endeavour* in the course of Captain Cook's 1770 voyage; in 1803, Lieutenant David Collins attempted to found a settlement on the shores of Port Phillip Bay but gave up and went on to Tasmania instead. For decades, only whalers and sealers landed along the coast. Then, in 1835, one John Batman from Tasmania sailed into the bay again and signed a treaty of dubious legality with the local Aborigines that gave him title to 600,000 acres of land. In spite of official attempts from Sydney to discourage settlement on the bay, Batman and others persisted; his famous phrase "This will be the place for a village" marked the founding of Melbourne.

Old Victorian building in Melbourne

92

Buckley's chance
One of the members of Lieutenant Collins' party, which tried and failed to establish a settlement at Sorrento on the Morningron Peninsula in 1803, was the Cheshire-born convict William Buckley. Taking a chance, he decamped and fled around Port Phillip Bay to the Barwon area, where he lived with the local Aborigines. Decades later, in 1835, some of John Batman's associates were amazed at the emergence of "a wild white man" at their encampment, hardly able to speak English any more. Buckley earned a pardon, a government pension and a place in the language ("Buckley's chance" means no chance at all).

The new settlers wanted nothing to do with the convict system, sending any ships that arrived with prisoners on to Sydney, and petitioning for separation from New South Wales. This was granted in 1851, and the new colony was given the Queen's name. Only weeks after this event, gold was found near Ballarat and at Clunes; other finds followed, the rush was on, and Melbourne and Victoria changed utterly in the process. Handsome new towns arose from the tent cities erected by the prospectors, and Melbourne boomed, fitting itself out with fine new buildings paid for by the profits made from the precious metal.

In spite of periodic slumps, the state has remained the financial and industrial powerhouse of the nation, boosted by massive immigration in the early 20th century from the British Isles, and after World War II from Europe and elsewhere. Melbourne is now perhaps the most cosmopolitan of all Australia's major cities, while other places within the state retain a pleasing atmosphere of bygone days.

Outdoor Victorians In spite of (or is it because of?) their unpredictable weather, the people of Victoria are great outdoor types, igniting the barbecue or flocking to the beaches at the slightest opportunity. *The* event in the racing calendar is the Melbourne Cup, when not only Victoria but the whole country seems to come to a stop. Australian Rules football is followed with passion. The accessibility of fine scenery brings out the bushwalkers in summer, while in winter the roads to the snowfields of the Alps are crowded with the cars of skiers.

Skiing in Victoria
Skiing began in the 1930s, when the first lift started taking people up to the high plateau country beneath Mount Buffalo. Nowadays Mount Donna Buang and Mount Baw Baw are even accessible to day-trippers from Melbourne. Mount Buller, further on in the Alps, is Australia's most popular winter resort; that at Mount Hotham is the highest in the country, with an award-winning, environmentally friendly complex at Dinner Plain, while Falls Creek in its sheltered bowl in the Alpine National Park has slopes suitable for every kind of skier.

93

Morning Star Creek, still with one foot in the past

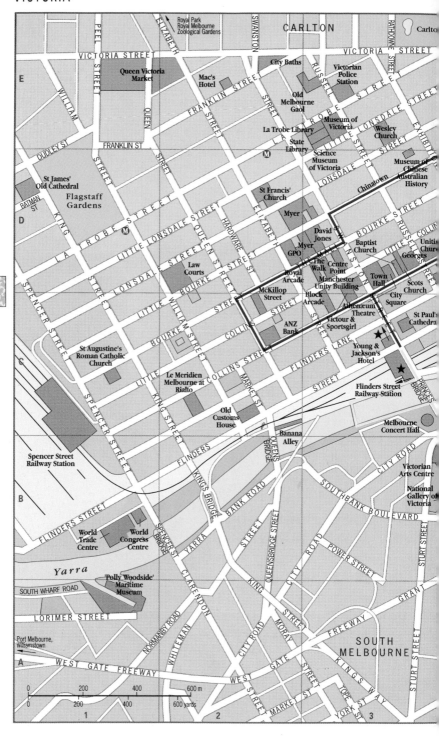

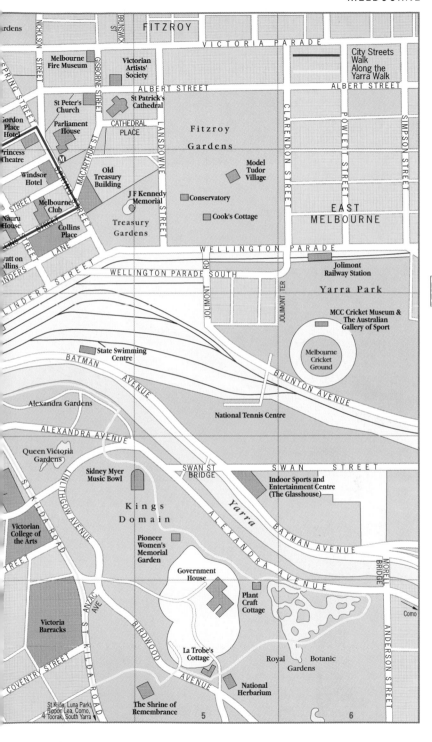

FITZROY

Melbourne Fire Museum

Victorian Artists' Society

VICTORIA PARADE

City Streets Walk Along the Yarra Walk

ALBERT STREET

ALBERT STREET

St Peter's Church

St Patrick's Cathedral

Gordon Place Hotel

Parliament House

CATHEDRAL PLACE

Fitzroy Gardens

Princess Theatre

Windsor Hotel

Old Treasury Building

Model Tudor Village

Conservatory

EAST MELBOURNE

Nauru House

Melbourne Club

J F Kennedy Memorial

Cook's Cottage

Collins Place

Treasury Gardens

Wyatt on Collins

WELLINGTON PARADE

Jolimont Railway Station

FLINDERS STREET

WELLINGTON PARADE SOUTH

Yarra Park

95

MCC Cricket Museum & The Australian Gallery of Sport

State Swimming Centre

BATMAN AVENUE

Melbourne Cricket Ground

Alexandra Gardens

BRUNTON AVENUE

National Tennis Centre

ALEXANDRA AVENUE

Queen Victoria Gardens

SWAN ST BRIDGE

SWAN STREET

Sidney Myer Music Bowl

Indoor Sports and Entertainment Centre (The Glasshouse)

Kings Domain

ST KILDA ROAD

Victorian College of the Arts

LITHGOW AVENUE

Pioneer Women's Memorial Garden

ALEXANDRA AVENUE

BATMAN AVENUE

Yarra

MORELL BRIDGE

Government House

Plant Craft Cottage

Como

Victoria Barracks

ANZAC AVE

ST KILDA ROAD

BIRDWOOD

La Trobe's Cottage

Royal Botanic Gardens

ANDERSON STREET

COVENTRY STREET

AVENUE

National Herbarium

St Kilda, Luna Park)
Rippon Lea, Como, Toorak, South Yarra

The Shrine of Remembrance

5

6

Moomba
The Melburnians' ability to let their hair down is demonstrated in the huge end-of-summer carnival known as Moomba, an Aboriginal word that can be translated as "let's get together and have fun." Ten days of sports, shows, concerts and performances of all kinds culminate in a monster multicultural procession watched by half a million people.

Batman's bargain
In exchange for 600,000 acres of Aboriginal land, John Batman delivered 40 blankets, 30 tomahawks, 100 knives, 50 pairs of scissors, 30 mirrors, 200 handkerchiefs, 100 pounds of flour and 6 shirts. The understanding that a similar quantity of useful items would be handed over annually was soon consigned to oblivion.

Outside the 1856 Parliament House

Untold goodies at Queen Victoria Market

Melbourne

Australia's second great metropolitan city sprawls around the head of Port Phillip Bay at the outlet of the muddy Yarra River. Hardly a generation ago, Melbourne was almost a synonym for dull respectability of a peculiarly British flavor, but since the 1960s Melbourne and its inhabitants have undergone a startling transformation. Much of the city center has been redeveloped with glittering office towers, to which the remaining treasures of 19th-century architecture act as a wonderful foil. Massive immigration, principally but by no means wholly from southern Europe, has enlivened the social scene. In addition to countless galleries, museums, theaters and movie houses, the city has a thriving nightlife not only of bars and discos but also of cabaret and comedians, jazz and rock. And whatever Sydney says, Melbourne is the gastronomic capital of Australia, with every kind of cuisine served, from Aussie to Vietnamese.

The early years Once John Batman's illegal treaty of 1835 had been accepted as a *fait accompli* by the authorities in Sydney, his "village" above the Yarra soon became an incipient city laid out on the usual grid pattern by an army surveyor. Within a few years, the wealthy were buying estates to the southeast of the river where they could set themselves up as country gentlemen and build elegant houses. Due to gold and land speculation, Melbourne boomed for most of the second half of the 19th century, leading a roistering kind of life characterized as "American" in contrast to Sydney's staid "Britishness." A great slump brought the era of "Marvellous Melbourne" to an end in the 1890s, and the city entered the long period of gloom from which its recent renaissance has so triumphantly rescued it.

Attractions today Melbourne is a wonderfully green city of parks and trees, but it is also renowned for its excellent 19th-century architecture. The best view of the city—and one of the finest panoramas in Australia—is from the south bank of the Yarra.

Melbourne has an extensive system of tramways

The city's inner suburbs have a strong and varied identity that makes them well worth exploring.

Just north of the city center, **Carlton** is home to the University of Melbourne and many examples of the row houses so characteristic of late 19th-century Melbourne. The suburb's largest landmark is the huge Exhibition Building dating from the International Exhibition of 1880.

Once decidedly "rough," **Fitzroy** has now turned Bohemian, its original inhabitants supplemented by students and artists. Brunswick Street is a fascinating mixture of cheap restaurants and alternative bookshops.

East Melbourne is a charming enclave of carefully restored row houses within walking distance of the city center via Fitzroy Gardens.

The suburb of **St. Kilda** became Melbourne's seaside in the 1880s, when the pier and the substantial villas of the rich were built. These days St. Kilda is fairly colorful, and Acland Street is hard to beat as a restaurant strip. The beaches stretching from here around to Port Melbourne are still popular, though the water tends to be of dubious quality. The fun palace of Luna Park has been here since 1912. On Sundays, St. Kilda hosts a big arts and crafts market.

South Melbourne has one of the most attractive of all inner city residential areas; in St. Vincent's Square, fine houses in a variety of styles were laid out around central gardens from the 1860s onward.

One of the richest inner suburbs east along the Yarra, **Toorak** is synonymous with a certain kind of trendiness.

Beyond the Yarra to the west, **Williamstown** has a superb view of the city center across the water. A stroll along the Strand is well worthwhile, and railroad buffs will enjoy the Railway Museum. On the way here, at Spotswood on the western side of the Westgate Bridge, is the recently opened Scienceworks, an annex of the Museum of Victoria. It has an amazing array of interactive exhibits on the theme of science and technology in the past, present, and future.

Melbourne's trams
One of the emblems of the city, the network of green and yellow trams covers much of the Melbourne metropolitan area. The older trams are classified by the National Trust, while a new line speeds commuters and workers between the city center and Port Melbourne. There are round trips for tourists by tram, and you can even dine aboard a vintage model; the Colonial Tramcar Restaurant is fitted with specially smooth suspension to keep your Yarra Valley red in its glass and has one-way windows to maintain your privacy while you glide gondolalike through the streets.

Collins Street

This has always been the best address in town, ever since professional men set up here in the late 1840s. The upper, eastern end of the street, tree-planted and close to parklands and government buildings, was more salubrious than the western end, down by the railroad tracks of Spencer Street Station. Not quite all the buildings from the era of "Marvellous Melbourne" have been replaced by developments like twin-towered Collins Place (No. 45) or the harsh precast concrete panels of Nauru House (No. 80); the Melbourne Club, most exclusive of such institutions, still stands (No. 36), as do a number of dignified banks, office buildings, churches and theaters.

▶▶ **A.N.Z. (Australia and New Zealand) Bank**   *94C2*

386 Collins Street

One of the finest examples of Gothic revival architecture in the country, the building of what used to be the English, Scottish and Australian Bank is more Venetian than the Doges Palace in Venice, with a magnificently elaborate interior whose blue décor is enhanced by lavish use of gold leaf.

The A.N.Z. Banking Museum has changing exhibitions on the history of Australian banking.

▶ **Chinatown**   *94D3*

Centered on Little Bourke Street, Melbourne's Chinatown has existed ever since Chinese prospectors joined the rush to the goldfields in the 1850s. It expanded later in the 19th century as the goldfields contracted and miners drifted back to the big city. Today it still flourishes as a haven for the Chinese community and for diners in search of cheap and excellent food and groceries, and has been fitted out with the usual archways that supposedly enhance its identity.

An interesting addition to the area is the **Museum of Chinese Australian History**▶▶ in an old warehouse in Cohen Place, just off Little Bourke Street. Its displays bring alive the whole of the considerable Chinese contribution to Australian history. Star exhibits include a life-size replica of a warrior-general of the 2nd century BC and Dai Loong, the 328-foot, 100-legged dragon that emerges once a year for the Chinese New Year parade.

▶▶ **Como**   *95A6*

Como Avenue, South Yarra

Begun in 1847, this delicious white mansion crowning the rise in the middle of its richly landscaped gardens is a

The gateway to flourishing Chinatown

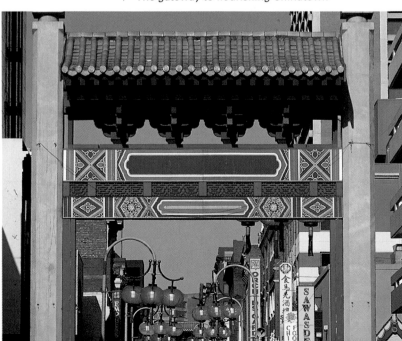

wonderful example of the gracious buildings of Melbourne's pre-boom period. Behind the nicely proportioned façade in South Yarra are a series of furnished rooms evoking the comfortable and very sociable life lived here in the 19th century; to the side are outbuildings containing the original laundry. Como's unselfconscious elegance was not imitated by the nouveau-riche owners of the next generation of villas to be built in the suburb of Toorak; they preferred something altogether more ostentatious, usually combining a number of architectural styles. Most of these pompous residences have now given way to apartment buildings, but Como, thankfully, passed into the hands of the National Trust in 1959.

▶▶ Fitzroy Gardens   95E5

Just to the east of the city center and consequently a favorite place for lunchtime sandwiches and assignations are the sweeping lawns and splendid trees of these 19th-century gardens, complementing the spires of St. Patrick's Cathedral in the background. Toward the southern end of the park is **Cooks' Cottage▶▶**. A modest stone building of the mid-18th century with the characteristic Yorkshire pantiled roof, this was the home of the great navigator's parents; it was dismantled and brought here in 1934 to mark the centenary of the founding of Melbourne. It is open to the public, as is another reminder of Anglo-Australian ties, the miniature Tudor Village, a gift from the citizens of the London borough of Lambeth in thanks for World War II food parcels.

▶▶ Kings Domain   95B5

A splendid tract of parkland sweeps southeast along the Yarra from the city center through Victoria and Alexandra Gardens to the Kings Domain and beyond to the Royal Botanic Gardens (see page 101). Alexandra Gardens has a fine riverside view of the city center, and Queen Victoria Gardens has an elaborate floral clock. Altogether more functional is the **Sidney Myer Music Bowl**, whose soaring canopy shelters all kinds of open-air musical events. Crowning the higher ground in the Domain is the great white **Government House**, the fourth to be built on this site (see panel). Its square tower rises above the trees and is a well-known city landmark. In contrast to this magnificence is the very first Government House, **La Trobe's Cottage**, a prefabricated two-story cottage brought from England, erected in Jolimont in 1839, and moved here in 1963.

▶ Melbourne Cricket Ground   95C6

Jolimont Terrace, Jolimont
To the southeast of the city center at Jolimont, divided up by roads and railroad tracks, are sports grounds of all kinds, many of them laid out for the 1956 Olympics. The central site for the games was the great M.C.G.—the Melbourne Cricket Ground—a vast stadium with a capacity well in excess of 100,000, just as much associated with football ("Aussie Rules") as with cricket. Here, too, is the M.C.C. Cricket Museum, the Australian Gallery of Sport, and the Olympic Museum, recalling the triumphs and disappointments that have attended the modern games since their revival in 1896.

Government House
Built appropriately enough by government architect William Wardell in the 1870s, the present Government House was modeled on Queen Victoria's Osborne House on England's Isle of Wight. That monarch is supposed to have been rather miffed that Melbourne's ballroom was twice as big as the one in Buckingham Palace.

99

One of the greatest stadiums, the Melbourne Cricket Ground at Jolimont creates an incredible atmosphere

The Sydney sneer
The rivalry between Sydney and Melbourne is long-standing and will probably never go away, though these days the tone of exchanges between Sydneysiders and Melburnians is bantering rather than bitter. The 1955 painting by John Brack entitled *Collins Street, 5 o'clock,* showing grim-faced commuters marching along Melbourne's main artery, has given much pleasure to Sydneysiders by confirming their view of Melburnians as archetypal killjoys.

Restored Polly Woodside *at the Maritime Museum*

The National Gallery is also the site for international traveling exhibitions

▶▶ **Museum of Victoria**   94E3

328 Swanston Street

At present housed next to the State Library, the state's most comprehensive museum is in the process of re-organization. The science and technology sections have been moved to the far side of the Westgate Bridge (see Williamstown on page 97) and natural history and anthropology are likely to have a home elsewhere in the city center, but the **Planetarium** and fascinating **Children's Museum** have remained on the present site. Whatever happens, the pride of place is still likely to be occupied by Phar Lap, the famous racehorse of the 1930s, believed to have been poisoned while in California.

▶▶▶ **National Gallery of Victoria**   95B4

180 St. Kilda Road

The somber bluestone building rising from pools and fountains on St. Kilda Road is in striking contrast to the other edifices making up the Victorian Arts Centre. Completed in 1968, the gallery houses some of the finest artworks to be seen in Australia. The collection of Australian art is possibly the most comprehensive in the country, from John Glover's charming scenes of colonial Tasmania to the story pictures of the later 19th century and the works of Sidney Nolan and Jeffrey Smart. In addition, there is a good selection of European Old Masters, pre-Columbian, Aboriginal and American art, and the courtyards contain a number of fine modern sculptures.

▶▶ **Old Melbourne Gaol**   94E3

Russell Street

Of all the countless jails that are such a feature of Australian townscapes, this grim bluestone building is one not to be missed. Its chilling interior seems to sum up the harshness of 19th-century concepts of justice and punishment. Here you can see the death mask of Ned Kelly, made in 1880. The most notorious and defiant of Australia's bushrangers looks peaceful enough, his wayward spirit expressed perhaps more strongly by the home made suit of armor displayed alongside.

► Parliament House 95E4
Spring Street
Begun in 1856, this great neo-Grecian palace of government was planned on such an ambitious scale that it has never been completed. The state government was moved from its grandiose home here in 1901 to make way for the newly established Federal Parliament, which sat in Melbourne until finally persuaded to make the move to Canberra in 1927. There are guided tours of the splendid interior when parliament is not in session; the Legislative Council Chamber was described by that connoisseur of Victorian architecture, John Betjeman, as "the best Corinthian room in the world."

► Polly Woodside Maritime Museum 94A1
South Wharf Road, South Melbourne
Built in Belfast in 1885, the sailing barque *Polly Woodside* ended her working days as a rusty, dilapidated, coal hulk in the Port of Melbourne. Fortunately she was immaculately restored and is now moored in an old dock basin in South Melbourne, as the proud centerpiece of this maritime museum, which has numerous other exhibits evoking the age of sail.

►► Queen Victoria Market 94E1
Victoria Street
Melbourne's sole surviving 19th-century market is an exciting place to shop or just wander. Trading has been carried on here since 1859, and there are now more than a thousand stalls selling everything imaginable at affordable prices in an exuberant multicultural atmosphere.

►► Rippon Lea 95A4
192 Hotham Street, Elsternwick
Begun in 1868 by the Walworth (London)-born Frederick Thomas Sargood, this polychrome brick house is perhaps the most splendid late-Victorian mansion to have survived in the Melbourne suburbs. On completion in 1887 its opulent interior had no fewer than 33 rooms. There are extensive and popular gardens.

►►► Royal Botanic Gardens 95A6
The jewel in the crown of parkland extending along the Yarra from the city center, these superb gardens are some of the finest of their kind in the world.
The site was chosen as early as 1845 by La Trobe, and the gardens were laid out and stocked with an incredible range of plants by successive directors. Ferdinand von Mueller (Director, 1852–73) preferred a formal layout, while his successor, William Guilfoyle, redesigned the gardens in a more romantic, English style with sweeping lawns, informal lakes and curving pathways.

Continued on page 103.

Dream on Elm Street
Some of the prestige of the top end of Collins Street in early days was due to the fact that it was one of the few places to have any street trees. Early photographs of Melbourne show the young city, once the bush had been cleared to build it, to have been a virtually treeless town. This was eventually remedied, and today's city enjoys the benefit of the countless trees, now fully mature, that were planted towards the end of the 19th century. Scorning the rich array of native trees, city fathers planted to remind themselves of "home," and as a result, streets and parks are graced with wonderful specimens of oaks, elms and poplars.

101

The Botanic Gardens: a fine example of 19th-century English landscaping

Early European Australia was not distinguished by its architecture. No architect sailed with the First Fleet, and the very first structures erected were primitive affairs of wattle and daub, bark or whatever materials came quickly and easily to hand. Some prefabricated structures were shipped out from England and reassembled on site, sometimes by guesswork.

102

The first proper edifice in Sydney was Government House, a two-story brick dwelling that amazed the Aborigines when they found people walking around above their heads. A sense of restraint and emphasis on good proportion contributed toward simple but effective structures like Elizabeth Farm at Parramatta, built in 1793. Its veranda, destined to become a persistent motif in Australian building, was derived from British practice in India. But architecture capable of making some kind of civic statement had to await the rule of Governor Macquarie and his forger-turned-architect, Francis Greenway. Thanks to buildings like **Hyde Park Barracks** and **St. James' Church**, Sydney began to take on the airs of a real city for the first time.

The development of the terrace Gold was the making of Melbourne, and of many architects, too. Melbourne is still one of the world's great 19th-century cities in terms of building, with grand self-confident edifices in a variety of revived styles—Gothic for churches, Romanesque and Venetian for offices and banks, and classical for public buildings. This was the period when row houses reached a high point of development, their elegance and cast-iron decoration helping to make the inner suburbs of both Melbourne and Sydney some of the most livable of their kind in the world.

Australia's own
What has been described as the most original local contribution to Australian architecture is the tropical house of Queensland. Raised above ground for ventilation, it is liberally provided with verandas and with a roof of corrugated iron—handsome, cheap and durable, although noisy!

Pride of place in the end, however, must go to the Sydney Opera House, a world-class building.

An Aussie style The row house was replaced after the turn of the century by the detached villa, built for a decade or so in "Federation" style, with a wealth of varied forms and features like terracotta kangaroos on the roof line and eucalyptus leaves in the barge boards.

The later, 20th-century suburbs are undistinguished. The interwar Californian bungalow has given way to brick veneer dwellings, or to bizarre neo-Grecian palaces. Similarly, the redeveloped city centers do not seem to have a particularly Australian style either.

Right: Old Victorian building in downtown Melbourne

One of the inhabitants of Melbourne Zoo

Continued from page 101.

Plants from many parts of the world thrive here in Melbourne's kind climate; there are more than 6,000 tree species, from cool temperate regions through to subtropical areas. English elms and oaks contrast with grass trees and river red gums. The Australian Lawn is planted with eucalypts from all over the country, and the Australian Border is the place to enjoy other native flora; it features a fine modern rockery, designed by the aptly named landscaper Ellis Stones. There is also the Oak Lawn, the Rose Garden, a cactus and succulent garden and a bulb garden. A number of buildings complement the plantings; they include the classical Temple of the Winds and the 1930s Visitor Centre and Herbarium with its excellent modern extension. A good way to get to know at least some of the riches of these wonderful gardens is to take one of the free guided walks that start at the visitor center (10AM and 11AM daily except Monday and Saturday).

▶▶ Royal Melbourne Zoological Gardens   *94E2*

Elliott Avenue, Parkville
This vast zoo with its progressive approach to introducing visitors and animals to each other is located in Royal Park, the city's largest tract of open space. Most of the old cages have been done away with, and visitors move easily through large enclosures simulating the native habitat of the creatures within. The whole range of Australian fauna is on show, from birds in their giant aviary, to fur seals in their tank and platypuses in their platypusary.

▶ St. Patrick's Cathedral   *95E4*

Cathedral Place, East Melbourne
Less hemmed in by modern buildings than the Anglican Cathedral, the 338-foot central spire of the great Roman Catholic cathedral features in many city views. It was designed by William Wardell, the state's official architect, who also built the fabulous Venetian-style A.N.Z. Bank.

The Separation Tree
This is the name given to one of the fine river red gums in the Royal Botanic Gardens, since it was beneath its branches that the grand public celebration took place in 1851 to mark the independence of Victoria from New South Wales.

Inside St. Patrick's
St. Patrick's has a splendidly soaring interior, with magnificent stained-glass windows. Long regarded as an Irish stronghold, it also has a statue of Daniel O'Connell—the great 19th-century Irish patriot known as "the Liberator"—in the churchyard.

On guard at the impressive Shrine of Remembrance

Arts tour
The Victorian Arts Centre complex is adorned inside and out with numerous works of art, many of them specially commissioned. These can best be experienced in the course of the center's guided tours.

Nellie Melba's Melbourne Memorial
Born in the Melbourne suburb of Richmond in 1861, world-famous soprano Helen Mitchell changed her name to Melba to honor her native city. Like so many Australian artists of the period, she made her reputation abroad, her association with London's Covent Garden lasting for three decades. The Performing Arts Museum has much Melba memorabilia.

► **St. Paul's Cathedral**   94C3

Corner of Swanston and Flinders Streets
No longer the dominant element in the cityscape, this fine church in Gothic Revival style still has a commanding presence. Standing on the site where the first official church service in Melbourne took place in 1836, it was built in 1880–91 to a design by the British architect William Butterfield, also responsible for the Chapter House and Diocesan Offices in the cathedral complex.

►►► **Shrine of Remembrance**   95A5

Off St. Kilda Road
This huge temple to the dead forms a dramatic terminus for the long vista that starts in the city center. Modeled on the Parthenon, the shrine sits massively on top of a rise in the ground in Kings Domain. Completed in 1934 to honor the 114,000 Victorians who served in World War I, of whom 19,000 died, its central chamber has a Stone of Remembrance illuminated by a shaft of light at 11AM every November 11. Deep below is the crypt, displaying regimental colors, and high above is a gallery with fine panoramas over the city and its environs. The immaculate surroundings of the shrine have been laid out to commemorate those who fell in other wars.

►►► **Victorian Arts Centre**   94B3

St. Kilda Road
No cultural ghetto, but a vibrant part of city life, the modern Arts Centre comprises a complex of exciting buildings on the south bank of the Yarra.

Next to the National Gallery is the **Theatres** building, topped by a stunning 377-foot-high spire and one of modern Melbourne's new landmarks. The three theaters themselves are built below ground: the State Theatre is the home of the Australian Ballet; the Melbourne Theatre Company performs in the Playhouse; and the third is a highly adaptable studio space. The great drum of the **Concert Hall** has a spectacular interior whose mineral colors reflect the geology of the Australian continent. The center also embraces the Performing Arts Museum and, in Kings Domain, the Sidney Myer Music Bowl.

Walk Melbourne's city streets

See map on pages 94–5.

From the traditional meeting place of Melburnians—"under the clocks" at Flinders Street station—to grandiose Parliament House, this walk of about 1¾ miles conveys the feeling of civic and commercial Melbourne.

The station steps open onto the bustle of the city center. Cleared of motor traffic, Swanston Street is a calm setting for the Gothic grandeur of **St. Paul's Cathedral**. Modern City Square, with its elaborate water features, marks the junction with Collins Street, dominated by the splendid Town Hall. Commercial dynamism has taken many shapes along this prestigious artery, from American deco of the 1930s to Victorian Gothic.

In Queen Street the elaborate Safe Deposit Building (Nos. 88–92) is dwarfed by the **A.N.Z. Tower** shooting skyward. Trams and shoppers throng Bourke Street Mall, off which runs the city's oldest shopping gallery, Royal Arcade, with its 1870 figures of Gog and Magog. Colorful archways signal the entry to Chinatown.

The grid of city streets ends where Little Bourke Street emerges into Spring Street, overlooked by the imposing colonnade of Victoria's **Parliament House**, and the Windsor Hotel of 1883. Nearby, the **Old Treasury Building**, built in 1857, contains the Melbourne Exhibition on the city's social and architectural history.

You can call a halt here, or return to Flinders Street station via the eastern end of Collins Street.

Walk Along the Yarra

See map on pages 94–5.

A 3-mile walk along Melbourne's River Yarra into the green spaces of Kings Domain and the Botanic Gardens.

Downstream from Princes Bridge, the Yarra is crossed by a sprightly new footbridge incorporating a surprising neon sculpture. Avoiding the temptation of the continuous line of riverside cafes, you are rewarded with one of the very best views of the city skyline from the far side of Princes Bridge.

Negotiate the crossing of Alexandra Avenue with care and enjoy the calm of **Kings Domain**, with its various focal points like the Sidney Myer Music Bowl and the Pioneer Women's Memorial Garden. The far bank of the lake in the **Royal Botanic Gardens** marks the outermost point of the walk, excuse enough for a pause at the lakeside café. Beyond the Herbarium and Visitor Centre is the

Shrine of Remembrance, whose outside gallery gives a wonderful vista back to the city center.

The return to Flinders Street station can be made on foot or by tram along St. Kilda Road.

The Yarra River: locals' playground

National parks

From high alps to rolling downlands, from luxuriant rainforests to desert scrub and from the spreading floodplains of the Murray River in the north to some of the country's most dramatic coastline in the south, Victoria's landscape is as varied as its climate. A relatively high rainfall over much of the state contributes to the luxuriance of the forest cover as well as to the productivity of grasslands and other farmed areas; by contrast, the far northwest is extremely arid.

Victorian Alps The dominating physical feature of the state is its mountain backbone, the southernmost stretch of Australia's Great Dividing Range. Majestic alpine summits rise to almost 6,560 feet, while foothills and lower ranges stretch southward and westward to form a hilly backdrop to the metropolitan area of Melbourne. Many of the highest and most spectacular parts of the Victorian Alps are protected as national parks; they include **Mount Buffalo** (5,646 feet), whose characteristic hump-backed shape was first seen by the explorers Hume and Hovell in 1824. Beneath the summit stretches a vast upland plateau bounded by cliffs falling abruptly to the plains below. A skier's paradise in winter, the plateau becomes an elaborate embroidery of wildflowers in spring.

As in the highlands generally, the vegetation cover varies with altitude, the dense wet forest of the valleys becoming more open farther up the slope, with peppermint gums giving way to alpine ash and finally to snow gums. In the early days of white settlement, cattlemen drove their beasts high into the uplands to feed off the summer pastures, building stone huts for shelter. Many of the huts remain, but grazing has been forbidden because of erosion. A number of physically separate national parks has since been grouped together to form the exhilarating **Alpine National Park**.

The birds of Wyperfeld
Much of the park is alive with great flocks of birds: white and pink cockatoos, galahs, and regent parrots. The most curious bird, though, is the mallee-fowl, builder of underground nests in which its young are hatched in meticulously controlled incubation conditions.

At Point Nepean—the entrance to Port Phillip Bay

The aptly named Organ Pipes National Park

Southeastern Victoria Along the border with New South Wales there is some of the most unspoiled scenery in the state. Inland are a number of national parks. At **Errinundra National Park** there is a large tract of cool, temperate woodland, and there are other pockets of rain forest at **Lind** and **Alfred National Parks**. The splendid gorges along the course of the **Snowy River** offer exciting whitewater canoeing; this park is also the habitat of the rare brush-tailed rock wallaby. Running from Sydenham Inlet to the N.S.W. boundary is one of the country's finest coastal reserves, the **Croajingolong National Park**, with savage cliffs and headlands protecting pristine beaches and tranquil inlets. In complete contrast are **The Lakes** to the west, where the seemingly infinite Ninety Mile Beach is backed by lagoons and waterways.

As well as the Dandenongs, day trips from Melbourne can take in **Point Nepean** at the tip of the Mornington Peninsula, the **Brisbane Ranges**, the forests and fern gullies of **Kinglake National Park** to the northeast, and the strange basalt columns of **Organ Pipes National Park** to the northwest. The rugged **Grampians** to the west are just about reachable in a day, but merit a longer stay.

Victoria's southwestern coastline The best can be seen in two contrasting parks: between Lorne and Cape Otway the high ranges of the **Otways**, still covered in glorious rain forest, rise steeply from the sea; farther west, the breakers are constantly resculpting the cliffs of the **Port Campbell National Park**, creating some of the most spectacular coastal scenery to be seen anywhere in the world. Inland, volcanic activity has given rise to fertile farmland interspersed with crater lakes and worn-down volcanic cones, as at **Mount Eccles**.

Far from the coast and the wooded uplands is **Wyperfeld National Park**, a complex system of normally dry lakes and lagoons, with mallee (see panel) stretching to the horizon.

Mastering the mallee
Much of northwestern Victoria was once covered in mallee, "a blue and level sea stretching to the horizon." Mallee is an Aboriginal word describing the fire-resistant scrub composed of 20 or so species of low-growing eucalyptus. The mallee burns fiercely, but quickly regenerates from the surviving roots, making it difficult for farmers to clear. Its demise came about with the invention of mullenization; a heavy roller was dragged through the scrub by oxen, followed by an ingenious "stump-jump" plow. Years of burning and cropping finally eradicated the troublesome mallee, except in areas like Wyperfeld, itself threatened with clearance as late as the 1960s.

The ideal way to travel outside the state capital

By air Melbourne's Tullamarine Airport is 13½ miles northwest of the city center and is connected to many overseas destinations as well as to all major cities in Australia. Domestic and international flights share the same terminal. Frequent buses link the airport to Spencer Street station downtown, from where a shuttle distributes passengers to city center hotels.

By bus Express buses travel to major destinations in Australia and within Victoria. Because of the (relatively!) small size of the state, public transportation is a reasonable proposition for most journeys. Many places in Victoria are accessible in a day's outing from Melbourne. There is the usual excellent range of organized bus tours —remember that it is worth shopping around for the one that suits your requirements exactly.

By rail Apart from the extensive mileage served by the Met (see below), quite a number of towns in Victoria can be reached by **V-Line train** (sometimes supplemented by a V-Line bus). There are interstate services to Adelaide and Sydney as well as to Perth (changing at Adelaide or Port Pirie).

Greater Melbourne's comprehensive public transportation network is marketed under the name of **the Met**. Electric suburban railroads are supplemented by one of the world's most extensive systems of tramways and by urban buses. Through-ticketing is based on a zoning system, and there are a number of special deals like day tickets or weekly passes that are worth considering. The principal station is Flinders Street, and most trains travel around the underground loop that circles the city center with useful stops at Flagstaff, Museum, Parliament and Spencer Street.

By car Highway conditions in Victoria are generally good. The grandiose freeway plan for Melbourne was only partly implemented, but traffic still seems to flow more freely than in Sydney. If you wish to visit the more inaccessible national parks, it is best to rent a car.

The unpredictable state
The weather in Victoria is notoriously changeable; desert influences may be felt one moment, with searing dry winds and high temperatures, giving way suddenly to cold and wet air from the ocean to the south. If you don't like our weather, say Melburnians, just hold on—it's bound to change!

►► **Apollo Bay**   90A2

This little fishing port about 75 miles to the west of Port Phillip Bay has magnificent beaches and makes an excellent base for exploring the superb forests of the Otway Ranges. The hills reach the sea at Cape Otway, the "fearful coastline" described by the explorer Matthew Flinders, with a lighthouse rising from 328-foot cliffs.

► **Ararat**   90B2

The town (125 miles west of Melbourne) owes its foundation to the gold strike of 1857, when 3,000 ounces of alluvial gold were found in the space of three weeks. Then Ararat's population was more than double its present total; now sheep outnumber people by about 150 to one. To the north is the world-famous **Great Western Winery**, where the champagne is stored in underground galleries originally dug out by the gold miners.

► **Avoca**   90B2

On the Pyrenees Highway between Ararat and Castlemaine, Avoca was once a gold town and is now the center of an agricultural area. Since the 1960s, vineyards have been replanted on the north-facing slopes of the foothills, making this one of the state's newer wine districts. The solid Court House complex with bluestone jail, powder magazine and police residence remains from earlier times.

►►► **Ballarat**   90B2

No bigger than in its gold-rush heyday, Ballarat has preserved much of its 19th-century townscape and still exudes the atmosphere of those heady times.

Gold was first found in 1851, and within a few months thousands of ill-assorted diggers were frantically prospecting in spite of mud, cold and frequent bitter disappointment. Surface deposits were soon exhausted, and individual miners were succeeded by companies with sufficient clout to dig deep mines and buy the machinery to run them. Gold may have made Melbourne, but it made Ballarat too; profits seem not to have been gambled or drunk away, but to have been invested respectably in bricks and mortar, giving the town as splendid an array of fine 19th-century building as can be seen anywhere in the country. Banks, churches, a synagogue, clubs, a mining exchange, a splendid town hall and an art gallery all demonstrate how quickly the raw life of the diggings was transmuted into civic respectability.

109

Ballarat's botanics
By the side of beautiful Lake Wendouree, the Botanic Gardens in Ballarat are a perfect example of High Victorian taste, with white marble statuary among the pretty pavilions and bedding plants. On plinths beneath the trees stand the busts of former prime ministers, some, like Gough Whitlam and Malcolm Fraser, none too comfortable at seeing each other in such close proximity again.

The gold-rush town of Ballarat

Eureka!
By 1854, passions were running high in Ballarat's goldfields. Grim working and living conditions and encroachment by bigger mining companies were compounded by high license fees, extracted from resentful diggers by heavy-handed and much hated special police. Eventually, a band of Irish-led miners staged the only major revolt by whites in Australian history. Licenses were burned in a joyous conflagration, and the rebels, armed with pikes, assembled in the Eureka Stockade under the banner of the Southern Cross. But in a savage example of overkill, they were swiftly overcome by government soldiers, who left 30 dead. Australia's "Civil War" had lasted 15 minutes; it is convincingly recreated, using advanced *son et lumière* techniques, at Sovereign Hill.

Bred in Ballarat
Ballarat Wildlife Park has a wonderful selection of mostly Antipodean animals in its park-like setting. It is one of the few places where Tasmanian Devils are successfully bred; if you are so inclined, you can see these thugs of the animal world being fed their daily ration of white mice.

Sovereign Hill▶▶▶ is a superb re-creation of life and work on the goldfields in the 1850s. It is justifiably popular with its many visitors, who can pan for gold, ride Cobb & Co.'s stagecoach, shop in the emporiums of Main Street, savor the unique world of the Chinese Village, or even spend the night in the tents and officers' quarters of the Government Camp. Other major features include the Mine Museum, with 1,970 feet of underground workings, and the Gold Museum, with exciting displays on the history of the precious metal.

▶▶ **Beechworth**   91B4

This exceptionally well-preserved gold town in the foothills of the Australian Alps, 168 miles northeast of Melbourne, has a fine array of old buildings, many of them constructed from warm, honey-colored stone. As well as the post office with its imposing tower and the survivors of the 61 hotels of gold-rush times (the carriage house of one is home to a coach museum), there is also the Burke Museum. Named after the ill-fated explorer, the museum is packed with memorabilia, including mementoes of Ned Kelly who spent a night in the cell beneath the town hall.

▶▶ **Bellarine Peninsula**   90A3

Stretching eastward into Port Phillip Bay, this broad peninsula, with its fine surf beaches and popular resorts like Ocean Grove and Barwon Heads, has become the summer playground for the inhabitants of Geelong.

Ballarat: well worth the 68-mile trip from Melbourne

▶▶ **Bendigo** *90B2*

Like Ballarat, Bendigo began as a gold-rush town, expanding rapidly from 1851 onward to become one of the state's largest inland towns. Again like Ballarat, it has kept many of the fine late 19th-century buildings that were erected with the wealth won from the ground. These include the vast Shamrock Hotel, a number of imposing churches and a fine group of public buildings. The work that paid for all this architectural splendor is celebrated in the completely preserved **Central Deborah Goldmine▶▶**, with its impressive underground galleries, while the special contribution of Chinese miners is recalled in the delightful **Joss House** at Emu Point. The best way to get acquainted with this fascinating town is to take the "Talking Tram," which runs along a 5-mile route and gives a full commentary on all the sights.

▶ **Brisbane Ranges National Park** *90A2*

This extensive block of slate and sandstone has been eroded in places to form deep defiles like Anakie Gorge, a favored spot for not-too-demanding bush walks. Gold was once mined in quantity at the ghost town of Steiglitz, now a historic park.

▶ **Camperdown** *90A2*

This township is located on the sweeping plains formed from lava and ash that run from the South Australian border to Port Phillip Bay and have long been the basis of a prosperous grazing industry. Now silent, the volcanic cones responsible for all this fertility are scattered over the area. Mount Leura and Mount Sugarloaf are to the southeast of town, while to the west there are two examples of crater lakes—Lake Bullen Merri (fresh water) and Lake Gnotuk (salt water).

▶▶ **Castlemaine** *90B2*

Once gold had been discovered here in Specimen Gully by a shepherd, 25,000 diggers joined the rush, although Castlemaine declined fairly quickly because of the lack of reef gold. Today it is an attractive township, popular with folk seeking refuge from the metropolitan stresses of Melbourne to the south, and full of interesting old buildings. Most striking is the classical market hall, an almost exact reproduction of a Greek temple, which now contains the local museum. Castlemaine is also home to an excellent art gallery, some fine botanic gardens and the mansion known as Buda, begun in 1857.

The Castlemaine and Maldon Railway is a steam train ride that is very popular with children. It is based at Maldon station, 11 miles west along Highway 122 (see also page 117).

▶▶ **Coal Creek Historical Park** *90A3*

The railroads of Victoria used to run on Korumburra coal, and after the last mine had been closed down in the late 1950s it was decided that the days of coal and steam should be recreated at Coal Creek Mine just outside town (about 62 miles southeast of Melbourne). As well as the gallery of the mine, the popular 99-acre site has a railroad station, tradesmen plying their crafts, old stores and settlers' cottages.

The Gippsland whopper
Of the 100 or so species of Australian worms, *Megascolides australis* is easily the biggest, measuring up to 12 feet long and 1 inch thick. This extraordinary creature has its own museum, in a predictably worm-shaped building, near the turn-off for Phillip Island on the Bass Highway.

Castlemaine is a former mining town about 25 miles north of Daylesford along the Midland Highway

For much of its 1,615-mile length, the mighty Murray forms the boundary between Victoria and New South Wales. The longest river in Australia rises in the Great Dividing Range near Mount Kosciusko, flowing past stands of red gums and irrigating the semi-arid country around Mildura before entering the sea at Encounter Bay.

Barmah Forest
Spreading for 116 square miles over the floodplain of the Murray upstream from Echuca is this magnificent forest of river red gum trees, some of them 500 years old. Australia was largely built on the extraordinarily durable wood of these majestic trees, which was used for railroad construction, bridges, mines, fences, wharves and so on. When the river spills over its banks in the Wet, the forest comes alive with the calls of more than 200 species of migrating birds.

112

For thousands of years the rich wildlife of the Murray and its tributaries gave sustenance to the Aborigines who lived along its banks. It was discovered by Hume and Hovell in 1824, and explored more thoroughly by Charles Sturt in the course of his expedition of 1829–30. As settlers moved in, in the beginning strongly opposed by the Aborigines, the river took on great importance as a transportation route. A spirited contest took place in 1853 between the *Mary Ann* and the *Lady Augusta*, to see which would be the first steamboat to make it up the Murray as far as Swan Hill. With the prize money of £4,000, the master of the winning steamboat founded the Murray River Navigation Co., whose sternwheelers dominated river traffic for many years until the coming of the railway rendered them obsolete.

The greatest handicap to navigation was the irregularity of the Murray's flow; for many months of the year there would not be enough water to float a boat of any size, and the risk of running aground was constant. A number of proud vessels survive to carry cargoes of nostalgic tourists rather than the bales of wool that filled the holds in their 19th-century heyday.

Attractions Upstream from the twin towns of Albury (N.S.W.) and Wodonga (Victoria) is **Lake Hume**, several times the size of Sydney Harbour. Built to regulate river flow, it is now an ideal location for watersports. Downstream are the wineries around **Rutherglen**, while **Yarrawonga**, thanks to Lake Mulwala, has become a major inland water recreation area. Around **Cobram** are dozens of surprisingly fine sandy beaches.

Paddle steamers can be explored...

Echuca was once Australia's busiest inland port, with a truly magnificent wharf more than a mile long built from the timber of red gums. The people of the town are very proud of its heritage, and have taken pains to preserve it for the pleasure of visitors. The port area has been fully restored and has a whole series of visitor attractions, including the Cargo Shed with life-like dioramas. The Bridge Hotel is full of period furniture,

...and ridden at many places along the Murray

and the old Customs House has been put to use as the information center. It is rare to see so many steamboats, either under restoration or in action.

To the northwest of the Kerang lakes is another river port, **Swan Hill**, named by explorer Thomas Mitchell who was kept awake at night by the swans on a nearby lagoon. The town's outstanding attraction is the **Swan Hill Pioneer Settlement**, a painstaking riverside re-creation put together using original buildings as well as accurate replicas, and brought alive by the presence of craftspeople practicing traditional trades. A strong sense of the past can also be experienced in two fine old properties, the **Tyntynder Homestead** to the north, and **Murray Downs** to the east, the latter designed to repel Aborigine attack.

Red to green At the heart of the irrigated area, **Mildura** was originally laid out on the American pattern, with streets given numbers rather than names. In the language of the Kulkyne Aborigines, Mildura meant "dry red earth," but here red has been turned to green ever since the Chaffey brothers arrived in 1885 from North America to apply their advanced irrigation engineering techniques (see panel). Avocados, melons, oranges and grapes—both for the table and for wine-making—are all grown here, as is a whole range of fruit for drying. A number of establishments are happy to share their production secrets with you, among them Orange World and Sultana Sam Vineyard. Alternatively, you could take a trip on the river, since paddlesteamers also operate from here.

The Chaffeys
Canadians George and William Chaffey pioneered artificially irrigated settlements in California before being invited to bring their expertise to the Murray. They both succeeded and failed; from the 1880s on, thousands of new settlers flocked to the newly irrigated areas around Mildura, and the town itself prospered, but there were floods, problems with leaching and salinity, and the great slump of the 1890s. By 1896 George had had enough and borrowed his fare home, but William stayed on, helping to put the area's economy on a firmer footing once the railroad arrived in 1903. The water pumps George had designed continued to work into the 1950s.

The lovely Olinda Rhododendron Gardens in the Dandenong Ranges

A feathered philanderer
The forests and gullies of the Dandenongs provide a habitat for *Menura novae-hollandiae*, the superb lyrebird, a wonderful singer and mimic of the calls of other birds. The rather ordinary looking male of the species comes into his own in winter, when he senses that female lyrebirds are ready to respond to his advances. Having built a series of mounds through-out his territory, the male mounts one and undergoes an extraordinary transfor-mation, fanning out his lyre-shaped tail-feathers so that his body disappears in a froth of plumage, at the same time pouring forth a cascade of song. The more impressive the display, the greater the bird's chances of winning his way with a succession of females.

► **Colac** 90A2

Colac is the market town for the agricultural wealth of the surrounding basalt plains. This area incorporates a lake district of some 50 to 60 water bodies. Those that have formed in deep craters contain fresh water, while the shallower lakes contain salty water because the rate of evaporation from them exceeds the rate of replenish-ment; Lake Corangamite is a saline lake, and is also Victoria's largest.

►► **The Dandenong Ranges** 90A3

Melbourne is fortunate to have these magnificently wooded hills on the eastern edge of the metropolitan area, a wonderful destination for a day's outing. The high-est point is **Mount Dandenong**►► (2,077 feet), with fan-tastic views over the sprawling city to the west and the further hills to the east.

Because of their accessibility, the Dandenongs have long been a favorite residential area, and there are pretty townships and many fine mansions, some of which have been converted into hotels and restaurants. There are lush gardens, too, like the **Olinda Rhododendron Gardens**►, whose exotic shrubs contrast with the native vegetation of towering mountain ash trees, massive tree ferns and rampant creepers. At Belgrave is the terminus of **"Puffing Billy"**►►, the vintage narrow-gauge steam locomotive that pulls trainloads of tourists on an 8-mile scenic railroad line through the forest.

►► **Daylesford** 90B2

Between them, Daylesford (62 miles northwest of Melbourne) and Hepburn Springs contain half of Aust-ralia's mineral springs. The supposedly therapeutic waters were discovered in the course of gold mining in the 1850s and 1860s, and by the turn of the century the place had taken on the character of the spa resorts so common in Europe, perhaps because many of the early inhabitants were originally immigrants from the Swiss canton of Ticino. At the Hepburn Spa Complex, the old spa building is still intact; you can acquire bottled water, take various treatments and enjoy relaxing walks. The excellent **Daylesford Historical Society Museum**▶ is housed in the old School of Mines, and there are attractive botanical gardens. To the north is the old volcanic cone of Mount Franklin with a fine view from its summit.

▶ **Dunolly** 90B2

The area around Dunolly, 125 miles northwest of Melbourne, yielded more nuggets than any other Australian goldfield, including the Welcome Stranger, weighing 2,505 ounces. Reproductions of this and other mega-nuggets can be seen in the quiet little town's Goldfields Museum.

▶ **Geelong** 90A2

This industrial port city, Victoria's second largest, once saw itself as a rival to Melbourne, but has long since given up the struggle, though its harbor still exports the rich produce of its agricultural hinterland. In spite of much redevelopment, there is plenty of evidence of 19th-century grandeur; pompous public buildings adorn the city center and the prosperity of Geelong's merchant class is reflected in the many elegant properties, such as Barwon Grange overlooking the Barwon River. Corio Villa above Eastern Beach was prefabricated in Scotland and reassembled here by guesswork after the plans and instructions had been destroyed. One of the fine old bluestone woolstores has been splendidly restored to house the excellent **National Wool Museum**▶▶. This is the place to come if you want to understand how Australia "rode to prosperity on the sheep's back."

▶▶ **Gippsland** 91A4

Named in the 1840s by Polish explorer Count Strzelecki after the Governor of N.S.W., Gippsland is the loosely defined region comprising most of southeastern Victoria between the highlands of the Great Dividing Range and the coastline of Bass Strait. The superb temperate rain forest that once blanketed the area has mostly been cut down to yield rich dairying and fruit-growing land, though fine tracts of woodland remain in the state forests and national parks along the N.S.W. border in the far east. This is one of the areas where protest action by conservationists has focused public attention on the fact that the glories of Australia's natural heritage are not inexhaustible. The La Trobe Valley in the heart of Gippsland has the world's biggest deposits of brown coal, burned here in power stations to provide something like 90 percent of the state's electric power, while oil and gas is extracted in quantity from offshore wells in Bass Strait.

The scale of contemporary opencast mining can be appreciated in the course of tours from the **Morwell Visitor Centre**▶, while more traditional activities can be contemplated in the **Old Gippstown Pioneer Folk Museum**▶ at Moe, with its collection of old buildings from many parts of Gippsland. Inland is some of Victoria's most attractive countryside, running up into the alpine foothills of the Great Dividing Range, while the Gippsland Lakes (see panel) lie landward of Ninety Mile Beach.

115

Gippsland Lakes
Sometimes described as "the best example of a coastal lagoon in the world," and with a near-Mediterranean climate, this area offers unrivaled opportunites for sailing, cruising, fishing or just taking it easy. Both beach and lakes are protected as national parks.

Rich dairy lands make for fine Gippsland cheeses

VICTORIA

Many native Australians now prefer to be called Kooris (meaning "our people") rather than Aborigines

Our people
Following the 1988 Bicentenary, the natives of Australia decided to try to replace the overall term "Aborigine" with names from their own languages. "Koori," meaning "our people," is now widely in use in southeastern Australia. The Grampians are an outdoor gallery of Koori art, to be seen in the Billimina, Larngibunja and Ngamadjidj shelters and at Flat Rock.

▶   **Goulburn Valley**   90B3

The Goulburn River runs northwest from artificial Lake Eildon in the foothills of the Victorian Alps through a rich fruit- and vine-growing area to join the Murray River near Echuca. With an indented shoreline more than 300 miles long, the lake is an immensely popular place for water-sports of all kinds. To the west of the river, Rushworth is a fine example of a gold-rush town of the 1850s.

▶▶   **The Grampians**   90B1

The Aborigines, who left many traces of their rock art here, knew the Grampians as Gariwerd. Forming the largest national park in Victoria, the region consists of a succession of sandstone ridges sloping gently to the west, ending in sheer cliffs and jagged rock formations to the east. The area is rich in wildlife and is carpeted with wildflowers in summer.

The park has an excellent network of trails and paths, and can also be appreciated by car thanks to a series of scenic roads. There are any number of spectacular view-points; **Boroka Lookout**▶▶ gives a fine panorama over the tourist center of Halls Gap, where there is a visitor center and the **Brambuk Living Cultural Centre**▶, which is intended to bring the history and culture of local Aborigines to life. To the west are two of the most spectacular sights of the ranges; the rock formation known as the **Balconies** and the grandiose water staircase of the **Mackenzie Falls.**

▶   **Hamilton**   90A1

Focal point of much of the prosperous agricultural plains of central western Victoria, Hamilton likes to style itself the "Wool Capital of the World." Its outstanding attraction is the **City of Hamilton Art Gallery**▶, with a large and varied collection including wonderful examples of the

The huge overhanging rocks known as the Balconies

Maldon's wide main street slopes gently downhill

applied arts of many countries, plus a splendid array of the watercolors and etchings of the British topographical artist Paul Sandby.

►► Healesville 90B3
Nestling among its green hills in the Yarra Valley, this attractive township is a good place for walks and picnics, but it is mostly visited now for the **Healesville Sanctuary►►**. A visit to this world-class wildlife park is an excellent way to appreciate the strange and wonderful fauna of the Antipodes, in a range of cleverly recreated habitats and walk-through enclosures.

►► Lorne 90A2
Protected from the north by the steep and beautifully forested slopes of the Otways, this charming little place facing onto the curving beach of Loutit Bay has enjoyed a high reputation as a beach resort for over a century. There are also delightful walks in the forest park.

►► Maldon 90B2
Among the many old gold-rush townships of central Victoria, Maldon is outstanding—"the best preserved town in Australia of the gold-mining era" according to the National Trust. It is certainly full of charm; the scale of the place is modest and the tone is set by delightful cottages, many of them with pretty gardens.

► Marysville 90B3
Pleasantly located in the foothills of the Victorian Alps, the township of Marysville has long been favored by week-ending Melburnians. In summer there is wonderful bush-walking to the Steavenson Falls, some of the highest in Victoria, or to the Cumberland Valley where the state's tallest trees grow. In winter, there is good cross-country skiing to be enjoyed, particularly on the popular snow-fields of Lake Mountain.

Duckbilled denizen
Even the normally bashful platypus can be observed going about its daily life at Healesville. The sanctuary has the distinction of being the first place to success-fully breed this normally diffident creature in captivity.

Penguins on parade
The endearing little fairy penguins that live along the coasts of southern Australia are the smallest of the species in the world, being only about a foot in length. They spend their days feeding and frolicking at sea, then as evening falls they gather in groups to waddle to their burrows at the back of the beach on Phillip Island. They maintain this routine with apparent complete indifference to the floodlighting and to the countless tourists huddled in the stands watching one of Australia's most popular wildlife spectacles.

▶▶ **Mornington Peninsula**   90A3

Melbourne's favorite weekend and vacation area embraces Port Phillip Bay in a great curve of sheltered beaches before ending at Point Nepean overlooking the dangerous currents of the narrow entrance to the bay known as The Rip.

Much of the peninsula is suburban in character, with dwellings crowding along the main road and spreading out from the residential and resort towns like Frankston and Mornington. In the season, the foreshore is crowded with campers and R.V.'s. Towards the tip, refined Sorrento and exclusive Portsea have retained more of the feeling of early days, when paddlesteamers brought vacationers across the bay from Melbourne. Once off limits as a naval base, Point Nepean is now a national park, reached from the visitor center by shuttle. The "front" beaches facing the bay tend to be calm but busy, while the "back" beaches looking out onto the Bass Strait are wild—no place for inexperienced swimmers.

The peninsula's importance in Victoria's history is recalled by the graves of the "early settlers" at **Sorrento**, and by the 1844 **McCrae Homestead▶**, the home of the first permanent settler family. The best overall view is from 1,000-foot high **Arthur's Seat**, reached by road or, more excitingly, by chairlift.

▶▶ **Phillip Island**   90A3

Bounded to the west by the Mornington Peninsula, the great tidal estuary of Westernport Bay is broken up by a number of islands. French Island and Little Churchill Island are rich in wildlife, but the most famous of the

The dramatic Twelve Apostles near Port Campbell

islands is Phillip Island, whose irresistible **Fairy Penguin Parade** pulls in hundreds of thousands of onlookers.

Reached by bridge and about 80 miles from Melbourne, Phillip Island is generally flat, but has a splendidly varied coastline that includes rugged cliffs, rock outcrops and long surf beaches. Muttonbirds nest on Cape Woolamai, the highest point on the island, thousands of seals can be seen off the basalt cliffs of Point Grant, and a number of sanctuaries harbor koalas, which were introduced to the island in the 1870s. Cowes is the main resort, with boat trips to the seals and to French Island and a ferry to Stony Point on the Mornington Peninsula.

▶▶▶ Port Campbell National Park   90A2

Backed by the Great Ocean Road running west from Geelong, this park comprises 19 miles of some of the world's most spectacular coastal scenery, a succession of high cliffs, headlands and strange rock formations standing out to sea. Cookie-like beds of limestone, sand, mud and seashells formed beneath the sea and then uplifted 25 million years ago are now being eaten away by the breakers rolling in from the Southern Ocean. Because the rock varies in strength and texture, the sea advances more rapidly in some places than others, leaving behind isolated features that have been given evocative names like the Twelve Apostles (at Port Campbell). In a dramatic demonstration of the rate of erosion, the arch of "London Bridge" collapsed into the surf in 1990, stranding the walkers who had ventured out onto it. Quickly rescued, they were luckier than the many passengers and crewmen who perished along what was named the "Shipwreck Coast" in the days of sail (see pages 242–3).

▶▶ Port Fairy   90A1

This delightful little fishing port and beach resort at the mouth of the Moyne River is one of the oldest settlements in Victoria, having been home to sealers and whalers in the early years of the 19th century. There are 50 buildings classified as historic by the National Trust, including Mott's Cottage and a wooden house erected by a whaling skipper in the 1830s.

▶ Portland   90A1

Founded a year earlier than Port Fairy, in 1834, this busy deep-water port is the oldest permanent settlement in Victoria. To the southwest are the spectacular seascapes of Cape Nelson and the blowholes and petrified forest of Cape Bridgewater.

▶▶ Queenscliff   90A3

Separated from Point Nepean only by the treacherous waters of The Rip, Queenscliff is a splendidly old-fashioned kind of place, with a harbor, a fort (1882), grand hotels and the Black Lighthouse, prefabricated in Scotland and shipped here in 1863.

▶▶ Strzelecki Ranges   91A3

The best way to see these ridges is to follow the Grand Ridge Road from Nyora to Carrajung (about 80 miles), passing through some of Victoria's finest upland scenery and numerous pretty towns and villages.

Queenscliff: a quiet and popular retreat for Melburnians

119

Count the consonants
His name unpronounceable to Anglo-Saxons, the Pole Paul Edmund de Strzelecki styled himself "Count," a claim with little apparent substance. Although it was Angus McMillan who had first blazed a trail through the almost impenetrable rain forest jungle of southeast Victoria, it was not his name for the area ("New South Caledonia") that was adopted, but Strzelecki's "Gippsland." Strzelecki's own venture into Gippsland was only saved from disaster by the skill of his Aboriginal guide, Tarra, after whom the Tarra Bulga National Park has been named.

Gum trees

Gum trees, or to give them their more digni-fied name, eucalypts, are the trees most closely identified with Australia. They comprise more than 500 different species, and grow in most parts of the country; some three-quarters of all Australian trees are eucalypts, many of them with wonderfully descriptive names like peppermint, ironbark, lemon-scented, bloodwood or blackbutt.

Eucalyptus leaves
All eucalyptus leaves contain a fragrant oil that is used in medicines and flavorings. Their indigestible look doesn't deter the koala either, which in fact depends entirely on one eucalyptus species for its food source.

120

Early settlers didn't much like the look of the unfamiliar eucalypts, with their peeling, untidy bark hanging in strips and tatters and the unseasonal failure of their dull gray leaves to fall at the proper time of year. Many farmers and sheep raisers brought cuttings of other trees from home, and elm, oak, willow and poplar grace many a rural scene. The same was true of townsfolk, who preferred the more orderly European trees for their parks.

Forests and felling But eucalypts have their own distinct allure, individually or in mass, forming magnificent forests or growing with other trees, shrubs and grasses to form the surprisingly park-like landscapes of many parts of the interior. Over the millenia, eucalypts have also learned to live with fire, regenerating after a bush blaze from buds concealed within their bark. Many species, like jarrah and messmate, yield first-rate wood, and in consequence were felled ruthlessly until quite recently. Others are logged, somewhat demeaningly, to be turned into wood-chip for foreign pulp mills.

World-beater
The confusingly named mountain ash (*Eucalyptus regnans*) is the tallest flowering plant in the world, reaching an extraordinary height of up to 328 feet in the forests of Victoria and Tasmania.

Varieties There are many types of eucalypts, from the Tasmanian blue gum that provided the wood for railroad ties, to the river red gum of semi-arid areas, the ghost gum of deserts, and the snow gum, symbol of the Australian Alps.

The great river red gum forest at Yarrawonga

Southern Right whales playing off Warrnambool

▶ **Walhalla** 91A4

Tucked away in the deep wooded valleys north of Moe, isolated Walhalla boomed in the late 19th century when more gold was extracted here than from any other area in Victoria. By the time the railroad reached here in 1910 via a series of spectacular tunnels and trestle bridges the gold had more or less run out. A stroll along the crooked main street recalls some of the atmosphere of former days, and you can visit the Long Tunnel Extended Mine.

▶ **Wangaratta** 90B3

The Hume Highway is the main route north from Melbourne to Sydney. About 150 miles from Melbourne is flourishing Wangaratta, a service center for the surrounding agricultural area. The body of the notorious bushranger Mad Dan Morgan is buried here minus his head, the latter having been sent to Melbourne in order to establish whether he really was mad, or just plain bad. The town's other attraction is the **Airworld Museum**▶▶, with a splendid collection of vintage aircraft.

▶ **Warrnambool** 90A1

The biggest town on Victoria's southwest coast, Warrnambool benefits from superb beaches. Founded by whalers in the 1840s, it is still frequented by Southern Right whales, which come here in winter to calve (see panel). **Flagstaff Hill Maritime Village**▶▶ is a conscientiously re-created port village with several historic vessels and other fascinating displays.

▶▶ **Wilsons Promontory National Park** 91A4

The southernmost point of mainland Australia, this wild and mountainous granite peninsula protruding into Bass Strait is perhaps Victoria's favorite national park. Many of its rocky headlands, splendid beaches and dense forests are only accessible on foot, and in spite of its popularity it is always possible to find whatever degree of isolation you want (though you may have kangaroos for company). The only settlement is at Tidal River, where the road ends and a network of wonderful hiking trails begins.

The Warrnambool whales
Between May and August Southern Right whales gather off Logan's Beach to bear their young. A special viewing platform has been built from which you can observe these magnificent creatures, once hunted to near-extinction, as they dive and play, making spectacular fountains from their blowholes or leaping bodily from the waves.

Drive The Dandenong Ranges

Less than an hour from the center of Melbourne, the "Blue Dandenongs" are a favorite recreation area and summer retreat for the inhabitants of the city.

Canterbury Road leads to Montrose at the northern end of the Dandenong Tourist Road. Those with time to spare could continue another 19 miles to **Healesville Sanctuary**, one of the best places in which to see Australian wildlife at close quarters. **Mount Dandenong**, at 2,077 feet

the highest point of the range, and the sculptures of the **William Ricketts Sanctuary** are accessible from the Tourist Road. The route to the village of Kallista passes the Nicholas Memorial Gardens and **Sherbrooke Forest Park**, where you can see the tree-ferns and the magnificent mountain ash trees for which the area is famous. **Belgrave** is the terminus for the irresistible "Puffing Billy," a restored steam train that hauls delighted passengers through the forest along its narrow-gauge

Drive Mornington Peninsula

The 62-mile drive to Point Nepean National Park at the far tip of the Mornington Peninsula passes residential areas and resorts enjoying the beaches of Port Phillip Bay.

Frankston marks the end of the commuter railroad line from Melbourne.

Beyond **Dromana** with its excellent Tourist Information Centre the coast is lined with vacation homes and campsites, while above the town **Arthur's Seat** rises 1,000 feet to give a fine panorama over bay and ocean. On its northern slope is the little **McCrae Homestead**, built in 1844 and still evocative of pioneer days, in spite of its suburban neighbors. Listed as an historic site by the National Trust, the original furniture is on display and guides give tours of the property.

With its broad main street, **Sorrento**, bearing little resemblance to its Italian namesake, has a charm all of its own, while posh **Portsea** does its best to maintain its exclusivity. On the outer rim of the peninsula, the "back beaches" face the ocean surf of Bass Strait. For a long time off limits as defense land, **Point Nepean** can now be explored, if not by car, then by transportation based at the National Park Orientation Centre.

The Peninsula Freeway and South Eastern Arterial can be used to speed your return to Melbourne.

Right: Port Phillip Bay begins at the tip of the Mornington Peninsula

VICTORIA DRIVES

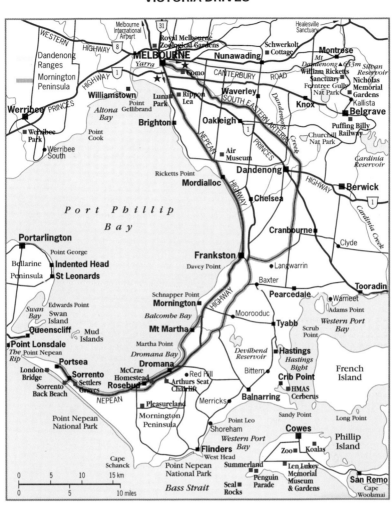

Western Highway
Melbourne International Airport
31
8
MELBOURNE
Yarra
Royal Melbourne Zoological Gardens
Nunawading
Healesville Sanctuary
Schwerkolt Cottage
Montrose
Mt
Dandenong 633m
Silvan Reservoir
William Ricketts Sanctuary
Ferntree Gully Nat Park
Nicholas Memorial Gardens
Kallista
CANTERBURY ROAD
SOUTH EASTERN ARTERIAL
Knox
Belgrave
Puffing Billy Railway
Dandenong Creek
Churchill Nat Park
Cardinia Reservoir

Dandenong Ranges
Mornington Peninsula
Williamstown
Como
Luna Park
Rippon Lea
Waverley
Oakleigh
PRINCES
Werribee
Altona Bay
Point Gellibrand
Brighton
Air Museum
NEPEAN
Werribee Park
Point Cook
Werribee South
Ricketts Point
Mordialloc
HIGHWAY
Dandenong
Berwick
1
Chelsea
Cranbourne
Clyde
Cardinia Creek

Port Phillip Bay

Portarlington
Point George
Bellarine Peninsula
Indented Head
St Leonards
Frankston
Davey Point
Langwarrin
Baxter
Pearcedale
Warneet
Adams Point
Tooradin
Western Port Bay

Swan Bay
Edwards Point
Swan Island
Queenscliff
Mud Islands
Schnapper Point
Mornington
Balcombe Bay
Mt Martha
Moorooduc
Tyabb
Scrub Point

Point Lonsdale
The Rip
Point Nepean
Portsea
London Bridge
Sorrento
Sorrento Back Beach
NEPEAN
Martha Point
Dromana Bay
McCrae Homestead
Settlers
Dromana
Rosebud
Arthurs Seat Chairlift
Red Hill
Pleasureland
Merricks
Martha Point
Devilbend Reservoir
Bittern
Hastings
Hastings Bight
Crib Point
HMAS Cerberus
French Island

Mornington Peninsula
Point Leo
Shoreham
Western Port Bay
Flinders
West Head
Point Nepean National Park
Cape Schanck
Summerland
Seal Rocks
Penguin Parade
Balnarring
Sandy Point
Long Point
Cowes
Zoo
Koalas
Len Lukey Memorial Museum & Gardens
San Remo
Cape Woolamai
Phillip Island

Point Nepean National Park

Bass Strait

0   5   10   15 km
0   5   10 miles

SOUTH AUSTRALIA

NORTHERN   TERRITORY

Stevenson Creek

Witjira National Park

▲ 1231m

Amata ●
Pukatja ●

1440m
Mt Woodroffe
Musgrave Ranges

Fregon ●

Everard Range

Granite Downs

Alberga River

Macumba ●

Marla ●

Nedes

87

Oodnadatta ●

E

Great Victoria Desert

Roadhouse ●

OODNADATTA TRACK

WESTERN

AUSTRALIA

Dey-Dey Lake

Lake Maurice

Coober Pedy ●

Ranges

STUART HIGHWAY

D

Maralinga ●

Trans-Australian Railway

Cook ●

Tarcoola ●

Kingoonya ●
Lake Harris

Glendambo ●

Koonalda Cave

Nullarbor Plain

Nullarbor ●

EYRE   HIGHWAY

1

Yalata ●

Lake Gairdner

Lake Everard

Nundroo ●

Head of Bight

Coorabie ●

Penong ●

Ceduna ■

Lake Acraman

Gawler Ranges

Cactus Beach ■

Yardea ●

Nullarbor National Park

Streaky Bay ●

1

EYRE   HIGHWAY

C

Port Kenny ●

FLINDERS HIGHWAY

Kyancutta ●

Eyre

Venus Bay

Elliston ●

Lock ●

Peninsula

Flinders Island

Mount Hope ●

Tumby Bay

Coffin Bay Nat Park

Port Lincoln ●
Cape Carnot

Lincoln Nat Park

Great   Australian   Bight

B

A

0   100   200   300 km

0   50   100   150   200 miles

1   2   3

SOUTH AUSTRALIA

QUEENSLAND

Simpson   Desert

Cordillo
Downs

Goyder
Lagoon

Sturt
Stony
Desert

Ephemeral
Lakes

Clifton Hills

The Macumba

The Warburton

Innamincka

Lake Eyre
North

Tirari
Desert

Lake
Moonba

Cooper Creek

BIRDSVILLE TRACK

Lake Eyre
Nat Park

Strzelecki   Desert

Lake
Gregory

Lake
Blanche

STRZELECKI TRACK

Lake Eyre
South

Coward
Springs

Marree

Lake
Callabonna

Roxby
Downs

Lyndhurst

Arkaroola

Andamooka

Leigh
Creek

Gammon Ranges
Nat Park

Balcanoona

Lake Frome

Busworth

Lake

NEW

Beltana

Torrens

SOUTH

Wonoona

Pimba

Blinman

Flinders Ranges
Nat Park

WALES

Island
Lagoon

Wilpena
1165m

Lake
Macfarlane

Booaloo

Hawker

Curnamona

Cradock

Cockburn

Port
Augusta

Quorn

Waukaringa

BARRIER   HIGHWAY

Lake
Gilles

Iron
Knob

Mt Remarkable
Nat Park

Yunta

Kimba

Whyalla

Peterborough

Port
Pirie

Jamestown

LINCOLN HIGHWAY

Cleve

Cowell

Crystal
Brook

32

Clare

Burra

Riverland

Wallaroo

Kadina

Moonta

Balaklava

Morgan

Spencer

Kapunda

Murray

Renmark

Gulf

Maitland

Gawler

Barossa Valley

Berri

20

STURT Hwy

Yorke

Port

Loxton

Yorketown

Peninsula

Adelaide
Hills

Birdwood

Innes
NP

Adelaide

Gulf

Hahndorf

Inneston

St Vincent

ADELAIDE

Murray Bridge

Investigator Strait

Strathalbyn

Kingscote

Fleurieu
Pen

12

Pinnaroo

Victor
Harbor

Goolwa

Kelly Hill
Caves

Coorong
Nat Park

DUKES HIGHWAY

VICTORIA

Flinders
Chase
Nat Park

Kangaroo
Island

Keith

8

Bordertown

PRINCES HIGHWAY

Kingston SE

Robe

1

Bool
Lagoon

Naracoorte

Coonawarra

Beachport

Millicent

Mount
Gambier

Canunda Nat Park

Cape
Northumberland

4

5

Wowsers no more
A wowser originally meant someone who didn't know how to enjoy himself. The epithet was maliciously applied to the good citizens of Adelaide because of their supposed piety and apparent aversion to letting their hair down. The visitor to South Australia is unlikely to see much trace of this today, least of all in Adelaide. It may still be a city of churches, but it is now also a city of restaurants, watered by the products of its wineries. And it was in South Australia that the country's first nudist beach was opened, at Maslins on the coast south of Adelaide.

South Australia Virtually all the inhabitants of Australia's third largest state live along the fertile coasts of its gulf lands and southeastern plains, three-quarters of them in Greater Adelaide. Northward from this tamed littoral with its almost Mediterranean climate stretches an immense and arid area of Outback and desert, some of it bearing the traces of failed European settlement, and huge tracts of it returned to the Aborigines. This is a land of sharp differences, with a capital that is the most elegant and obviously cultured of all Australian cities.

In the beginning South Australia was not a prison colony but a "province," settled by free people (mostly from the south of England, but many also from Germany) under the auspices of the South Australia Company. The first group landed from the *Buffalo* in 1836, but the true founding father was Colonel William Light, a brilliant and unorthodox character whose visionary plan for Adelaide has shaped the city to the present day. The development of the colony was erratic. Within a few years of its foundation it was only saved from economic collapse by the discovery of copper at Kapunda and Burra. Attempts to push the frontier of agriculture north were defeated by long years of drought, although the peninsula's corn lands flourished.

For many years Adelaide remained simply the center of a vast agricultural and mining area, its affairs conducted by merchants who lived sober lives ("wowsers" to other Australians). Much of the tone of South Australian life was indeed set by the seriousness with which its Nonconformist (British) or Lutheran (German) citizens took their religion; not for nothing was Adelaide known as the city of churches.

The vulnerability of what was an almost entirely rural economy became apparent in the years of the great Depression, and following World War II the state underwent an industrial transformation, with shipyards at Whyalla and car factories at Adelaide's satellite town of Elizabeth. In the 1970s, these activities showed themselves to be vulnerable in their turn, and South Australia, along with much of the rest of the country, continues to suffer economic and financial troubles.

Given the state's range of landscapes, it is not surprising that tourism is of increasing importance. Adelaide attracts visitors with its biennial Arts Festival, as well as by the elegance of its townscape and its reputation for good living. It is no longer possible to take a luxury cruise from Port Adelaide around the two great inlets that bring the sea far into the heart of the state, Spencer Gulf and Gulf St. Vincent, but an immensely long coastline offers endless opportunites for water-based activities of all kinds at unspoiled towns such as **Robe**, south of the spectacular Coorong National Park. Coastal landscapes vary from the wild isolation of rugged headlands to delightful little fishing ports and resorts. Offshore islands invite those with a taste for escapism, the biggest of them, Kangaroo Island, having a superb range of (accessible) wildlife.

South Australia is the starting point for many of the country's great tourist itineraries. Tarcoola is the junction for two trains of almost legendary reputation—the *Ghan*, on its way north to Alice Springs in the Red Centre, and the *Indian Pacific*, pausing here on its transcontinental run westward across the Nullarbor.

Bethany's Lutheran church and hall in the Barossa Valley

127

It is possible to tour some of the Naracoorte Caves

Dashing Don's derring-do
South Australia's Premier from 1967–8 and again from 1970–9, Don Dunstan not only cultivated a progressive and dynamic image, but was instrumental in dragging his state into the late 20th century. Under his leadership, South Australia passed legislation outlawing racial and sexual discrimination. Pastor Sir Douglas Nicholls, a distinguished Aborigine, became Governor, while a police chief who refused to reveal who had instructed him to keep secret files on M.P.s and other potential subversives was dismissed.

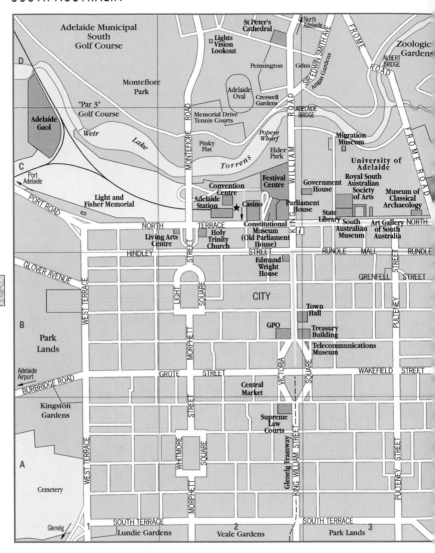

Adelaide

Australia's fifth largest city likes to be known for its biennial Festival of the Arts, its restaurants and its generally
high cultural tone. Many of its early citizens were religious
dissenters escaping from persecution in their home countries; without the "convict stain" and lacking the "Irish
element," people pursued both work and recreation with
a kind of earnest dullness, in rationally planned surroundings of dignified elegance.

These surroundings were the vision of one man,
Colonel William Light, who, as South Australia's
Surveyor-General, drew up a brilliant plan in 1836, to
which the city has adhered ever since. Having found a
suitable site on the banks of the little River Torrens, he set
out a square-mile grid of streets on the south bank. The

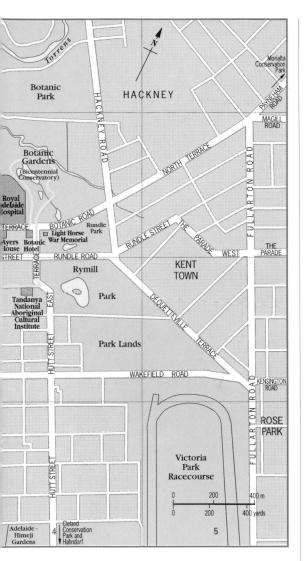

Torrens

Botanic Park

HACKNEY

Morialta Conservation Park

PAYNEHAM ROAD

MAGILL ROAD

NORTH TERRACE

FULLARTON ROAD

Botanic Gardens (Bicentennial Conservatory)

Royal Adelaide Hospital

TERRACE

BOTANIC ROAD

Light Horse War Memorial

Rundle Park

Ayers House

Botanic Hotel

RUNDLE STREET

THE PARADE

WEST

THE PARADE

STREET

RUNDLE ROAD

Rymill Park

KENT TOWN

Tandanya National Aboriginal Cultural Institute

EAST

DEQUETTEVILLE TERRACE

Park Lands

WAKEFIELD ROAD

KENSINGTON ROAD

ROSE PARK

FULLARTON ROAD

HUTT STREET

Victoria Park Racecourse

0   200   400 m
0   200   400 yards

Adelaide - Himeji Gardens

4

Cleland Conservation Park and Hahndorf

5

What a bastard!
Although 19th-century Britain produced a number of plans for ideal towns, most Australian cities developed in a totally chaotic way. It was left to an army officer, illegitimate offspring of the English founder of Pinang in Malaysia and a Eurasian woman, to conceive and implement the ambitious plan for Adelaide. William Light had served as an intelligence officer with the Duke of Wellington, gaining his rank of colonel on a temporary posting in Spain; he reveled in the commission to survey and plan not only the site of Adelaide but much of the rest of the new province. Married to the daughter (also illegitimate) of the Duke of Richmond, he left his wife at home in England, and when he died (probably from overwork) in 1839, was refused the last rites because he was living in open sin with another lady.

central thoroughfare was impressively wide, and the whole was enlivened with a series of squares. A green belt around the city was to remain parkland in perpetuity, a fit setting for public buildings such as Government House; on the far bank of the river was the fine suburb of North Adelaide. In spite of opposition at the time, in spite of the building boom of the 1970s and 1980s, and in spite of the automobile, all these elements are in place today, helping make Adelaide a most agreeable city.

It is rare in a metropolis to be able to live in a Victorian villa looking onto parkland, walk or cycle to work in the city center, spend the evening at the theater, then walk home again, but here people can. The majority however, inhabit the suburbs that have spread across the coastal plain between the magnificent beaches along the gulf and the Adelaide Hills to the east.

Time for a leisurely sail in quiet Port Adelaide

Festive season
They say in Adelaide that the Festival Centre cost less to build than it did to carpet Sydney's Opera House. The center is busy all year round, with two major theaters and two outdoor performance areas. Its plaza, designed by the German environmental sculptor Otto Hajek, has been described as Australia's biggest outdoor art work.

Adelaide's Festival of the Arts is held every two years for a period of three weeks in February/March. Warm days and mild nights help create the right atmosphere for a wonderful choice of events—opera, ballet, concerts, theater, exhibitions, children's activities and a literary festival—all within walking distance of each other in this compact city.

▶▶ **Adelaide Botanic Gardens**   *129C4*

North Terrace
Founded in 1855, these 49 acres of trees, shrubs, lawns and lakes glitter with an array of heritage buildings. As well as the Museum of Economic Botany, there is the Simpson Shade House, the 1868 Victoria House with its giant waterlily, and the wonderful Palm House, brought out from Germany in the 1870s. But most extraordinary of all is the soaring **Bicentennial Conservatory**, an environmental capsule of great sophistication, within whose high-tech skin there flourishes a profusion of plants from the tropical rain forests of North Australia and its neighbors.

▶▶▶ **Art Gallery of South Australia**   *128C3*

North Terrace
Behind its classical portico this refined building houses one of the country's most important collections of Australian, European and Asian art. Some of the paintings by Australian artists are familiar, seeming to encapsulate key aspects of the country's character, like the stampeding sheep in Tom Roberts' *The Breakaway* of 1891 or the subtle beach flirtation depicted in Charles Conder's *Holiday at Mentone* (1888).

▶ **Glenelg**   *128A1*

Once Adelaide's rather exclusive seaside center, with splendid sandy beaches stretching far in either direction, suburban Glenelg still has plenty of charm, epitomized by the 1920s trams that link it to the city's Victoria Square. It was here that Governor Hindmarsh and the first band of settlers landed in 1836.

▶▶ **Migration Museum**   *128C3*

82 Kintore Avenue
Housed in the restored buildings of the city's Destitute Asylum, this innovative institution presents the story of the immigrant groups who founded South Australia. Visitors are invited to trace their own background by using the museum's considerable resources. Despite the tendency to dwell on disappointment rather than optimism and achievement, this is an essential visit for anyone trying to understand how Australia has evolved.

▶ North Adelaide   128D3

Adelaide's classiest and oldest suburb has many fine houses. Melbourne Street has the kind of shops, restaurants and boutiques you might expect, while St. Peter's Cathedral boasts the heaviest bells in the southern hemisphere. At Light's Vision Lookout, a statue of the good colonel surveys the city he created.

▶▶ Port Adelaide   128C1

Some 6 miles northwest of the landlocked city center, Adelaide's harbor town has been deserted by most of its maritime traffic, leaving it free to concentrate on its fascinating past; it has South Australia's largest collection of distinguished 19th-century buildings. Among the long quayside sheds is the bright red 1869 lighthouse, overlooking a number of historic ships when they are in dock. A short distance inland on Lipson Street are a couple of first-rate museums, each on its own well worth the bus or train trip out from the city center. The main building of the fascinating **South Australian Maritime Museum▶▶** is an old bond store, while the **Port Dock Station Railway Museum▶▶** is the biggest of its kind in the country.

▶▶▶ South Australian Museum   128C3
North Terrace

This is the state's museum of natural history, with all the geological and zoological displays one would expect, but its main attraction is probably its outstanding collection of Aboriginal artifacts. These are presented in an imaginative and accessible fashion, making the museum the best such place in the country to study the past life of the original Australians.

▶ Tandanya National Aboriginal Cultural Institute   129B4
Grenfell Street

A recent addition to Adelaide's developing East End, this offers an exceptional opportunity to learn about contemporary Aboriginal culture. There are dance and theater performances, meetings, talks and celebrations, constantly changing exhibitions, and demonstrations and sales of arts and crafts.

Impressive Ayers House, now open to the public

Other Adelaide sights
The 19th-century Ayers House with its curving bays is perhaps the most elegant structure in North Terrace. Seven times premier of South Australia, Sir Henry Ayers used his home for state functions; the hub of city life, its ballroom was washed down with milk to give it a smooth and fast surface.
   Not to be confused with Parliament House up the street (still lacking the dome planned for it), the Tudor-style Old Parliament House in North Terrace was home to South Australia's first parliament. Now a museum of political and state history, it has lively multimedia displays.

131

Ngurunderi's dreaming track
An extensive display in the South Australian Museum tells the story of Ngurunderi, one of the great ancestral dreaming figures of the Ngarrindjeri people. His travels from high up the Murray River to Kangaroo Island in pursuit of his miscreant wives explain many of the features of the river and coastal landscape. The bends and meanders of the Murray were made by the giant cod Ponde sweeping his tail, while Long Island near Murray Bridge is Ngurunderi's spear, which missed its target. At Middleton he killed a seal, whose dying gasps can still be heard among the rocks today. Another spear thrust created the islands off Victor Harbor, while his abandoned club became the Bluff. As his wives fled west along the causeway that then connected Kangaroo Island to the mainland, Ngurunderi caused the waters to rise and drown them. They turned into the rocky Pages Islands, while Ngurunderi rose to become a star in the Milky Way.

The National Tandanya Aboriginal Cultural Institute in Adelaide's East End

Walk **Green spaces and old buildings**

See map on page 128.

Linking some of Adelaide's splendid green spaces with North Terrace, the city's boulevard, this walk passes through the central shopping mall before ending in Victoria Square, the geographical heart of the city.

A walkway leads to North Terrace from the controversial **Festival Centre** complex overlooking parkland along the River Torrens. Stay on the leafy north side of North Terrace to admire the sequence of historic buildings and monuments revealed as you walk eastward. The post-modern forecourt of the Hyatt Hotel contrasts with the grandiose railroad station building now housing the city's Casino. The **Old Parliament House** of 1855 seems very modest compared with its successor, the latter ultra-conservative in design though it was only completed in 1939. **Government House** behind its garden wall gives way to the State Library (1884), the **South Australian Museum** (1895), and the **Art Gallery of South Australia** (opened in 1881). The south side of the Terrace presents a more or less continuous wall of imposing edifices, ending with the fine colonial mansion of **Ayers House** and the exuberant Botanic Hotel with its tiers of verandas.

The detour into the **Botanic Gardens** should take in the elegant Old Palm House and the truly remarkable Bicentennial Conservatory. In Rundle Street are the East End Market Buildings, but you should not miss the **Tandanya National Aboriginal Cultural Institute** in Grenfell Street just to the south. Rundle Mall is a cheerful pedestrian precinct, the main focus of city shopping. It leads into King William Street, Adelaide's main north–south route. The General Post Office and Town Hall stand at the northern end of Victoria Square, where the city's last surviving original tramway waits to take its passengers down to the sea at **Glenelg**.

Dry as dust The interminable flatness of the interior is broken only by two mountain ranges worthy of the name. Part of the vast Pitjantjatjara Aboriginal Lands, the Musgrave Ranges in the far northwest parallel the other ridges of the Red Centre just over the boundary with the Northern Territory. The ancient Flinders Ranges run some 300 miles from near the head of Spencer Gulf toward Lake Eyre, their most spectacular single feature being the magnificent natural fortress of **Wilpena Pound**. Northward are the interminable sand ridges of the **Simpson Desert**, laid down by winds that ceased to blow in prehistoric times. In the rare bouts of rain, its sparse cover of spinifex is supplemented by a sudden tapestry of wildflowers, while its inhabitants include unique creatures like hopping mice and marsupial moles. The Sturt Stony Desert is a virtually impassable plain of wind-polished stones known as gibbers, while **Mount Remarkable** has deep gorges.

The wildlife-rich south Toward the sea, the near-total aridity of South Australia's interior gives way to a Mediterranean-type climate, whose hot summers are relieved by relatively cool and moist winters. A century and a half of settlement has converted much of the area into productive farmland. However, there is still plenty of wildness left, particularly along the coast from Cottin Bay and Lincoln National Park at the tip of the Eyre Peninsula in the west to **Coorong National Park** in the far southeast. In between are the dunes and cliffs of **Innes National Park** on the toe of Yorke Peninsula and the wonders of **Kangaroo Island**. The extraordinary Coorong begins at the mouth of the Murray where the great river has broken through to the sea. A 60-mile beach stretches eastward, backed by superb sand dunes and a long, shallow lagoon. The haunt of a multitude of birds, this is one of the best places for observing the habits of the pelican.

Australia's dead sea
Much of the huge expanse of Lake Eyre is below sea level. On the map it appears to be fed by rivers over 600 miles long, but their waters usually run dry long before they reach the lake. Its salty surface, flat and featureless, made it ideal for Donald Campbell's successful attempt on the world land-speed record in 1964. When filled with water, an event that has only occurred three times in living memory, the lake becomes alive with birds.

133

The Remarkable Rocks on peaceful Kangaroo Island

How to travel

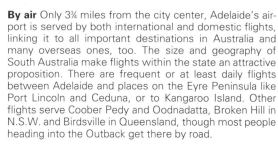

By air Only 3¾ miles from the city center, Adelaide's airport is served by both international and domestic flights, linking it to all important destinations in Australia and many overseas ones, too. The size and geography of South Australia make flights within the state an attractive proposition. There are frequent or at least daily flights between Adelaide and places on the Eyre Peninsula like Port Lincoln and Ceduna, or to Kangaroo Island. Other flights serve Coober Pedy and Oodnadatta, Broken Hill in N.S.W. and Birdsville in Queensland, though most people heading into the Outback get there by road.

By bus Adelaide has a comprehensive metropolitan transportation system with integrated ticketing, mostly based on buses, but also including suburban trains. A free bus service runs frequently between the main railroad station and the Glenelg tram terminus in Victoria Square. The State Transport Authority office in King William Street is helpful in planning tours around Greater Adelaide. The Glenelg Tram (a vintage 1929 model) and the replica Adelaide Explorer Tram are excellent as an introduction to Adelaide's sights. Long-distance buses operate express services to all major destinations, and even quite remote places in the Outback may have a bus service of some kind, albeit an infrequent one. If you have a little time to spare, a fun way to travel between Adelaide and Melbourne or Alice Springs and take in many of the good things *en route* is by the **Wayward Bus** (three days to Melbourne and 10 to Alice).

By rail Long-distance trains leave the modern Keswick terminus at the southwestern edge of Adelaide city center for Perth, Alice Springs, Melbourne, Broken Hill and Sydney. There are also services to Port Pirie and Mount Gambier. Adelaide's suburban network based at the main station on North Terrace is quite extensive, with services to places of interest like Port Adelaide and Belair in the Adelaide Hills.

A diesel commuter bus on Adelaide's "O-Bahn" line

By car
Roads in the relatively densely populated coastal area are good and the main interstate highways are all paved, including the Stuart Highway north to Alice Springs. In the Outback, roads are of variable quality and you must check conditions first and take adequate provisions (see page 143).

134

By water
You can take the car ferry to Kangaroo Island, either from Port Adelaide (weekly) or Cape Jervis.

Visitors and inmate at Cleland Conservation Park

▶▶ Adelaide Hills 125B4

Sprawling over the coastal plain, Greater Adelaide is defined to the west by the beaches of Gulf St. Vincent and to the east by the gorges and steep slopes of these beautiful hills. Laced with scenic drives and hiking trails through wild bushland, this is an area of richly varied landscapes, with some of the oldest settlements in South Australia. The forest has regrown since "Black Sunday" of January 2, 1955, when an uncontrollable bush fire raged for days. As well as the occasional vineyard, there are market gardens, orchards and any number of recreational attractions. The latter include the **Toy Factory**, its emblem the biggest rocking horse in the world, and the animals of the **Cleland Conservation Park** on the slopes of Mount Lofty, 12½ miles southeast of Adelaide.

▶▶ Arkaroola 125D4

Formerly a vast sheep station, the Outback resort and wildlife sanctuary of Arkaroola is now the center for exploring the northern parts of the spectacular Flinders Ranges. The rugged ridges of the **Gammon Ranges National Park▶▶** glint and glitter in the piercing light with quartz, fluorspar, hematites and other minerals; there are hot springs and a vast salt lake.

▶▶ Birdwood 125B4

The National Motor Museum is a good excuse for a 30-mile leisurely drive through the Adelaide Hills. Australia's biggest collection of vintage, veteran and classic cars is housed in the stone-built Birdwood Mill of 1852.

▶▶ Burra 125B4

In the 1840s, the discovery of rich copper deposits in Kapunda and Burra rescued the ailing South Australian economy from its doldrums. Miners flocked to Burra from Britain's Celtic fringe, and within 10 years had created the Monster Mine, 8 miles long and 3¾ miles across. Today, a 7-mile heritage trail includes a museum, a Cornish engine house, a mine captain's cottage, the inevitable jail, and the extraordinary riverbed dugouts in which as many as 2,000 miners once lived.

Deutschland Down Under
Germans sailed into Sydney Harbour with the First Fleet, and many thousands have come since. South Australia was the destination in the 1830s and 1840s for whole communities from Brandenburg and Silesia suffering religious intolerance at the hands of the Prussian authorities. The first settlements were Klemzig, now overwhelmed by Adelaide's suburbia, Hahndorf and Lobethal in the Adelaide Hills, then in the Barossa Valley, originally called Neuschlesien (New Silesia).

135

Hooray for Holden
Australia became one of the world's great car-owning nations from early on; by the beginning of the 1960s there was one car per family. Sir Edward Holden's car body firm merged with General Motors in 1931, initially assembling British and American vehicles. "Australia's Own Car," the first Holden rolled off the production line in 1948, the millionth in 1962. With the advent of the cheap and reliable Japanese cars that now dominate whole sectors of the Australian market, Holden faltered, but in recent years has made something of a comeback.

It is possible to visit the Old Times Opal Mine at Coober Pedy

136

The Aussie Wave

When you're watching an Australian game of cricket on T.V., why do the spectators always seem to be waving casual greetings to unseen friends? It's not friends, but the persistent flies—as noted by Dutch Commander Pelsaert in 1629: "Such a host of flies came to sit in the mouth and eyes that they could not be beaten off." This early observation would seem to disprove the theory that the plague is due to the dung dropped in quantity by all those cattle in the Outback. Australians protect themselves from this nuisance with door and window screens at home and, outside, with as nonchalant a wave as possible, since frantic swatting seems only to encourage the fly. No one, but no one (except some Japanese tourists) wears a Ned Kelly hat with dangling corks to keep the brutes away.

▶▶ **Coober Pedy** *124D3*

The lunar landscape of mounds and holes in the ground greeting travelers on the Stuart Highway some 560 miles northwest of Adelaide is the result of several decades of searching for opals. The name Coober Pedy comes from the Aboriginal *kupa piti* meaning something like "white fellow's burrow"; since opals were discovered here in 1915, enterprising folk from all over the world have been hacking away in the hope of making their fortune, living underground in order to escape the intolerable conditions on the surface, which include temperatures in excess of 104°F. As well as comfortable troglodyte homes, there are underground shops, restaurants, hotels and even a couple of churches. Several working mines in the area can be visited.

▶ **Eyre Peninsula** *124B3*

This vast triangle faces the breakers of the Great Australian Bight to the west and the sheltered waters of the Spencer Gulf to the east. The northern base of the triangle is formed by the uninhabited Gawler Ranges, while its southern apex is near the deep-water harbor of Port Lincoln. The sandy soils of the peninsula support wheat and sheep, while the subsoil yields iron ore, which is converted into steel in the coke ovens and rolling mills of Whyalla, South Australia's second city. The Eyre Highway runs in a great loop from the communications center of Port Augusta at the head of the Gulf toward the township of Ceduna, then on toward the Western Australian border. The trip southward along the Flinders and Lincoln Highways takes in any number of fishing villages, wild seascapes and unspoiled beaches. Both sea lions and great white sharks may be seen at **Dangerous Reef▶**, some 12 miles off the cliffs and sand dunes that support the rich wildlife of **Lincoln National Park▶**.

▶▶ **Fleurieu Peninsula** *125B4*

Rolling countryside, attractive vineyards and a superb coastline of wild cliffs and fine beaches provide a wonderful vacation region right on Adelaide's doorstep. Within half an hour's drive south of the city is the **McLaren Vale Wine District▶▶**, centered on the township of McLaren Vale in a setting of delightful hills. Farther south, around Willunga, the crop changes to almonds, a froth of blossom in July. Studded with sandy beaches, including the country's first official nudist one, Maslins, the coast runs southwestward along the gulf to terminate in rugged terrain around Cape Jervis. The far shore of Backstairs Passage belongs to Kangaroo Island, reached from here by ferry.

Around the corner of the Cape the scenery is no less spectacular, particularly at **Deep Creek Conservation Park▶** where the land falls sheer into the ocean. The pleasant resort of **Victor Harbor** (see page 142) is guarded by the massive lump of rock known as Rosetta Head. From here the vintage Cockle Train chuffs eastward past the breakers crashing on the beaches of Port Elliot to the charming town of Goolwa near the mouth of the Murray River (see page 138). The story of the Murray, its history and its current problems, are told at the impressive interpretive center at Signal Point (see page 138).

▶▶▶ **Flinders Ranges** *125C4*

These ranges are made up of some of the world's most ancient rocks, marking the landscape northeast of Port Augusta with steep ridges and rugged gorges. Of no great height, the ranges owe their popularity to their vivid mineral coloring, dramatic landforms, fascinating plant and animal life, and the incredibly clear sunlight that reveals everything with visionary intensity. One of the gateways to the main part of the ranges is the township of Quorn; here is the terminus of the **Pichi Richi steam railroad▶**, part of the old Ghan line. Beyond Quorn, the road to Hawker passes close to the ruins of the old **Kanyaka Homestead** as well as the **Yourambulla Caves** with their Aboriginal wall-paintings.

The road to one of the country's great geological curiosities, the mighty natural stronghold of **Wilpena Pound▶▶▶**, turns off at Hawker. The Pound is a great oval, 12½ miles long by about 5 miles wide, protected from the outside world by sheer 3,280-foot high walls, sloping steeply to a park-like interior where the flat floor is rich in sugar gums and, in spring, wildflowers. Like any great fortress, the Pound has only one way in, a narrow gorge cut by the Wilpena Creek, sometimes a torrent but usually just a trickle. A number of marked trails of varying difficulty lead from the tourist center near this entrance; anyone capable of walking 12½ miles lengthwise and 1,640 feet vertically should consider the trek across the Pound and up to its highest point, St. Marys Peak. The reward is a stunning panorama over the whole area, including the dazzling white surface of salty Lake Torrens.

Beyond Wilpena on unpaved roads is the main part of the Flinders Ranges National Park, less spectacular perhaps but equally rewarding. Its wildlife includes hosts of birds and two types of kangaroo, as well as the rare yellow-footed rock wallaby.

Typical scenery in the Flinders Ranges

Reptilian ramparts
Like so many features of the Aboriginal landscape, the walls of Wilpena Pound are perceived to be the petrified forms of the animal ancestors who assisted at their creation. Two giant serpents were lying in wait here for those who gathered to celebrate the very first ceremony of initiation of a young man into adulthood by circumcision. The serpents devoured them all, save for Wala the wild turkey, Yulu the kingfisher, and the young man himself, who all escaped and founded new tribes. The serpents expired, their bodies curling round to enclose the Pound for ever.

137

Take time for a trip up the Murray River...

Sir Hans Heysen
Young Hans came to South Australia in 1884 at the age of seven. He is one of the best loved painters of the Australian landscape, whose natural features, particularly its trees and the play of light on them, he studied with great meticulousness. His charming works grace many an Australian gallery, and several can be seen at Hahndorf (where he lived for 60 years) in the gallery of the Academy. Sir Hans is honored by having the long-distance walking trail from the Fleurieu Peninsula to the Flinders Ranges named after him as well as part of the ranges themselves.

Australian seals
Of the three species of seal that inhabit Australian waters, two live around Kangaroo Island: the New Zealand fur seal and the Australian sea lion. The former were almost hunted to extinction in the 19th century; now protected, their numbers are recovering. Sea lions had an easier time, largely because they lack the warm coat of the fur seal.

▶ **Goolwa** *125B4*

This little riverport on the lower reaches of the mighty Murray River is the terminus for two trips in time: the old-timer Cockle Train that runs along the coast, and the paddlesteamer *Mundoo* that heads upriver. The **Signal Point Interpretive Centre▶**, a model of its kind, has comprehensive displays on the theme of the Murray River yesterday and today.

▶ **Hahndorf** *125B4*

South Australia's second oldest German settlement (1839) can be found in a pretty location in the Adelaide Hills. Conveniently close to the South Eastern Freeway, Hahndorf makes the most of Teutonic tradition, with sausages, a Schutzenfest and waitresses in dirndls. You can still see how the first settlers laid out their homes in orderly fashion along the main street.

▶▶▶ **Kangaroo Island** *125B4*

Separated from the Fleurieu Peninsula by the deep straits known as Backstairs Passage, this is Australia's third largest island, a paradise for lovers of nature, with wild coastal landscapes and a particularly rich animal life. The island was named by the redoubtable Matthew Flinders; when the *Investigator* called here in 1802, his crew bagged a few of the locals, members of the subspecies of gray kangaroo still present in large numbers.

Most visitors arrive by ferry from the mainland at the little fishing port of Penneshaw on the Dudley Peninsula at the eastern end of the island. Fairy penguins frequent Christmas Cove just to the west of the harbor. Situated on Nepean Bay, Kingscote preserves some traces of its past in its oldest building, Hope Cottage of 1858. A paved main road heads past the airport into the interior, but the island's unique sights lie on the south coast.

Seal Bay▶▶ is home to the country's largest colony of sea lions, seemingly indifferent to their many human visitors. Inland is the spectacular underground world of **Kelly Hill Caves**, discovered by a horse of that name that disappeared for ever into their still unexplored depths (Kelly's rider was saved). The surging waters around Cape du Couedic at the southwestern tip of the island are often visited by another marine mammal, the New Zealand fur seal. At the cape itself is awesome **Admirals Arch**, a natural bridge hollowed out in the limestone cliffs, while to the east are the aptly named **Remarkable Rocks▶▶**. Crowning a smoothly planed promontory, great blocks of granite have been eroded into strange shapes as if by the chisel of an abstract sculptor at his most imaginative.

Flinders Chase National Park▶ in the west is a reminder of how most of the island once looked—a wilderness of low-growing eucalyptus and shrubs. The headquarters of the park is at Rocky River, where friendly kangaroos, wallabies and emus are likely to pester you for your sandwiches. Koalas can be seen in the trees nearby, and platypuses sometimes reveal themselves to the patient observer. The northwestern tip of the island is marked by the isolated lighthouse at Cape Borda. To the east, accessible by a rough road, stretches a spectacular coastline of cliffs sometimes rising to over 650 feet and relieved by the occasional sandy bay.

▶   **Mount Gambier**   *125A5*

The most important town in the southeast of South Australia had a turbulent volcanic past that only came to an end in relatively recent times. This has left a legacy of cones and craters, one water-filled hole being in the very center of town. Blue Lake, just outside town, changes color mysteriously according to the season.

▶   **Murray River**   *125B5*

The sluggish Murray (see pages 112–13) meanders into South Australia near Renmark. From here to where it meets the sea at Lake Alexandrina, the river has become a mecca for those seeking lazy water-based holidays.

...it's a wonderfully relaxing way to travel

Along the mighty Murray
Massive irrigation projects have transformed the area into a vast orchard and vineyard, producing oranges, apples, pears and some 40 percent of the state's grape harvest. Loxton Historical Village recreates life as it was in the difficult early days of settlement. Many of the places along the river have a poignant feel about them, now that the great days of river trade have gone. There is another evocation of bygone times at the Old Tailem Town Pioneer Village, and the paddlesteamer *Marion* moored at Mannum has been transformed into a floating museum.

139

Vine cuttings were among the plants imported with the First Fleet, though it seems that the very first attempts to produce an Australian wine met with failure. However, persistence paid off, and today Australian wines enjoy a high reputation at home and abroad.

Amber fluid in ice-cold tubes Despite the rise in wine consumption, Australians remain some of the most committed beer drinkers in the world. A century ago, most beers tended to be top-fermented on the model of British ales and stouts, but these have steadily been displaced by bottom-fermented, lager types. More suited to the local climate, these were first brewed by Melbourne Germans as well as by the Foster brothers, originally from New York, who gave their name to Foster's Lager, the country's best-known beer. Americans used to six-packs may be surprised at the standard-sized "slab" (a 24-pack!).

In the early days, the colonists seem to have preferred rum; later it was the country's excellent beer that was rated highly, in contrast to its wines, which foreigners wrote off as crude imitations utterly failing to fulfill the promise of their labels.

Since the 1960s, however, things have changed—a result of increased prosperity, greater sophistication and, not least, the wine-drinking habits of many of the country's recent immigrants. A visit to a well-stocked wine merchant reveals a whole world of home-grown wine waiting to be discovered; like other great wine countries, Australia has no real need to import.

New South Wales This state has the most venerable vineyards, in the highly reputed Hunter Valley only a short journey north of Sydney. Quality is the keynote here, whereas far to the southwest, in the irrigated valley of the Murrumbidgee River, producers concentrate on making as great a quantity as possible for distilling or fortifying.

Victoria Here there were once as many vineyards as N.S.W. and S.A. had put together, but most were wiped

A winery at Nuriootpa in the Barossa Valley

out by phylloxera in the last century and have never been replanted. Victorian wines could now be described as up and coming; there are many "boutique" wines, some of the best from the **Yarra Valley** near Melbourne. The Great Western area is famous for sparkling wine.

Western Australia This state has its old vineyards too, planted along the Swan Valley in the early days of settlement. Perhaps the most interesting wines produced since the 1980s come from the **Margaret River** area.

Tasmania Lying closer to the South Pole, Tasmania is benefiting from a fashion for growing vines over a long ripening period in a cool climate, and there is an increasing number of vineyards (mostly around Hobart and Launceston) producing wines of fine quality.

South Australia This perhaps is the heartland of Australian wine, contributing about two-thirds of the country's total production. Most of the original vineyards of the Adelaide Plains have disappeared beneath suburban sprawl, and the huge quantities of grapes grown in the Riverland area along the Murray are mostly turned into alcohol, but other districts make wines of the highest reputation. Far-off **Coonawarra** in the southeast produces wonderful reds on a tiny band of ultra-fertile volcanic soil, while **Adelaide Hills** is the most successful of the newer, cool climate regions. The boutique wines made among the rolling hills of the **McLaren Vale Wine District** are much in vogue, but perhaps the best of all wine districts is the **Barossa Valley**, north of Adelaide. The combination of suitable soils, summer sun and reliable winter rain makes for an excellent product, grown amid a delightful landscape of old-established towns and well-ordered countryside.

Tastings Australian vintners welcome visitors to their wineries. Tastings have become a popular pastime, though choosing can be difficult. The name of a reputable maker is generally reckoned to be a good starting point.

A rum corps
In the early days of New South Wales, the colony seems to have been kept afloat on an ocean of Bengal rum. Coinage was short, and in its absence rum took over many of the functions of the currency. Its sale was controlled by the officers of the New South Wales Corps, perhaps the least prestigious of the British regiments of the time. With little to occupy them in the way of genuine military activity, these gentlemen devoted their time to enriching themselves by all possible means, only stirring into martial action when their monopoly on rum was threatened by Governor Bligh. Their march on Government House on January 26, 1808, and arrest of the governor has become known disparagingly as the "Rum Rebellion."

141

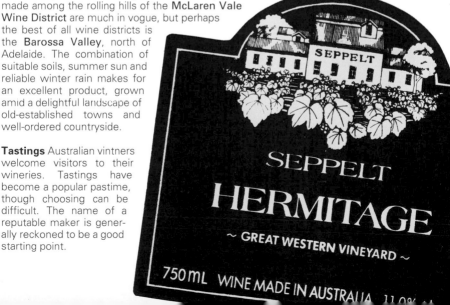

SEPPELT

SEPPELT

HERMITAGE

~ GREAT WESTERN VINEYARD ~

750 mL WINE MADE IN AUSTRALIA 11.0%

Petrel Cove at Victor Harbor

► **Naracoorte** 125A5

This southeastern town celebrates the prosperity of its pastoral surroundings in the excellent Sheep's Back Wool Museum. But most visitors come to marvel at the beauty of the World Heritage-listed **Naracoorte Caves►**. Only a few of the 60 or so known caves are accessible; there are guided tours into Blanche Cave and Alexandra Cave. In 1969, the bones of hitherto unknown marsupials, giant kangaroos and wombats were found in Victoria Cave.

► **Strathalbyn** 125B4

Strathalbyn, at the neck of the Fleurieu Peninsula, has something indefinably Scottish about its dignified public buildings and neat public gardens on the banks of the Angas River. The town's past has been tidily gathered up and presented by the National Trust in two buildings, the 1858 police station and the 1867 court house.

► **Victor Harbor** 125B4

Victor Harbor's setting on Encounter Bay is superb, protected as it is from the ocean by both Rosetta Head ("the Bluff") and Granite Island, the latter reached across a causeway by horse-drawn tram and then by chairlift to its highest point. The island's colony of fairy penguins generally puts in an appearance in the evening.

► **Yorke Peninsula** 125B4

Some 150 miles long, this boot-shaped peninsula projects southward, bounded by Spencer Gulf on the west and Gulf St. Vincent to the east. South Australians come here for quiet vacations, fishing, boating and all kinds of water activities. Because there were few good roads in the past, little ports and landing places were dotted all along the coast, and you are sure to find an appealing place. Toward the tip of the peninsula the coastline becomes more rugged, though there are still splendid beaches for swimming, surfing and diving.

Strangely compelling, South Australia's 230,000 square miles of Outback include some of the least hospitable parts of the earth's surface. Distances are vast, water is sparse and summer temperatures are almost unbearable. Human life is spread thinly over cattle stations the size of small European states and "towns" no bigger than hamlets. But the Outback exerts its own fascination; its arid beauty is liable to sudden and miraculous change when rain falls, as salt lakes fill with water and wildflowers carpet the surface of the land.

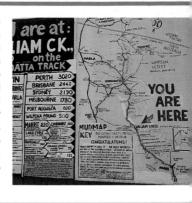

The great vastness of the South Australian Outback is penetrated by a small number of roads, tying together the isolated stations and settlements. Some are paved throughout, while others are still rightly referred to as "tracks" and set a challenge for the more adventurous.

The Oodnadatta Track This track is part of a route north from Adelaide to Alice Springs, an alternative to the Stuart Highway. Beginning at Marree near the southern end of Lake Eyre, it follows the route taken by the explorer John McDouall Stuart and subsequently by the Overland Telegraph and the original Ghan railroad line. Before the line was completed to the Alice, Oodnadatta was the railhead, goods being carried on from here on the backs of camels. The old station, now a museum, still stands.

The Strzelecki Track Named in honor of the Polish explorer Count Paul Strzelecki, this track runs northeast from Lyndhurst towards the Queensland border, following the trail used by the notorious Captain Starlight to drive stolen cattle down to southern markets. The track fringes the northern Flinders Ranges before crossing the interminable sandhills of the Strzelecki Desert and ending at Innamincka where the unfortunate Burke and Wills finally expired.

The Birdsville Track Also a cattle-driving route, this track was traced out by stockmen possibly more law-abiding than Captain Starlight but equally tough. Like the Oodnadatta Track it begins at Marree, but this track ends up in Queensland's Birdsville some 320 miles later.

Above: William Creek, on the Oodnadatta Track

143

Birdsville Track sights
Along the track's course are hot springs, deserted homesteads, 30-foot-high sandhills and the wind-polished pebbles of the Sturt Stony Desert stretching to the horizon. The old frontier post of Birdsville with its famous pub comes alive every year when its race meeting is held, an event yielding up to 50,000 empty beer cans!

BAROSSA VALLEY DRIVE

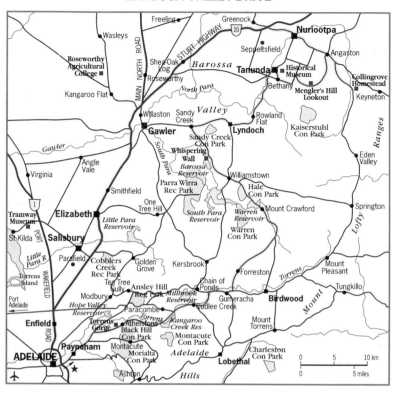

Map labels: Freeling, Greenock, Nuriootpa, Wasleys, Sturt Highway, 20, Seppeltsfield, Angaston, Roseworthy Agricultural College, Shea-Oak Log, Barossa, Tanunda, Historical Museum, Collingrove Homestead, Main North Road, Roseworthy, Bethany, Mengler's Hill Lookout, Keyneton, Kangaroo Flat, North Para, Valley, Willaston, Sandy Creek, Rowland Flat, Kaiserstuhl Con Park, Ranges, Gawler, Gawler, Lyndoch, Eden Valley, Sandy Creek Con Park, Whispering Wall, Angle Vale, Barossa Reservoir, Williamstown, Virginia, South Para, Parra Wirra Rec Park, Hale Con Park, Smithfield, One Tree Hill, South Para Reservoir, Warren Reservoir, Mount Crawford, Springton, Tramway Museum, 1, Elizabeth, Little Para Reservoir, Warren Con Park, Lofty, St Kilda, Salisbury, Port Wakefield Road, Little Para R, Parafield, Cobblers Creek Rec Park, Golden Grove, Kersbrook, Forreston, Torrens, Mount Pleasant, Torrens Island, Tea Tree Gully, Ansley Hill, Chain of Ponds, Tungkillo, Port Adelaide, Modbury, Reg Park, Millbrook Reservoir, Gumeracha, Birdwood, Mount, Hope Valley Reservoir, Paracombe, Cudlee Creek, Enfield, Torrens Gorge, Athelstone, Black Hill Con Park, Kangaroo Creek Res, Mount Torrens, Charleston, Payneham, Montacute, Montacute Con Park, Moriata Con Park, Adelaide, Con Park, ADELAIDE, Ashton, Hills, Lobethal. Scale: 0 5 10 km, 0 5 miles

Drive Barossa Valley

The world-famous wine-growing district of the Barossa Valley is reached by an indirect but rewarding route through the varied countryside of the northern Adelaide Hills.

Adelaide's Payneham Road, then Gorge Road lead to the rocky defile followed by the River Torrens, and so into the orchard country around **Gumeracha**. Among the many dams built to take advantage of the relatively high rainfall of these uplands, the **Barossa Reservoir** is a popular stopping point because of the curious sound effects produced by its "Whispering Wall." The little town of Lyndoch is the gateway to the Barossa Valley, while **Tanunda**, with its Historical Museum, is the cultural center of what was Australia's most important German-settled area. All around are inviting wineries. **Bethany**, founded in 1842, the valley's oldest village, sits beneath Mengler's Hill Lookout, which offers a splendid panorama over the neatly ordered countryside. It is worth taking a detour to the **Collingrove Homestead,** now managed by the National Trust but once the center of the million-acre estate belonging to the Angas family, early pioneers of South Australia.

The route back to Adelaide passes through **Nuriootpa**, the commercial heart of the Barossa, the prosperous agricultural center of **Gawler** and the satellite town of **Elizabeth**, home to many British immigrants in the post-war years.

MCLAREN VALE WINE REGION and FLEURIEU PENINSULA DRIVE

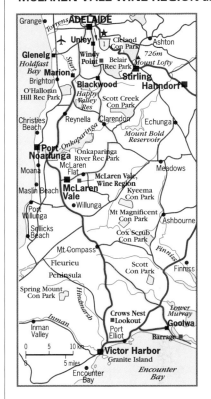

Insect-pollinated banksia

Drive **McLaren Vale Wine Region and Fleurieu Peninsula**

This drive leads through the attractive wine-growing countryside of the McLaren Vale Wine Region, across the rolling farmland of the Fleurieu Peninsula to the mouth of the Murray River and the dramatic ocean setting of Victor Harbor.

From Adelaide, Unley Road soon reaches the surrounding hills and climbs to the **Windy Point Lookout**, from where there is a fine panorama of city and suburbs sprawling over the coastal plain. The uplands are a favored residential area for the city's more affluent commuters, but suburban housing soon gives way to farmland and forest, and to the vineyards and welcoming wineries around McLaren Flat and McLaren Vale.

A beautifully engineered highway speeds you towards the coast through the broad "waist" of the **Fleurieu Peninsula** to the small town of Goolwa. Here the excellent **Signal Point Interpretive Centre** tells all you could possibly want to know about the longest river in Australia, the Murray, whose waters flow through the bird-thronged barrage to the east of the town.

A short drive along the shore of Encounter Bay leads to **Victor Harbor** with its causeway linking the resort to Granite Island. The view of town and ocean is well worth the 330-foot climb up the **Bluff**, just to the west of the town.

Return to Adelaide by the direct route to complete a 125-mile drive.

146

Perth's Swan River
was named (in 1697)
after the black swans
that still live here

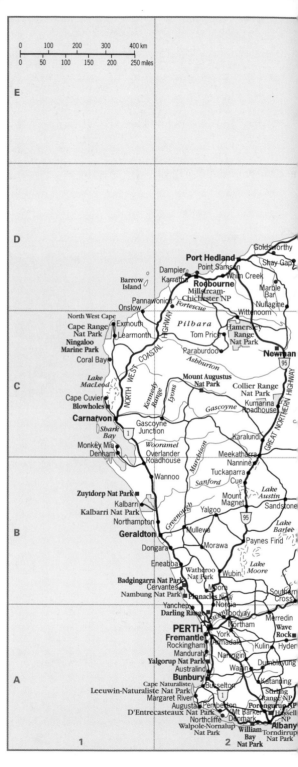

Cape Londonderry

Cape Bougainville
Admiralty Gulf
Port Warrender

Kalumburu
Joseph Bonaparte Gulf
Drysdale River Nat Park

Ord
Wyndham
Mirima (Hidden Valley) National Park

Kuri Bay
Collier Bay
Kununurra

K i m b e r l e y
Gibb River
Lake Argyle

Cape Leveque

Beagle Bay

Windjana Gorge Nat Park 937m
■ Mt Ord Geikie Gorge
Bungle Bungle (Purnululu) Nat Park

Derby
Tunnel Creek Nat Park
■ Geikie Gorge Nat Park
Halls Creek

Camballin
Fitzroy Crossing
Fitzroy

Broome
Roebuck Bay

Wolfe Creek Crater ■ Nat Park

King Sound

NORTHERN HIGHWAY

Tanami Desert
Balgo

N O R T H E R N   T E R R I T O R Y

Great Sandy Desert

CANNING STOCK ROUTE

Percival Lakes

Oakover

Paterson Range
Telfer

Lake Muckay

Minjoo

Rudall River Nat Park

Gibson Desert

Jigalong

Lake Disappointment

Little Sandy Desert

...ere Range

Giles

Lake Carnegie

Warburton
1013m ▲ Mt Hinckley

S O U T H   A U S T R A L I A

Wiluna

Lake Wells

Cosmo Newbery

Leinster

Agnew

Laverton

Great Victoria Desert

Leonora
Lake Carey

Malcolm

Menzies

Lake Rebecca

Goongarrie Nat Park

Trans-Australian Railway

Kalgoorlie ■ Kanowna

Coolgardie ● Boulder
94
Kambalda
Lake Lefroy

Nullarbor Plain

Eucla Nat Park ■

Madura
1
Eucla ■

Boorabin Nat Park

Lake Cowan

Mundrabilla

Norseman

Cocklebiddy

Frank Hann Nat Park
1
Ralladonia
Lake Dundas
EYRE HIGHWAY
Caiguna

Peak Charles Nat Park
Cape Arid Nat Park

Great Australian Bight

Ravensthorpe

Esperance

Hopetoun Cape Le Grand Nat Park

Fitzgerald River Nat Park
Archipelago of the Recherche

3   4

Virgin karri forests at Warren National Park, southwest of Pemberton

Tropical north
Parts of the Kimberley are subject to monsoonal rainfall; rivers that may have been reduced to a few pools in the Dry quickly fill and spill over the surrounding plains. In the far north are habitats of such biological value that their national park status, far from opening them up to the public, has led to the banning of all access.

Western Australia Devotees of this state, Australia's largest, are fond of producing maps showing how much of Europe or the U.S.A. might be fitted into its 965,250 square miles. Western Australia is undoubtedly *big*. It is also very empty, much of it consisting of variations on the theme of desert—voids of various kinds extend from the desert beaches of the Indian Ocean in the far northwest to the cliffs of the Nullarbor being eaten away by the Southern Ocean. A further factor is its isolation. Perth is generally reckoned to be the most remote city on earth; its nearest neighbor Adelaide is 1,678 miles away and Sydney is 2,610 miles away. For all this, the West provides some of Australia's great vacation destinations.

Friendly, sunny **Perth** is every Australian's second favorite city, next to Sydney; until recently, this was the place other Australians migrated to in search of the good life at an affordable price. It certainly ranks high in the hierarchy of Australian cities, not least because of its stunning site on the beautiful Swan River just inland from its port of **Fremantle**, one of the country's most atmospheric historic towns.

Perth and its metropolitan region dominate the coastal plain spreading westward from the **Darling Range**, Western Australia's modest equivalent of the Great Dividing Range. With a Mediterranean climate, an often spectacularly rugged coastline, fine forests and the lion's share of fertile farmland, this is the most densely inhabited part of the state. Inland stretches the Wheat Belt, its yields of grain dependent on a variable rainfall, gradually merging into the scrublands that herald the desert itself. Straggling along the desert rim is a line of gold-rush towns, some defunct, some, like **Kalgoorlie-Boulder**, still with plenty of kick in them.

In the rest of the state, people are thinly spread. Towns, none of them of any size, are widely spaced along the immensely long coast. The old pearling base of **Broome** is enjoying a revival as a tourist center, while **Port Hedland** deals efficiently with the iron ore being extracted in huge quantities from its Pilbara hinterland. Here are strange new settlements of prefabricated buildings, erected quickly to create air-conditioned shelter from the fierce temperatures for miners and prospectors.

But far more than urban amenities, it is the grandeur of Western Australia's natural landscapes that visitors will want to experience. The paving of the highways to the north and the northwest of the state has encouraged visitors to explore areas previously considered to be well off the beaten track. Even more than the harsh vastness of the **Hamersley Range** in the Pilbara, the far-off tropical **Kimberley** is attracting tourists to its wealth of natural wonders, sometimes as part of a trip to the adjoining Northern Territory.

History New Holland was the unlikely name bestowed in the early 1600s on the western rim of the unknown continent by Dutch seamen on their way to their country's possessions in the East Indies. They would race eastward across the Indian Ocean, then sail along the Australian coast towards Java. Sometimes they were traveling too fast, and Western Australia's earliest European history is studded with the names of famous ships such as the *Zeewijk* and *Batavia* wrecked on the reefs and shoals of its treacherous coastline.

The first British impressions were not favorable either; William Dampier's reports in 1688–9 on the barren north-west were distinctly discouraging. It was a (largely imaginary) French threat in the 1820s that impelled the British to add the west of the continent to the Empire; the port of Albany was founded on the south coast in 1826, and in 1829 Lieutenant-Governor Stirling and his band of free settlers established the Swan River colony where Perth now stands. Progress was fitful, and the colony was only saved by a massive infusion of convict labor in the 1850s and 1860s, then in the 1880s and 1890s by the opening up of the Eastern Goldfields.

In the early 20th century, Western Australia's adherence to the Federation was only secured by a promise to link it to the rest of the country by the construction of the Transcontinental Railway. Even as late as the 1930s, a referendum revealed a majority in favor of secession. Today, in spite of extraordinary financial mismanagement, the west's position seems to be secure, based on massive postwar immigration and seemingly unlimited mineral wealth.

On top of the state
The Stirling Range is the highest mountain range in southwestern Australia, and is carpeted by wild-flowers during the spring (September through October). The area has numerous hiking trails, but don't forget your water-proofs, because sudden rainstorms are common.

149

The Stirling Range National Park in the southwest

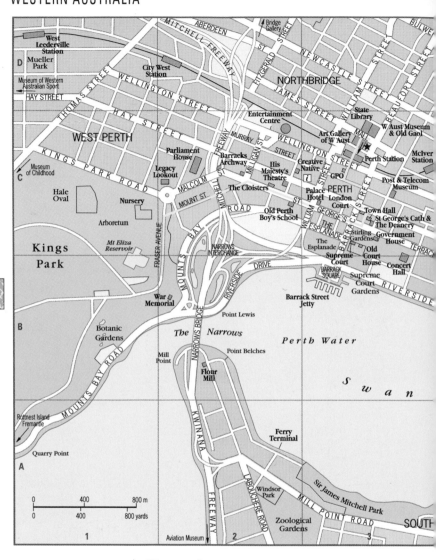

Perth

Perth, like Sydney, is an inspired fusion of fine building in a splendid natural setting. The view eastward from **Kings Park** reveals one of the world's great urban panoramas— to the left the office towers of the city center glittering in the constant bright sunlight, to the right the glorious stretch of Perth Water alive with pleasure craft.

The city seems to offer its citizens most of the ingredients of the good life: a Californian climate unspoiled by smog; attractive homes in every price category in suburbs that range from the merely pleasant to the opulent; and every kind of outdoor playground, from the generous sweeps of the Swan River and superb ocean beaches, to lavish parklands that bring the bush almost into the city center.

Suburbs

The plush succession of waterside suburbs you pass if you take the ferry from South Perth (see panel opposite) may tempt you to sell up and move here without further ado. This is where the millionaires of the "Golden West" choose to live, with easy access to their yachts at the marina or yacht club.

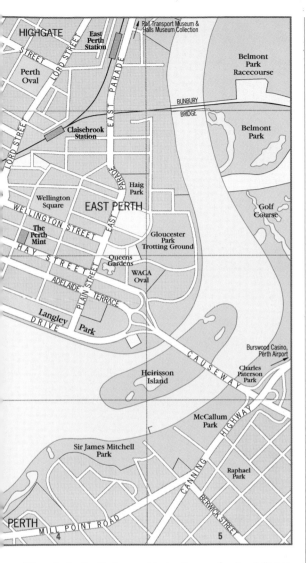

Rail Transport Museum &
Halls Museum Collection

HIGHGATE

East
Perth
Station

Perth
Oval

EAST PARADE

LORD STREET

STREET

Belmont
Park
Racecourse

BUNBURY
BRIDGE

Claisebrook
Station

Belmont
Park

Haig
Park

PARADE

Wellington
Square

EAST PERTH

Golf
Course

WELLINGTON STREET

The
Perth
Mint

Gloucester
Park
Trotting Ground

HAY STREET

Queens
Gardens

PLAIN STREET

EAST

WACA
Oval

ADELAIDE TERRACE

Langley
Park

DRIVE

Park

CAUSEWAY

Burswood Casino,
Perth Airport

Heirisson
Island

Charles
Paterson
Park

McCallum
Park

CANNING HIGHWAY

Sir James Mitchell
Park

Raphael
Park

PERTH

MILL POINT ROAD

BERWICK STREET

4

5

*Kings Park in the
center of Perth*

City of plenty Perth used to be known for its dullness. True or false, this is certainly no longer the case. Contrasting with the historic and lavishly restored **His Majesty's Theatre**, the home of Western Australian opera and dance, the **Concert Hall** and the **Entertainment Centre** have been major recent additions to the city's cultural life. Another new landmark is the white tower of the **Burswood Casino**, biggest in the southern hemisphere. New buildings of high cultural significance (the Art Gallery and State Library) have been grouped together to form a new urban focal point. The city center is quite compact. A network of futuristic walkways straddles streets and tunnels through buildings, linking transportation terminals, shopping arcades, pedestrian precincts and civic plazas. Spectacular sights may be few, but there are a host of minor urban pleasures.

Riverside Perth
True Perth is a synthesis of city and river, and you should make sure that you enjoy this not only from Kings Park but from the river itself. At the very least, take the ferry across to South Perth (and back again!), but better still return by ferry from Rottnest Island or Fremantle. For much of the latter part of the journey, your eye will return again and again to the unforgettable image of the city's clustering towers rising over the functionally elegant Narrows Bridge.

Perth: a most attractive city

▶▶ Art Gallery of Western Australia 150C3
Perth Cultural Centre, James Street
Generously housed in a spacious new building, the gallery has a fine collection of mostly Australian artworks, including an acclaimed array of Aboriginal art. There are also collections of traditional and contemporary crafts, ceramics, textiles, jewelry, woodwork and glass, and the museum extends its influence beyond its doors with sculpture gracing the plaza linking the city center to Northbridge.

▶ Aviation Museum 150A2
Bull Creek
Australia's largest collection of historic aircraft and aviation memorabilia is to be found in the southern suburb of Bull Creek. The aggressive elegance of war winners like the Avro Lancaster and Supermarine Spitfire contrasts with the workaday lines of the famous Dakota, first built in the 1930s and still flying today.

▶▶ Kings Park 150C1
Few cities in the world enjoy anything like this great swath of natural landscape on the very edge of the city center. From the founding of the colony in 1829 it was always intended that this area, known as Mount Eliza, should be kept as an open space. About two-thirds of the park is bushland, glorious with wildflowers in the spring, and accessible by scenic drive as well as on foot. Fraser Avenue, with its monuments, memorials and lines of lemon gums, gives an unequaled panorama of Perth in its Swan River setting, while the **Botanic Gardens** encapsulate the incomparable floral wealth of Western Australia in a series of richly planted gardens.

▶ Perth Zoological Gardens 150A2
South Perth
An excellent reason for taking the ferry to South Perth, the city's zoo has a fine collection of exotic animals as

Sightsee by water
Ferries connect the jetty at Barrack Square in Perth with South Perth, Fremantle and Rottnest Island, and there are trips upstream, too, visiting the early colonial landscapes of the upper reaches of the Swan River. Cruise ships still occasionally call at Fremantle.

well as Australian creatures like emus, koalas and kanga-roos, which you can meet in the wildlife park. One resident of Western Australia now on the endangered list, the little termite-eating numbat, is provided with its own quarters. The zoo is constantly developing; there are innovative features like Harmony Farm (which demonstrates earth-friendly techniques for living harmoniously on Planet Earth), the Conservation Discovery Centre and the African savannah, a complete reconstruction of an African ecosystem.

▶▶▶ Western Australian Museum   150C3

James Street
This fascinating museum complex comprises a cluster of buildings of many different dates and styles contributing in their various ways to the attractive ambience of Perth's Cultural Centre. Half a day spent here is no substitute for a month spent exploring the natural wonders and human heritage of Western Australia, but it will go a long way towards it!

The centerpiece of the complex is the modern Francis Street building, which has a **Marine Gallery** dominated by the awesome 79-foot skeleton of a blue whale, as well as an **Aboriginal Gallery** that is a magnificent attempt to review in a comprehensive and sympathetic way the art, religion and culture of the first Australians. Traditional displays of mammals and fossils are in the old Beaufort Street building, while the history of white settlement of the west is evoked in the cool spaces of the stone-built jail, the **Old Gaol**.

The mock-Tudor London Court, built in 1937, runs between the Hay Street Mall and St. George's Terrace

A girl's best friend
Perth is home to several shops that sell precious and semiprecious stones. You can buy pearls from Broome, opals from Coober Pedy and, not least, pink diamonds from the Argyle diamond mines.

153

Walk Perth city center

See map on page 150.

This walk of about 2½ miles takes in many of the contrasts of old and new that make Perth such a stimulating capital city.

A few steps north of Perth's City Railway Station are the buildings and plazas of the **Cultural Centre**. The pedestrian mall south of the station is dominated by the handsome sandstone **General Post Office** (1925). The junction of Hay Street Mall with Barrack Street is overlooked by the tower of the **Town Hall**, behind which is **St. George's Cathedral** and the cottage-style **Deanery** (1859) facing onto **St. George's Terrace**.

Government House was built in the mid-19th century and enclosed in luxuriant gardens. Following the slope down toward The Esplanade fronting the Swan River are **Stirling Gardens**, laid out as a botanical garden in 1829, and **Supreme Court Gardens**, laid out on reclaimed land. Next to the Supreme Court itself is the city's oldest surviving building, the **Old Court House** (1837).

The mock-Tudor arcade known as **London Court** links St. George's Terrace with Hay Street Mall. In spite of its ecclesiastical Gothic appearance, No. 139 St. George's Terrace is not a church but the **Old Perth Boy's School**, now the home of the National Trust. Further west, next to a splendid Port Jackson fig tree is **The Cloisters**, founded in 1858 as Perth's first secondary school and now tastefully converted to offices.

You can complete your walk here, or continue on foot or by Clipper bus past **Barracks Archway** to the city viewpoints in **Kings Park**.

Drive The southwest

This full day's outing from Perth follows the coastline south of Fremantle toward the southwestern tip of Western Australia, an area rich in flowers, splendid forests and vineyards.

Beyond the resort of **Mandurah**, the old coast road passes close to the lakes, swamps and woodland of **Yalgorup National Park**. Bunbury has fine beaches; between here and Busselton on Geographe Bay the highway runs through fine stands of tuart trees, some of the few remaining after the uncontrolled felling that took place in colonial days.

The coastline of the **Leeuwin-Naturaliste National Park** stretches for about 75 miles between Cape Naturaliste in the north and Augusta in the south. The backbone of the

area is formed by a granite ridge capped by limestone; erosion by water has given rise to hundreds of caves, some of which are open.

Some two dozen vineyards cluster around the little township of Margaret River. To the south are the wonderful karri trees of the **Boranup Forest**, best seen from the forest drive and the **Boranup Lookout**. There are fine coastal views at Prevelly Park at the mouth of the Margaret River.

If time permits, the tour can be extended to **Augusta** and to **Cape Leeuwin**. The return to Perth is faster via the South Western Highway beyond Bunbury.

Drive

Mundaring Weir

This short excursion enters the heavily wooded Darling Range.

The Great Eastern Highway soon leaves the city behind as it winds up the Darling scarp. The **John Forrest National Park** is a popular recreation area, with streams, waterfalls and a pool, while the dam and reservoir of **Mundaring Weir** have an attractive bushland setting. Return via Lesmurdie Falls and Kalamunda.

PERTH DRIVES

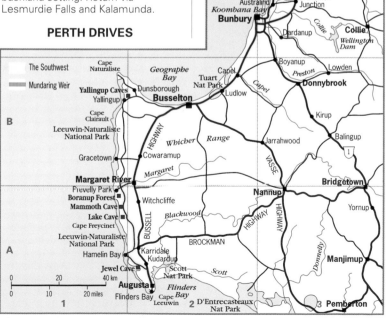

155

The eerie Pinnacles, 152 miles north of Perth

The immense spaces of Western Australia include great swaths of unvarying country of little obvious interest, but there are also any number of landscapes well deserving of their national-park or special-interest designation.

The southwest Facing the meeting point of the Southern and Indian Oceans, the southwest of the state enjoys a reasonably high rainfall that favors the growth of magnificent forests, notably of the karri tree. Its numbers much reduced by the 19th century's insatiable appetite for wood, this forest giant nevertheless survives in substantial patches in a number of national parks. In the southwest, these include the Stirling and Porongurup Ranges, the Boranup Forest in the Margaret River area, and the **Walpole-Nornalup National Park**, a coastal park beautifully sited around the Nornalup Inlet, where deep rivers wind seaward through heath-covered dunes.

Battered by breakers, these southwestern coasts have a rugged quality, well exemplified in the wild cliffs and rocky shoreline of the **Leeuwin-Naturaliste National Park**. On the shoreline farther north resorts mix with wildlife-rich lagoons and lakes, as at **Yalgorup National Park**. The backdrop to the coastal plain is formed by the escarpment of the Darling Range, whose jarrah woods and bushland make a useful playground for Perth weekenders. The jarrah (a eucalyptus) is one of the characteristic trees of the southwest, much logged in the past and sawed up for railroad ties. The range is accessible at any number of points along its 186-mile length, from the **John Forrest National Park** east of Perth, or **Lane Pool** on the Murray River, to **Marrinup** and **Pinjarra**.

One of the privileges of life in Perth is easy access to unspoiled nature. Only 22 miles out of the city to the northeast is **Walyunga National Park**, an area of wild bushland where the Swan and Avon Rivers have cut through the Darling Range. Equally near the city, but due north, is **Yanchep National Park** where the bush is home

Grass-trees
Among the oddest of Australian plants are the grass-trees. They used to be known as blackboys, from their supposed resemblance to an Aborigine brandishing a spear, but this term has been discarded, at least officially. Resin exudes from the blackened, stubby trunk above which flares a skirt of grass-like leaves and a spectacular flower spike (the "spear"). Grass-trees depend on fire for their growth, reaching a maximum height of about 16 feet.

to honey possums, kangaroos and bandicoots, and there are a loch and limestone caves to be explored. Few sights are as compelling as the countless limestone pillars known as **The Pinnacles** in the Nambung National Park.

The northwest There is a great contrast of natural landscapes in the vast northwest. Some of the most stunning scenery is on the coast. Among the inlets and peninsulas of Shark Bay is unique Shell Beach, 37 miles long and built up of a 33-foot depth of crushed and compacted shells. The North West Cape has twin parks of outstanding interest. To the east are the parched plateau and deep rocky gorges of the **Cape Range National Park**, descending to the west through fossil reefs and sand dunes to Australia's "other" barrier reef, the **Ningaloo Marine Park**, 162 miles of coral reef sheltering a shallow lagoon. Running inland from the tidal flats and mangrove swamps of the coast is the **Pilbara**, a spectacular upland deeply incised by river valleys and culminating in the vividly colored gorges of the **Hamersley Range National Park**.

Between the Pilbara and the Kimberley, the Great Sandy Desert claims part of the coastline. Where it merges with the Little Sandy Desert, far inland, are the salt lakes of the **Rudall River National Park**, accessible only to the well-equipped (contact the tourist office for information).

The Kimberley Beyond the desert, dramatic landforms include **Geikie Gorge, Windjana Gorge**, the world's second largest meteorite crater at **Wolfe Creek**, and the strange beehive rock formations of the **Bungle Bungles**. Plant life ranges from sparse spinifex to scenes of great luxuriance in spots with a guaranteed water supply.

A possum—part of the myriad wildlife of the state

The soft sandstone forms of the Bungle Bungles are best seen from April through October

A rare bird
In 1894 Windjana Gorge was the scene of a gun battle between heavily armed police and a band of Aborigines led by Jundumurra, known to his adversaries as Pigeon. A skillful horseman and tracker, Pigeon had been compelled to work for the police against his own people. Eventually turning against his masters, he shot a constable, set prisoners free, and for years waged a minor guerilla war. He was finally hunted down and killed at Tunnel Creek on April 1, 1897.

Kalbarri National Park is best seen by helicopter

Eyre travel
The 1,678 miles of the Eyre Highway between Adelaide and Perth are less of an obstacle than might be supposed. Plenty of Australians refuse to be deterred by such distances and plan their driving accordingly, settling down to a steady pace and accepting the discipline of distance. At vacation periods it's wise to reserve ahead if you plan to stay in any of the motels along the route. Your vehicle should be absolutely roadworthy before setting out, since repair facilities are limited. Two hazards to remember: articulated trucks ("semi-trailers") may be difficult to pass, especially if traveling at speed in convoy or if the road edge breaks away sharply; and when traveling west, you will have the setting sun to reckon with for long and disagreeable periods. One solution (reserve well in advance!) is to put the car on the train for the westward journey and drive back to the east.

By air The remoteness and sheer size of Western Australia mean that air travel is often used, not only for traveling between major cities but also to reach faraway places of interest or for day and half-day trips. Perth has direct connections to numerous overseas destinations, as well as daily flights to all state capitals and a number of other Australian cities.

By bus Express buses link Perth to the rest of the state, and to other Australian cities (given time!). The metropolitan area of Perth has a comprehensive network of buses, some of them operating out of the futuristic terminal near the Narrows. The capital also enjoys free services in the central area: clippers of various colors (red, yellow, blue and green) roam the central streets, a great boon once you've got the hang of their routes.

By rail Perth has a three-pronged suburban rail service, connecting City Station with Guildford, Armadale and, usefully for the visitor, Fremantle. Fares are reasonable, and the service is generally efficient. Most of Western Australia's railroads now carry freight only, though there are passenger trains from Perth to Bunbury in the south (the *Australind*) and west to Kalgoorlie (the *Prospector*). One of the world's great trains runs from Perth Terminal Station, the twice-weekly *Indian Pacific* to Adelaide (and, once a week, to Sydney). Linking west and east across the Nullarbor Plain, this train is the railroad experience of a lifetime.

By car The alternative routes north from Perth to Port Hedland, the **North West Coastal Highway** and the **Great Northern Highway,** are both paved, as is their continuation onward to the Kimberley and the Northern Territory. It's a long way, though! The road network around Perth and in much of the southwest is well developed, but many places can only be reached on unpaved roads, in varying states of upkeep. Some particular favorites, like the **Gibb River Road** through the Kimberley, can definitely only be negotiated by 4WD.

▶▶ Albany 146A2

Albany was the first European settlement in Western Australia, founded on King George Sound in 1826 by Major Edmund Lockyer to preempt any possible French interest in this quarter of the continent. It became an important base for whalers, then a coaling station for ships on the India-Sydney run; it is now a popular vacation town. The 19th-century buildings include the **Old Gaol**, built in 1851 as a convict hiring depot; **Patrick Taylor Cottage▶** of 1832, probably the town's oldest building and now a folk museum; the old **Post Office▶**, now the Inter-Colonial Communications Museum; and the excellent **Residency Museum▶**. Nearby is the **Amity Replica**, a full-size reproduction of Major Lockyer's brig.

The town nestles between Mount Clarence and Mount Melville, the summits of which give terrific views over coast and countryside. Further inland are the granite domes and karri forests of Porongurup National Park, and farther still the high Stirling Range. To east and west lies one of Australia's finest stretches of coastline, and protecting the sound to the south is the rugged peninsula of **Torndirrup National Park▶▶**, with spectacular features like the **Blowholes▶**, **The Gap▶** and **Natural Bridge▶**. The old whaling station on Frenchman Bay is now **Whaleworld▶**, which claims to be the world's largest whaling museum.

▶ Armadale 146A2

Armadale, 19 miles to the south of Perth, is famous for **Pioneer World▶▶**, a conscientious reproduction of a 19th-century village. Old-timers, including prospectors and blacksmiths, work in authentic-looking old buildings.

▶ Augusta 146A2

Overlooking the mouth of the Blackwood River, pleasant Augusta has spectacular **Jewel Cave▶**, with strange rock formations and a mysterious underground river.

Enjoy yourself at Armadale's Pioneer World

Diggers on horseback
Australia's Desert Mounted Corps distinguished itself in the Middle East in the course of World War I. Albany was the port of embarkation for many of its troops, and they and their mounts are commemorated by the dramatic statue on top of Mount Clarence. This is a recast of the bronze erected on the banks of the Suez Canal in 1932, which came to a sorry end during the Suez crisis of 1956. The original of the horse's head was recovered, however, and, a bit battered, is on view in the Residency Museum.

A lady lion
The map of Australia reveals a number of names of obviously Dutch origin. Perhaps the most famous of these is Cape Leeuwin, the "land's end" of south-western Australia, with its lighthouse overlooking the meeting point of the Indian and Southern oceans. Its name recalls the Dutch vessel that first put it on the map, the *Leeuwin*, or lioness, which passed this way in 1622, and which is also commemorated in a national park and a famous winery.

159

►► Broome   147D3

The tourist's southwestern gateway to the Kimberley, Broome makes the most of its colorful past, when divers from all over Asia braved the bends and fierce rivalry to harvest precious mother-of-pearl from the sea bed (see page 161). Although only a few luggers still sail today, cultured pearls are farmed in the vicinity.

The authentic past can best be savored in the **Broome Historical Society Museum►**, or in the **cemetery**, its graves a grim record of the dangers of life as a diver. The restored Japanese section is particularly impressive. The town overlooks the mud flats and mangroves of Roebuck Bay, a rich haven for birdlife. The tidal range at Broome is exceptional, up to 33 feet, and at very low tide the footprints of dinosaurs can be seen at Gantheaume Point to the south of the town. From here the splendid white sands of Cable Beach stretch north for 18 miles.

► Bunbury   146A2

With its population of 25,000 inhabitants making it one of Western Australia's largest settlements, Bunbury serves as the urban center for much of the southwest of the state. The viewpoint known as Boulter's Heights provides a panorama over the town and its surroundings. As well as a port, Bunbury is a popular resort, with good fishing, a fine string of beaches along the 5-mile Ocean Drive and, a recent phenomenon, a friendly school of dolphins that enjoy the company of visitors to Koombana Beach.

►► Bungle Bungle National Park   147E4

The soft sandstone of this part of the East Kimberley has been eroded into spectacularly strange rock formations resembling domes, turrets and beehives. Access to the national park is by 4WD only and there are no facilities. Most visitors prefer to view the park by plane or helicopter; the aerial perspective reveals clearly nature's weird beauty and striking colors. The park also has numerous examples of the art of the tribes who lived here, plus a number of burial sites.

Bunbury, major seaport and center of the southwest

Broome's zero hour
It was not only Darwin that suffered Japanese air raids in World War II. On March 3, 1942, a squadron of Japanese Zero fighter planes spent a leisurely hour attacking a number of Allied flying boats moored off Mangrove Point. At very low tides, the remains of some of these machines can be seen in the bay.

A stairway to the sky
Another effect of Broome's exceptional tidal range is the optical illusion known as "The Golden Staircase to the Moon," visible only at certain times of the year when the rays of the moon are reflected off the exposed bed of the ocean.

FOCUS ON — *Pearling*

Pearl oysters thrive in the tropical seas from Cape York in northern Queensland right around to Shark Bay in the west of Western Australia, a distance of some 1,865 miles. There is a particularly large concentration between Derby and Cossack in the northwest. From early on, the pearls themselves were a bonus, the mainstay of the industry being mother-of-pearl shell, used for jewelry and, above all, for humble buttons.

Commercial exploitation This began in the 1860s, when Aborigines were more or less forced by pearling masters into diving for the shell on the sea bed, an often lethal task; even if drowning was avoided, there were shark attacks, and many boats and their crews were lost in the frequent cyclones. With the expansion of the trade and the introduction of diving suits later in the century, there was an influx of Chinese, Filipinos, Malays, Koepangers from Timor and, above all, the most expert of all pearlers, the Japanese. In the 1920s Broome, one of the world centers of pearling, had a population of about 3,000, some 600 of them of British and 1,200 of Japanese descent. A typical pearling lugger might have had a European master, a pair of Japanese divers, a Japanese engineer and a crew from Timor. The different races lived in sometimes uneasy proximity in Broome, with occasional outbreaks of violence.

Broome's pearling year
The pearl farmer's year is split up into three distinct seasons. In the winter (December through March) there is little to do, for this is the region's wet season; from April through August the young oysters are seeded so that they produce pearls; during the remainder of the year the large oysters are removed and their shells used for mother-of-pearl.

161

Pearling today By the 1930s the shell beds had been seriously depleted and, later, mother-of-pearl was displaced by plastic in the manufacture of buttons. Nowadays a few luggers still set off for the oyster beds some 4 miles off the coast, but most of Broome's current output comes from cultured pearls, raised in "farms" away from public view. Pearling's colorful history is explained in the **Broome Historical Society Museum**, while an old pearling lugger can be seen outside the **Maritime Museum** in Fremantle. A real curiosity connected with this exotic trade is the Catholic mission at Beagle Bay, 80 miles north of Broome, its altar shimmering with mother-of-pearl decoration.

Until recently, Broome relied on pearling for its livelihood

Western rock

Mount Augustus, 280 miles inland from Carnarvon, perhaps lacks the unique beauty of Ayers Rock but beats it hands-down for size. This is the world's largest monocline, created according to the Aborigines when a man called Burringurrah was speared by his enemies in the Dreamtime. From a viewpoint southeast of the rock his form can still be made out, with the stump of the spear in his leg.

Watering the goldfields

Extracting gold from the fields of Western Australia posed fewer difficulties than finding water in this utterly arid area. The Irish-born engineer Charles Yelverton O'Connor solved the problem. Already responsible for the construction of Fremantle Harbour and the building of much of the state's railroad system, this late-Victorian genius built one of the wonders of the age, known as the Goldfields and Agricultural Water Supply Scheme. Beginning at the splendid dam at Mundaring Weir near Perth, O'Connor's great pipe sucked water 340 miles eastward in sufficient quantities to quench the miners' thirst and leave some over to irrigate the farms of the Wheat Belt. Attacked by landed interests and ridiculed by critics, O'Connor lost heart, and he committed suicide a year before completion of the project.

► Busselton 146A2

Busselton is a pleasant family resort with good beaches, facing north across Geographe Bay and sheltered from the west. Fishermen still frequent the remains of what was—until Cyclone Alby in 1978—the longest (1¼ miles) wooden jetty in Australia.

The approach to the town from the north passes through a splendid forest of tuarts, a tree unique to Western Australia. Just off the highway is the long and low tin-roofed colonial mansion known as **Wonnerup House►**, furnished in period style and open to the public.

► Carnarvon 146C1

Only about 90 miles south of the Tropic of Capricorn, Carnarvon wears a tropical air, with palm trees lining its fascine promenade and hibiscus and bougainvillea blooming in its elegantly broad main street. Famous for its fishing industries (you can visit the shrimp and scallop processing plant), it is also the center of a prosperous fruit and vegetable growing area, the Gascoyne district.

The **Bibbawarra Bore►**, 10 miles to the north of town, produces a constant gush of water at 149°F. There is another demonstration of the power of water at **The Blowholes►**, 43 miles north, where jets of water spout 65 feet into the air.

► Coolgardie 147B3

A classic boom-and-bust town 348 miles east of Perth, Coolgardie was the center of Australia's most frantic gold rush, with a peak population in the 1890s of 15,000, its needs catered to by two stock exchanges, three breweries and a couple of dozen hotels. Now a tenth of its former size, it still has symbols of its former glory.

Looking like an exceptionally grand railroad terminus, the old Government Buildings are now the home of the **Goldfields Exhibition►**, with extensive displays including a model of the town at its height. Opposite is the weird **Open Air Museum**, its scrapped machinery and statues of Australian heroes standing out surrealistically in the implacable sun. More abandoned machinery, rolling stock and a locomotive have been preserved in Coolgardie's **Railway Station Museum**.

► Darling Range 146A2

The unbroken line of this wooded escarpment stretches far to the north and south of Perth, rising to a height of about 985 feet and defining the boundary of the coastal plain. Not far from the city are several popular recreation areas, like the bushland and streams of the John Forrest National

Coolgardie—model of Ned Kelly

Park or Mundaring Weir. The reservoir here was built in 1898–1902 to supply the far-off Eastern Goldfields with water; attractively landscaped, it is a favorite picnic spot. The **O'Connor Museum▶** at the reservoir is named after the engineer who oversaw this vast project and tells the story of its construction (see panel opposite).

▶ **Denmark**   *146A2*

Rugged coastal scenery contrasting with the tranquil Denmark River and attractive farmlands makes the small town of Denmark in the extreme southwest a popular place for family vacations. Wilson Inlet is one of the largest areas of sheltered water on the south coast, with fine fishing, boating and other aquatic pleasures. To the west, **William Bay National Park▶** has sand dunes and pristine beaches, as well as heathland and karri forest.

▶ **Derby**   *147E3*

On the shores of King Sound to the north of the mouth of the Fitzroy River, and within striking distance of the West Kimberley, Derby likes to describe itself as the "Gateway to the Gorges;" indeed, Windjana Gorge is only about 87 miles east of the town. Nearer at hand (5 miles away) is a famous boab tree, popularly supposed to have served as a lock-up for a small part of its 1,000-year life.

▶ **Esperance**   *147A3*

This deep-water port on the south coast flourished and declined in parallel to the boom and bust in the goldfields to its north. Now tourism has discovered Esperance, not least because of the magnificent beaches and the islands of the Recherche Archipelago. A scenic drive takes in part of the fine coastline and leads to **Pink Lake▶**, an extraordinary salt lake, genuinely pink in color. Some of the best coastal scenery is some 30 miles to the east; here is the **Cape Le Grand National Park▶**, with stunning bays of blue water and white sand set between rocky headlands.

▶▶ **Fremantle**   *146A2*

Now part of the built-up area of Greater Perth, the old harbor town of Fremantle continues to serve as Western Australia's principal port. Founded in 1829, Fremantle owes some of its attractive appearance to the convict craftsmen shipped in to save the colony's faltering fortunes in the gold-rush building boom of the 1890s. These were Fremantle's great days, when the harbor was improved out of all recognition by the great engineer O'Connor (see panel opposite).

The center of town is compact, its venerable (by Australian standards!) townscape best enjoyed on foot. Good places to get your bearings include the viewing platform on top of the Port Authority Building or the **Round House▶**, erected in 1831 as the new colony's prison. The **Western Australian Maritime Museum▶▶** has a pearling lugger drawn up outside the old Commissariat Store in which it is housed; inside are excellent maritime history displays. The town's other major museum, the **Fremantle Museum▶**, occupies a neo-Gothic edifice on the far side of town. In between are any number of places worth a visit, including the famous **Fremantle Markets**, alive with dealers and (some) bargains.

The fine city of Fremantle lies southwest of Perth, where the Swan River meets the Indian Ocean

163

How Fremantle got its name
Fremantle is named after the commander of the British naval force sent here to claim the west before anyone else. Captain Charles Howe Fremantle planted the Union Jack here on May 2, 1829, a month before the first settlers arrived to found the Swan River colony. An optimist, he believed that the colony would become "in time, a place of consequence," in spite of "its sandy and uncompromising appearance."

▶▶ Geikie Gorge National Park   *147D4*

The tiny settlement at **Fitzroy Crossing** has grown up around the point where the Northern Highway traverses the 340-mile-long river that drains much of the Kimberley. Reduced to a series of pools in the dry season, the Fitzroy rises an extraordinary 53 feet in the Wet, flooding vast areas. The effects of this phenomenal difference in water level can be observed (in the Dry!) by taking a boat trip up nearby Geikie Gorge, where the lower parts of the sheer 100–165-foot cliffs have been dramatically scoured by the annual floodwaters. Cut by the river through the limestone that eons ago was an ocean reef, the gorge is home to many tropical aquatic life forms, and is fringed by reeds and dense forest supporting a rich range of birdlife.

▶ Geraldton   *146B2*

This prosperous harbor town to the north of Perth, noted for its export of locally caught lobsters, is popular with visitors year round but particularly in winter because of its excellent sunshine record. Some 35 miles off shore is the archipelago aptly named the Houtman Abrolhos (derived from the Portuguese for "Keep your eyes open!") Islands, notorious as a death trap for ships heading eastward across the Indian Ocean. Relics from famous wrecks are the mainstay of the Maritime Display Building, part of the **Geraldton Museum**▶; the Museum's other sections are housed in the nearby Old Railway Building.

▶ Halls Creek   *147D4*

Halfway through the Kimberley on the Northern Highway, Halls Creek seems the archetypal Outback town, center of a vast area thinly populated by cattlemen and mineral prospectors. A short distance away is Old Halls Creek, with its evocative remains of an 1880s gold rush. Between the two settlements is a natural curiosity, a vein of white quartz standing clear of its surroundings and inevitably named the China Wall.

The crumbling rugged cliffs around Kalbarri

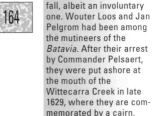

Unwilling immigrants
It was on the shores of Kalbarri that Australia's first known European settlers made their landfall, albeit an involuntary one. Wouter Loos and Jan Pelgrom had been among the mutineers of the *Batavia*. After their arrest by Commander Pelsaert, they were put ashore at the mouth of the Wittecarra Creek in late 1629, where they are commemorated by a cairn. Their further story is unknown; ordered to look for them in 1644, Abel Tasman could find no trace.

Instead of horses, cars now front Kalgoorlie's hotels

▶ **Kalbarri**   *146B1*

The gorges in the **Kalbarri National Park**▶▶ are up to 50 miles long and 558 feet deep, cut into the vivid red and wonderfully named tumblagooda sandstone. A number of easily accessible viewpoints like Hawk's Head Lookout overlook this landscape in its setting of sandy plains. The coastal scenery has its drama, too, with high red cliffs dropping sheer into the ocean.

▶▶▶ **Kalgoorlie–Boulder**   *147B3*

The classic gold-rush towns of Kalgoorlie and Boulder were amalgamated in 1989. Gold was first found at nearby Coolgardie; not long after, on June 10, 1893, Patrick (Paddy) Hannan and two mates made the greatest find of all—known for ever after as Hannan's Reward—and within a year tens of thousands of eager prospectors had swarmed to the "Golden Mile." In under a decade, both places had been transformed from ragged settlements to solid-seeming municipalities.

Hannan's slightly bemused statue sits outside the massive 1908 Town Hall on the sidewalk of the street named after him. This gently sloping roadway is of boulevard dimensions, wide enough to turn a camel train. On either side are monuments to the town's great days: canopied shopfronts; grandiose public edifices like the colonnaded government buildings; and the swaggeringly self-confident hotels, the **Exchange** (1894), the **Palace** (1897), the **Old Australia** (1896) and the **York** (1900).

▶▶▶ **The Kimberley**   *147E4*

See page 173.

▶ **Kununurra**   *147C4*

This town in the East Kimberley was created in the 1960s to act as an urban center for the Ord River Irrigation Scheme (see panel). A solitary relic of the past, the **Argyle Downs Homestead** was rescued when the land on which it stood was flooded, and is now a pioneer museum. Outside town at **Mirima (Hidden Valley) National Park**▶, 300 million years of erosion have created spectacular patterns in the red sandstone.

See page 173.

Lawlessness
Kalgoorlie always was a rip-roaring kind of place, and even today takes a perverse pride in being labeled the most crime-ridden of Australia's smaller towns. In 1926, gold thieves hacked to death the detectives sent after them, and 10 years later anti-immigrant riots raged for two days before a trainload of police could be brought up from Perth. Many of today's misdeeds seem to be the result of enthusiastic weekend drinking getting out of hand rather than anything more serious.

Out of order
Frustrated at seeing the floodwaters of the Ord River in the Kimberley running uselessly into the sea while for the rest of the year the land lay scorched and thirsty, the goverment spent huge sums on the Ord River Irrigation Scheme. Completed in 1972, its dams held back the muddy tide and distributed it among thousands of acres of irrigated cropland. But the desert, on the whole, failed to bloom. The cotton crop was killed by caterpillars, and other crops have been only partially successful, while D.D.T.-resistant insects seem to enjoy life in the 280 square miles of the project's main water body, Lake Argyle.

"We can make this country a quarry to serve the whole world," enthused Henry Bolte, the Premier of Victoria (1955–72). All the Australian states and territories either have built or are building much of their prosperity on the abundant mineral resources locked up in their ancient rocks.

People still pan for gold at Sovereign Hill, Victoria

Ironing out the landscape
Long suspected, the existence of unbelievably rich deposits of iron ore in the Pilbara were confirmed almost by accident in the 1950s. Forced by poor weather to fly low over one of the area's many gorges, Lang Hancock noticed that its walls gave off a metallic sheen. Subsequent investigation revealed what proved to be the world's greatest concentration of iron ore. The topography of whole tracts of land has been transformed by its removal, for example at the Mount Whaleback Mine near Newman, the biggest opencast pit in the world.

A wealth of minerals Western Australia really came alive with the discovery of gold in unprecedented abundance in the Eastern Goldfields at the end of the 19th century, but the state also has (or had) reserves of antimony, bismuth, asbestos, coal, tin, copper, iron and nickel, as well as such rarities as tungsten, tantalite and beryl. Exploration and prospecting are very much a matter of the present as well as of history; the world's biggest iron mountain was discovered by accident in the Pilbara in the 1950s (see panel), while the incredibly productive diamond mine near Kununurra only came on board in the 1980s.

The first rush But it is the lure of gold that still catches the imagination most. The gold rushes, here as everywhere, were epic events, with their extraordinary mixture of greed, determination and endurance amounting to heroism. The first rush in W.A. was to Halls Creek in the Kimberley, in 1885, when Charlie Hall's Christmas present to himself was a 28-ounce nugget. Conditions in this utterly remote and harsh area were perhaps the worst anywhere; one devoted mate, Russian Jack, carted a sick friend 200 miles in a wheelbarrow in search of a doctor.

Halls Creek failed to live up to its promise, and the prospectors soon abandoned the Kimberley for the infinitely greater pickings to be found in the Eastern Goldfields. In 1892 Arthur Bayley rode into Southern Cross with 554 ounces of gold that he and his partner, Bill Ford, had found at Fly Flat 125 miles to the east; bars emptied as the news got around, and within hours the greatest rush in the colony's history had begun. Fly Flat was renamed Coolgardie; within six months thousands were living in a city of tents, having trekked through the waterless waste

on foot or horseback, while supplies were brought up by dray or camel train. A year later the biggest find of all was made at Boulder. The rush increased Western Australia's population by leaps and bounds and was an immense stimulus to the colony's development. Terrible conditions endured for a while, with plagues of flies, outbreaks of typhoid, and water that sometimes cost as much as champagne. Before the completion of O'Connor's 340-mile pipeline from Perth in 1903 (see panel on page 162), traders in water often became richer than prospectors.

Companies move in Within the space of a few years, individual prospectors had scarred most of the Eastern Goldfields area with their shallow diggings ("specking") and extracted most of the alluvial gold. From now on it became necessary to mine more deeply, requiring the use of sophisticated machinery and the outlay of capital. Companies took over from rugged individuals.

Contemporary opencast methods of gold extraction and the extraordinary landscape they are creating can be observed from the viewing platform overlooking Kalgoorlie's **Super Pit**, which will eventually stretch for several miles and reach a depth of 1,640 feet.

Paddy's patter
A "living" Paddy Hannan recounts the tale of the Eastern Goldfields at Hannan's North Mine in Boulder, a faithful reconstruction of a mine and its surroundings in its heyday. Here you can drop underground in the cramped miners' cage and have the mysteries and miseries and sheer hard work of extraction explained to you by a veteran miner. Back on the surface, a railroad meanders around the extensive site with its many authentic old buildings.

Other mine museums in Kalgoorlie–Boulder are the School of Mines Mineral Museum, the Goldfields War Museum, which commemorates World War I volunteers from the goldfields, and the Museum of the Goldfields.

167

Pilbara: giant trucks are used to transport the iron ore

The beaches around Mandurah are always popular

Rails through the forest
In the early part of the century the jarrah forests inland from Mandurah echoed to the hiss of steam and the toot of whistles as narrow-gauge locomotives hauled timber to the mills. One of these forestry railroads, the Hotham Valley Tourist Railway, running between Pinjarra and Dwellingup, has been kept alive by enthusiasts, and steam trains meet passengers off the modern Australind train from Perth. The enthusiasm is such that an additional line, the Etmilyn Forest Tramway, was opened in 1986, leading deep into the heart of the atmospheric jarrah woodlands.

▶ **Mandurah** 146A2

Less than an hour's drive south of Perth, Mandurah is deservedly popular with city weekenders. Vast areas of sheltered water along the Murray and Serpentine Rivers and the Peel Inlet, 25 miles of beaches and an abundance of shady picnic spots help distribute the crowds and keep at least some of the town's tranquil atmosphere.

▶▶ **Margaret River** 146A2

The township of Margaret River is the center of the attractive district named after it, where the manicured landscape of prestige wineries contrasts with the savagery of surf pounding a rugged coastline and with a mysterious underground world of limestone caves. Arts and crafts abound in the town itself, while music (of the highest caliber, but only once a year) is performed in the delightful grounds of the Leeuwin Winery.

Among the more sheltered places along the coast, most of which forms part of the Leeuwin-Naturaliste National Park, is **Prevelly Park▶**. Only a few of the hundreds of caves are accessible, among them Mammoth Cave▶ (named for its size) and Lake Cave▶. The **Boranup Forest▶** is a good place to see the extraordinary massed ranks of karri trees, standing like cathedral columns.

▶ **Monkey Mia** 146C1

Some of the several hundred dolphins living in Shark Bay mix with humans and accept fresh fish. To stand in the water of Monkey Mia beach and be nuzzled by a dolphin is an experience that few can resist, but do check first with the rangers at the Dolphin Information Centre.

▶ **New Norcia** 146B2

The Benedictines came to Western Australia as early as 1846, leaving the unmistakable imprint of Mediterranean Catholicism here in the bush 80 miles north of Perth, where they established a mission for the Aborigines. As well as the Abbey Church and Monastery, there is a museum and an art gallery with a fine collection of paintings and monastic belongings.

Wildflowers

The "strangeness" of Australian plants—including eucalypts in all their glorious variety, wattles and banksias—fascinates visitors from the northern hemisphere. Australia's vegetation provides a constant and stimulating backdrop, and is a continual reminder that you really are somewhere else.

Early settlers tackled the isolation of this unfamiliar land by manipulating its appearance to recall the landscapes left behind. Planted in uncountable numbers, oaks, elms, willows and poplars transformed whole tracts of countryside—particularly in Tasmania—into a version of lowland England; the occasional eucalyptus looked like an intruder.

A great variety One of the joys of springtime is the abundance of wildflowers, particularly in Western Australia. Here a twofold isolation, not only from the rest of the world but from the rest of the continent, has resulted in flora of extraordinary variety. The state has some 8,000 named species, plus a further 2,000 that are still anonymous, three-quarters of them unique to the area though not necessarily unrelated to plants elsewhere in Australia.

Springtime spectacular Wildflowers pattern the ground from north to south as springtime advances. At the **Kalbarri National Park**, 375 miles north of Perth, flowers begin to bloom in July. Some of the most spectacular displays occur in the heathlands of the southwest, where there are more species of plants than in the rain forest. In places like the **Stirling** and **Porongurup Ranges**, spring arrives much later than in the north, with November being the most rewarding month. For those unable to leave Perth, **Kings Park** makes a splendid substitute, with its extensive areas of natural bushland and its special section devoted to Australian trees, shrubs and wildflowers.

Below: The peak wildflower season in coastal Western Australia runs from September through October

Above: Trailing orchid in bloom

Harold Heights

Named after former Prime Minister Harold E. Holt, the joint U.S./Australian Naval Communications Station keeps in touch with what is going on around the oceans with an extraordinary cluster of tall towers, the central one of which, at 1,273 feet, is taller than the Empire State Building. American accents can be heard in the streets of Exmouth, founded in 1964 as the support town for the base, but visitors come here mostly for the excellent fishing; North West Cape is the nearest point in Australia to the teeming marine life of the continental shelf.

▶▶ **Ningaloo Marine Park** *146C1*

A long detour leads off the North West Coastal Highway to far-off North West Cape, whose backbone is formed by the rugged **Cape Range**. This national park is made up of a high limestone plateau cut into by gorges and ravines, some containing deep pools. To the west stretch rarely visited dunes and beaches, protected from the ocean rollers by a barrier reef, 162 miles long and extending some 10 miles from the coast. With its 220 species of coral and more than 500 varieties of tropical fish, the reef of Ningaloo Marine Park is one of the great natural wonders of Australia, as yet hardly exploited; there is fishing, camping, diving and swimming, and glass-bottomed boats operate from Coral Bay and Exmouth. The best place to begin your exploration is at the innovative Milyering Visitor Centre.

▶ **Northam** *146A2*

An important road and rail junction and depot for the Goldfields Water Scheme, this Wheat Belt town is the regional center for much of the attractive Avon Valley. The railway up from Perth about 60 miles away used to terminate here, so Northam was the point at which prospectors would begin their thirsty trek to the Goldfields 280 miles to the east; the old railroad station is now a museum with evocative memorabilia of those days.

▶ **Northcliffe** *146A2*

This tiny place lost among the magnificent karri forests of the extreme southwest began as one of the townships of the ill-fated Group Settlement Scheme of the 1920s, whose hopes and failures are documented in the excellent **Pioneer Museum▶**. A good base for viewing the karris (some of the tallest of them grow in the nearby Forest Park), Northcliffe is also the starting point for a 17-mile road leading to Windy Harbour, the only readily accessible beach between Augusta and Walpole.

Ningaloo Reef is home to over 500 varieties of fish

A forest of karris, the tallest of the eucalypts

►   **Nullarbor Plain**   147B4

Renowned for its utter desolation, the world's largest flat surface stretches interminably eastward into South Australia, covering an area of more than 96,525 square miles. Few plants (other than saltbush) and fewer animals flourish in this unyielding environment—the name Nullarbor means "no tree."

The explorer Edward John Eyre survived his terrible journey across the plain from east to west in 1840–1 by keeping close to the coast, where brackish water could occasionally be found beneath patches of sand dunes. The highway named after him also follows a southern route, while the transcontinental railroad strikes off boldly from the goldfields far inland. The landscape along the highway is not entirely without incident, since only a relatively short section traverses the Nullarbor proper, but the 90-mile continuous straight between the Balladonia Roadhouse and Caiguna tests any driver's ability to stay alert!

►►   **Pemberton**   146A2

Steeped in logging lore, the township of Pemberton in the southwest corner of the state is the best place to experience the magic of the magnificent karri forest growing all around. Its wonders can be appreciated in a variety of ways—by car, on foot or aboard a tramcar along a 23-mile railroad line. One tree can be walked through, another, the Gloucester Tree► (see panel) can be climbed. You can visit a restored 1865 sawpit, take a guided tour around a huge modern sawmill, or trace the area's history in the nearby **Manjimup Regional Timber Park►**. The beauty of the forest is enhanced by clear streams and pretty cascades, and by a wealth of wildflowers in the spring.

The Gloucester Tree
It was difficult to build fire-watch towers of sufficient height to rise above the canopy of the giant karris. The answer was to wind a peg ladder around the trunk of a suitable tree and make a lookout cabin at the top. Planes perform the lookout function nowadays, but the Gloucester Tree near Pemberton has been kept for fearless tourists to climb its 153 rungs and be rewarded with a stupendous view over the treetops. It's the loftiest fire lookout tree in the world, but at around 195 feet, it is by no means the tallest karri.

Rails across the desert
Passengers aboard a transcontinental train have an altogether different experience of the Nullarbor. This is one of the world's few railroad journeys where the view from your sleeping berth in the morning is identical to the one on which you closed the curtain the night before! Imposing-sounding stations turn out to be nothing more than a marker planted in the wilderness, or at the very most a huddle of railroad paraphernalia with a section of loop allowing trains to pass. The 297-mile "Long Straight" between Ooldea and Watson tests the patience of even the most disciplined driver of the big diesel hauling its train of stainless steel cars.

Porongurup National Park in the Albany hinterland

Karried to extremes
The tallest of all eucalypts is the karri (*Eucalyptus diversicolor*), a magnificent tree reaching a height of 280 feet, and with a life-span of up to 1,000 years. Growing together in the forest, the soaring stems of the karris create the stately atmosphere of a Gothic church. The finest tracts of karri forest are found in the well-watered south, inland from the coast between Augusta and Albany; much of it was cleared after both world wars to make small-holdings for returned soldiers. Most of these settlements failed, since the deep loamy soil preferred by the karris was good for trees but not for crops.

► **Pilbara**   *147C2*

Until the 1960s, a few cattlemen were the only inhabitants of this wasteland in the northwest. The accidental discovery in the 1950s of what proved to be the world's largest deposit of iron ore (see page 166) was the stimulus for the construction of mining cities like Tom Price and Newman and of deep-water harbors like Dampier and Port Hedland. Trains 6,550 feet long haul the ore from the huge opencast pits down hundreds of miles of track to the sea. Much of this exported raw material is later returned to Australia in the form of Japanese cars.

Tourists come this way for winter sun and for the stunning landscapes of the **Karijini (Hamersley Range) National Park►►**. The vividly colored rocks of this ancient plateau have been bitten into deeply by the action of rivers, forming splendid gorges where intensely cold water gathers in pools and where a surprisingly lush vegetation flourishes. Even more luxuriant plants are a feature of the **Millstream-Chichester National Park►**, where there is permanently flowing water, nourishing the palm trees of a relict rain forest.

►► **The Pinnacles (Nambung National Park)**   *146B2*

The thousands of limestone monoliths scattered around the sandy plain south of the coastal township of Cervantes 155 miles from Perth were mistaken by Dutch sailors for the remains of an ancient city. Varying in size from 19-foot giants to finger-thick pieces of piping, they may well be the fossilized roots of long-dead trees and shrubs. Whatever their origin, they remain compelling presences in their desert setting.

► **Porongurup National Park**   *146A2*

The ancient granites of this range of hills in the Albany hinterland have been eroded into domes and curious formations like Balancing Rock. Castle Rock (1,870 feet) gives stunning views over karri forest and the country beyond. In spring, the forest floor is brilliant with wildflowers.

The Kimberley

This remote land in the far north of Western Australia was explored in 1879 by Alexander Forrest, who thought that some of it might sustain grazing animals. Million-acre stations still graze their stock on the sparse vegetation. There is diamond mining at Argyle, and now tourism has arrived; visitors pass through on around-Australia trips or make the Kimberley their prime destination, drawn by the lure of a "last frontier."

East Kimberley The modern township of Kununurra is the gateway to the East Kimberley, a region of ancient volcanic rocks and sandstone ranges. Tropical rainfall fills the rivers in the Wet, supporting a rich pattern of vegetation and wildlife, while mangrove swamps clad the margins of estuaries. The Ord River Irrigation Scheme has attempted to harness the river's summer flow to irrigate vast areas of cropland, with only limited success; **Wyndham**, the state's northernmost harbor, exports cattle as well as whatever crops the project produces. Persistence will lead the determined visitor to natural wonders like the **Mitchell Falls**, or even (with a permit) along the Kalumburu Road to the far off Aboriginal Reserve and Mission near the mouth of the King Edward River. Some areas, like the Drysdale River National Park, of unresearched biological value, may not be visited at all.

West Kimberley Entered via Broome and Derby, the west has spectacular inland gorges, cut through the limestones of an ancient barrier reef, long since hoisted high above sea level. The river running through **Windjana Gorge** is reduced to a series of pools in the dry season, while the mighty Fitzroy River manages to maintain an all-year flow through the much longer **Geikie Gorge**.

How to get there
Most traffic takes the long way around from Derby to Kununurra via the main highway. This gives access to Wolfe Creek Crater National Park as well as the magical Bungle Bungles (though both of these extraordinary natural phenomena are perhaps best seen from the air). The shorter route is the Gibb River Road, rougher but more rewarding, with well-vegetated creeks, gorges and waterholes.

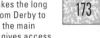

Argyle Diamond Mine, East Kimberley

A nest of rats
Rottnest Island, meaning rats' nest island, was named in 1696 by Dutchman Willem de Vlamingh who found the place infested with what he took to be large rodents. The rats were in fact the hare-sized marsupials known as quokkas, a kind of pademelon wallaby, found here on "Rotto" and on parts of the mainland.

▶   **Rottnest Island**   155E2

Situated 12 miles off the Fremantle coast, and measuring a mere 7 miles long by a maximum of 3 miles across, Perth's weekend paradise has the special charm of all islands, enormously enhanced by the lack of cars; bikes are the main mode for exploring the delightful bays and white beaches along the rugged coastline. The clear waters are ideal for diving and snorkeling.

▶   **Shark Bay**   146C1

Divided into a series of inlets by peninsulas and islands, Shark Bay was named in 1699 by the adventurer William Dampier. The waters of the bay provide excellent swimming, fishing and other watersports, and there are spectacular dunes of red sand, high limestone cliffs, and extraordinary beaches as well. Shell Beach, 37 miles long, is made up of countless shells to a depth of 33 feet; naturally compacted at this depth, this strange material can be cut into blocks and used in buildings. The little resort of Denham is the westernmost town in Australia; on the opposite side of the Peron Peninsula are the famous dolphins of Monkey Mia (see page 168).

▶   **Southern Cross**   146B2

The streets of Southern Cross, founded by gold prospectors in 1888, are still wide enough to turn a camel train. There are mementoes of the old days in the 1891 court house.

▶   **Stirling Range National Park**   146A2

A scenic highway threads through this 40-mile-long range, whose peaks rise abruptly 325 feet above the surrounding country. As well as being southwestern Australia's highest mountains, with occasional snowfall, they are a botanical reserve of first importance and great beauty, with no less than 1,000 wildflower species.

Some of the hundreds of dolphins in Shark Bay

Wave Rock: another ancient geological curiosity

▶▶ **Wave Rock** *146A2*

One of Australia's great tourist attractions, Wave Rock remains forever a surfer's dream turned to stone. More than 325 feet long and 50 feet high, the petrified breaker's resemblance to the real thing is emphasized by the colorful vertical streaking, the result of natural chemicals in the granite reacting with rainwater.

Other curiosities near the little Wheat Belt town of Hyden (211 miles inland from Perth) include further odd rock formations with names like the Humps and the Hippo's Yawn; there are Aboriginal wall paintings in Mulka's Cave.

▶ **Yanchep** *146A2*

Days out from Perth often take in the coastline to the north of the city with its fine beaches, sand dunes and chain of lakes just inland. Yanchep itself is a resort, but around it stretches the **Yanchep National Park▶**, with colorful limestone caves, a lake, eucalyptus woods and a wealth of wildflowers in the spring.

▶ **York** *146A2*

With Northam and Toodyay, York is one of a trio of much-visited towns located in the picturesque Avon Valley 60 miles northeast of Perth. Western Australia's most historic inland town, York was founded in 1831, and many of its old buildings have survived the ravages of time, including an earthquake in 1968. The **Residency Museum▶** evokes the early days, as does the **Balladong Farm▶**, a living museum of agriculture with animals galore. More than 200 classic vehicles are on display in the **York Motor Museum▶▶**.

Hotel sign in the small, respectable town of York

River of the black swans
The Avon is a tributary of the Swan River, given its name ("Swarte Swanne Drift") in 1696 by Willem de Vlamingh in honor of the black swans that so impressed him (and still do impress visitors from the northern hemisphere). Both rivers formed a corridor for early settlement, and the old town of Guildford includes many venerable buildings and historic houses like Woodbridge, built in 1885 and now impeccably restored and authentically furnished (open to the public). The Swan Valley is also famous for its wine. A tour of the wineries is a popular excursion, not only for the product but for the attractive setting of many of the vineyards.

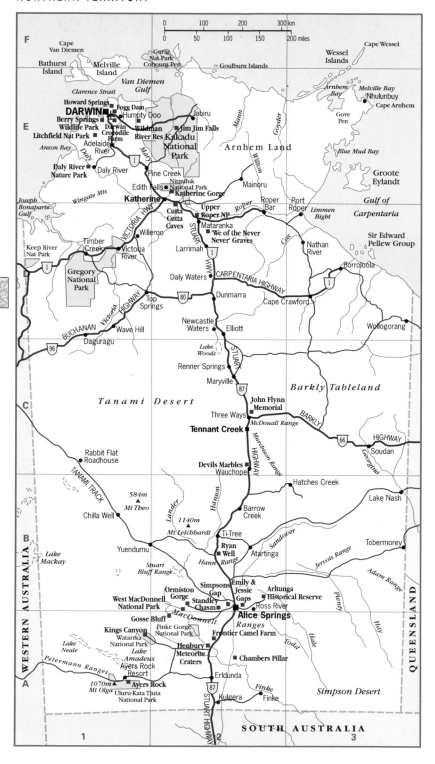

A ghost gum, easily recognizable by its white trunk

The Northern Territory With the thin bitumen ribbon of the Stuart Highway as its backbone, the third largest territorial area in Australia stretches from the country's desert heart, the "Red Centre," to the coast and islands of the tropical north, the "Top End." The cattle rearing that used to form the basis of the territory's economy is still important, but has been overtaken by mining (bauxite, manganese, uranium) and by tourism; more and more visitors are drawn here, not only to the mysterious landforms of the desert, of which **Ayers Rock** is just one, but to Darwin; to the natural riches of the north; and, above all, to the incomparable World Heritage wilderness of **Kakadu National Park**.

First settlement The first European sighting of the coast of the Northern Territory seems to have been made in 1623 by the Dutchman Jan Carstenzoon on board the *Arnhem*, but it was not until the 1820s that the British felt the need to deny the remote northern end of the continent to the French and Dutch. First attempts to found settlements came to grief; Port Essington (1824) on the Cobourg Peninsula had no fresh water, Fort Dundas (1824–9) on Melville Island had hostile Aborigines, and Raffles Bay (1827), also on the Cobourg Peninsula, was abandoned after only two years. Victoria (on an inlet of Port Essington) was established in 1838, and in spite of cyclones and earthquakes, managed to last until 1849, when it too was given up. The splendid natural harbor of Port Darwin was given its name in 1839 by Captain J. C. Wickham of the *Beagle*, thereby honoring Charles Darwin, a member of an earlier voyage. However, it was not until three decades later, in 1869, that the site of the present capital of the territory was surveyed and a start made on building. The choice was a propitious one, and Darwin, originally named Palmerston, has survived and prospered in spite of cyclones and Japanese air raids.

Conquering the interior The interminable and arid spaces of the center resisted attempts to cross them until 1862 when, undeterred by several heroic failures, John McDouall Stuart finally blazed a trail from south to north; Stuart's route is followed by the highway named after him. Before the road was built, the famous Overland Telegraph, spanning the unmapped wilderness between Port Augusta on the coast of South Australia and Darwin, had been completed in less than two years. Linked at Darwin to the submarine cable from Java in 1872, the Australian colonies were thus connected with the "grand electric chain that unites the nations of the earth." The repeater stations constructed along its 1,800-mile length became focal points for travelers. Pastoralists then moved into the territory, and it became part of South Australia in 1863. The telegraph station at Alice Springs still stands, though the town itself has moved south.

Into the 20th century In 1911 the Northern Territory, a drain on the meager resources of South Australia, became the responsibility of the Commonwealth. Though self-governing since 1978, it has still not acquired full statehood, and some of its affairs (Aboriginal matters and uranium mining) continue to be handled by Canberra. For many years it stayed a backwater; few drivers braved the horrible surface of its unpaved roads and there were very few tourists. However, World War II changed all that. In a series of heavy raids, Japanese aircraft inflicted severe damage not only on Darwin but on the Australian psyche. Acutely aware of the country's vulnerability via the empty and remote north, government and armed forces paved the road from the railhead at Alice Springs to the coast, and built a chain of depots, bases and airfields, remains of which can be seen along the highway.

The Northern Territory was hauled bodily into the life of the nation by these events.

Road trains
Taking 51 days on its arduous trip from Adelaide to Darwin, the first car to cross the desert center signaled the beginning of the end for the horses, camels and buffalo-drawn carts that had served the Northern Territory's needs until then. In the 1930s, a cumbersome A.E.C. diesel and trailer formed what was called the Government Road Train, hauling supplies to isolated communities. After World War II, Kurt Johannsen used an old army tank transporter to pull no less than eight cattle trailers. Today's road trains are limited to a maximum of three "dogs" or trailers, a formidable sight as they roar along the highways of the Northern Territory and Western Australia.

One of the lovely gorges cut by the Katherine River

To travel along the Stuart Highway between the arid Red Centre and tropical Top End is to experience some of the most dramatic contrasts nature has to offer in Australia.

The Red Centre Geological processes at their most primeval have shaped the red rocks of the center, creating an almost abstract world of crater and boulder, jagged ridge and lonely monolith, starkly defined against a background of sandy plain or pebbly desert. Etched into this awesome pattern are the winding beds of watercourses, filled only when rare rainstorms rage. Ancestors of the present rivers were fed more generously, and they carved chasm, gorge and canyon, niches in this hostile world for a surprisingly rich and varied wildlife. The rugged **MacDonnell Ranges** to the west and east of Alice Springs are breached by many a gap filled with ferns, palms and other exotic plants, some of them descendants of the flora that flourished on the shore of the vast sea that once covered much of central Australia. Waterholes may persist here long after rivers have dried up, creating a refuge for both animals and humans.

Experiencing the desert is not difficult (unless you want it that way!). The National Parks and Wildlife Service and Conservation Commission are improving facilities while preserving the landscapes entrusted to them. Their management of Ayers Rock is a model of its kind.

The more verdant north Toward the northern rim of the center, permanently flowing rivers are a reminder of a more abundant, monsoon rainfall (up to 63 inches a year compared with around 4¾ inches in the south). Many rivers have their source on the high plateau of Arnhem Land; the Katherine River has cut a series of spectacular gorges, while the **Kakadu National Park** teems with an almost vulgar profusion of wildlife. The Top End has some of Australia's remotest places, like the Cobourg Peninsula, which closes off Van Diemen Gulf, while Darwin itself enjoys a superabundance of natural areas in its hinterland.

Darwin's territorial waters
At Doctors Gully at the end of the Esplanade, thousands of fish and no small number of tourists come together at Aquascene during every high tide—the former to be fed and the latter to do the feeding.

Another place for seeing fish as well as a recreated coral reef is at the Indo Pacific Marine.

179

Rainforest and rivers
An easy day's outing from Darwin, Berry Springs has both a nature park with natural swimming pools and the splendid Territory Wildlife Park. This tract of bushland is aimed at introducing visitors to the N.T.'s varied wildlife.

Well off the beaten track down the Daly River Road, the Daly River Nature Park is a favorite spot for barramundi fishing and boating, although the large number of salties (saltwater crocodiles) precludes swimming.

The Gregory National Park has a spectacular gorge and boat trips along the Victoria River.

East Point
Military Museum

Darwin
Airport

DICK WARD DRIVE

Ross Smith
Memorial

Fannie Bay
Racecourse

Fannie Bay
Gaol Museum

Richardson
Park

BAGOT ROAD

ROSS

SMITH

AVENUE

Australian Aviation Heritage
Centre

D

Vesteys
Beach

EAST POINT ROAD

PARAP

PARAP ROAD

STUART

HIGHWAY

WOOLNER ROAD

TIGER BRENNAN DRIVE

Recreation
Reserve

FANNIE
BAY

CONACHER ST

Fannie
Bay

GOYDER RD

Museum and Art
Gallery of the
Northern Territory

Bullocky
Point

GILRUTH AVENUE

HIGHWAY

Botanic
Gardens

C

Mindil
Beach Reserve

Mindil
Beach

Gardens
Oval

Amphitheatre

STUART
PARK

Myilly
Point

National
Trust HQ

Casino

Palmerston
Park
Oval

THE
GARDENS

Reserve

Indo-
Pacific
Marine
Aquarium

Golf

Course

GARDENS ROAD

STUART

Dinah
Oval

Dinah
Beach

Cullen Bay
Marina

Northern
Territory
University

SMITH STREET

DALY

MITCHELL STREET

McMINN

WOODS STREET

CAVENAGH

STREET

TIGER BRENNAN DRIVE

Marina

Frances
Bay

LARRAKEYAH

Kahlin
Oval

Military
Area

Aquascene

B

Doctors
Gully

Leichhardt
Memorial

ESPLANADE

MITCHELL

SMITH

KNUCKEY STREET

DARWIN CITY

Chinese
Temple

Beaufort
Darwin
Centre

GPO

Victoria
i Hotel

Port
Darwin

Lyons House

Lameroo
Beach

Commercial
Bank

Old
Admiralty
House

Brown's Mart
(Theatre)

Old Town Hall

Old Post Office
(Legislative Assembly)

The Tree of Knowledge

Stokes
Hill

A

Government
House

Fort
Hill

Darwin
Harbour

Stokes Hill
Wharf

0   400   800 m

0   400   800 yards

Iron Ore
Wharf

Fort Hill
Wharf

1

2

3

Darwin

The capital of the Northern Territory clings precariously to the peninsula protruding into Port Darwin, a superb natural anchorage twice the size of Sydney Harbour. Darwin has almost disappeared from the map no less than four times. Cyclones flattened the place in 1897, 1937 and again with great thoroughness in 1974. In between, the aviators of the Imperial Japanese forces did their best to imitate nature at her most furious in the course of no less than 60 air raids. But Darwin's resilience is legendary; after each disaster, the evacuated population has returned to rebuild. In 1974, Cyclone Tracy destroyed

Getting around

The best way to orient yourself is to take a trip on the Tour Tub, an open circulating minibus that allows you to get on and off at any point along its route.

Government House, Darwin's oldest building

nearly all the town's old buildings, including elegant old stilt houses; their replacements were conceived with cyclone-proofing in mind more than beauty.

Diverse community Advertised as Australia's front door, Darwin has looked for much of its life more like the country's back yard. Its appeal is that it is on the edge, a place in touch with other places. Founded in 1869, it became a base for "fabulous old-timers—pearlers, buffalo hunters, trepangers, prospectors, cattlemen and overlanders." The city's population is extraordinarily mixed; the number of ethnic groups varies between 49 and 61 according to who is doing the counting. Many are Asians, and of all Australian cities, Darwin is the most conscious of the lands just to the north; Singapore is no further away than Sydney and Jakarta is closer.

Most visitors pass through Darwin with other destinations in mind, either abroad or in the Northern Territory, many of whose attractions are within easy reach. However, they should beware the place's insidious allure, one based less on visual appeal than on an utterly relaxed, tropical lifestyle.

City sights and orientation Small enough to walk around, the center of the city has a number of surviving (or reconstructed) buildings from early days. Some of these face the parkland of the west-facing Esplanade; here is **Government House** of 1883 as well as **Old Admiralty House**, a fine example of a tropical building on stilts dating from the 1920s. Among the grid of streets further inland is the much rebuilt **Victoria Hotel**, the **Chinese Temple** or Joss House and, in the courtyard of the Civic Centre, an ancient banyan, the "**Tree of Knowledge**," one of Darwin's most resilient landmarks. Other sights lie farther afield, many of them overlooking beautiful Fannie Bay to the north. Here is the Diamond Beach Casino, close to Mindil Beach where a famous market is held from April to October.

Toping in the tropics
The tropical heat provides the people of Darwin with an excellent reason to drink more beer than anywhere else in what, after all, is not an abstemious country. Discarded beer bottles once used to litter the streets and highways, but an ingenious solution has been found for the disposal of the cans in which the amber fluid comes—the Beercan Regatta. Held every August at Mindil Beach, this weird event featuring bizarre craft ingeniously constructed from the humble "tinnie" has become one of the highlights of Darwin's social calendar, attracting thousands of spectators. Beer consumption during the festivities helps provide the raw material for the following year's event.

Meet Sweetheart at the Museum and Art Gallery

►   **Botanic Gardens**   *180C2*
Gardens Road
Plants grow rapidly in Darwin's climate, and the damage done to these fine gardens in 1974 has been made good. The opportunity was taken to add new features, including collections of orchids, figs, ferns, and a quite exceptional array of palms. As much a park as a scientific institution, the gardens are the city's favorite cool retreat.

►   **East Point Military Museum**   *180D2*
East Point Road
Concrete bunkers and items of military hardware lie scattered around East Point headland. The 9-inch guns installed here to repel an invader who never came were, ironically, finally removed by a Japanese scrap metal dealer.

►   **Fannie Bay Gaol Museum**   *180D2*
East Point Road
With no history of convictism, Darwin nevertheless stresses the importance of its prison, built in 1883 and in use until 1979. The museum features a gallows, used for the Territory's last execution in 1952.

►►►   **Museum and Art Gallery
of the Northern Territory**   *180C2*
Conacher Street, Fannie Bay
This modern complex on Fannie Bay emphasizes the unique geographical position of the territory and its capital. In addition to an excellent collection of traditional and contemporary Aboriginal art and artifacts, there is a wealth of fascinating objects from Southeast Asia and the Southwest Pacific, and the Cyclone Tracy gallery. A huge shed houses original seagoing vessels, among them sinister war canoes, dugouts, fantastic outriggers, a lipa-lipa, proas and the last of Darwin's pearling luggers, the *Vivienne*. But pride of place should perhaps go to Sweetheart, a monster among crocodiles, now stuffed and harmless.

FOCUS ON *Crocodiles*

A morbid fascination with crocodiles has no doubt something to do with seeing one-self as the potential prey of a large and aggressive reptile. The crocodiles of the Northern Territory, Western Australia and Queensland have loomed large in the public mind not only because of the movie *Crocodile Dundee* but also because of their increasing numbers (a result of effective conservation measures), the opening-up of their habitat to wilderness tourism, and the readiness of the media to make a meal out of any crocodile attack.

Two kinds of crocodile live in Australia. Harmless to humans, the relatively small freshwater crocodile frequents rivers and billabongs between the Gulf of Carpentaria and Broome in Western Australia. Double its size (20 foot specimens are not uncommon), and distinguished by a broader snout, the saltwater or estuarine crocodile prefers the brackish waters of tidal rivers though it is quite capable of penetrating far inland as well as out into the ocean. It occurs from India to the western Pacific, and in Australia from the central Queensland coast around Rockhampton to the Broome area.

Salties prey on fish and animals of all sizes, including human beings. Many victims are taken unawares at the water's edge; the crocodile makes its approach underwater, then uses the massive muscle of its tail to propel itself from the deep like a Polaris missile. The prey is dragged underwater and drowned rather than immediately torn apart; the croc can stay below the surface for up to an hour. Male crocodiles lord it over a territory they defend from other males. Much of their time is spent lying log-like in the shallows, conserving energy that is rapidly expended in violent maneuvers to secure dinner.

Look before you dive Darwin's swimming pools and ornamental waters have to be checked before they are opened to the public. Swimming or paddling in areas frequented by crocodiles could well be fatal. Remember, too, that crocodiles are amphibians, capable of reaching high speeds on land. Always obey the signs forbidding swimming (if they haven't been removed as souvenirs!) and seek local advice if in doubt. The best way to see these intimidating creatures is to take a conducted tour in a steel-bottomed boat (one legendary beast—long since dealt with—developed a taste for the more chewy kind of outboard motor, so don't trail your hand in the water!) Craft of this kind ply Yellow Water in Kakadu and, nearer Darwin, the Adelaide River.

Darwin Crocodile Farm
This establishment 25 miles south of Darwin is home to thousands of crocodiles reared for their skins. Feeding time is always spectacular.

183

Warning
Crocodiles respect neither man nor beast, so take no chances. Just because you can't see them, it doesn't mean they're not there.

Albert Namatjira
Born at Hermannsburg Mission in 1902, this member of the Aranda tribe became a talented watercolorist in the European tradition, his subject the stunning landscapes of his native MacDonnell Ranges. He and his work were acclaimed; he was presented to the Queen during a royal visit, and in 1957 he was given the extraordinary privilege (for the time) of full citizenship. But Namatjira was destroyed by the tension between white and Aboriginal society and by alcohol; imprisoned for supplying drink to a fellow Aborigine, his morale collapsed and he died in 1959 at the age of 57. His wonderfully fresh paintings can be seen in many Australian galleries.

184

▶ **Alice Springs**   *176B2*

Bang in the middle of the continent, The Alice (as it is widely known) has transformed itself from a dusty outpost to an indispensable stop on the tourist itinerary. Equipped with all modern amenities, it makes an excellent base for exploring the wonders of the Red Centre.

The township began in 1871 as a convenient place for a repeater station on the Overland Telegraph between Adelaide and Darwin. Development was slow until the arrival of the railroad from Adelaide in 1929, the famous but rickety "Ghan," named after the Afghan camel drivers it supplanted. In World War II, the railhead acquired enormous strategic value, particularly after the Stuart Highway leading on up to Darwin had been given its first coat of bitumen. But it was the advent of mass tourism from the 1970s onward that persuaded the town to provide what had previously been lacking: comfortable hotels, sophisticated restaurants and even a tastefully landscaped shopping mall. All this came as something of a surprise to the old-timers, who not so long ago would ride in for an evening's drinking and hitch their horse to the rail in the main street.

The best place to get an overall impression of the Alice in its desert setting is to climb (or drive up) **Anzac Hill**▶ with its obelisk memorial. The town center stretches out on the west bank of the bed of the Todd River. The fact that it rarely contains any water has not stopped the hilarious Henley-on-Todd Regatta becoming a major annual event, with legs rather than oars supplying the motive power for the bottomless craft. For much of the rest of the year the dry river bed serves as a camping ground for some of the Alice's substantial Aboriginal population. To the south are the long ridges of the MacDonnell Ranges, pierced by the Heavitree Gap, through which run road and railroad. Beyond is the airport, and then the top-secret U.S./Australian Pine Gap communications base.

Alice Springs has a number of memorials to...

...and reminders of the Royal Flying Doctor Service

Although visitors come to Alice Springs more because of where it is than for what it is, there are a fair number of attractions in the town and its immediate vicinity. A few older buildings recall its beginnings; the **Stuart Town Gaol** is the most venerable of these, a jail dating all the way back to 1907! **Adelaide House** was built in 1920–6 to serve as a hospital and had natural air-conditioning. For a short time in the 1920s the administration of the N.T. was split between Darwin and Alice Springs. The **Residency**▶ dates from this period, and now houses a small but well-presented museum of local history. The town's main museum is the **Spencer and Gillen Museum**▶ on the upper floor of the modern mall; it has extensive exhibits on the art and natural history of central Australia.

Transportation and communications are one theme of Alice Springs, if not *the* theme. The place's *raison d'être* was the **Old Telegraph Station**▶▶, and its plain but evocative stone buildings still stand just north of the town. Both the **School of the Air** and the **Royal Flying Doctor Service** have bases in town that are open to the public. To the west is the **Museum of Technology, Transport and Communications**, which celebrates early flight in the Outback as well as the history of automobile transportation, while off the Stuart Highway beyond the Heavitree Gap is the **Ghan Preservation Society**, dedicated to rehabilitating the rolling stock of the original, narrow-gauge railway line. In pioneering days, the arid interior relied on camel trains for supplies; at the **Frontier Camel Farm** you can ride one of these ships of the desert and find out about them and their Afghan masters.

Alice Springs is one of the places where the overseas visitor cannot fail to become aware of the Aboriginal presence. Part of the town's living comes from money spent by Aborigines, even more from the merchandising of Aboriginal souvenirs, though you are unlikely to be able to buy a painting by Albert Namatjira (see panel opposite). A particularly poignant story about the European/Aboriginal relationship is told in the modern **Strehlow Research Centre,** which celebrates the culture of the Aranda people and the German missionary's son who lived and worked among them.

They both feed and *entertain you in The Alice*

How to travel

186

The Stuart Highway
This 1,865-mile road unrolls its thin band of bitumen through the vast and deserted spaces of central Australia between Adelaide and Darwin. Known to all as "The Track", it follows the route first traced in 1862 by the tough Scotsman John McDouall Stuart. For many years it was a notorious axle-breaker, but nothing was done until Australia's war situation became desperate in 1942 when, with U.S. Forces' help, the road was speedily asphalted from the railhead at Alice Springs to Darwin. Several decades passed before the southern half of the highway was completely paved, and the adventure of gravel, rock and bulldust replaced by the predictability of bitumen.

By air Darwin's international airport acquired a bright new terminal in 1991, less colorful than the tin shed it replaced but infinitely more convenient. From here there are connections to many overseas destinations and to all major Australian cities. Alice Springs also has a modern airport, again linked to a variety of Australian destinations. Connellan Airport, serving Ayers Rock and its resort, has a more limited range of connections. Light aircraft will take you virtually anywhere you want to go in the territory; the traveler in a hurry will almost certainly make use of some of the services and day tours available. The desert looks at its most dramatic from the air; try the hot-air balloon operation at Alice Springs.

By bus Long-distance buses link Darwin, Alice Springs, Ayers Rock and other points in the territory with major Australian cities (though it takes time!). Tour operators offer any number of trips, particularly in the Red Centre. Some day trips, like Darwin–Kakadu–Darwin, are not recommended for the faint-hearted. Only Darwin has any sort of local bus service.

By rail The rebuilt line north from Tarcoola in South Australia carries the revived "Ghan," a luxury train connecting Adelaide and Alice Springs; this is the only railway within the Northern Territory. There are bus and air connections from various towns to the railhead at Mount Isa, terminus for the "Inlander" train from Townsville, almost 620 miles away on the Queensland coast.

By car From Darwin, the **Stuart Highway** runs south through Alice Springs to Port Augusta and Adelaide (1,906 miles); at Three Ways the **Barkly Highway** leaves the Stuart for Mount Isa and on to Townsville (1,588 miles); at Katherine, the **Victoria Highway** branches off towards the Kimberley and thence to Perth (2,536 miles). Paved roads reach Ayers Rock and Jabiru in Kakadu National Park, and all-weather roads will take you to most major tourist destinations.

One of the huge road trains that span the continent

The domes of the Olgas, just waiting to be explored

▶ ▬▬▬ **Arnhem Land** *176E2*

Beyond Kakadu a rugged sandstone escarpment seems to bar the way to this mysterious and inaccessible area. Given the name of the Dutch ship whose crew were the first Europeans to sight it, Arnhem Land stretches spectacularly eastward to form the western coastline of the Gulf of Carpentaria. Now in the hands of its Aboriginal owners, most of it can only be entered by permit, though a limited number of guided tours do take place.

▶ ▶ ▶ **Ayers Rock (Uluru) and**
Mount Olga (Kata Tjuta) *176A1*

Reproduced a million times on film, tape and glossy brochures, the great red monolith of Ayers Rock has become one of the world's tourist clichés, yet it still retains the power to stir the spirits of all those who visit it. Not surprisingly, Uluru (to give the Rock its Aboriginal name) occupied a central place in the spiritual lives of local tribespeople whose ancestors may have frequented the area for as long as 20,000 years. A number of sacred sites around the base are protected, and must not be entered or photographed.

The Rock was first sighted by the surveyor Ernest Giles in 1872. In 1985 the land, which includes the Uluru–Kata Tjuta National Park, was ceremonially handed back to an Aboriginal trust on behalf of the traditional owners, then immediately leased for 99 years to the National Parks and Wildlife Service. It had been intended to demolish the resort that had grown up in a haphazard way near the base of the Rock, but in the event this too passed into the hands of the Aborigines. Its replacement is the **Ayers Rock Resort▶**, a respectful distance away.

The sediments making up Ayers Rock and the neighboring Olgas were laid down some 500–600 million years ago and then tilted almost vertically by earth movements. Ayers Rock rises 1,142 feet above the plain and Mount Olga rises 1,791 feet, but their foundations go far deeper.

Continued on page 190.

Aboriginal place-names
While many Australian place-names were borrowed from the "old country," the early settlers were also happy to use Aboriginal names. Parramatta was the first town to be designated in this way, and others can be seen all over the map, often sounding more appropriate than names recalling the villages, suburbs or shire towns of faraway England. Who could resist Woolloomooloo? A trend nowadays is to replace an English name with an Aboriginal one; the Olgas (named after a 19th-century queen of Spain) are now officially Kata Tjuta ("many heads") and Ayers Rock is called Uluru, though one suspects that these English names will prove difficult to eradicate, such is their resonance worldwide.

Railroads helped shape Australia. In such a vast country, the battle to overcome "the tyranny of distance" was a long and difficult one, and the role of the railroad in helping the country to both grow economically and grow together politically was of outstanding importance.

A long short cut

Once the Transcontinental Railway had linked west to east, travelers from Europe who were in a hurry to get to Melbourne or Sydney would leave their ship at Fremantle and continue their journey by rail. In spite of having to change trains each time there was a break of gauge (at Kalgoorlie, Port Augusta, and again at Albury), the advantage was that a day or two would be saved. The fare, just as on the ocean liner, included all meals—as it still does—but today you no longer need to change trains as the standard gauge stretches right across the continent from Perth to Sydney (you do, however, still have to change for broad-gauge Melbourne).

There is plenty of time to study the route

Gauging success The first iron road in Australia was a short line in Adelaide for horse-drawn traffic. The earliest steam railroads were those linking Melbourne to its port (September 1854) and Sydney to Parramatta (a year later). But already there was trouble. What track gauge should be adopted?

The colonies initially agreed among themselves that the gauge should be George Stephenson's standard of 4 feet 8½ inches, then a preference was expressed for a broader gap between the rails of 5 feet 3 inches as used in Ireland. In the end each colony went its own way, Victoria and South Australia adopting the broad gauge and New South Wales adopting the standard gauge. South Australia fell for the comfort and spaciousness implied by the broad gauge, while Queensland and Western Australia came up with a different idea altogether, that of systems built entirely on the narrow gauge of 3 feet 6 inches. Tasmania began with standard gauge, then converted to narrow gauge.

This was fine as long as each system remained self-contained, but eventually the tracks reached out to connect (or rather not connect) with those of the neighboring network. Through-passengers had to disembark, goods had to be unloaded and re-loaded, and the most hated three words in all Australia at the time were supposed to have been "All change! Albury!", the name of the station on the border between New South Wales and Victoria. In 1897, Mark Twain was more than vexed to have to change trains here, not least because it involved a tedious walk along a lengthy track.

Natural hazards Railroads were often difficult and expensive to build in Australia, because of the distances that had to be covered, the variety of natural obstacles that had to be overcome, and the high cost of importing rails and other materials from England. The capricious nature of the landscape didn't help, and flooding often occurred in places where no rain had fallen for years, washing the track away.

To keep costs down, many country lines were built to a low standard, resulting in irksome speed restrictions. Bridges remained unbuilt; the train ferry that for years carried the coaches and wagons of Sydney–Brisbane trains over the Clarence River was only replaced by a bridge in 1932. Secondary lines were built not only to the 3 feet 6 inches gauge but to an even narrower 2 feet 6 inches standard, virtually a miniature railroad of the kind that still chuffs between Ferntree Gully and Belgrave in the Dandenongs today (the famous Puffing Billy). Narrower still—a mere 2 feet—are the sugarcane

railroads that wander through the plantations of Queensland.

From time to time some parts of Australia have toyed with the idea of going their own way. Such a stance was taken up by Western Australia at the end of the 19th century, when it only joined the Federation on condition that it was physically linked to the rest of the country by a transcontinental railroad (paid for by the Federation). It took years to lay the rails across the 298 miles of the waterless Nullarbor, but the line was ready for traffic in 1917 and is now traversed by the world-famous *Indian Pacific*.

The Ghan A still incomplete but nevertheless fascinating railroad project was the South Australia–Northern Territory link. Shakily built narrow-gauge tracks snaked out from Port Augusta in the south and from Darwin in the north. The southern section was called the Ghan because it replaced the Afghan camel trains that had hitherto been the most effective means of transportation along the route. Reaching Oodnadatta in 1890, it took another 39 years to get as far as Alice Springs, and the top section only went as far as Birdum, 311 miles south of Darwin. Both lines were ripped up in the 1970s, the northern section disappearing altogether and the southern section being rebuilt along a less flood-prone alignment that now carries a luxury train. Also called the Ghan, this train offers standards of comfort that would have been quite alien to Wilfred Thomas's traveling companions (see panel).

Afghan nights
An early traveler on the Ghan, Wilfred Thomas, settled down to try to get some sleep, but was amazed when his fellow-travelers—a tough looking bunch of miners and stockmen—cleared the seats away brusquely, brought out the drink and some bagpipes, and then danced the night away together.

189

The luxury Ghan connects Adelaide and The Alice

An Outback dragon
The fearsome-looking thorny devil is one of the most astonishing denizens of the desert, well deserving its zoological name *Moloch horridus*. In spite of its bulbous spine-covered body and multicolored blotches, it is an inoffensive creature, relying on its unappetizing appearance to deter any predator.

AYERS ROCK RESORT
CENTRAL AUSTRALIA

The spectacular view from the top of Ayers Rock

Continued from page 187.

Much is made of the mysterious responsiveness of both Ayers Rock and the Olgas to lighting conditions, and few visitors will want to miss the uncanny changes produced by dawn and sunset; the basic red color is due to the presence of iron.

Most visitors rush to climb the Rock, but the expedition should not be undertaken lightly, least of all by the elderly or by those with a medical condition. Take the advice of rangers and tour guides concerning timing, water supplies and the route (the only one) that must be followed. You might even bow to the Aborigines' expressed preference that the Rock should not be climbed, but experienced in a more respectful way by a circular walk or tour around its 6-mile base. This is worth doing in any case, revealing as it does a wealth of fascinating detail, the strange, almost cookie-like texture of the stone, or the way in which the almost vertical lower slopes have been eroded into deep furrows. If you are really lucky, you could experience a storm and the subsequent extraordinary spectacle of myriad waterfalls standing out against a sinister black background.

Of geologically related origin, the 30 or so domes of the **Olgas** offer a quite different but no less fascinating experience, not least because of the rich vegetation and wildlife that flourish in the sheltered gorges between the individual summits. All those able to undertake one of the somewhat stony walks through the area should certainly do so, though perhaps the most spectacular way to view these sleeping dinosaurs (as they have been called) is aboard a light plane on one of the short flights that also takes in the Rock. As well as revealing the isolated table mountain known as Mount Conner, perfectly aligned with the Rock and Olgas, this aerial perspective is also a good way to appreciate the layout of the Ayers Rock Resort (see panel). Designed in 1981, its architecture, planning and landscaping are a remarkably sensitive response to its desert environment.

The visitor to Ayers Rock will find an array of organized tours available, ranging from double-deck bus trips to a personalized commentary given while riding pillion on a Harley-Davidson. The **Uluru Experience►** aims to bring small groups of participants into more intimate contact with the plants and animals of the desert, as well as with Aboriginal life and lore.

► Bathurst and Melville Islands   *176E1*

Lying off the coast to the north of Darwin and separated from each other by the narrow Apsley Strait, these two large islands are the home of the Tiwi people. Lacking contact with the Aborigines of the mainland, they developed their own very distinct culture, including the making of the extraordinary and highly decorated Pukamani burial poles. The British settlement at Fort Dundas, the first to be attempted on the north Australian coast (1824–9), was a failure. A Catholic mission was set up in the early 1900s, but the islands have now been returned to their traditional owners and can only be visited on an organized tour.

► Chambers Pillar   *176A2*

This 112-foot sandstone monolith rises abruptly from its spreading foundation to make one of the desert's most striking landmarks. Few visitors can resist the temptation to etch their initials in its soft surface.

► Cutta Cutta Caves   *176D2*

South of Katherine on the Stuart Highway, these limestone chambers linked by narrow passages are the home of the orange horseshoe bat, once believed to be extinct.

The rare orange horseshoe bat can be found in the Cutta Cutta Caves

Green on red
Deserts are fragile environments, whose ecological balance and visual appeal can easily be degraded when visitors arrive in large numbers. The collection of motels and other facilities that had accumulated at the base of Ayers Rock was no triumph of design. Its replacement, the Ayers Rock Resort, is distinguished both architecturally and ecologically. Sited 12 miles away from the Rock, its visual impact on its unique surroundings is minimal, partly because of skillful landscaping using the characteristic landforms and plants of the desert. The hotel and other buildings of the resort have thick masonry walls for insulation, while bull-nose verandas and eaves shield windows and walkways from the sun. The huge shade sails rising over the main hotel have become the emblem of the place, but they too play a role in energy conservation.

Barramundi
This fine tropical freshwater fish is Australia's favorite catch, making an excellent meal as well as providing good sport. Barramundi can grow to huge sizes; specimens 6 feet long weighing up to 22½ pounds are not uncommon. They live in most aquatic environments, traveling to river estuaries to breed. A big barramundi will fiercely resist being taken. Barramundi are still plentiful but there are Northern Territory restrictions on how many may be caught.

The Devils Marbles, 56 miles south of Tennant Creek

▶▶ **Devils Marbles** 176C2

Hundreds of granite boulders lie scattered across the plain, some huge, some tiny and some perched in impossible positions. To the geologist they are all that remains of the ancient mountains that once rose here, but to the Aborigines they are the eggs of the Rainbow Serpent, Wanambi. The best time to see them is early morning.

▶▶ **Finke Gorge National Park** 176A2

Access to the famous gorge in the western MacDonnell Ranges known as Palm Valley is along the rocky bed of the Finke River, normally dry but impassable after rain. In utter contrast to the desert is the lush vegetation thriving in the protected environment of the gorge. The 3,000 or so cabbage palms are unique to the area, the descendants of prehistoric trees that grew on the shore of what was then a tropical sea. A good way to get a general view of the rugged sandstone gorge is to climb up to **Initiation Rock**, where youths of the Aranda people were once introduced to the mysteries of manhood.

▶▶ **Gurig National Park** 176F2

Now returned to its traditional Aboriginal owners, this national park covers the whole of the remote Cobourg Peninsula protruding westward from Arnhem Land. There is splendid sailing and fishing, as well as the experience of utter isolation, since the number of visitor permits issued is strictly limited. The superb natural harbor of **Port Essington** was the site of Victoria, one of the early British settlements later replaced by Darwin.

▶ **Henbury Meteorite Craters Conservation Reserve** 176A2

At the end of a dirt road off the Stuart Highway south of Alice Springs is a genuine curiosity: a swarm of craters formed about 5,000 years ago when a big meteorite split into pieces on entering the earth's atmosphere. The largest crater is 590 feet across and 49 feet deep.

▶▶▶ Kakadu National Park   *176E2*

Some 155 miles east of Darwin, Australia's largest national park joined Unesco's World Heritage Area list in 1987 on account of the Aboriginal art sites it contains and its almost unbelievably rich and varied wildlife.

Kakadu extends over a number of very distinct landscapes. The tidal zone along the shore of Van Diemen's Gulf is pierced by the estuaries of four great rivers, the East, West and South Alligator Rivers and the Wildman River. Here the gray of tidal mudflats contrasts with the bright green of mangrove swamps, breeding grounds for the well-known barramundi (see panel on page 191). The floodplains of the rivers become a vast freshwater sea in the Wet, teeming with migratory birds and other waterfowl, including magpie geese, kites, egrets, brolgas, pelicans, cormorants, ibises and the handsome jabiru. Salt and freshwater crocodiles lurk in creek and billabong. As the land rises gradually southwards, eucalyptus woodland develops, interspersed with myriad termite mounds or dramatically interrupted by massive rock outcrops, isolated fragments of the formidable sandstone escarpment marking the western edge of Arnhem Land. This rugged north–south barrier runs for 310 miles, broken by gorges cut by the streams draining the vast interior, the scene of spectacular waterfalls in the wet season. Two of the best known of these are **Jim Jim Falls▶** and **Twin Falls▶**, in the south of the park, both with abundant tropical wildlife.

Scores of natural galleries in the escarpment sandstone contain some of the country's choicest examples of early Aboriginal art. The most visited are those at **Ubirr▶▶**, where there are "X-ray" paintings as well as other styles, and at **Nourlangie Rock▶**. The Bowali Visitor Center for the park is near Jabiru. It is just possible to get some idea of Kakadu in the course of a day visit by air from Darwin (there are bus trips too, in spite of the distance).

Art of the Outback
Aboriginal art is traditionally connected to ritual and ceremony rather than self-expression, and is ephemeral or renewable. Much of the art of central Australia is abstract and symbolic. The artist's canvas could be a rock wall or the ground itself, with sand paintings executed in colored earths, pebbles, feathers and so on. The wall paintings at Kakadu are representational. Some of them, depicting hunting scenes, are incredibly old, dating from the pre-estuarine period up to 23,000 years ago. The X-ray style, showing the internal organs and bone structure of fish and animals, dates from the estuarine period, which followed a rise in sea level some 7,000–9,000 years ago. More recent depictions of Europeans and their accoutrements belong to the so-called contact period.

193

Dawn over Kakadu—a sight to remember

In the early part of the 20th century, it seemed as if the Aborigines of Australia were doomed as a race. Their numbers had diminished drastically from an estimated population of a half million at the onset of European colonization to perhaps 60,000 in the 1920s; and many of these were of mixed blood.

Good grub
While Aboriginal men hunted game with boomerang and fire, women and children foraged for smaller animals, lizards, insects, seeds and fruit. A particular delicacy is the witchetty grub. With a buttery taste when cold, the grubs are said to resemble pork scratchings when cooked in hot ashes. Initiation into the delights of "bush tucker" can be a fascinating experience.

194

These children live near a school; for those too far away there is always the radio-transmitted School of the Air

Christian missions established in the Outback destroyed the Aborigines' ancient religious links with the land, government "Protectors" moved them around at will, and mixed-race children were removed from their parents and brought up in homes or by foster parents. Devastated by alcoholism, wasted by white men's diseases, seldom in steady employment and universally despised, it seemed to some as if it would only be a matter of time before mainland Aborigines suffered the fate of the Tasmanians.

A genius not extinguished As the end of the century approaches, however, the situation has become more hopeful. A once silent people has found a voice, one moreover that is listened to and sometimes acted on. The Aboriginal plight has been noticed, thanks to protests like the "tent embassy" established for years in front of the Canberra Parliament, or the march of 30,000 people through the streets of Sydney, part of a boycott of the 1988 Bicentennial celebrations. On a small scale, Aboriginal voices are heard over the air on Aboriginal-owned radio and television stations.

In the realm of politics, reforms have been carried out and, in part, implemented. The almost incredible situation in which Aborigines were not classed as citizens or even counted in the official census of population was rectified

by the 1967 referendum that gave the Federal Government overall responsibility for Aboriginal affairs. One outcome was the drafting and passing of the Aboriginal Land Rights Act of 1976 that enabled Crown lands to be handed back to the "traditional owners." A dramatic illustration of the effect of this took place in 1985, when **Ayers Rock** and the **Uluru National Park** formally became the property of the Uluru–Kata Tjuta Land Trust on behalf of the traditional owners. Entry to such lands is now only possible by means of a permit. In the case of a world-famous national park, this is obtained both instantly and easily; in the case of less well-known places it is by no means automatic, a fact resented by many white Australians.

As seen by others White attitudes have undergone change, even transformation. In an age of environmental devastation and loss of religious direction, the way in which Aborigines lived for thousands of years in material and religious harmony with their surroundings has earned respect and even wonder. Aboriginal art, both traditional and contemporary, is widely admired. There is a widespread wish, expressed by politicians as well as by ordinary people, to make restitution for the injustices perpetrated over 200 years. But problems remain, even if they no longer seem so insurmountable. While some younger people of Aboriginal descent try to combine old ways of living with some of the benefits of European civilization, others fail to find a place anywhere and continue to live on the margins of society. In the face of widespread petty criminality and alcohol-related offenses, a repressive police culture persists; a shameful number of young blacks have died while in police custody. Rejection and contempt live on in many white hearts.

It may be that a certain degree of separation must take place before the races can come together again in harmony, and the right of refusal of entry to Aboriginal lands should be seen in this light, rather than denounced as incipient apartheid. In any case, there is a wish on the part of many Aborigines to share their growing pride in themselves and their heritage with their fellow Australians and with visitors. Contemporary Aboriginal art, of variable quality, is available everywhere, while traditional rock paintings are best experienced in the company of an Aboriginal ranger, who will be able to explain at least some of their mysteries. Music, dance and ritual are performed in many places, but the high point of many people's experience of Australia could be a visit to an Aboriginal community.

A right to land
Since 1976, Northern Territory Aborigines have owned the land in what were formerly reserves and in addition have been able to lay claim to vacant Crown Land. Many of these claims have been opposed, and even when successful do not necessarily inhibit mining and quarrying. But royalties have to be paid to the owners, and quite a few communities in areas like Arnhem Land now have no shortage of funds.

195

Some communities are willing to share and explain their traditions

The total number of sheep in Australia today amounts to more than 160 million, more than three-quarters of them the resilient merino with a fleece of up to 4½ pounds in weight. Australia accounts for about a quarter of the world's wool and is the biggest exporter of lamb and mutton. In some places the sheep/people ratio begs belief: one million sheep roam South Australia's Kangaroo Island, for example, compared with only 4,000 humans.

Record shearing
Traditionally working in teams that moved from station to station during the shearing season, shearers honed their skills to an almost incredible pitch; in 1892 a Queensland man, Jackie Howe, set the record for hand-shearing, having shorn 321 sheep in 7 hours 40 minutes. Even with electric clippers, today's shearers find this difficult to match.

A tough breed Second only to kangaroos as the animals most closely identified with Australia, sheep were among the passengers of the first fleet, though 59 of Governor Phillip's 90 beasts soon perished. A certain Captain Macarthur had better luck; he cannily bred Bengal ewes with English rams, then crossed them with Spanish merinos. This mixed breed flourished in the new environment, yielding a fleece of fine quality and good weight and providing the foundation of Australia's wool industry, a mainstay of the national economy even today. In the 19th century, it was sheep as much as men that colonized the vast spaces of the new country; by 1900 there were nearly 100 million of them.

Sheep shearers Watching sheep shearers at work is quite a spectacle. The sheep is driven into the shearing shed, thrown to the ground by the shearer and held fast between his or her legs. The clippers run swiftly through the fleece, this being removed in one piece if possible. The heaps of wool are sorted according to quality and are then dispatched in huge bales.

Will this be a new sheep-shearing record?

Kings Canyon, good walking country

► Katherine   *176E2*

An important stopping place on the Stuart Highway, this township is the center of the vast and remote territory described by Jeannie Gunn in her classic 1908 novel of the Outback *We of the Never Never*. The area derives its name from the saying that those who live there can "never never" leave. You can visit the Northern Territory's oldest surviving homestead, Springvale, but most of the town's 250,000 annual visitors come for the spectacular Katherine Gorge at **Nitmiluk National Park►►**, about 18 miles to the east. Rising in Arnhem Land, the Katherine River has cut a series of stunning gorges through the sandstone plateau, providing a refuge for a surprising variety of flora and fauna. The first two gorges can be seen aboard tourist boats, the defiles farther upstream in your own canoe. There are a number of walks from the information center to points along the gorge.

►► Kings Canyon   *176A1*

One of the most spectacular natural landscapes of Central Australia, this deep canyon (officially called Watarrka National Park and located some 220 miles southwest from Alice), with its rugged sandstone cliffs rising 650 feet above the dry river bed, has only recently become well frequented by visitors. A short walk leads up the floor of the canyon to a lookout point, but anyone with proper walking shoes who is reasonably fit should not miss the more challenging (3¾ miles) walk up onto the plateau and around the rim of the canyon. Steep to start with, it gives panoramic views over the canyon and a distant glimpse of Ayers Rock.

►► Litchfield National Park   *176E1*

This 250-square-mile tract of sandstone plateau and lush rain forest is becoming increasingly popular with both tourists and local people from the Darwin area, not least because of the excellent swimming in the clear pools at the foot of its numerous waterfalls. Access is via the pleasant tree-shaded township of Batchelor.

Spinifex
Early explorers cursed the spiky tussocks of spinifex as its spear-like blades impeded their progress through the desert, causing pain and bleeding to horses and camels. Spinifex grasses are great survivors, often the only plants able to withstand the extreme heat and aridity of the center, thanks to a deep tap root that manages to extract moisture from far below the surface. Growing outward into hollow clumps, the plants provide a habitat for other forms of desert life—insects, dragons, skinks and even a species of pigeon.

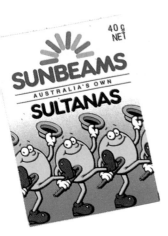

▶▶▶ **MacDonnell Ranges** 176A2

These parallel ridges of red quartzite and sandstone extend their corrugations hundreds of miles across Central Australia, an almost frightening panorama of total desolation when seen from the air. But this was home to the Aranda people until well after the arrival of the white man, and in the gorges cut long ago by the now infrequently flowing rivers there flourishes a lush vegetation of palms and ferns, descendants of the flora that grew on the shore of an ancient tropical sea.

Some of the most spectacular landscapes of the **West MacDonnell National Park** are easily accessible from Alice Springs via Namatjira Drive. Overlooking the Alice itself from a height of 3,084 feet is the distinctive peak of Mount Gillen. Only a little farther out is **Simpsons Gap**▶▶, where the steep-sided gorge, pale sands and fine specimens of river red gums and ghost gums make an excellent introduction to the landscape of the ranges. The reserve is accessible by vehicle but, as always, the best way to explore is on foot, using one of several marked hiking tracks. Among the wildlife of the gorge is a colony of black-footed wallabies.

In dramatic contrast to the impressively wide gorge at Simpsons Gap is **Standley Chasm**▶▶, an incredibly narrow cleft between 330-foot quartzite cliffs. For a short period around midday the sun fills the gorge with vibrant light, a popular spectacle for visitors who have walked the half-mile or so along the bed of the creek. At **Ellery Creek Big Hole**▶▶, high red cliffs frame the water-filled gorge, which is a favorite spot for swimming and fishing. **Serpentine Gorge**▶ consists of a narrow winding defile with semi-permanent waterholes, and has been left deliberately undeveloped. **Ormiston Gorge and Pound**▶▶ is the largest of the

The blue lagoon of the Glen Helen Gorge

A noble face, first imported but now native

reserves in West MacDonnell National Park with permanent waterholes and magical ghost gums, while **Glen Helen Gorge▶▶** has rugged rust-colored cliffs contrasting with the blue of the water that forms a deep lagoon in the bed of the Finke River. Farther west is **Redbank▶** with its chilly rockpools. Further on still, Tylers Pass leads to Gosses Bluff, then back towards Alice Springs via the old Hermannsburg Mission, a possible short detour is to spectacular **Palm Valley▶**.

In the MacDonnells east of Alice Springs, **Emily and Jessie Gaps Nature Park▶** has semi-permanent waterholes and Aboriginal paintings, while in **Trephina Gorge Nature Park▶▶** the pale stems of splendid ghost gums stand out starkly against the rugged cliffs. High above **John Hayes Rockhole▶** is what must be one of the finest views in the whole of Central Australia. **Ross River**, where there is a resort, makes a good base for further exploration, to **Arltunga Historical Reserve** for example.

▶   **Mataranka**   *176D2*

Just off the Stuart Highway, 60 miles southeast of Katherine, is the Mataranka Homestead and the nearby thermal pool, a popular stop-off. Every minute, 4,500 gallons of water at a constant temperature of 93°F gush into a crystal-clear waterhole fringed by palm trees.

▶▶▶   **Mount Olga/Kata Tjuta**   *176A1*

See pages 187 and 190.

▶   **Pine Creek**   *176E1*

Ah Toy's store in this tiny Stuart Highway township is a reminder of the gold-rush days of the 1870s, when the Chinese population outnumbered Europeans 15 to 1. The old times are recalled in the **Pine Creek Miners' Park**.

▶   **Tennant Creek**   *176C2*

Legend has it that Tennant Creek came into existence in the 1930s when the axle broke on a wagon carting beer and building materials for a new hotel farther north. Moving on seemed too much bother, so once the beer had been drunk the building was put up here. Then gold was found and Tennant Creek became one of the roughest places along the track. Relatively calm now, the town has plenty of amenities for the passer-by.

Not a mirage

Camels may have become a tourist curiosity in today's Australia, but right up to the 1930s these tough beasts played an indispensable part in opening up the center of the continent. Explorers, surveyors, miners and pastoralists all used camel trains to transport food, equipment, building materials, barbed wire and metal ores. Their equally tough attendants all acquired the epithet "Afghan," though many of them were from India. Turned loose when trucks, jeeps and planes took over their work, the camels adapted easily to the wild and today are numbered in the thousands. In captivity, they are successfully bred for export to Arabia, as well as giving many visitors the thrill of a humpback ride. The Frontier Camel Farm 3¾ miles south of Alice Springs is one of the best known of such establishments.

Idyllic Green Island

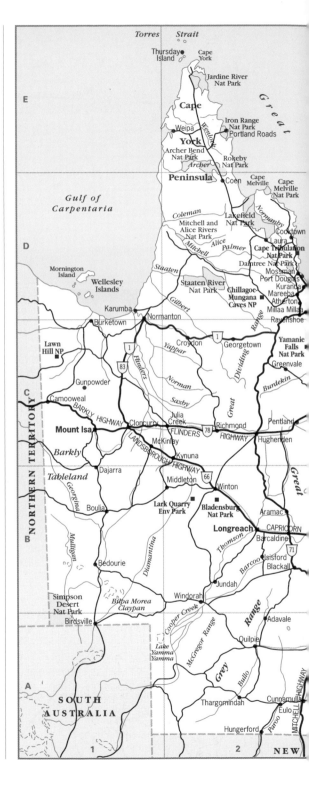

Torres Strait

Thursday Island   Cape York

Jardine River Nat Park

E

Great

Cape

Weipa   Iron Range Nat Park
Portland Roads

York

Archer Bend Nat Park   Rokeby Nat Park

Archer

Coen   Cape Melville

Cape Melville Nat Park

Peninsula

Gulf of Carpentaria

Coleman

Lakefield Nat Park

Mitchell and Alice Rivers Nat Park   *Mitchell*   *Palmer*   *Alice*

Cooktown

Laura   Cape Tribulation Nat Park

Daintree Nat Park
Mossman
Port Douglas

D

Mornington Island

Staaten

Staaten River Nat Park

Chillagoe Mungana Caves NP   Kuranda
Mareeba
Atherton
Millaa Millaa

Wellesley Islands

Gilbert

Karumba

Burketown   Normanton

Ravenshoe

Range

Croydon   Georgetown   **Yamanie Falls Nat Park**

1

Lawn Hill NP   *Yappar*   Greenvale

C   **1**

Flinders   *Norman*   *Great*   *Burdekin*

Gunpowder   *Saxby*

Camooweal

BARKLY HIGHWAY   Cloncurry   Julia Creek   Richmond   **78**   Pentland

Mount Isa   *FLINDERS*   **HIGHWAY**   Hughenden

Dividing

McKinlay

LANDSBOROUGH   *HIGHWAY*

Barkly   Kynuna

Tableland   Dajarra   Middleton   **66**

Georgina   Winton   *Great*

Boulia   Lark Quarry Env Park   Bladensburg Nat Park   Aramac

B   **Longreach**   **CAPICORN**

Mulligan   *Thomson*   Barcaldine

Diamantina   *Barcoo*   Isisford
Blackall   **71**

Bedourie   Jundah

Simpson Desert Nat Park   Windorah

Bilpa Morea Claypan   *Cooper Creek*   *McGregor Range*   Adavale

Birdsville   *Range*

Lake Yamma Yamma   Quilpie

Grey   *Bullo*

A

SOUTH AUSTRALIA   Thargomindah   Cunnamulla

Hungerford   *Paroo*   Eulo

MITCHELL HIGHWAY

1   **2**   **NEW**

NORTHERN TERRITORY

(PNG)

| 0 | 100 | 200 | 300 | 400 km |
| 0 | 50 | 100 | 150 | 200 | 250 miles |

Cairns
Babinda
1612m
Innisfail
Mission Beach
Tully
Hinchinbrook Island
Ingham
Mt Spec Nat Park
Townsville
Barrier
Ayr
1834m
Cape Upstart Nat Park
Charters Towers
Bowen
Proserpine
Conway Nat Park
Collinsville
Whitsunday Group
Cape Hillsborough Nat Park
Eungella Nat Park
Mackay
Sarina
Moranbah
Belyando
Denham Range
BRUCE
Clermont
Dysart
Capella
Reef
Emerald
HIGHWAY
Blackwater
Rockhampton
Alpha
Three Moon
Springsure
Yeppoon
Drummond Range
Moura
Gladstone
Tambo
Carnarvon Nat Park
55
Biloela
Range
Monto
Bundaberg
Carnarvon Gorge
Robinson Gorge Nat Park
Dawson
Taroom
Hervey Bay
Great Sandy Nat Park
Augathella
Maranoa
Burnett
Childers
Fraser Island
Warrego
Dividing
Range
HIGHWAY
Auburn
Maryborough
71
Mitchell
Roma
Miles
17
Cooloola Nat Park
Charleville
Condamine
Bunya Mts Nat Park
Kingaroy
Gympie
Noosa
Nambour
Sunshine Coast
Wyandra
Surat
Dalby
Glass House Mts
Moreton Island NP
39
Toowoomba
Darling
Cunningham's Gap
Blue Lake NP
Bollon
St George
Downs
BRISBANE
Tamborine Mt NP
Gold Coast
Dirranbandi
Goondiwindi
Warwick
Surfers Paradise
Mungindi
Macintyre
Stanthorpe
Lamington Nat Park
SOUTH   WALES

NEXT 20 km

Sugar cane
One of the spectacles of Queensland is the fires that rage through the cane plantations in winter near towns such as Mossman (43 miles from Cairns), when the dry stalks are burned off to get rid of debris, snakes and insects. At other times the tall green crop presents a peaceful sight, often combined on the coastal plain with tropical fruits like pineapples, mangoes, paw-paws and guavas. Sugar production goes back to the mid-19th century, when South Sea Islanders were brought in in large numbers as indentured laborers (called "Kanakas"). Many of Queensland's sugar mills can now be visited.

Queensland Second only to Western Australia in area, the Sunshine State straddles the Tropic of Capricorn between the New South Wales border and the Torres Strait separating Australia from Papua New Guinea. The immensely long and fertile coastline, with its succession of incomparable beaches and island paradises, is mostly within sight of the hills and mountains of the **Great Dividing Range**. To the east, across the transparent waters of a broad lagoon, is the **Great Barrier Reef**, the largest structure in the world to have been built by living creatures. To the west, the subtropical rain forest covering the seaward slopes of the mountains gives way to plateau farmlands of gradually diminishing quality; here, where cattle stations sometimes provide the only names on the map, is some of the country's most authentic Outback, merging in the end with the sands, stones and spinifex of true desert. In the far north, the **Cape York Peninsula** remains one of the continent's strangest and most remote places.

Almost overendowed with natural beauty and a benign climate, Queensland has become a favorite destination with visitors from abroad as well as with Australians on vacation or in retirement. Together with a superabundance of mineral wealth, mined in such areas as **Mount Isa** (the world's largest city in terms of area), the growth of tourism has helped Queensland prosper when the economy of other states has languished. Agriculture maintains its importance; along the coastal plain it has created richly textured landscapes of tropical crops including sugar cane, which is delivered to the mill by a network of narrow-gauge agricultural railroads.

Convict roots Queensland's recent history began with the establishment of a convict settlement at Moreton Bay in 1824. This dumping ground for particularly recalcitrant offenders was soon transferred to an upriver site nearby, which was named Brisbane after the Governor of New South Wales at the time. In 1859 independence from New South Wales was granted, and the new colony was given its name in honor of Queen Victoria.

The population increased and settlement spread; timber workers took the best trees from the rain forest, leaving farmers to clear the resulting scrub. Gold and other mineral finds helped open up the country; Queensland's richest goldfield was the remote and disease-ridden Palmer River, scene of a rush in the 1870s. Immigrant labor has played a relatively minor role in Queensland's history, but at one point the gold-digging Chinese on the Palmer outnumbered the rest of the Far North's population. Tradition has it that the local Aborigines killed and ate these Chinese with more relish than they did Europeans. Another immigrant group were the Kanakas, shipped in in their thousands from the South Pacific and New Guinea to work in the canefields (see panel).

A high proportion of Australia's Aborigines lived in Queensland, perhaps more than 200,000 at the beginning of white settlement. Of a fiercer and more warlike disposition than their fellows elsewhere, they put up a spirited resistance to their dispossession. To little avail, however; by the turn of the century their numbers had been reduced to no more than 15,000.

Politics and people For a generation, Queensland was governed by the National Party, led from 1968 by the robust peanut farmer Sir Jo Bjelke-Petersen, a sworn opponent of moral permissiveness, conservation or anything that stood in the way of "development." Under his authoritarian rule, demonstrations were banned, books censored, homosexuals harrassed and protected buildings demolished. Building speculators prospered and foreign capital was encouraged to share in the state's wealth, with few strings attached or questions asked. Sir Joh's demise came with revelations of police misconduct and corruption.

The typical Queenslander is popularly supposed to be the most Australian of Australians. A manly frontier mentality lasted longer here than in the southern states; the metropolitan refinements of Sydney and Melbourne were looked down on, as were women, natives and "culture." Until quite recently, Brisbane took a positive pride in its decidedly provincial character. Much of this has now changed, but enough remains to make the state quite distinct.

View from the Cairns—Kuranda train

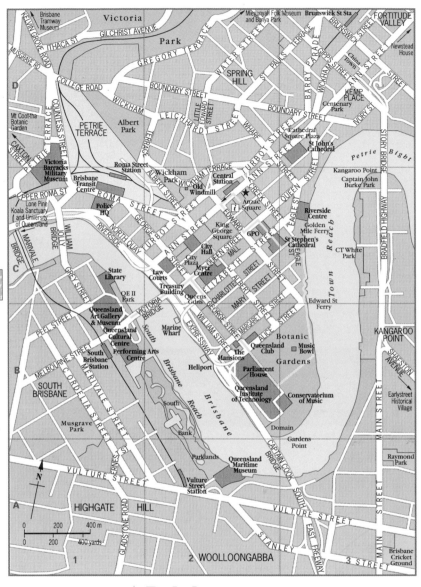

Brisbane

Australia's third largest city stands on the banks of the winding Brisbane River just inland from Moreton Bay. For long it was regarded as a provincial backwater, a kind of agricultural town that as recently as 1961 had hundreds of miles of unpaved streets. Perhaps in order to combat this image, Brisbane has recently embraced the idea of progress with an enthusiasm that some people find altogether regrettable.

Old-town sights Not all traces of an older charm have been erased in a misguided pursuit of modernity, however, and enough older buildings remain to tantalize the visitor with thoughts of the stylish tropical metropolis Brisbane perhaps never was but might have become. One such example is the corner of George and Alice Streets where the **Botanic Gardens** help frame the white stuccoed fronts of the **Queensland Club** and **Old Parliament House**. A more positive face of modernization than the new high-rise parliamentary annex can be seen on the south bank of the river at South Bank Parklands. **Expo 88** was held here, leaving behind a legacy of parkland and a number of cultural and recreational buildings of the very highest standard.

Suburban splendor The suburbs are perhaps the best places in which to savor the city's special quality. Spread over a vast and largely hilly area, they consist almost entirely of single-family houses, and in areas like Red Hill, Paddington and Bardon, the Queensland stilt house can be studied in all its variety.

City center orientation Brisbane's city center is surprisingly small and easily explored on foot, although a nice idea is to take the replica tram that wanders around most of the sights, allowing you to jump on and off whenever you wish for a flat fare. A boat cruise to **Newstead House** makes a pleasant excursion, too, while ferries link a number of destinations along the river bank.

The handsome 1868 Parliament House has been carefully restored to its former glory

---

 **Brisbane's buildings and Botanic Gardens**

See map opposite.

Allow a half-day for this long exploration of the peninsula on which the city of Brisbane is built.

Extending almost an entire city block, the **Central Railway Station** of 1901 faces **Anzac Square** with its **Shrine of Remembrance**. At the corner of Ann and Edward Streets stands the extraordinary **People's Palace** with its elaborate verandas and cast-iron balustrades. The **General Post Office** is an imposing building, and the G.P.O. arcade leads to Elizabeth Street, to **Old St. Stephen's Church** and to **St. Stephen's Cathedral** near the waterfront.

The riverside walk extends beyond the Edward Street gates of the **Botanic Gardens**, and the **Institute of Technology** flanks the gardens.

An intimation of the tropical paradise Brisbane might have been is given by the lovely building of the **Queensland Club** in its impeccably gardened setting. Opposite are **The Mansions**, a striking group of row houses in red brick and pale limestone, now housing stores and restaurants of the more refined type. Just off Queens Gardens in William Street are the **Commissariat Stores**, built in 1829 and one of only two convict-era buildings remaining intact in the city.

On the far side of Victoria Bridge are the modern buildings of the **Queensland Cultural Centre** and the **South Bank Parklands**. A visit here could easily last a whole day, though a quick tour could be made using the B.C.C. ferry to return to the city center.

Queen Street Mall is more commercial, though there are some fine late 19th-century and interwar buildings. The walk ends in **King George Square**, dominated by the tall tower of **City Hall**.

Parks and gardens
Brisbane is extremely fortunate in the number of green spaces in its center and immediate environs. The **Brisbane Forest Park** comprises 102 square miles of forests, hills and reservoirs, while the **Botanic Gardens** occupy the tip of the peninsula formed by the great bend in the Brisbane River. There is a riverside walk, and the gardens form an ideal setting for the buildings of the Queensland Institute of Technology, among them the Old Government House of 1860. At the foot of **Mount Coot-tha** (751 feet) there are more splendid botanic gardens. This is one of the best places in Australia to enjoy native plants, and there are stunning tropical greenhouses and a planetarium.

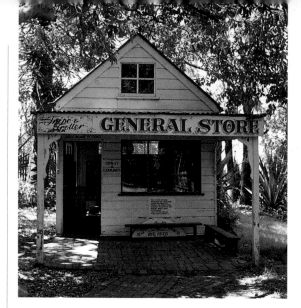

One of Earlystreet's authentic exhibits

▶   **City Hall**   *204C2*
King George Square
In the late 1920s, a determined attempt was made to overcome Brisbane's provincial image by the erection of this colossal edifice, whose 299-foot tower shoots up behind the array of columns facing King George Square. The gallery at the top offers a view of the city center. Inside, there is an art gallery and museum, with plenty of exhibits celebrating the city's importance.

▶   **Earlystreet Historical Village**   *204B3*
McIlwraith Avenue, Norman Park
This open-air museum to the east of the city center offers a chance to see some of Queensland's characteristic architecture. A number of buildings from all over the state have been rescued from demolition and re-erected here.

▶   **Miegunyah Folk Museum**   *204D2*
Jordan Terrace, Bowen Hills
Housed in a fine example of a stilt house dating from 1886, this museum takes as its theme the life led by women in colonial times.

▶   **Newstead House**   *204D3*
Breakfast Creek Road, Newstead
Built in 1846, this white mansion (2½ miles north of the center) with its elegant verandas is the oldest surviving house in Brisbane. Now a museum of colonial days, it was once owned by Captain John Wickham, commander of the *Beagle* during its survey of Australia's coastline, who made Newstead the center of the city's social life.

▶   **Old Windmill**   *204C2*
Wickham Terrace
This is Brisbane's oldest structure, overlooking the city from the pleasant heights of Wickham Terrace. What if its sails failed to work? No worries! Put in a treadmill! Plenty

of convict feet to keep it turning, and more reliable, too! It was later used as an observatory.

▶▶ Queensland Cultural Centre 204B1
Melbourne Street

"Culture" seems to have been something that Brisbane was content to leave for many years to the fancy folk down in Sydney. But times change and, once having decided that it was a good thing after all, Brisbane set about accommodating culture in as lavish a way as possible. The result is the impressive complex of buildings on the south bank spanning the area at the far end of the Victoria Bridge. Completed in 1985, it includes the Queensland Art Gallery, Queensland Museum, State Library and Performing Arts Complex, the latter with a 2,000-seat theater and an equally large concert hall.

The **Queensland Art Gallery**▶▶ has a good selection of Australian art, and a beginner's collection of European painting, some of it interestingly arranged by theme rather than by artist or country. But the pictures have little chance of competing with the architecture, which is on a huge scale and very concrete.

The exhibits in the **Queensland Museum**▶▶, particularly the dinosaurs and the aircraft, are more of a match for their surroundings and there is a major display on the history, art and culture of the Aborigines.

▶ South Bank Parklands 204B2

Once the international crowds have gone, Expo sites often become forlorn places. But many of the pavilions and facilities erected for Brisbane's 1988 bonanza are still here, bringing life to this extensive area of parkland stretching along the river across from the city center. Its **Gondwana Rainforest Sanctuary**▶ is an ambitious and imaginative re-creation of the Queensland jungle.

Modern Brisbane is Australia's third largest city

Koala capital
Brisbane styles itself the "koala capital," and the Bunya Park Wildlife Sanctuary and Lone Pine Koala Sanctuary are both good places to see these friendly marsupials.

207

Glass House Mountains scenery

208

Drive

The Sunshine Coast and hinterland

This full day's drive along Queensland's Sunshine Coast goes into the hinterland of farming and hill country along the Bruce Highway.

About 37 miles north of Brisbane, the **Glass House Mountains** interrupt the monotony of the coastal plain. These old volcanic hills are best viewed from the old main road north of Caboolture as well as from the Mary Cairncross Park near Maleny. The **Blackall Range** panoramic drive gives access to this superb upland country of undulating hills and verdant valleys, tea shops and craft studios. Just north of the little highland resort of Montville is the **Kondalilla National Park**, where splendid 330-foot waterfalls crash down through the rainforest. Equally spectacular falls can be experienced at **Mapleton Falls National Park**.

In **Nambour**, a center of tropical fruit production, a narrow-gauge sugar-cane train trundles nonchalantly through the streets. A sequence of splendid beaches unravels along the Sunshine Coast north of Coolum to the multicentered and highly fashionable community of Noosa Heads,

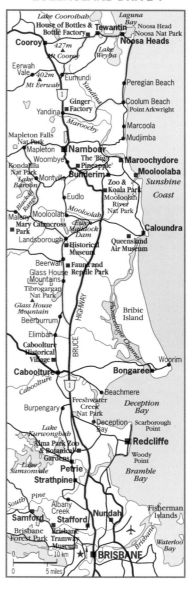

QUEENSLAND DRIVE 1

while **Tewantin** boasts a couple of curiosities—a house built of bottles and the Big Shell. Back inland, the charming village of **Eumundi** makes a good stopping place, though it will be packed if you visit on market day (Saturday).

The Bruce Highway is the best route for a swift return to Brisbane.

As may be expected in a state of its vast size, Queensland has an extraordinary variety of landscapes, many of them protected by designation as national or environmental parks.

Tropical coastline to desert heartlands Most visitors will become familiar with the reef and rain forest parks of the tropical and subtropical coastline, but the spectacular and often unique parks of the interior demand attention too. More than 745 miles to the west of the coast are the monotonous sandhills of the **Simpson Desert**, "stretching interminably like waves of the sea" according to the explorer Charles Sturt, who gave up his attempt to conquer them. Only crossed on foot in 1973, they still offer a challenge to anyone venturing into them today.

Further east, the sparse vegetation of the desert gives way to country characterized by grasslands, wattle scrub, eucalyptus woodland, or by scattered individuals of the strange Queensland bottle tree. Among the spinifex and rugged hills of the **Lark Quarry Environmental Park**, the footprints of dinosaurs that perished in a stampede 100 million years ago are preserved in mud that has long since turned to rock.

Further east still, a broad belt of sandstone gives rise to spectacular scenery. This is where many of Queensland's major rivers have their origin; their erosive action has formed deep gorges in which a rich flora thrives, including the cabbage palms of **Carnarvon National Park**, also well known for its strange rock formations. As the land rises and rainfall increases, the blue-green of eucalypts gives way to the dark green of tropical rain forest, with its incredible wealth of species including ferns, climbers and other epiphytes. In parts of far north Queensland the rainforest descends to the beaches fringing the Great Barrier Reef, whose cays and islands are now preserved as part of the **Great Barrier Reef Marine Park**.

Wild north to friendly south Cape York has some of the finest but least accessible of Queensland's national parks, where nature displays herself in all her savage unpredictability. In the wet season, rivers fill with fierce-flowing, silt-rich water, closing fords and cutting communications for weeks on end, only to dry up into a series of isolated pools when the rain has stopped. Strange termite mounds stud the inland landscape, while mangrove swamps grow from the mud of the coastal plain. In the southeast of the state, nature wears a kindlier air. Brisbane must be one of the world's best endowed capital cities in terms of grand scenery within easy reach; a crescent of gloriously wooded highlands extends from close to the city boundary to **Lamington National Park** on the New South Wales boundary.

Keep an eye out for the beautiful crimson rosella

Brisbane's Lone Pine Koala Sanctuary is the state's best-known animal park

209

In the south
Near the market center of Warwick, at Cunningham's Gap in the Main Range National Park, there are fine views and a number of trails through rain forest and eucalyptus woodland.

How to travel

The Pacific Highway to the south of Brisbane runs through eucalyptus country

A Queensland highland line
Half a million people travel the Cairns–Kuranda railroad line every year. Few are disappointed by the spectacular 21-mile ride from coast to mountain rainforest. The long train of period cars climbs from sea level to a summit at 1,076 feet via a series of tunnels and sharp bends, stopping for a breather at the spectacularly tall Barron Falls. The railroad was built in 1886–91 to link the Atherton Tableland with the port at Cairns; it immediately put an end to Port Douglas as a harbor of any significance. The terminus at Kuranda, planted with palms and shady with ferns, would win any international best-kept station award.

By air Uniquely among Australian states, Queensland has three international airports—Brisbane, Townsville and Cairns—all with regular connections to many overseas airports. A variety of airlines links cities elsewhere in Australia with many places in Queensland, for example with the airports serving the Gold Coast (Coolangatta) and Sunshine Coast (Maroochydore). Given the large size of the state, internal travel by air is well developed, and may sometimes be the only way of reaching remote northern destinations during the wet season. Smaller aircraft, including helicopters and seaplanes, spin a web of services spanning mainland and islands; some islands can only be reached in this way.

By water Visitors are bound to find themselves afloat at some point in their Queensland holiday, even if it is only for a day trip to part of the Great Barrier Reef aboard a high-speed wave piercer or a more humble craft hired locally. Most, but not all, of the islands are accessible by ferry or launch, which also carry vehicles if there are roads on your destination island. For short stays it may make sense to leave your car on the mainland. The best way of getting the feel of reef and islands might be to cruise; there are any number of operators competing for your business, some with liner-like vessels calling at luxury resorts, others offering a more adventurous experience involving camping on uninhabited islands. Do not forget a trip up the Brisbane River.

By bus Bus services link Brisbane with other Australian cities as well as with major destinations within Queensland. Local services are variable, though quite well developed on the Gold Coast.

By rail Queensland has the longest rail network in the country, with several well-promoted tourist services. These rail lines include: the luxury **Queenslander** (weekly Brisbane–Cairns); the **Sunlander** (more frequently Brisbane–Cairns); the **Inlander** (Townsville–Mount Isa); the **Spirit of the Outback** (Brisbane–Longreach via Rockhampton); the **Westlander** (Brisbane–Charleville), and the **Spirit of Capricorn** (Brisbane–Rockhampton). Australia's most popular tourist train labors up from Cairns to Kuranda (see panel), and there are two rail curiosities to attract the adventurous: the weekly run from Cairns to Forsayth in the deep interior, and the strange **Gulflander** running on an isolated section of line near the Gulf of Carpentaria. The only interstate rail link is with Sydney.

By car The road system in the densely populated coastal strip is well developed, and paved surface now reaches east–west across Queensland and into the Northern Territory via Mount Isa, but many places in the state are only accessible on unpaved roads. Cape York and other far northern places may be cut off in the wet season when fords become impassable and roads are swept away. Your own car or 4WD will be an almost indispensable asset if you want to visit many national parks, though with patience some sort of guided tour can be found for almost any destination.

► **Atherton Tableland** 200D2

From Cairns south for over 90 miles to near Innisfail, high tablelands rise steeply from the coastal plain. There are remnants of the once dense rainforest, but the area's rich volcanic soils now mostly support tobacco, maize and a whole range of exotic fruits. Southeast of Atherton on the Gillies Highway is **Yungaburra**►►, with extinct volcanoes and crater lakes.

►►► **Cairns** 201D3

Stretched out in the subtropical sun, Cairns, the key to far north Queensland, breathes in the balmy air of Trinity Bay as if there was no tomorrow. It helped open up the goldfields and tin mines of the interior, then became a major outlet for the booming agriculture of the area, particularly for sugar cane. But tomorrow seems to promise even more expansive times; because of the proximity of the Barrier Reef, superb beaches and the rivers and forests of the Daintree and the Atherton Tableland, tourism flourishes. Cairns International Airport, only relatively recently opened, is already fifth among Australian ports of entry in the amount of traffic it handles.

The town's founders laid out a generous grid of streets, whose width and relative absence of traffic contribute to the relaxed atmosphere. A walk at sunset along the broad Esplanade facing the bay, with its abundant birdlife, is an unforgettable experience. The waterfront complex housing boutiques, shops and a luxury hotel adds a sophisticated note, as do the ocean-going vessels of the super-rich in the adjacent marina.

Cairns Museum and Art Gallery► gives a fascinating insight into a colorful past populated by Aborigines, railroad workers, goldminers and Chinese laborers. For a different experience, journey just outside town to the **Flecker Botanic Gardens**►, with more than 200 varieties of palm trees and the tranquil Centenary Lakes.

The Esplanade and pier at sunny Cairns

Rum Bundaberg
The name of this substantial town about 185 miles north of Brisbane at the end of Hervey Bay is synonymous with its principal product—rum, distilled from the canefields of the coastal plain. Bundaberg is also the main gateway to the southern Barrier Reef. Mon Repos Environmental Park, a beach to the north, is a spot favored by turtles during their egg-laying season (November—February).

Birds and beaches
The wildfowl enjoying the muddy flats of Trinity Bay have won their battle against proposals to turn the flats into an artificial beach, but swimmers and sun-worshipers are more than well provided for in the string of beaches stretching along the 16-mile "Marlin Coast" to the north, each of them more paradisical than the last.

211

Drive The Daintree and Cape Tribulation

If you can resist the temptation of the glorious beaches along the way, this full day's drive will take you over the Daintree River to tropical rain forest and coral reef.

The **Captain Cook Highway** is without doubt one of the world's finest coastal roads. Rarely overburdened with traffic, it runs inland at first from Cairns, rejoining the shore north of the exclusive resort of Palm Cove. **Port Douglas**, the coastline's northernmost resort of any consequence, is home to the **Rainforest Habitat**, an ambitious re-creation of the tropical rain forest environment.

The canefields around **Mossman** feed the town's sugar mill via miles of narrow-gauge railroad. A short detour leads to the rain forest of the Mossman River Gorge in **Daintree National Park**, with its graded walking track, rapids and delightful swimming holes. At the turn leading to the ferry over the Daintree River the pavement comes to a (temporary) end; non-4WD vehicles proceed with caution or not at all in the wet season. The wide river is lined with mangrove swamp and crocodiles.

Beyond the ferry begins the tropical paradise of the **Cape Tribulation**

The goanna, or monitor lizard

National Park, some of it, incredibly, divided up into lots for sale and development. The unpaved road lurches crazily through the forest and across dry river beds, pale dust from vehicles coating the luxuriant vegetation with a thin film. The **Heights of Alexandra Lookout** gives a superb view over the forest tumbling down to the sea. The best initiation into the complex ecology and sheer beauty of the World Heritage Area is at the **Daintree Forest Environmental Centre** with its boardwalk leading deep into this mysterious realm.

Even if noxious stingers inhibit swimming, you should at least walk along one of the incomparable beaches of **Cape Tribulation**, several of which are easily accessible from the road. Beyond the cape itself, the 20-mile Bloomfield Track begins; it is only negotiable by 4WD.

QUEENSLAND DRIVE 2

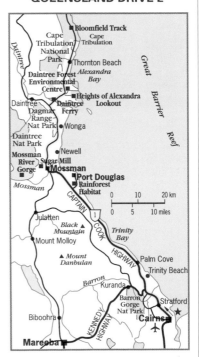

The bottle brush is native to Queensland

►► Cape York Peninsula   200E2

Often described as one of the world's last wildernesses, the great peninsula tapers northward for hundreds of miles to its tip at Cape York itself, overlooking the island-studded Torres Straits separating Australia from Papua New Guinea. A total of perhaps 10,000 people are thinly distributed over this vast area, most of them Aborigines whose ancestors left a legacy of remarkable rock painting, best seen around **Laura**. This little township straddles the lower end of the Peninsula Developmental Road, a less developed highway than its name implies, especially in the Wet when river crossings become impassable even for the most rugged of 4WDs.

In the Dry, the Cape becomes a fascinating destination for the more adventurous type of tourist. The rain forest along the Pacific coast gives way to savannah-like country farther inland, punctuated by the surreal turrets of termite mounds, some of them reaching an extraordinary 20 feet. The future of the peninsula probably lies in wilderness tourism; civilization's other activities, apart from bauxite mining at Weipa, have left little mark on the land.

►► Carnarvon National Park   201B3

Much of this spectacular park is difficult to get to, but the extraordinary gorges cut by the Carnarvon Creek and its tributaries into the soft sandstone of the plateau can be reached from the Carnarvon Development Road between Roma and Rolleston. Here 650-foot high cliffs tower over cabbage palms, ferns, mosses and orchids, a shady world quite different from the exposed plateau far above with its open eucalyptus woodland. A number of caves shelter mysterious and evocative Aboriginal rock paintings. A 6¼-mile footpath leads up the gorge from the ranger station, with side tracks giving access to all the park's delights.

► Charters Towers   201C3

In contrast to the sweltering heat at Townsville, 84 miles away, this modest-sized upland town enjoys an invigorating climate. It is a favored spot for boarding schools and has some of the best early Australian architecture to be seen anywhere (see panel).

Ancient home
Mount Moffat in Carnarvon National Park has strange sandstone formations as well as Kenniff Cave, lived in by Aboriginal people nearly 20,000 years ago and containing Aboriginal rock paintings.

213

Upland architecture
Following the discovery of gold in 1872 at Charters Towers, the town fitted itself out with some fine buildings. Some of these can still be seen today, including banks, the stock exchange, the School of Mines, the city hall and the courthouse.

If doctors could fly
Set up in 1927–8 by the Reverend John Flynn, the Royal Flying Doctor Service (R.F.D.S.) began operations in Cloncurry with a plane supplied by the Queensland and Northern Territory Aerial Service (QANTAS). The event is recalled in a memorial to Flynn, its missionary founder, and in the R.F.D.S. Museum in Cloncurry.

Saving the wilderness
Destruction of the Daintree by volcanic explosions and lava flows may have been avoided in the remote geological past; more recent threats have involved the dividing of the rain forest into handy packages for "development" and the construction of the controversial Bloomfield Track. World Heritage designation may have come just in time to save this irreplaceable tract of wild nature.

▶ **Chillagoe–Mungana Caves National Park** *200D2*

Around the old mining township of Chillagoe are extensive and spectacular caves eroded in the local limestone by the headwaters of the Mitchell River. Not all are accessible, but the Donna and Trezkinn caves are artificially lit to enhance the drama and strangeness of the limestone formations. On the surface, the same rock has been weathered into equally peculiar shapes—turrets, pinnacles and forms resembling animals.

▶ **Cloncurry** *200C1*

Once a bustling gold and copper town, Cloncurry sits astride the main road and railroad line from Mount Isa to the coast, earning its living nowadays from sheep and cattle grazing. It was here in 1928 that the Royal Flying Doctor Service began operating (see panel).

▶ **Cooktown** *200D2*

A late 19th-century boomtown in the rip-roaring days of gold strikes on the Palmer River, Cooktown was named for Captain James Cook. The great navigator beached the *Endeavour* here after she had been badly holed on the Barrier Reef. Though the peak population of 30,000 or more has shrunk to less than 1,000, enough traces of the past remain to make Cooktown an attractive tourist destination. The Captain's enforced stay is recalled in the Victorian villa housing the **Historical Museum,** as well as by his statue and by the annual reenactment in June of his landing. Cooktown is easily reached from Cairns by the inland road or, more picturesquely, by the mostly unpaved Cape Tribulation coast road. The town is also a useful base for expeditions into the Cape York interior.

▶▶▶ **Daintree National Park** *200D2*

The outstanding international significance of the Queensland rain forest has been recognized by the designation of the Daintree and Cape Tribulation area as a World Heritage Area. A relic of Cretaceous times over 100 million years ago, the jungle of far north Queensland escaped the volcanic eruptions that destroyed other primitive forests in the region, and consequently has a unique ecological value.

The tiny settlement of Daintree is located on the banks of the Daintree River, famous for its mangroves and crocodiles. The rain forest is penetrable only by the most experienced of bushwalkers; the best place for novices to appreciate its wonders is at the **Daintree Forest Environmental Centre**▶▶.

▶▶ **Fraser Island** *201B4*

This is the largest sand island in the world, stretching 90 miles along the south Queensland coast and partly enclosing Hervey Bay. With wonderful beaches, some dunes rising to an extraordinary 790 feet, heathland, rain forest, mangroves and dozens of freshwater lakes, it attracts many visitors, though formal facilities are few and access is only by 4WD (there are no roads). Most visitors will want to travel past the wreck of the *Maheno* and cliffs of colored sandstone to the resort villages of Eurong Beach and Happy Valley.

Fraser Island is easily reached by ferry from a number of points on the mainland (Inskip Point, Urangan and River Heads), or by air.

▶ Glass House Mountains 201A4

Inland from the Bruce Highway north of Brisbane rises a group of steep and strangely shaped peaks, the cores of old volcanoes. Given their enigmatic name by Captain Cook, they are a favorite with climbers; the inexperienced can best view them from the Old Gympie Road or from Mary Cairncross Park.

▶▶▶ Gold Coast 201A4

Between Tweed Heads on the New South Wales border and Paradise Point in the north stretches a 25-mile chain of glorious sandy beaches blessed by regular rolling surf and basking in equally regular sunshine. Everyone is catered to here. Swimming, surfing and sunbathing all have their place, but so do many other activities. There are any number of theme parks and similar establishments, among them the incredibly successful **Sea World** at Main Beach, smoothly entertaining its tidal wave of visitors.

Surfers Paradise, with its lavish malls, Cascade Gardens and Jupiters Casino, is where the full flavor of this seaside Arcadia can be relished. A somewhat quieter (and cheaper) ambience can be enjoyed to the south, around Currumbin or at wooded Burleigh Heads, where a discreet national park visitor center introduces what is left of the coast's natural environment.

High-rise buildings loom over Surfers Paradise

Unplanned Utopia
The sprawling Gold Coast is a textbook example of how not to plan an urban environment. The approach from Brisbane, an hour away, is reminiscent of the outskirts of Moscow, save that the high-rise buildings are more varied in shape and decorated in tasteful pastel shades. They jostle each other for a glimpse of the beach, which, because it is to the east and they are too close, is plunged into shade in the course of the afternoon. Through the wire fencing festooning the main highway an array of signs, each more lurid than the last, calls for your business; Charcoal Chicken competes with Korean Cooking, Cocktail Academy with Coastal Chiropracters, and Jesus is The Answer with the Drive-Thru Bottle Shop.

The reef, often called the eighth wonder of the world, is Australia's greatest tourist attraction, stretching for more than 1,240 miles along the east coast from the Gulf of Papua to a point near Gladstone.

Reef fish
The Reef is home to thousands of species of fish, from the greedy potato cod (see picture below), to colorful parrot fish, graceful rays and poisonous lion fish. It also harbors many types of shark—attacks are rare, however, and they will probably be more scared of you than you are of them!

Giant potato cod expect to be fed and stroked at Cod Hole, 12 miles off Lizard Island and one of the world's best diving sites

The coral of the reef's outer rim forms a steep submarine escarpment, dropping abruptly into the abyss of the Pacific; only some 19 miles out from Cairns, this Outer Reef gradually extends farther away from the mainland until, opposite Mackay, it is some 160 miles off shore. To landward is warm and shallow water forming a kind of lagoon broken up by more reefs and hundreds of islands, some of them true coral cays, most of them detached fragments of the mainland, separated from it when sea levels rose. They vary enormously in character, from exposed and unvegetated cays of sand and coral barely rising out of the water at low tide, to reef-fringed mountain ranges covered in splendid rain forest.

Creatures of the deep Hardly another ecosystem on earth can surpass the reef for sheer beauty or variety. Responsible for its formation are humble polyps, tiny organisms with limestone outer skeletons that form a coral reef's basic building blocks. With wildly differing shapes recalling trees, plates, fungi and even brains, the still living polyps paint the underwater scene with vivid color, to which is added a kaleidoscope of other living creatures. These include not only tropical fish of brilliant hue and intriguing personality, but also sponges, starfish, crabs, sharks, turtles, giant clams and an occasional dugong, a large and harmless creature also known as the sea-cow.

Another creature drawn to this watery paradise in large numbers is *Homo sapiens*, tourist variety. This medium-

The Reef is a great place to learn how to snorkel

sized, sometimes amphibious mammal can be observed gazing at the wonders of the reef from aircraft, wave piercers and vessels of all kinds, including flat-bottomed boats and semi-submersibles, or socializing with its other inhabitants while wearing a snorkel or wetsuit. Large numbers stay on the mainland, venturing out onto the Reef on day trips; others stay on the islands themselves, in exclusive resorts, and crowded hotels and apartments, or on uninhabited isles with no resources whatever.

Problems of conservation The reef is now a World Heritage Area, controlled and managed since 1976 by the Great Barrier Reef Marine Park Authority. Conservation problems arise not only through the influx of tourists and pressure from developers (who by 1989 had applied for permission to build no less than 250 new resorts along the Queensland coast), but because of agricultural and other pollutants washed into the sea from the rivers draining the interior. Exploratory drilling in the ocean may have been halted, but the petrochemical industry continues to keep a watchful eye on the reef's potential as an offshore oilfield.

A more immediate threat comes from a natural phenomenon. The crown-of-thorns starfish has a voracious appetite for the coral polyp, which it easily sucks out of its protective skeleton, and in recent years has devastated huge areas of coral. It is thought by some that overfishing of the starfish's natural predators may have caused its population to explode; scientists are at a loss for a cure.

Butterfly fish: one of the natives of the world's largest living organism

Great Barrier Reef map area

Flinders
Group
Cape Melville
Howick I
Lizard I
Laura
Cape Flattery
Cooktown
Cape Tribulation
Mossman
Port Douglas
Kuranda
Cairns
Green I
Fitzroy I
Gordonvale
1612m
Babinda
Innisfail
Tully
Mission Beach
Dunk I
Bedarra I
Cardwell
Hinchinbrook I
Orpheus I
Ingham
Great Palm I

Magnetic I
Townsville
Bowling Green Bay
Cape Bowling Green
1234m
Ayr
Upstart Bay
Cape Upstart
Bowen
Gloucester I
Hayman I
Shute Harbour
Hook I
Proserpine
Daydream I
South Molle
Whitsunday I
Hamilton I
Long I
Lindeman I
Repulse Is
Mackay
Carlisle I
Brampton I
Sarina
Northumberland Is

Percy Is
Broad Sound
Duke Is
St Lawrence
Marlborough

Yeppoon
Great Keppel I
Rockhampton
Curtis I
Gladstone
Biloela
Heron I
Rodds Bay
Miriam Vale
Lady Musgrave I
Monto
Lady Elliot I
Bundaberg
Hervey Bay
Fraser I
Maryborough

BRUCE HIGHWAY

100   200 km
0   50   100 miles

Great Barrier Reef

Blue semicircle angel fish seen around Heron Island

▶▶▶ **Great Barrier Reef**   *201C3*

The following information does not cover all the islands of the reef, but gives details of those that are more popular or accessible, dealing with them from south to north.

Southern Reef At the southernmost end of the reef, Lady Elliot Island▶▶ and uninhabited Lady Musgrave Island▶▶ are both small coral cays with excellent diving and snorkeling. The former is accessible by air from Bundaberg (50 miles) or Hervey Bay, while the latter, also with glass-bottomed boats and an underwater observatory, is accessible on a day trip by launch from Bundaberg (also 50 miles distant).

Heron Island▶▶ is part resort and part national park, famed for its teeming wildlife, with optimal diving and snorkeling, semi-submersibles and reef-walking. Access is by helicopter or launch from Gladstone (45 miles).

Large, wooded Great Keppel Island▶▶ is popular with young people and has glass-bottomed boats, a coral submarine, an underwater observatory, aqua-bikes and water-skiing, plus bush-walking and nightlife. It has some beautiful secluded beaches and is accessible by air from Rockhampton (35 miles) or by ferry from Rosslyn Bay.

Finally, Brampton Island▶▶ (part of the Cumberland group) is a favorite with honeymooners and other couples for its romantic setting. It has good facilities, including golf and walking tracks, and is accessible by air and launch from Mackay (20 miles).

Whitsunday Islands These hilly, wooded islands, usually fringed with reefs, once formed the tips of ancient mountains and lie scattered to either side of the Whitsunday Passage. Only seven of the 70-plus islands have been developed for tourism, the rest remaining uninhabited.

Numerous high-rise hotels and apartments characterize popular, medium-sized Hamilton Island▶▶. It has an international airport with flights from some southern Australian cities and Cairns; alternatively, access is by aircraft from Proserpine or Mackay, and by boat from Shute Harbour (10 miles).

Of the six other developed Whitsunday Islands, **Hayman Island** is luxurious and expensive, **Lindeman Island**, **South Molle** and **Daydream Island** cater to families, while **Hook Island** (with a splendid underwater observatory) and **Long Island** are casual and popular with the young. All offer day trips to the Outer Reef.

North Islands Large **Magnetic Island►►** (just off Townsville) has 1,640-foot granite hills, varied beaches and a shark aquarium. Access is by helicopter or ferry from Townsville (5½ miles) and the island has a bus service. Farther north, **Orpheus Island►►** is of volcanic origin and is densely wooded. It has fine beaches, exceptional coral and a biological research station. Access is by air or launch from Townsville (50 miles).

Largest and perhaps wildest of the Queensland islands, **Hinchinbrook Island►►** has peaks rising through rain forest to 3,746 feet. The Coastal Walk along the east coast takes experienced hikers several days to complete; access to the island is by launch from Cardwell or seaplane from Townsville (93 miles).

Medium-sized **Dunk Island►►** and smaller **Fitzroy Island►►** both have rain forest-clad hills. The former has wonderful beaches and rich wildlife, and is accessible by air from Townsville (100 miles) and Cairns (75 miles), and by launch from Clump Point. Fitzroy Island has excellent diving and snorkeling as well as superb views from its lighthouse, and is accessible by launch from Cairns (11 miles).

Green Island► can easily be reached from Cairns (17 miles) by boat and is therefore popular for a day trip. It has the reef's longest-established underwater observatory.

Northernmost of the resort islands, **Lizard Island►►** is sometimes called "the jewel of the Barrier Reef." Accessible by air from Cairns (150 miles), it has wonderful bays and fringing coral, and a superb view from Cook's Lookout.

Heron Island becomes a breeding ground for green and loggerhead turtles in October and November

Island accommodation
Basic and budget Lady Elliot Island (safari cabins and tents), Lady Musgrave Island (self-sufficient camping with permit from the National Parks and Wildlife Service), Great Keppel Island (youth resort and camping), Magnetic Island (backpackers' accommodation), Hinchinbrook Island (camping), Dunk Island (camping with permit) and Fitzroy Island (hostel).
Mid-range and moderate Great Keppel Island (resort and cabins), Brampton Island (resort), Hamilton Island (resorts), Magnetic Island (resorts), Hinchinbrook Island (resort), Dunk Island (resort) and Fitzroy Island (villas).
Exclusive and expensive Luxury resorts are located on Heron, Hayman, Orpheus, Bedarra and Lizard islands.

219

Innisfail 201D3

A useful gateway to far north Queensland with good access to the Barrier Reef and the Atherton Tableland, Innisfail is also well known as a sugar town. Cane was first planted in the 1880s, and the industry was boosted by a wave of Italian immigrants after World War II. Innisfail's Chinese community is of much longer standing; their joss-house (temple) is one of only two still in use in Australia.

▶▶ **Kuranda** 200D2

High up in the Atherton Tableland, this "village in the rain forest" is enormously popular with visitors, most of whom have taken the spectacular train ride up from Cairns. Kuranda is a full-blooded tourist paradise, with rides in amphibious ex-army "ducks" through the rain forest, a butterfly sanctuary, a noctarium, a huge open-air market, even bungee jumping—everything has been accommodated without damaging the town's character too much. Among all these attractions, one is unmissable: the Aboriginal troupe known as the Tjapukai Dance Theatre▶ puts on a daily show of great verve and seeming authenticity.

▶▶ **Lamington National Park** 201A4

In utter contrast to the glitz and concrete of the Gold Coast is its lush hinterland of upland farms and forests. Rising to 3,950 feet on the New South Wales border, the green mountains of Lamington National Park are remarkable for their superb stands of Antarctic beech trees, some of them thousands of years old. The forest, of which they form a part, is best experienced by braving the spectacular treetop walk near O'Reilly's Guesthouse. Between here and Binna Burra Lodge, the other main focal point of the park, there runs another famous walk, this one of 14 miles and with stupendous views out over the New South Wales border country.

Through the tropics by duck
Equally happy climbing a steep jungle track or crossing a turtle-thronged pool, the Kuranda ducks are really "D.U.K.W.s," the code name for a rugged amphibious vehicle developed for army use in World War II.

220

Lamington National Park, a birdwatcher's paradise

EMERALD
SURPRISE

QUEENSLAND KIWI FRUIT

ROUGH
AND READY

ROUGH LEAF PINEAPPLES

SUGAR MAKES
MANY FOODS MORE
ENJOYABLE TO EAT

A F
ST

Quite an experience – inside the "Big Pineapple"

▶ **Longreach** *200B2*

Far inland on the Capricorn Highway and railroad from Rockhampton, Longreach is the center for a vast pastoral area of the Outback. It was here that QANTAS made its base in the 1920s and here that Australia's first aircraft factory was established. Tourists come here now mostly to visit the splendid **Stockman's Hall of Fame▶▶**; opened for the Bicentenary in 1988, this large and lavish modern building houses every conceivable kind of display on Outback life.

▶ **Mackay** *201C3*

This city of nearly 40,000 people prides itself on its important sugar industry, shipping something like a third of Australia's total production from its deep-water harbor. But tourism is of growing significance, with good access to the adjacent Barrier Reef, mainland beaches and the wonderful **Eungella National Park▶▶** to the northwest. This tract of rain forest-covered upland ("land of the clouds" to the Aborigines) offers a cool contrast to the torrid coast, and has unusual—and sometimes unique—plants and animals, like the Eungella honeyeater. You may also catch sight of the normally elusive platypus.

▶ **Maryborough** *201A4*

Near the mouth of the Mary River, Maryborough serves a rich agricultural hinterland. Founded in 1843, it has a good number of surviving 19th-century buildings as well as parks and gardens of subtropical splendor.

▶ **Millaa Millaa** *200D2*

This tiny place is famous for the **Millaa Millaa Falls**, one of several picturesque waterfalls along the unpaved scenic route known as the Waterfall Circuit. West of the township is the **Millaa Millaa Lookout**, 3,608 feet up, with fantastic views over the Atherton Tableland.

Flamboyant fruit
One of Australia's most convincing examples of commercial kitsch is the "Big Pineapple." Almost 50 feet high, this fantastical fiberglass fruit cannot fail to catch your attention as you drive up the Bruce Highway inland from the Sunshine Coast. Advertising the attractions of an extensive pineapple plantation, it has become something of an unofficial emblem of the tropical fruit country centered on the town of Nambour, whose streets you must be prepared to share with the occasional cane train.

Greetings from
AUSTRA

Having been logged for its wood, cleared to make way for cane plantations, and threatened by roads, airports, reservoirs and tourist developments, Australia's magnificent rain forest is at last being recognized as a unique habitat, not only worthy of conservation for its own sake but also for its immense appeal to visitors who are enchanted by its exotic beauty.

Although it is both shy and rare, the cassowary is very powerful

222

Animal life
Rain forest is as abundant in animals as it is in plants. Some of the animals, like the tree kangaroo, the ringtail possum or the tiny musky rat kangaroo, are unique to this habitat. One endangered species is the cassowary, a flightless bird related to the emu, whose thuggish habits include a grunting cry, kicking to kill with its sharp toe, and an ability to head-butt its way through the densest undergrowth.

Subtropical rain forest in Bunya Mountains National Park

Remnants from the past Scattered along the east coast from Cape York to Tasmania, today's rain forest is a mere fragment of the ancient mosaic of vegetation that covered the whole of the continent millions of years ago. Rain forest flourishes in sheltered, moist conditions, and gradually perished as ancient Australia's climate became drier and drier. But splendid remnants still grace the surface of the land where the complex equation of rainfall, evaporation, soil and temperature balances out. The eastward-facing slopes of north Queensland's coastal mountains, for example, are sheltered by the high ridges of the Great Dividing Range from the parching winds of the interior and enjoy the benefit of moisture-rich onshore breezes. Here are the country's most luxuriant, and perhaps most spectacular rain forests.

Variety A variant, littoral rain forest occurs in unexpected locations close to the sea where sand dunes offer shelter from the scorching effects of salt spray, as on a number of Barrier Reef islands. Further south, into New South Wales and Victoria, the composition of the rain forest changes; its structure becomes simpler and there are fewer species. Nevertheless, the appearance is still one of great luxuriance, and a number of the New South Wales temperate and subtropical rain forests stretching from the Queensland border to the Newcastle area have been grouped together to form one of the country's World Heritage Areas. This type of forest merges imperceptibly with cool-temperate rain forest, characterized by the trees known as southern beech and Antarctic beech. These trees flourish in the cooler climate of Tasmania, although they can also be seen at high altitude in Queensland's **Lamington National Park**.

► Mission Beach 201C3

The fine beaches between Tully and Innisfail, known collectively as the Mission Beach area, stretch over 8 miles along the coast within sight of Dunk Island. Cassowaries frequent the nearby forest, and there is spectacular whitewater rafting on the upper reaches of the Tully River.

►► Noosa 201A4

Many-centered Noosa (Noosaville, Noosa Heads, Tewantin, and Sunshine Beach) at the northern tip of the Sunshine Coast 280 miles from Brisbane is the place to come if you crave sophistication but are repelled by the brazen style of the Gold Coast. It is the starting point for boat trips up the Noosa River and its lagoons or across the river into **Cooloola National Park►►**, where there is a 40-mile beach and the largest sand dune system in the world. Inland is the charming village of **Eumundi►** whose Saturday market is justly famous.

► Port Douglas 200D2

This little harbor town and resort 43 miles north of Cairns exudes a charm all its own, especially on a tropical evening when only the occasional car disturbs the calm of the broad streets, still lined with old colonial buildings. You can ride through the cane fields on the little Bally Hooley train or visit the fascinating **Rainforest Habitat**, and nearby is a Shipwreck Museum and a Gothic chapel with a view of the Pacific from behind the altar.

► Rockhampton 201B4

Australia's "Beef Capital" lies inland up the Fitzroy River astride the Tropic of Capricorn. A note of distinction is struck by the elegant late 19th-century buildings and tropical trees and shrubs; the Botanical Gardens are among the finest in the country. Nearby is the **Dreamtime Cultural Centre►**, with excellent displays on the life of Torres Strait Islanders as well as mainland Aborigines.

Coal from the tropics
Queensland makes an important contribution to Australia's coal production. In the Bowen Basin and adjoining country inland from Rockhampton, the coal is extracted on the opencast system from huge pits and exported worldwide through Gladstone and special coal ports like Hay Point. Several of the mines (Blackwater, Blair Athol, Goonyella and Peak Downs) welcome visitors.

Cruising home to Port Douglas harbor

Cattle

Today, steak-happy Australians bite into about half the 1½ million tons of the beef their country produces. The rest is exported, mostly to Canada, the U.S.A. and Japan.

The convicts and soldiers landed from the First Fleet seem to have subsisted on Bengal beef, meat from cattle brought out from India. Later, English breeds were introduced, and the colony became first self-sufficient, then embarrassed by the production of a surplus of beef that could not be consumed locally. Canning and refrigeration eventually solved this problem, enabling Australia to become a major exporter of beef; until the advent of the European Community, a good proportion of the roast beef of Olde England started life in the Outback.

Together with sheep, beef cattle were the companions of the white man in his conquest of the continent's vast interior spaces. Some treks were of epic quality; in 1883–5 the Durack family overlanded 10,000 head of stock 3,100 miles from Queensland to the Ord River in the Kimberley, a journey lasting more than two years.

Farming on a grand scale Most of Australia's beef cattle are Herefords or Shorthorns, though there has been cross-breeding with Brahmans in an attempt to increase resistance to extreme heat and pests. Numbers peaked in the 1970s at some 33½ million, but they have declined and today's total is about 18 million.

The majority of animals graze the arid lands of the center and north of the country, their thirst slaked by the water pumped up from artesian wells. Because of the poverty of the pasture, stocking rates are incredibly low and cattle stations are huge, some of them the size of European states. There are few fences to stop the beasts roaming freely until the time comes for round-up. From the stockyard they are taken by mammoth cattle trucks for the rest cure, which puts flesh on their often meager bones before they are finally slaughtered.

Beef cattle country in New South Wales

The round-up
At muster time the cattle are rounded up by a handful of cattlemen on horseback or, more likely these days, by men on motorbikes or in 4WD vehicles. Helicopters are often used to locate the more wily creatures and drive them from their hiding places.

224

▶▶ Sunshine Coast 201A4

This fabled strip of fine beaches stretches some 60 miles north of Brisbane from Bribie Island to Rainbow Beach and is much favored by those who enjoy a quieter alternative to the Gold Coast. Should you tire of sun and sand there is the garden-like hinterland to explore, including the green world of the Blackall Range.

▶ Toowoomba 201A4

High up among the grainfields and pastures of the fertile Darling Downs, Toowoomba is Queensland's largest inland city, distinguished by wide, tree-shaded streets and attractive parks and gardens. Nearby is the **Ravensbourne National Park▶**, rich in birdlife, and **Crows Nest Falls▶**, whose waters crash into a deep granite gorge.

▶ Townsville 201C3

Overlooked by its Castle Hill, Australia's largest tropical city is the outlet for an awesomely vast region stretching inland to Mount Isa and to the distant Gulf of Carpentaria. As well as a university city and a defense center, it is an important stop-off for tourists heading north or embarking for the Barrier Reef. Townsville has botanic gardens dating from the late 19th century and a number of buildings from the same period, but visitors are likely to be drawn first and foremost to the complex known as the **Great Barrier Reef Wonderland▶▶**. Here, the glass tunnel of the world's largest coral reef aquarium enables you to marvel at the wonders of the reef without donning wetsuit or snorkel, an experience not to be missed. Almost equally vivid are the films shown on the 360° screen of the **Omnimax Theatre▶**, while a branch of the **Queensland Museum▶** has displays on natural history, history and technology. As if this weren't enough, there is also the **Visitor Centre of the Marine Park Authority**, the body responsible for the management of the Reef.

▶ Warwick 201A4

A thriving market center for the southern Darling Downs, Warwick is Queensland's second oldest town (after Brisbane), dating back to 1848.

Caloundra, on the Sunshine Coast, is ideal for families

Cane toads
Not far behind the rabbit in nuisance value, these unlovely creatures are an example of an introduced animal that has become more of a menace than the pest it was supposed to control. The toad was originally imported from Hawaii in 1935 in the hope that it would eliminate the beetles attacking the cane fields. Unfortunately it has proved highly successful in reducing the numbers of many kinds of native animals, exuding toxins poisonous enough to kill most of its predators, apart from road vehicles; squashed toads are a common sight along Queensland highways.

TASMANIA

226

Curtis Group

Cape Wickham

Egg Lagoon
■ Lavinia Nature Reserve

King Island

Naracoopa

Currie

Grassy

Stokes Point

B a s s

S t r a i t

Hunter Island

Three Hummock Island

Robbins Island

Cape Grim

Stanley
Rocky Cape Nat Park
Montagu
Smithton
Boat Harbour Beach
Marrawah
Irishtown
■ **Wynyard**
Somerset
Calder **Burnie**
Arthur
Yolla
Penguin
Asbestos Range Nat Park
Ridgley
Ulverstone
Rebecca Lagoon ● Temma
Gunns Plains **Devonport**
Port Sorell
Latrobe
Arthur Pieman Protected Area
Savage
Leven Canyon
Sprent
Railton
Sandy Cape
Waratah
Sheffield
Savage River
1339m Black Bluff
Mole Creek
Lake Dove ■
1545m Cradle Mt
Marakoopa Cave
Tullah
Rosebery
Cradle Mt
Walls of Jerusalem Nat Park
Pieman
Lake St Clair
1617m Mt Ossa
Lake Augusta
Zeehan
Mt Lyell Copper Mines
Nat Park
1447m Lake St Clair
Queenstown
Mt Olympus
Derwent Bridge
Lake Echo
Strahan
West Coast Range
L King William
Cape Sorell
Franklin-Gordon
1443m Frenchmans Cap
Tarraleah
Lake Binney
Macquarie Harbour
Wild Rivers Nat Park
Wayatinah
Franklin
Sarah Island ■
Mt Field Nat Park
Point Hibbs
Gordon
Lake Gordon
Strathgordon
Maydena
Lake Pedder
Frankland Range
Low Rocky Point
Southwest
Arthur Range
National
Park
Port Davey

See Drive page 246

South West Cape
Maatsuyker Group

0 20 40 60 80 100 km
0 10 20 30 40 50 60 miles

Kent
Group

Sister
Islands

Stanley Point

Cape Frankland

**Flinders
Island**

Babel Island

**Furneaux
Group**

Emita
**Wybalenna
Historic Site**

Whitemark

Strzelecki
Nat Park
Chappell Islands
Lady Barron

**Cape Barren
Island**

Cape
Barren

Clarke Island

Banks Strait

Cape
Portland

Waterhouse
**Mt William
National Park**

Bridport
Gladstone
Eddystone
Point

George
Town
Winnaleah
Scottsdale

Bell Bay
Beauty Point
Beaconsfield
Derby
Binalong Bay

Lilydale
Pyengana
St Helens
Point

Exeter
St Helens

Hadspen
Scamander

Launceston
Kings
Meadow
1573m Mathinna

Deloraine
**Ben Lomond
Nat Park**
St Marys

Longford
Clarendon

Cressy
Rossarden
Fingal

Liffey Falls
South Esk

Conara
Avoca
St Pauls

Lake
Macquarie
**Douglas-Apsley
Nat Park**
Bicheno

*Great
Lake*
*Arthurs
Lake*
Campbell Town

Miena
Cranbrook

Country
Ross

*Lake
Sorell*
Coles Bay

*Lake
Crescent*
Tunbridge
Swansea
**Freycinet
National
Park**

*Great
Oyster
Bay*

Bothwell
Oatlands
Little
Swanport
Schouten
Island

Ouse
Melton
Mowbray
Coal
Triabunna

Ouse
Hamilton
Colebrook
Orford

Kempton
Buckland
**Maria Island
National Park**

Derwent
Pontville
Brighton
Richmond

**New
Norfolk**
Risdon
Cove
Sorell
*Marion
Bay*

Glenorchy
Dunalley

HOBART
Lauderdale
Forestier Peninsula

Huonville
**Blowhole, Arch &
Devil's Kitchen**

Huon
Kingston

Franklin
Snug
*Storm
Bay*
**Tasmanian Devil
Wildlife Park**

Geeveston
Cygnet
Port Arthur
Tasman Peninsula

**Hartz Mts
Nat Park**
Dover
Cape Pillar

Hastings

Lune
River
Southport
Bruny Island

Adventure Bay

Tasman
Head

South East Cape

4   5

Tasmania This green and mountainous island's intimate links with mainland Australia are celebrated each summer by one of the world's great spectacles of sail, the Sydney to Hobart race, an exciting sprint down the coast of New South Wales and across the often turbulent waters of Bass Strait. Early explorers assumed Van Diemen's Land (Tasmania's name until 1856) to be part of the mainland, but this error was rectified by George Bass and Matthew Flinders in 1798, and by 1804 Hobart had become the capital of the second British colony to be founded in Australia.

Small is beautiful "Tassie" certainly is different. It's a fully functioning state of the Australian Commonwealth, but everything else about it conspires to distinguish it from the rest of the country. Australia's smallest state, about the size of Scotland, Bavaria or West Virginia, it revels in a temperate climate that nourishes its forests with an abundant rainfall while providing blue skies often enough for all but the most fanatical of sun-worshippers. In the interior, stone-built bridges, villages, townships and Georgian mansions are set among neat farmlands where hedgerows and deciduous trees recall the early settlers' British origin. Beyond the pastures and orchards rise rugged uplands, with clear lakes, rushing rivers and the continent's most magnificent mountain scenery, some of it still hardly explored. The three great national parks of Tasmania's southwest have been declared a World Heritage Area, a wilderness of high peaks, deep gorges and dense rain forest of unequaled grandeur.

Visitors welcome Tasmania's relatively long history has left an exceptional wealth of old settlements and historic buildings, including what for many people is the most compellingly poignant of all Australia's monuments to

Conflict
In recent years bitter conflict has arisen between narrowly conceived economic interests and the environment. Unique Lake Pedder was destroyed by the construction of a dam, but public opinion saved the Franklin and Gordon Rivers from going the same way. The environment seems to be winning at the moment.

228

NEXT
3 km

convict days, the Port Arthur complex in its evocative setting of sea inlet and parkland. Hobart is a city of European style and dignity, its deep-water harbor opening onto the broad Derwent River against a backdrop of splendid green hills and mountains.

Perhaps it is the island's small size and relative isolation that have made it a welcoming place, even by the exceptional standards of Australian friendliness. The pace of life is slow, the locals are usually happy to pass the time of day with a stranger; "no worries" is even more applicable here than in the rest of the country. (This openness has not stopped Tassie's 470,000 inhabitants becoming the butt of jokes for other Australians.)

All this, together with generally lower prices, has helped tourism become an important bastion of the local economy, though surprisingly few foreigners make the short journey (150 miles) from the mainland. Visitors' dollars are particularly welcome; the island faces the perennial problems of an economy based mostly on primary products, and its unemployment rate has remained consistently higher than that of the mainland. Agriculture thrives in the Midlands, the southeast and along river valleys, though orcharding was dealt a devastating blow when the European Common Market began to exclude its products. Mining of metal ores continues in the thinly populated west, and around Queenstown has left a landscape of lunar weirdness. Forestry is a major industry, though its scope is increasingly restricted by awareness that trees have an ecological and scenic value as well as a short-term financial one. Despite some recent environmental destruction (see panel opposite and page 238), much wild nature survives to attract the visitor.

It is easy to find historic corners in Launceston

229

Lovely Freycinet National Park, on the east coast

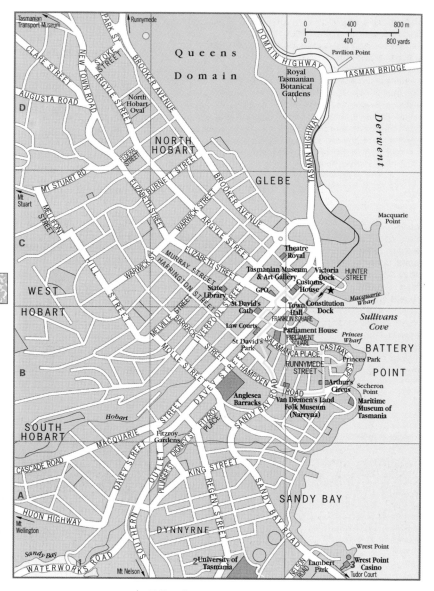

Hobart

Second in age only to Sydney, Hobart is the smallest of Australia's state capitals. It stretches out along both shores of the broad estuary of the River Derwent, one of the deepest harbors in the world and a sporting paradise, linked by the 336-foot span of the Tasman Bridge. The old city center, with its wealth of colonial buildings, clusters compactly around **Sullivans Cove** on the west bank, backed by wooded slopes rising to the often snow-capped peak of Mount Wellington. Its limited size, rich architectural heritage and incomparable setting make Hobart a delight to explore.

History The city was founded in 1804 by Lieutenant-Governor David Collins, after the first attempt at settlement at Risdon Cove just upstream had failed. For many years the population consisted mostly of convicts and their overseers, though the splendid harbor soon became a base for the whalers and sealers pursuing their prey in the Antarctic and South Pacific.

The city spread inland along the grid of streets leading uphill from the wharves and warehouses of Sullivans Cove, leaving a legacy of fine building; individual monuments abound, but it is the almost European quality of the townscape as a whole that makes Hobart virtually unique in Australia. Streets dominated by splendid Victorian structures like the town hall or the Theatre Royal of 1837 contrast with the delightful informality of the village suburb of **Battery Point**.

Laid-back lifestyle Life in Hobart proceeds at an easy pace, leavened by the good temper of its inhabitants, who seem perfectly content to live in this least metropolitan of capital cities. This is not to say that amenities are lacking; today's Hobart has a full range of facilities to keep both locals and visitors stimulated and entertained. Its hotels and eating places equal those found elsewhere, while the casino complex at Wrest Point (Australia's first) has introduced a note of sophistication previously lacking. Every Saturday the dignified sandstone warehouses of **Salamanca Place** look down on what is one of the country's liveliest and most colorful open-air markets, while December 31 and the first week in January are enlivened by the excitement of the Sydney–Hobart yacht race, when thousands of spectators line the shore.

Life revolves around the harbor in Hobart

Tasmania discovered
Dutch mariner Abel Tasman caught sight of an uncharted shore on November 24, 1642 and named it Van Diemen's Land after Anthony van Diemen, Governor-General of the East Indies. Mounts Heemskerk and Zeehan in the west of the island recall the name of his expedition's two ships. Unaware that his discovery was not part of the mainland, much less that it would eventually bear his name, he sailed off, leaving George Bass and Matthew Flinders to circumnavigate the island more than a century and a half later, in 1798. Evidence of French interest was provided by the scientific voyage of Nicolas Baudin in 1800, and it was partly in order to forestall any French designs on the island that Lieutenant John Bowen was sent to plant the Union Jack on the shores of Risdon Cove in 1803.

231

▶ Anglesea Barracks 230B2

Davey Street

Well-sited on rising ground to the west of the city center, the barracks are outstanding examples of early 19th-century military architecture, a stern assemblage of buildings including drill hall, messes and officers' quarters.

▶▶ Battery Point 230B3

This is the name given to the promontory separating Sullivans Cove on the north from Sandy Bay to the south. Its commanding position made it a natural site for the battery of guns placed here in 1818 to protect the approach to the harbor. Battery Point's interest today is in its delightfully domesticated 19th-century townscape. There are cottages and villas, and little row houses looking (apart from their tin roofs) as if they have just been transplanted from late-Georgian England. Grander altogether is "Narryna," a solid, pilastered stone-fronted home of 1836, protected from the street by fine iron railings. Housing the **Van Diemen's Land Folk Museum**, the interior has been authentically refurnished to evoke the more elegant side of life in 19th-century Hobart, and the gardens and outbuildings are being restored in the same spirit.

▶▶ Harbor area 230B3

The true spirit of Hobart can still be sensed along the wharves and quaysides of the harbor fronting Sullivans Cove, although the whalers have long since sailed away. Fishing boats and pleasure craft tie up in the twin basins

Church landmarks
Hobart's churches were mostly built on prominent sites to act as city landmarks. With its commanding octagonal tower, St. George's Church at Battery Point is no exception, although its Egyptian-style stonework, fashionable during the early 19th-century when the church was built, is most unusual.

The Botanical Gardens: well-kept and beautiful

known as Victoria Dock and Constitution Dock, the name of the latter a reminder of the great day in 1853 when the granting of a constitution marked the end of convictism in Tasmania. A venerable Sydney ferry contrasts with trim trawlers and with the spick-and-span survey ship of the Commonwealth Scientific and Industrial Research Organisation (C.S.I.R.O.) tied up at Battery Point to the west. The buildings around the harbor are some of the best in Hobart; they include the **Customs House** and the restored warehouses along Hunter Street. You will have to make your own mind up about the controversial Sheraton Hotel.

▶ **Maritime Museum of Tasmania**   *230B3*
Secheron Road, Battery Point
This delightfully old-fashioned museum is housed in "Secheron," a fine Battery Point residence dating back to the 1830s, and has a comprehensive collection of maritime memorabilia showing how intimately Tasmania's history has been linked with the sea.

▶ **Royal Tasmanian Botanical Gardens** *230D3*
Sloping steeply down to the Derwent near the Tasman Bridge, the lawns of these superlative gardens are studded with fine specimen trees as well as with structures like the wooden Fernery or the Conservatory with its changing floral displays, each more dazzling than the last. Not only keen botanists will be fascinated by the carefully maintained array of specifically Tasmanian plants, some still awaiting classification and some under threat of extinction.

The 1837 Theatre Royal has been carefully restored

233

▶▶ **Salamanca Place**   *230B3*
In the 1830s the stony slopes of Battery Point were quarried away to build the wharf to the west of Sullivans Cove, and warehouses of magnificently solid appearance were erected to serve the ships docked there. Long since vacated, these superb sandstone structures have happily found new users: boutiques, craft studios, galleries, restaurants, antiques dealers and bookstores. Every Saturday morning the place is transformed by the arrival of an army of stallholders offering wares of incredible variety, a must for every visitor.

▶▶ **Tasmanian Museum and Art Gallery** *230C3*
Macquarie Street
Tasmania's principal museum is housed in a complex of buildings of various dates, including 40 Macquarie Street, erected in 1808 and supposedly the oldest continuously occupied building in Australia. Within, the Natural History section has displays on Tasmanian creatures (and their ancestors, the megafauna of Pleistocene times that included 10-foot kangaroos and giant wombats); Ethnography tells the sad story of the island's Aborigines; and Colonial's exhibits, guarded by a redcoat, bring to life the part-epic, part-sordid decades dominated by convictism. The gallery naturally enough features colonial art; of more than passing interest are John Glover's depictions of Tasmania as a paradise populated by Aborigines, and the famous *Conciliation* by Benjamin Duterrau, marking the fateful meeting that led to their exile and death.

Hobart's mountains
In clear weather both Mount Nelson and Mount Wellington give sensational views of Hobart in its incomparable setting. Mount Nelson (1,115 feet), the residences of the privileged dotting its slopes, rises over Sandy Bay; a little signal station still stands at the summit, though the signalman's house has become a tearoom. Mount Wellington (4,167 feet) is reached via the panoramic road built in 1937 to enable the lazy to enjoy the views that were previously only accessible to determined hikers. At the summit is a boardwalk as well as a shelter with notices explaining exactly what it is you are looking at, though most visitors will probably be quite content to gaze in mindless wonder at the glorious prospect before them.

Constitution Dock, mooring point for sailboats in the Sydney–Hobart race

Walk Sullivans Cove to Battery Point

This walk from Sullivans Cove begins at the north end of the harbor by the memorial commemorating the city's foundation in 1804 and links Hobart's waterfront to the charming old quarter of Battery Point.

The handsome old warehouses flanking Hunter Street contrast with the modern hotel overlooking Victoria Dock. Take time to enjoy the activity around the **harbor**.

Inland from the harbor are the old buildings of the **Tasmanian Museum and Art Gallery** whose new entrance is around the corner in Macquarie Street, where you will also find the 1864 Town Hall and the tall-towered **General Post Office** of 1905. Now planted with fine trees and with a fountain at its center, **Franklin Square** was once a parade ground fronting the first Government House. The intersection formed by Murray Street and Macquarie Street is unique in Australia in having retained all its early buildings: **St. David's Cathedral**, the old **Law Courts**, and a number of mid-19th-century row houses.

Opposite St. David's Park is a real curiosity, a royal-tennis court, still in use by players of what has become a very exclusive indoor game. The park itself, with its sweeping lawns and fine native and exotic trees, was once the city's cemetery. A memorial recalls John Woodcock Graves, author of the song "Do ye ken John Peel?", who visited Tasmania in 1886.

Beyond Harrington Street is **Hampden Road**, the artery of Battery Point, with a pleasingly variegated collection of 19th- and early 20th-century buildings. Princes Park descends abruptly to the 1818 **Signal Station**. Beyond Castray Esplanade, the modern C.S.I.R.O. laboratories occupy the headland, but it is still possible to find a way through and enjoy views across the Derwent.

The Esplanade leads back toward the city center. Inland from Princes Wharf is the magnificent set of 19th-century warehouses fronting **Salamanca Place**, a fine conclusion to your walk.

By air Tasmania is linked to the mainland by a large variety of air services from airports such as Hobart, Launceston, Burnie/Wynyard and Devonport. There are also more limited services to airfields at Queenstown, Smithton and Strahan, as well as to Flinders and King Islands. The only direct international link is with Christchurch, New Zealand. Regular internal flights between all these airfields are supplemented by any number of local firms operating tourist flights; of these, the seaplane trip that takes off from Strahan to fly over Macquarie Harbour and Frenchman's Cap to land in the gorge of the Lower Gordon River cannot be recommended too highly.

By sea Bringing passengers and their vehicles to Tasmania: the *Spirit of Tasmania* takes about 15 hours on alternate days between Melbourne (departs Monday, Wednesday and Friday) and Devonport (departs Sunday, Tuesday, Thursday). This modern, luxurious ship offers a wide range of accommodations in its 467 cabins and can carry more than 300 vehicles.

By car Most visitors bring their own vehicle with them or rent a car once here. Distances are relatively short and roads mostly good, though occasionally clogged with logging trucks in a hurry to deliver their load. The freedom you get from your own car is particularly useful in Tasmania where there is really only the skeleton of a public transportation system.

By rail Although a narrow-gauge network still exists, passenger trains (except for enthusiasts' specials) stopped running a while ago.

By bus Every settlement of any size has its bus service, though its frequency may be strictly limited. The island's main operator is **Tasmanian Redline Coaches**, who issue "Tassie Passes" valid for varying periods. A vital link to the wilderness is maintained by **Tasmanian Wilderness Transport and Tours**, whose robust minibuses will get you into the heart of the major national parks and out again.

235

Traveling on foot
Anyone who comes to Tasmania should be prepared to walk, even if it is only for a short distance along the numerous marked boardwalks and nature trails. The adventurous will want to climb the more accessible peaks like Cradle Mountain, walk the five-day Overland Track, or enjoy a guided adventure rafting down the Franklin River.

Prime bushwalking country

National parks

Over a fifth of Tasmania's land is designated as national parks or state reserves.

World Heritage Area The largest tract of protected land (about 5,400 square miles) was declared the World Heritage Area in the 1980s, and stretches from Cradle Mountain to South West Cape taking in several parks and reserves. One of the world's last great temperate wildernesses, its pristine rivers, rain forest and rugged mountain ranges can be appreciated from the Lyell Highway or by flights and cruises from Strahan, but its deepest secrets will only be revealed to the dedicated bushwalker or whitewater rafter. Cradle Mountain, Lake St. Clair, the Franklin-Gordon Wild Rivers and the Southwest national parks are all described separately below, but the wild heart of the island also includes the great natural amphitheater of the **Walls of Jerusalem** as well as the "land of a thousand lakes," as the Central Plateau area is sometimes known. Through it passes the Lake Highway linking Deloraine with Melton Mowbray, a fascinating and unhurried alternative to the usual Midland Highway for north–south journeys.

236

The Franklin River is great for whitewater rafting

Beautiful and protected National park or reserve designation applies to many more of Tasmania's outstanding natural landscapes: beaches, caves, lakes and forests. Together with the granite hills of the Freycinet Peninsula, the alpine moorlands, tree ferns and waterfalls of Mount Field were the first to be listed as a national park. In the northeast of Tasmania rise the bare ridges of Ben Lomond, its ski slopes reached by a twisting mountain road. The eucalypts of the island's last major tract of dry sclerophyll forest are protected within the **Douglas-Apsley National Park**. Most of the smaller islands have important conservation areas: King Island's **Lavinia Nature Reserve** is the abode of the endangered orange-bellied parrot, while Wybalenna Historic Site on Flinders Island preserves what is left of the ill-fated attempt to re-settle the last of Tasmania's Aborigines between 1833 and 1847.

The lush rain forest of the Wild Rivers National Park

The alpine scenery of Cradle Mountain

►   **Bicheno**   *227C5*

Pronounced Bee-sheno, this little place on the east coast was once a base for sealers and whalers as well as a port for exporting coal from the nearby mines. Nowadays its boats bring in crayfish and abalone, and the township is popular with fishermen, artists and beach-lovers.

►   **Bothwell**   *227B4*

Pleasantly set in the beautiful Clyde Valley, Bothwell is of considerable historic interest in its own right, containing numerous colonial buildings, as well as acting as the southern gateway to Tasmania's mountainous Central Highlands.

►   **Burnie**   *226D3*

Most visitors hurry through Tasmania's fourth largest town, but workaday Burnie makes an interesting contrast to the rather self-conscious rusticity of much of the island. There are industrial plants, a huge paper mill ("The Pulp") and great trainloads of ore.

►►►   **Cradle Mountain–Lake St. Clair**   *226C3*

Part of Tasmania's World Heritage Area, this national park of rugged mountain peaks and high moorlands is one of the great landscapes of Australia. The gateways to the park are **Cradle Valley►►►** to the north and Lake St. Clair near the Lyell Highway in the south. At Cradle Valley the spacious visitor center introduces the national park to its public with displays, talks and events; a boardwalk penetrates the depths of the rain forest and gives a fine view of the Pencil Pine Creek waterfall. A number of shorter or longer walks radiate from the center, but most visitors will want to press on up the gravel road to the north shore of **Lake Dove►►►**. Bearing in mind that the park generally receives no less than 103 inches of rain each year and that most days will bring at least some, let us hope that you will see the unforgettable outline of Cradle Mountain reflected in the clear waters of the lake.

Source of the River Derwent, **Lake St. Clair►►►** is the deepest (656 feet) body of freshwater in Australia and certainly one of the clearest. It is easy to escape into wild nature, even if it is only as far as Watersmeet, confluence of the Cuvier and Hugel Rivers.

Weindorfer's "Home in the Woods"

In 1912, deep in the primeval woodland, an Austrian called Gustav Weindorfer built himself a chalet of King Billy pine and named it "Waldheim" (Forest Home). It was Weindorfer's enthusiasm that was largely responsible for the area's designation, first in 1922 as a scenic reserve, then later as a national park. Waldheim still stands, albeit rebuilt, but it has been joined by other forms of accommodation ranging from the comfort of Cradle Mountain Lodge to the more basic amenities of a campsite, all designed to harmonize with their incomparable surroundings.

The Overland Track

The route from Cradle Valley to Cynthia Bay on Lake St. Clair is 53 miles long. Walking it is perhaps the best way to savor to the utmost the varied landscapes of the national park —wild open heaths, forested valleys, deep gorges, lakes and tarns, and rocky peaks, among them Mount Ossa (5,305 feet), Tasmania's highest point. The trek takes a minimum of five days, but it is better to allow longer to avoid rushing and to be able to explore a little at will. There are huts along the way, but their capacity is limited and you should be prepared to camp. Always check with a ranger before setting off into the wilderness.

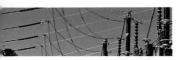

With its abundant rainfall and mountainous terrain, Tasmania's potential for the generation of hydroelectricity is easily the greatest of all the Australian states.

One of the many Tasmanian dams

Water power
Tasmania developed its hydroelectric power supplies partly so that it could expand its aluminum processing industry. It takes huge quantities of electricity to turn aluminum ore (bauxite) into the metal. Hydroelectric power is economical, so it must have seemed the ideal solution. Bell Bay in northern Tasmania was selected as a suitable site for an aluminum plant in the 1950s, lying as it does between the cheap power produced in Tasmania's interior and Queensland's large deposits of bauxite.

Early developments The first projects were built before World War I, but it was in the interwar period that grandiose visions were expounded of Tasmania becoming Australia's Ruhr, whose new industries would feed off cut-price electricity and solve the island's economic problems forever. Founded in 1930, the **Hydro-Electric Commission** (H.E.C.) became a kind of state-within-a-state, Tasmania's biggest employer, capable of overcoming whatever technical challenges might be involved in wresting power from the trackless wilderness.

By the late 1960s the H.E.C. had its eye on glacial **Lake Pedder**, and was able to flood this unique ecosystem in the face of gathering protests from a growing minority of people concerned about the impact of hydro-power on the environment. The destruction of Lake Pedder was described by Unesco as "the greatest ecological tragedy since European settlement in Tasmania."

Power or greenery The H.E.C.'s next major proposal was the transformation of the Franklin and Lower Gordon Rivers and the surrounding temperate rain forest.

Tasmanian society was bitterly divided, but opposition was better organized this time in the shape of the **Tasmanian Wilderness Society**. A referendum showed the extent of concern, the construction site was blockaded, 1,500 arrests were made, and the project was finally halted in 1983 by a newly elected Federal Labor government anxious to cultivate the "Green vote." The wild rivers of the southwest, once described by Premier Gray as "brown and leech-ridden," were saved; in the end it may well be that Tasmania will gain more from tourists drawn to one of the world's great wildernesses than from any extra wattage that might have been generated.

▶ **Deloraine** 227C4

Now bypassed, but well worth the detour, this attractive and somewhat self-conscious old township lies in fertile country on the Meander River halfway between Launceston and Devonport. In and around the town are any number of interesting colonial buildings, including Bonney's Inn (1831).

▶ **Devonport** 226D3

Devonport is one of the principal gateways into Tasmania. It is here that the *Spirit of Tasmania* vehicle ferry ties up after crossing Bass Strait from Melbourne; and there is an airfield, too. Just inland from the 1889 lighthouse, on the rocky promontory of Mersey Bluff, is the **Tiagarra Aboriginal Cultural and Arts Centre▶**, with excellent displays on the life led by the first Tasmanians as well as a guided walk around the enigmatic carvings that are a feature of the area. Other places to visit include the Maritime Museum as well as **Home Hill▶**, the white house that belonged to Joseph Lyons, the only Australian to have been both State Premier and Prime Minister. Outside the town to the west is the terminus of the **Don River Railway▶** where you will find Tasmania's largest collection of veteran locomotives and rolling stock.

▶▶ **Flinders Island** 227E5

Guarding the eastern end of Bass Strait, Flinders is the largest island of the Furneaux Group. Once the abode of sealers, then the site of G. A. Robinson's ill-fated Aboriginal refuge (see page 241), it is a lonely place, with an agricultural and fishing population of less than 1,000. But there is an abundance of wildlife (including the famed muttonbirds—see panel), as well as splendid white beaches contrasting with the rugged granite outcrops of the Strzelecki National Park▶▶.

Muttonbirds
The islands of the Bass Strait are the breeding ground of the short-tailed shearwater, a rather non-descript brown bird that migrates in a clockwise direction around the Pacific. The nestlings, chubby creatures rich in fat and oil, are bred in yard-long burrows, then left to their own devices by their careless parents. This made them easy prey for the Aborigines, who would harvest them in huge numbers.

239

The Liffey Falls near Deloraine are well worth a visit

The beautiful beaches of the Freycinet Peninsula

▶▶▶ Franklin–Gordon Wild Rivers National Park
226B3

This glorious tract of rain forest, wild rivers and rugged uplands extends from the sheltered waters of Macquarie Harbour to the Lyell Highway, forming the central portion of Tasmania's World Heritage Area. Its highest point (4,734 feet) is the spectacular quartzite monolith known as **Frenchmans Cap▶▶▶**, whose sheer eastern face drops an alarming 985 feet. Experienced bushwalkers can make the round trip to Frenchmans Cap in four days; others must content themselves with views from the highway. The adventurous can go whitewater rafting on the Franklin River, an immensely rewarding trip through gorges and over rapids that takes more than a week to reach the little jetty near the mouth of the Gordon. This point is also accessible by launch from Strahan or, more excitingly, by a seaplane that drifts down the gorge to land gracefully on the limpid, tea-colored stream. A boardwalk leads deep into the damp and mossy forest where, among the tree ferns, Huon pines and Antarctic beeches, a waterfall crashes into its pool.

▶▶ Freycinet National Park
227B5

Approached via the fishing township of Coles Bay, the Freycinet Peninsula extends southward into the azure waters of the Tasman Sea towards little Schouten Island. With its backbone of red granite peaks, immaculate beaches of white sand, forests of eucalyptus and wealth of wildflowers, this was one of Tasmania's very first national parks and has long been popular with locals.

▶ Geeveston
227A4

At Geeveston is the **Esperance Forest and Heritage Centre▶**, a not-to-be-missed starting point for explorations of the woodland area. The **Arve Road▶▶** has picnic areas and lookouts, and a little further inland is **Hartz Mountains National Park▶▶**.

Huon pines
Easily identified because of its feathery foliage and trailing branches, this is a uniquely Tasmanian conifer, occurring mainly in the wetter areas of the far southwest. Extraordinarily slow-growing, it is also extraordinarily long-lived—some specimens still alive may go back to the pre-Christian era. Respect for age meant little in colonial days, when the "piners" prized the Huon for its exceptionally resilient timber. Today it is valued more for its beauty when converted into ornamental objects such as fruitbowls, and has become a mainstay of the Tasmanian souvenir industry.

Tasmanian Aborigines

In December 1642, the crew of Abel Tasman's *Heemskerk* heard human voices calling in the forest fringing their landing place near Cape Sorell on the west coast, but the owners of the voices failed to show themselves. Perhaps they had premonitions about the fate of their descendants at the hands of later colonists.

Early conflict Tasmanian Aborigines were quite distinct in character from their mainland counterparts. Thinly spread around the island, they totaled an estimated 4,000–5,000 at the start of white settlement in 1803. The usual complicated relationships arose between the two races. There was plenty of cooperation; Aboriginal women in particular gave freely of their skills in the seal hunts that formed such a staple of Tasmania's early economy. But conflict inevitably grew, in spite of earnest professions of concern on the part of white officialdom; the natives' living patterns were disrupted as their hunting grounds were turned into fenced-off farmland In the face of the destruction of their way of life, some resisted violently, to be met with more effective violence by the settlers. Within 20 years Aboriginal numbers had been halved.

The end of a race The most fateful episode was reconciliation. The undoubtedly well-meaning George Augustus Robinson traveled the island, making contact with all remaining Aborigines, winning their trust and persuading them to settle in a kind of Christian protectorate on Flinders Island. Here, religion, drink, disease and the loss of their land and culture gradually destroyed those who had survived thus far. The last full-blooded Tasmanian Aborigine, a woman called Trucanini, died in 1876.

Above: Aboriginal rock carving in Devonport

Lost but not forgotten
The disappearance of Tasmania's Aborigines is often characterized as genocide, though the processes involved were essentially the same as those at work on the mainland. Though full-blooded Tasmanian Aborigines are no more, many people of mixed blood remain, some of them seemingly indistinguishable from other Australians.

John Glover's 1836 painting, The Last Muster

Hazards aplenty presented themselves to early mariners negotiating the uncharted coastal waters of the great southern continent: vicious storms, unexpected islands, hidden reefs and no hope of succor from land. Even the careful Captain Cook ran aground on the coral of the Barrier Reef, though his disciplined crew was able to refloat the stranded *Endeavour* on the next high tide.

Captain Bligh

Often called "Bligh of the Bounty," the naval officer William Bligh (1754–1817) was also known to his contemporaries as "Breadfruit Bligh," since one of his tasks had been to introduce that fruit to the West Indies. Strict to the point of harshness and beyond, he had the misfortune to suffer not one, but two mutinies. The first, aboard the *Bounty*, is part of popular history. The second rebellion against his rule, in 1808, was led by the officers of the "Rum Corps," as the New South Wales Corps was disparagingly known. Bligh, as Governor of the colony, had attempted to curb what he saw as the Corps' excessive influence over the colony's commercial life (including a monopoly on the sale of spirits). A *coup d'état* was staged, and Bligh was arrested by his own guards. Undaunted, he refused to return to London as a prisoner, and was later completely cleared of any misconduct.

A Dutch disaster The first to experience the inhospitable aspect of Australia were the Dutch, who favored an indirect but rapid route to their possessions in the East Indies. This led them around the Cape of Good Hope, then swiftly eastward with the winds of the Roaring Forties filling their sails, turning north before reaching the coast of Western Australia (which they named Nova Hollandia—New Holland).

However, not every captain made the turn in time, among them Commandant Pelsaert; his vessel the *Batavia* was named after the chief town of a Dutch colony (now Jakarta) and her cargo included the carefully chiseled stones for the town's main gate. On a fateful morning of 1629, the *Batavia* ran aground on one of the low coral atolls of the Houtman Abrolhos Islands, some 40 miles off Geraldton. Crew and passengers struggled ashore, rescuing what provisions they could. Once a degree of organization had been established, Pelsaert set sail for distant Java in a small boat to fetch help. His departure gave the signal for the mutiny that had long been brewing aboard the *Batavia*. Disaffected sailors and marines set up a reign of terror; rape and casual murder became the order of the day, though some managed to flee to neighboring islands and hold out against the mutineers. By a miracle, Pelsaert's frail craft survived the ocean voyage, and he returned, arresting the rebels and executing the ringleaders on the spot.

This improbable tale is told in full detail in the **Western Australian Maritime Museum** at Fremantle. Many of the *Batavia's* timbers have been recovered, and enough of them put together again to make up her stern, a most impressive and evocative sight. Here, too, the ready-cut masonry from her hold has been erected to form the classical gateway once intended to adorn the approach to the city of Batavia.

The Shipwreck Coast The *Batavia* was not alone in coming to grief off Western Australia, but it is probably Bass Strait between Victoria and Tasmania that has been responsible for the greatest number of Australian shipwrecks. In the last century, the stormy waters of the Strait formed the principal approach for vessels making for eastern Australia; King Island was only provided with a lighthouse in 1861, and until then ships would hug the rocky coast of the mainland, frequently running aground.

Shipwrecks

The most famous wreck occurred in 1878, when the iron clipper *Loch Ard* foundered on rocks near Port Campbell in Victoria. Of the 50 or so souls aboard, only two survived. Apprentice-boy Tom Pearce clung to a lifeboat and was swept into a narrow cliff-bound gorge. Badly knocked about, he was nevertheless able to rescue young Eva Carmichael whom the current had also brought into the gorge. Leaving the semi-conscious Eva on the beach, Tom somehow managed to climb the cliff and stagger for help. Only four bodies were recovered from the *Loch Ard*; their graves are in the nearby cemetery, one of several containing the remains of victims of this treacherous shore, which bears the name of the Shipwreck Coast.

Between Princetown in the east and Port Fairy in the west, the Historic Shipwreck Trail has markers and information boards indicating the locations of 25 wrecks of coasters, cargo boats, and ships full of hopeful immigrants. At Warrnambool the re-created port called **Flagstaff Hill Maritime Village** has many objects recovered from these wrecks, and there are other maritime displays at the **Old Cable Station Museum** at Apollo Bay and the **Blackwood Gully Centre** at Lavers Hill.

The waters around Flinders Island are treacherous

Above: The rugged cliffs of Cape Raoul on the Tasman Peninsula

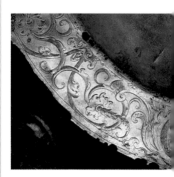

Above and below: Precious objects have been salvaged from the 17th-century Batavia

TASMANIA

Devils...
One of Tasmania's unofficial emblems is *Sarcophilus harrisii*, the stocky little predator known commonly as a devil. Invariably shown with a snarl on its less than endearing features, the black and white devil uses its powerful jaws to make short work of the carrion on which it prefers to feed. Devils genuinely do seem to suffer from bad temper, quarreling fiercely with each other at meal times and not hesitating to eat their own young if no other food is available. You may see them in the wild or, more reliably, in somewhere like the beautiful Bonorong Park Wildlife Centre at Brighton, 25 minutes north of Hobart.

An old windmill attracts visitors in Launceston

► **George Town**   *227D4*

A center for historic sites, unspoiled beaches, and gentle scenery, George Town stands near the mouth of the beautiful Tamar River, the 30-mile-long combined estuary of the North Esk, South Esk and Macquarie rivers. One of the oldest towns in Australia, it has several early colonial buildings, including the elegant Georgian house known as **The Grove**, built in the early 1830s for port officer and magistrate Mathew (Curling) Friend.

► **Hamilton**   *227B4*

A useful stopping point on the way to the west from Hobart, this charming little place of sandstone cottages and a few larger buildings never realized the ambitions of those early colonists who predicted a great future for it as a minor metropolis. Even Jackson's Emporium has been reduced from two stories to one.

►► **King Island**   *226E1*

Far out in the stormy waters of Bass Strait to the northwest of Tasmania, verdant King Island has an enviable reputation for dairy products, though much of the 36-mile-long island consists of unpopulated bushland teeming with wildlife. In the early 19th century it was one of the great battlefields in what has been called "Man's War on Animals," when the rough and ready "Straitsmen" butchered vast numbers of seals for their oil and skins.

►► **Launceston**   *227C4*

Located at the point where the North and South Esk Rivers combine to form the beautiful Tamar, Tasmania's second city is the unofficial capital of the northern part of the island. It has retained much of its Georgian and Victorian heritage and offers continuous pleasures to the urban stroller, even though few buildings are outstanding in themselves.

The city was laid out on the usual grid pattern of streets, some of which, like the Mall and Civic Square, have been given over to pedestrian use. In Civic Square is an intriguing sculpture of Tasmanian wildlife, including tail-biting thylacines (tigers—see panel opposite), as well as **Macquarie House►**, an excellently restored stone, iron and wooden structure dating from very early colonial days and now housing the local museum. Nearby are other reminders of the past—the red-brick Queen Anne-style post office, the Italianate town hall and St. Andrew's Kirk in brilliant white stucco, while the Old Umbrella Shop in George Street, now the National Trust shop, has retained its authentic 1860s frontage.

Launceston's other major attractions lie to the east of the city center. In a prettily landscaped setting, the **Queen Victoria Museum and Art Gallery►** rivals Hobart's Tasmanian Museum for the interest of its collections and innovative displays (don't tell Hobart!), reminding us with the title of one gallery that Tasmania is indeed "A Special Island." Close to King's Bridge over the South Esk is **Penny Royal World►**, with an array of re-erected and reproduced 19th-century buildings including water mills and windmills, as well as a fully operational gunpowder mill, reached by vintage tramway. Upstream is the most dramatic of Launceston's many parklands, **Cataract**

Gorge Reserve►►, a wild and rocky canyon in miniature, crossed by chairlift suspension bridge.

A collection of fine country houses (all open to the public) graces Launceston's hinterland. Finely proportioned **Franklin House►** near Kings Meadow would not have been out of place in the countryside of Georgian England, while single-storied **Entally House►** at Hadspen, with its veranda, seems much more rooted, more "Tasmanian." **Clarendon►**, behind its restored Ionic portico, is on a grander scale altogether, one of the great rural residences of Australia, overlooking its grounds and the South Esk River with a haughty eye.

► **Maria Island National Park**   227B5

Reached by ferry from Triabunna, this east coast island will appeal to those seeking undisturbed nature. Though pre-dating Port Arthur as a penal settlement and once exploited for various commercial purposes, the island is now an oasis of tranquility, with an abundant wildlife enjoying total freedom from motor vehicles. Visitors will need to take their own staples.

► **Mole Creek**   226C3

The limestone rock around this tiny township is riddled with caves, most of them inaccessible. But two of the more spectacular can be reached: **King Solomon Cave►**, where a limestone formation recalls the biblical monarch, and the longer **Marakoopa Cave►**, watered by two streams and lit by glow-worms.

...and tigers
Devils are not an endangered species, but the thylacine or Tasmanian tiger is officially extinct. What is generally thought to have been the last of the race died in Hobart Zoo in 1936, ironically within three months of tigers being declared a protected species. Thylacines were wolf-like marsupials, with stripy backs and wide-opening jaws; their liking for sheep and lambs didn't endear them to farmers. The question of whether or not the tiger lives on in seclusion somewhere has divided Tasmanians into believers and skeptics; there have been plenty of supposed sightings, but no definite proof.

The delights of Cataract Gorge, near Launceston

Drive Through the wilderness on the Lyell Highway

See map on pages 226–7

Allow a day for this trip from Hobart across the glorious mountain core of Tasmania on the Lyell Highway to the remote fishing port and resort of Strahan.

The first section of the drive runs up the valley of the Derwent, through well-tamed countryside of fields and farms and pleasant towns like English-looking New Norfolk and historic Hamilton. More rugged country follows, with increasing evidence of

The attractively wooded Derwent Valley and its villages lie just a short drive from Hobart

Tasmania's highly developed hydro-electricity industry—signs point down side-roads to dams, there is a surprise of a canal, and huge pipelines snake up and down the slopes. After Lake Binney the forest thins and gives way to featureless button-grass plains.

Shortly before Derwent Bridge, **Mount Olympus** comes into view; this grand mountain overlooks the clear waters of **Lake St. Clair,** which is reached via a short side-road from Derwent Bridge. The ranger station at Cynthia Bay marks one end of the famous Overland Track between here and Cradle Mountain. The recommended time to complete this famous trek is five days, but shorter hikes are also available.

One of the world's great mountain roads, the Lyell Highway was only completed in 1932. There are several, mostly well-marked stopping points along the way between Derwent Bridge and Queenstown: King William Saddle marks the watershed between the Derwent and Franklin–Gordon river systems, while Surprise Valley Lookout has a view of the imposing peak known as **Frenchmans Cap**. A number of short walks can be made from the Franklin River Bridge along part of the Frenchmans Cap Walking Track to the Donaghy's Hill Wilderness Lookout, to the Alma River Crossing or to Nelson Falls.

A new road has been built to circumvent the recently flooded valley bottom at **Lake Burbury**, a mountain scene of incomparable grandeur. Equally extraordinary, albeit in an utterly different way, is the "moon-scape" of devastated uplands around the mining center of Queenstown. The final leg of the journey is along the twisting but otherwise uneventful road through the forest and down into the little port of **Strahan**, one of the best starting points for further exploration of the wild western coast or the rain forest, rivers and mountains of the interior.

▶ New Norfolk
227B4

Upstream from Hobart, the Derwent Valley recalls the landscapes of southern England, with rolling hills as a background to a countryside of big deciduous trees and, around historic New Norfolk, hops fields and their attendant oast houses, one of which is now a museum.

▶ Oatlands
227B4

Extension of British power into the interior of Tasmania was marked by the construction of highways; one of the most important was the road now known as the Midland Highway, linking Hobart with Launceston. A small number of strategic settlements were planned along the route, of which Oatlands was one. First surveyed in 1832, the township is no bigger than a modest village, but nevertheless boasts a good number of fine colonial buildings.

▶▶▶ Port Arthur
227A5

Port Arthur is the most evocative of all the places recalling the days of the convict system, offering an experience that no visitor should miss.

The Tasman Peninsula is virtually an island, linked to the rest of Tasmania only by a slender isthmus; with sharks patrolling the surrounding waters and with this narrow neck of land guarded by vicious dogs, the peninsula could be made escape-proof. The first prisoners were brought here in 1830 to fell and saw the wood that formed the basis of the first of Port Arthur's thriving industries. As more convicts and those sent to guard them arrived, a vast range of activities began to flourish: ship building, tile, and brick-making, footwear and clothing manufacture, as well as coal mining at Plunkett Point. In time the place became virtually self-sufficient, supporting a population of more than 2,000, housed, working and worshiping in an array of handsome brick and stone structures. To make soldiers and officials feel more at home, touches of Old England were contrived; oaks and elms were planted and blackbirds released to sing from their branches.

Both extreme cruelty and weird forms of enlightenment were features of life at Port Arthur. Floggings were given for the slightest offense, but it was also here, at Point Puer, that juvenile delinquents received the first compulsory education in the world. By the mid-19th century, the desire to reform rather than punish led to the building of the Model Prison, whose inmates spent their time in total "solitary." However, madness rather than rehabilitation was the frequent outcome.

With the end of the convict era, Port Arthur was closed down as a penal colony, and in the late 19th century became a tourist attraction. Many of its more substantial structures remain to intrigue the visitor. They include the 1844 penitentiary, Australia's largest building at the time of its construction; guard towers; the sinister Model Prison and, looking down on the site from landward, the fine church with tower and pinnacles.

The Tasman Peninsula also has many other attractions, including strange coastal rock formations and Bush Mill, an authentically recreated logging settlement.

New Norfolk firsts
The town boasts a number of "firsts:" St. Matthew's, the island's oldest surviving church; the Bush Inn, Australia's oldest continuously licensed inn (you are likely to come across several of these); and the nearby salmon ponds, where a batch of ice-packed eggs survived the long trip from England to hatch into the first trout and salmon to swim the streams of the southern hemisphere.

The gentleman bushranger
Filled with "a deep and concentrated hatred of that power which was undeservedly persecuting me," the Irish convict Martin Cash and two companions braved the sharks in about 1840 by swimming to freedom from the Tasman Peninsula. Recognized in the course of an overconfident visit to a lady friend in Hobart in 1843, Cash managed to shoot a constable while being re-arrested, but somehow avoided execution, and eventually settled down to the life of a farmer.

VISIT MUSEUM HERE
Port Arthur's Convict Exhibition
ACCLAIMED LARGEST RELIC COLLECTION EVER SEEN

Eroded hills behind Queenstown

Leatherwood honey
One of Tasmania's most distinctive trees is *Eucryphia lucida* or leatherwood, a characteristic species of the temperate rain forest. For many years, local beekeepers have hung hives in the vicinity of leatherwoods in order to take advantage of the bees' liking for the nectar-rich flowers that bloom in spring and early summer. The nectar is converted into a particularly delicious honey.

▶▶ **Queenstown** 226B2

Few scenes of industrial devastation are quite as spectacular as the lunar highlands surrounding this mining town in western Tasmania. For visitors approaching from the east, the contrast between the vast tracts of luxuriant rainforest to either side of the Lyell Highway and the utterly denuded slopes around Queenstown could not come as more of a surprise.

The miners who came here from the early 1880s onward were prospecting for gold, but it was not long before copper extraction took precedence. The copper smelters' insatiable demand for fuel was responsible for the wholesale clearance of the rain forest all around, while their emissions poisoned any regrowth that might have occurred. With no vegetative cover to bind it together, the soil was quickly washed away by the abundant rainfall (up to 118 inches each year), leaving deep gullies and bare rock faces.

Queenstown is not without a certain quiet pride in this horror story, which undoubtedly gave it a distinctive identity, commemorated by the rather odd collection of sculptures at the **Miners Siding**, together with a sturdy little rack-and-pinion locomotive. The Mount Lyell Mining and Railway Company still processes copper here, and the mine and its museum can be visited in the course of a guided tour. It is likely that the mine will eventually become a "living" museum of mining history.

▶▶ **Richmond** 227B4

For Tasmanians, tiny Richmond embodies all that is "historical" about their island. Along the township's main street are a number of fine old buildings from colonial days, some of them dating from the 1820s.

Two attractions in particular capture visitors' imaginations: the jail and the bridge, built in the local sandstone in 1823–5. The bridge carried the highway that for many years linked Hobart with Port Arthur, and now benefits from its picturesque setting of riverside lawns, trees and ducks.

►► Ross 227C4

Driving the Midland Highway is an almost continuous pleasure; the well-engineered road speeds you past a background of blue hills through a countryside that was remade by the early settlers into a facsimile of the England they had left behind. Ross is one of a number of strategic settlements established along the route in the 1820s to act as staging posts for travelers. Church Street, with its attractive old stone buildings, is nicely shaded by the ubiquitous elms, but it is Ross's stone bridge that is quite exceptional. An elegant structure dating from 1836, it is decorated with carvings of such virtuosity that they earned their convict stonemason his freedom.

► St. Helens 227C5

The most populous place on Tasmania's east coast, the fishing port of St. Helens is also the most popular, with vacationers outnumbering locals five to one in the height of summer. As well as attracting game fishermen, it makes an excellent base for exploring the magnificent northeastern coast of the island, where there are splendid sand dunes, white sandy beaches and bands of Forester kangaroos.

►►► Southwest National Park 226A3

Forming the southern part of Tasmania's World Heritage Area, this is a vast wilderness of mountain ranges rising from virgin forest of southern beech and Huon pine, with great sweeps of buttongrass, glacial lakes and wild rivers, and a wonderful coastline of deserted sandy beaches.

   Until quite recently only the more hardy type of bushwalker, mountaineer or canoeist ventured into this remote and unspoiled world. But in the late 1960s, Tasmania's Hydroelectric Commission drove a road deep into the heart of the area, a harbinger of its plan to drown Lake Pedder beneath an artificial water body 20 times its size.

   The outrage this provoked, not only among conservationists but also in a wider public, turned out to be in vain; Lake Pedder, with its unique fauna and beach of brilliant white sand, was duly submerged in the interest of generating marginally cheaper electricity. The advantage for the visitor is that it is possible to taste, if not fully experience, something of one of the world's last temperate wildernesses by driving up the Strathgordon and Scotts Peak Roads. Both highways give spectacular views of the new Lake Pedder in its rugged setting. For those wishing to penetrate farther, the track from Scotts Peak Dam via the coastal inlet of Port Davey to South East Cape will take up to two weeks' strenuous trekking; there are several specialist tour operators.

► Stanley 226D2

On its peninsula protruding into Bass Strait, this historic port and vacation center nestles beneath its famous landmark, the Nut; properly known as **Circular Head**, this 470-foot basalt outcrop is the core of an ancient volcano. Walk or take the chairlift to the breezy summit for terrific views along the northwest coastline.

Fishing in Tasmania
Fishing is one of Tasmania's main industries and fresh seafood is one of the delights of eating out on the island. There are plenty of opportunities for visiting enthusiasts to go sea fishing, particularly for tuna and marlin from the little ports of the east coast. But it is probably the lure of the trout that will most entice the angler from abroad. Ever since trout spawn from England was successfully hatched in 1864 in the famous Salmon Ponds hatchery near New Norfolk, the island's unpolluted streams and lakes have proved an ideal habitat for both brown and salmon trout. These are not lethargic, farmed fish, but wild creatures whose desire to escape capture is a guarantee of good sport.

249

Catching tuna the "kind" way off the Tasman Peninsula

▶▶ Strahan   226B2

A small settlement on the inland sea of Macquarie Harbour, Strahan grew to export the wood and minerals of the western interior. Its main functions today are fishing and tourism. The visitor's center on the waterside has deliberately tendentious displays on the history of the area.

Hell's Gates, as the narrow and dangerous entrance to Macquarie Harbour is known, were so named because they guarded Sarah Island, from 1822 to 1834 one of Britain's most brutally administered penal colonies.

▶ Swansea   227B5

From the beach there is a wonderful prospect across Great Oyster Bay toward the Freycinet Peninsula. One of the best places to stay along the Suncoast, Swansea has such visitor attractions as the imposing three-story brick General Store constructed around 1838 and the unusual Bark Mill.

▶ Wynyard   226D3

Linked to the mainland by flights from its own airport, this fishing port at the mouth of the Inglis River is a useful gateway to Tasmania's scenic northwest coast and its fertile farming hinterland. To the east are the wonderful white sands of **Boat Harbour** and **Sisters Beach**, as well as the rugged coastline of the **Rocky Cape National Park▶▶** backed by heath and hill land. The headland at Table Cape has a lighthouse and offers splendid views.

▶ Zeehan   226C2

Named after one of Abel Tasman's ships, this isolated mining town in Tasmania's far west saw both boom and bust before beginning a modest recovery in recent years. Legacies of turn-of-the-century prosperity based on silver-lead extraction include the **Gaiety Theatre** and the **West Coast Pioneers Memorial Museum▶** (see panel).

Georges Bay at St. Helens is still a bustling fishing port despite an influx of summer visitors

250

Railroad delights
The West Coast Pioneers Museum in Zeehan is home to a comprehensive array of local exhibits as well as locomotives built long ago in Glasgow, Manchester and Germany. These were shipped across the seas to work the ore trains of one of the most mineralized areas on earth.

Arriving

All visitors to Australia must have a valid passport and, with the exception of New Zealanders, a visa. Visas must be obtained in advance from an Australian High Commission, Embassy, or Consulate; a fee is only charged if you intend to stay more than three months or if you require a multiple-entry visa.

A Working Holiday Maker visa (valid for 12 months) allows you to take employment of a casual nature during your stay, and also carries a charge.

By air All Australian state capitals with the exception of Hobart have direct connections with destinations abroad, and there are also international flights from Darwin, Cairns and Townsville. There are many opportunities for combining a visit to Australia with stopovers at intermediate destinations or by buying a "round-the-world" flight. Many visitors will want to take advantage of the option of arriving at one point in Australia and departing from another.

Fares vary considerably among the 30 or so international airlines serving Australia and also fluctuate according to the time of year; the cheapest fare may turn out to be a false economy if it involves an exhaustingly long flight with several stops. Check prices and availability well in advance through a travel agent or reputable media outlets; there are some real bargains, particularly in charter flights.

By sea Those with time to spare can travel to Australia on board the cruise ships of operators like C.T.C., Cunard, P & O, and Royal Viking, albeit at a price. Some freighters carry a small number of passengers too, but this is by no means a cheap alternative.

Camping

Despite the risks of insect nuisance, Australia is usually a wonderful land in which to camp, not just because of its climate but also because of its excep-

tionally generous and varied provision of campsites, both on the edge of town and in the bush. Site equipment is generally good, and might include electricity hook-up, hot and cold water, showers, lavatories and laundromats. Some sites offer pre-erected tents, and many more have trailers and cabins for rent. Operators range from town councils to commercial chains or national park authorities. Some of the national park sites are "basic." Camping on your own in the wild is also possible, but discretion is advisable; check that your presence will not annoy a landowner.

Camper-vans and motorhomes are increasingly popular among Australians exploring their own country in a leisurely way. Renting such a vehicle should be considered by visitors from abroad who intend to spend most or part of their time touring rather than visiting city sights.

Car breakdown

When renting a car, check with the rental company about emergency road service; they will normally arrange help for you. Membership in a motoring association in your own country will in many cases give you access to the facilities of the various state motoring

The Overland Train runs between Adelaide and Melbourne

clubs (contact the Australian Automobile Association for details).

Breaking down in the Outback is potentially fatal and should be avoided by making sensible preparations for your journey (see Driving tips on pages 257–8).

● **Australian Automobile Association** G.P.O. Box 1555, Canberra City, A.C.T./2601 (tel: 06 247 7311).

Car rental

Car rental is well developed in Australia, with vehicles available from a range of agencies (both international and local) at most airports as well as from town and city centers. To rent a car you will need to have a valid driving license and, normally, be more than 21 years old. One-way rentals between major cities are possible, but they are not cheap. The total cost of the rental will consist of the basic daily or weekly rate plus various additions like a collision damage waiver and possibly a mileage charge. Choice of vehicle is very much an individual matter; 4WDs and camper-vans are available, and you might find a six-cylinder home-grown model more restful for long trips than a hatchback. There may be restrictions on taking a vehicle over a state boundary, into "country" or "remote" areas, or driving it on unpaved roads.

Climate

As befits a country that is also a continent, Australia has a variety of climates. Visitors from the northern hemisphere will need to get used to the seasons being reversed (summer is from December through February, and winter is from June through August). In very general terms, the best time to visit the southwest and southeast is between September and April, and the north and center between May and October.

The southwest and southeast (southwest Western Australia, much of South Australia, Victoria, much of New South Wales, Australian Capital Territory and Tasmania) are at their best in spring and summer, although midsummer temperatures can get very high. Winters here can be dull and rainy, though frost is rare except at high altitudes where snow can be expected – as in the Snowy Mountains.

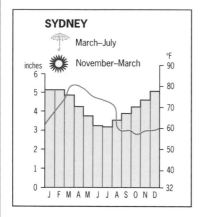

SYDNEY
☂ March–July
☀ November–March

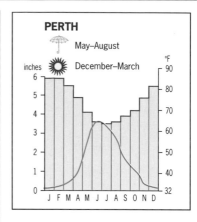

PERTH
☂ May–August
☀ December–March

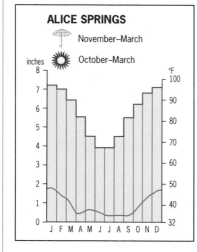

ALICE SPRINGS
☂ November–March
☀ October–March

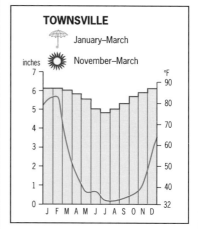

TOWNSVILLE
☂ January–March
☀ November–March

Many Australians enjoy a winter vacation in the Red Centre or north-western Western Australia, where there is likely to be an endless succession of bright sunny days with temperatures around the 68–77°F mark, although nights will be cold. Summer in these areas can be unbearably hot, with temperatures of 113°F not uncommon.

The subtropical and tropical parts of the country (much of Queensland, Western Australia and the Northern Territory) are at their least comfortable in the Wet (usually November through April), when heavy rainfall and high humidity prevail. This is also the season when box jellyfish make the sea unsafe for swimmers, and when roads may be washed away. In the Dry (May through October) conditions are much more pleasant, with warm (but not too hot) and sunny days.

Crime
Political and business scandals of sometimes spectacular dimensions, and the activities of a well-organized criminal underworld dominate the headlines in Australia more than casual offenses against the person. Thieves and muggers do exist, but Australian cities are still among the safest in the world, and no more than the normal precautions against pickpockets, muggers and car thieves are necessary.

Customs regulations
Personal effects can be brought into Australia without payment of duty, as can 250 cigarettes and a liter (about

CONVERSION CHARTS

FROM	TO	MULTIPLY BY
Inches	Centimeters	2.54
Centimeters	Inches	0.3937
Feet	Meters	0.3048
Meters	Feet	3.2810
Yards	Meters	0.9144
Meters	Yards	1.0940
Miles	Kilometers	1.6090
Kilometers	Miles	0.6214
Acres	Hectares	0.4047
Hectares	Acres	2.4710
U.S. Gallons	Liters	3.7854
Liters	U.S.Gallons	0.2642
Ounces	Grams	28.35
Grams	Ounces	0.0353
Pounds	Grams	453.6
Grams	Pounds	0.0022
Pounds	Kilograms	0.4536
Kilograms	Pounds	2.205
U.S. Tons	Tonnes	0.9072
Tonnes	U.S. Tons	1.1023

MEN'S SUITS

U.K	36	38	40	42	44	46	48
Europe	46	48	50	52	54	56	58
U.S.	36	38	40	42	44	46	48
Australia	92	97	102	107	112	117	122

DRESS SIZES

U.K.	8	10	12	14	16	18
France	36	38	40	42	44	46
Rest of Europe	34	36	38	40	42	44
U.S.	6	8	10	12	14	16
Australia	8	10	12	14	16	18

MEN'S SHIRTS

U.K.	14	14.5	15	15.5	16	16.5	17
Europe	36	37	38	39/40	41	42	43
U.S.	14	14.5	15	15.5	16	16.5	17
Australia	36	37	38	39	41	42	43

MEN'S SHOES

U.K.	7	7.5	8.5	9.5	10.5	11
Europe	41	42	43	44	45	46
U.S.	8	8.5	9.5	10.5	11.5	12
Australia	7	7.5	8.5	9.5	10.5	11

WOMEN'S SHOES

U.K.	4.5	5	5.5	6	6.5	7
Europe	38	38	39	39	40	41
U.S.	6	6.5	7	7.5	8	8.5
Australia	6.5	7	7.5	8	8.5	9

one U.S. quart) of liquor (beer, wine, or spirits), and gifts up to a value of A$400. There are tough penalties for importing weapons, drugs (soft or hard), and for attempting to bring in quarantinable articles, particularly plants that may be disease carriers.

Visitors with disabilities

Conscientious efforts are made by public bodies and by the tourist industry to make life easier for people with disabilities. Modern buildings and facilities are designed to high standards of accessibility for wheelchairs, pedestrian crossings have audible signals when the way is clear, and many national parks have special trails for people with disabilities. They will find Australia one of the most helpful countries to visit, although it would be wise to give advance notice when planning your itinerary. The **Australian Council for Rehabilitation of the Disabled,** (P.O. Box 60, Curtin, A.C.T. /2605 (tel: 06 282 4333) will provide detailed information about facilities.

Renting a 4WD is sensible if you wish to journey into the Outback

Domestic travel

By air As you would expect in such a huge country, Australia is very air-minded, with more than three-quarters of all long-distance journeys made by plane. There are few places that cannot be reached by aircraft, whether in the comfortable cabin of a large modern jet or riding the thermals next to the pilot in a single-engine machine of considerable vintage.

Internal airlines are now deregulated, with benefits to passengers in terms of good prices and availability of services. In addition to a number of regional airlines, the main carriers are **Ansett Australia** and **Qantas Airways**, both of which offer visitors from abroad discounts on ordinary fares. Travelers using Qantas to get to Australia can usually make discounted internal flights with that company. Check on what offers are available when planning your journey and bear in mind that flights fill up quickly during the main holiday periods. Student discounts are available, as are standby fares. Smoking is not permitted on internal flights, and you will have to have a dollar or two ready if you want a luggage cart at the larger airports.

● Ansett Australia 501 Swanston Street, Melbourne, Victoria (tel: 03 9623 3333).
● Qantas Airways 203 Coward Street, Mascot, N.S.W. 2020 (tel: 02 9691 3636).

By car Australia's roads are of variable quality. In the metropolitan areas around the great cities they compare well with those anywhere in the developed world, while in remote areas they may consist of dirt tracks liable to disappear altogether in the Wet. Expressways are confined to relatively short sections leading out of the major cities. Most main roads have two lanes, although some still consist of a single strip of bitumen with gravel shoulders and others are made entirely of gravel. The recent asphalting of main roads in Western Australia and the Northern Territory has made it possible to drive all around the country "on the bitumen."

Having your own vehicle offers the usual flexibility and independence, but you should never forget the great distances likely to be involved in any extensive traveling around Australia. The great majority of the popular tourist areas can be reached in an

Ansett Australia flights are frequently offered at discount rates

Australia is great for backpackers

ordinary car; a 4WD vehicle will only be necessary if you are contemplating traveling extensively on dirt roads in the Outback—for example, on one of the South Australian "tracks" (see page 143). A camper-van or similar vehicle offers even more flexibility.

An alternative to renting a vehicle (see Car rental on page 253) is to buy one, especially if your stay is going to be a long one. Secondhand vehicles can be obtained in the usual ways (dealers, auctions and so on), or from your fellow travelers. Noticeboards in backpackers' lodges may be a useful source of information here, and in some places dusty camper-vans displaying hopeful prices are lined up on the street. The stress of disposing of your vehicle at the end of your stay can be alleviated by purchasing it from a dealer who offers a guaranteed buy-back, although obviously this will not be the cheapest way.

By train A railroad map of Australia seems incomplete, with huge areas empty of any trace of tracks. However, the big cities are accessible by train, and some Australian rail journeys count among the great railroad experiences of the world. Among them are the three-night transcontinental trip aboard the *Indian Pacific* between Sydney (or Adelaide) and Perth across the aching emptiness of the Nullarbor Plain, or the famous *Ghan*, a 20-hour foray from Adelaide into the center of the continent at Alice Springs. These, together with trains like the *Sunlander* (Brisbane–Cairns), are a relaxing way of appreciating the vastness and diversity of Australia in great comfort (ingeniously luxurious sleeping cars, gourmet dining, attentive service and showers). Other railroad services are best developed in the east and southeast of the country, with extensive metropolitan networks around Sydney, Melbourne, Brisbane and Adelaide. Europeans, used to frequent services, may be surprised to find that trains may run only once a day. Speeds are less impressive than standards of comfort.

Visitors from abroad can buy an **Austrailpass**, giving unlimited travel for various periods over the whole network (only available outside the country). A **Kangaroo Road 'n' Rail Pass** supplements this with unlimited travel on the Australian Coachlines bus network.

Driving tips
The Australian smile sometimes becomes a snarl once its owner is behind the wheel of a vehicle. However, road safety is improving and Australia has one of the lowest road fatality rates compared to vehicle numbers and distances traveled. Drinking and driving were once very much part of ordinary life, and may still be so in Outback areas, but police crackdowns (using "booze buses" to conduct random tests) seem to be having a useful effect in major cities. The legal permitted limit for alcohol is 0.05 percent blood alcohol level (0.08 percent in the Northern Territory).

In principle, Australians drive on the left and pass on the right. However, this may not immediately be obvious on a multiple-lane highway where many drivers prefer to stay in the right-hand lane, impervious to the traffic passing them on the left. Driving down the central strip of bitumen on a partly paved highway is acceptable, but it can turn into a test of nerves as oncoming traffic approaches. The monstrous "road trains" to be encountered in Western Australia, Queensland and the Northern Territory expect you to give way to them at all times and have no strategy for coping if you don't. Passing a road train that may be 165 feet or more long and throwing up clouds of dust can be very tricky; if you can't see a long way ahead, it's better to give up altogether.

Driving on unpaved roads requires special skills that you are unlikely to have time to acquire. It's best to avoid them or take very special care. At dawn, dusk and at night many animals stray onto the highway; "roo bars" are not fitted to vehicles just for macho reasons but to minimize the damage that a collision with a large kangaroo can cause. Don't drive in the country at night if you can avoid it.

Road signs in Australia vary from those in other countries, but their meaning is clear!

Speed limits are 60 k.p.h. (37 m.p.h.) in urban areas and 100/110 k.p.h. (62/68 m.p.h.) elsewhere unless indicated. Some road signs are peculiar to Australia, but most of these will be immediately understandable to visitors; they may involve tortuous wordage rather than the use of symbols. On some stretches of winding road, long passing places are provided that should be used by slow traffic to enable other drivers to pass, but remember that the passing traffic has the right of way.

Visitors from abroad must have a valid driver's license with a translation if the license is not in English or, better still, an international driving license. Gas is sold (by the liter) in leaded and unleaded varieties. Gas stations are fairly numerous but tend to have restricted opening hours; there may be problems in some areas with filling up on Saturday afternoons and on Sundays.

Adequate preparations must be made for driving in the Outback. The vehicle must be in good condition and it is sensible to carry a selection of spare parts, including an emergency plastic windshield. Enough fuel and water (5 quarts of drinking water a day) to see you through is essential. On some routes you may be required to complete a police form, giving your itinerary and estimated time of arrival.

In case of breakdown it is vital that you stay in or near your vehicle, for it will offer shade and protection, and will also be much more visible than you are on your own.

Electricity
Current emerges at 240/250 volts A.C. from Australian sockets, these being of a three-pin type unlike those used in most countries. You will either need to bring an adapter for your appliances or simply fit them with an Australian plug on arrival. Most shaver points are of the universal type.

Embassies and consulates
● **British High Commission**
Commonwealth Avenue, Yarralumla, Canberra (tel: 06 270 6666).
● **Canadian High Commission**
Commonwealth Avenue, Yarralumla, Canberra (tel: 06 273 3844).

The best way to explore Simpsons Gap is on foot, but go prepared

● **New Zealand High Commission**
Commonwealth Avenue, Yarralumla, Canberra (tel: 06 270 4211).
● **United States Embassy** 21 Moonah Place, Yarralumla, Canberra (tel: 06 270 5000).
   There are U.S. consulates in Sydney and Melbourne, and British consulate-generals in Sydney, Melbourne, Perth and Brisbane.

Emergency telephone numbers
For police, ambulance or fire brigade services, dial 000.

Health
No special health precautions are required before visiting Australia. Standards of hygiene are high, and food and drinking water are safe. Sunburn is a common hazard; wear a broad-brimmed hat, a shirt with a collar and apply plenty of sunscreen.
   Free hospital medical treatment under the **Australian Medicare** plan is available to visitors from the United Kingdom and New Zealand, although ambulance charges and the cost of medicines must be paid. Medicare also covers the bulk of the cost of a visit to a doctor. Visitors from most other countries will need full medical insurance. Dental treatment has to be paid for in full.

Language
The peculiarities and delights of Australian English are widely known in the English-speaking world, not least through the efforts of the humorist Barry Humphries, creator of Dame Edna Everage, Sir Leslie Patterson ("Australian Cultural Attaché"), and Barry "Bazza" McKenzie.
   Having some affinities with Cockney, the rather nasal Australian accent is, however, quite distinctive and is spoken without any real regional variation throughout the whole country. Differences in speech are likely to be more a matter of occasion or class; the types you might meet in the bar on Friday night would probably pour scorn on the "posh" Australian Broadcasting Corporation voice still frequently heard, with its carefully articulated vowels and diphthongs. In turn, their speech would probably present difficulties to a non-native English speaker who has conscientiously learned the "standard" language. Many Australians speak with a rising intonation that makes their sentences sound like questions.

Enjoying a beaut barbie down under with a few mates

The Australian vocabulary contains a number of words of Aboriginal origin (mallee, didgeridoo and kangaroo), as well as plenty of invented terms to describe characteristic Australian phenomena (Outback, bottle brush and bloodwood), and not a few English words that have changed their original meaning (creek means river, mountain ash is a kind of eucalyptus and mob is a group of creatures such as sheep). But the real joy of "Strine" (Australian) is its slang. Anything that can be reduced to a more or less affectionate diminutive, is ("barbie" means barbecue, "cossie" is a swimming suit (costume), and "garbo" is a garbage collector), and there are any number of quirky inventions (dunny is an outside toilet, while bludger is a scrounger) that may be the remnants of the slang of Georgian England. A lot of slang is sexual, scatological, or connected with heavy drinking. Terms evocative of throwing up after a binge are plentiful ("to chunder," "have a liquid laugh," "speak into the big white telephone"). Insults are common, sometimes delivered with affectionate intent ("you old bastard"); a recently devised university course instructed "New Aussies" on how to swear acceptably.

Although Strine is based on British English, the biggest influence on it today is American English—in terms of pronunciation ("quarder" instead of quarter), of vocabulary ("take on board" and "yuppie"), and in spelling ("program"), although the A.L.P. has been the "Labor" Party since its foundation in the late 19th century.

The following is a short and highly selective list of words, phrases and abbreviations a visitor might encounter:

A.B.C.	Australian Broadcasting Corporation
A.C.T.	Australian Capital Territory (Canberra area)
The Alice	Alice Springs
A.L.P.	Australian Labor Party
A.N.Z.A.C.	Australian and New Zealand Army Corps
arvo	afternoon
barbie	barbecue
beaut	wonderful

billabong	cut-off river bend
billy	tin used for brewing tea
bloke	man
bludger	scrounger
blue	a fight, a redhead
bottle shop	liquor store
bush	countryside
bushranger	outlaw
B.Y.O.	bring your own (drink to a restaurant)
cask	wine-box
chook	chicken
chunder	to vomit
crook	ill
dag, daggy	tangled dirty wool at the rear end of a sheep, used abusively of persons or things
daks	trousers
dinkum	genuine
drongo	a slow-witted person
Dry	the dry season
dunny	outside lavatory
fossicking	hunting for precious stones
galah	a kind of parrot, an idiot
garbo	garbage collector
g'day	good morning, good afternoon, hello
greenie	conservationist
hoon	hooligan
international	foreign (as in "international visitors")
interstate	anything to do with the other Australian states ("he's interstate" means the person referred to is away from his home state)
joey	baby kangaroo
journo	journalist
larrikin	rogue, hoodlum
migrant	immigrant
mob	group of persons or animals, for example sheep
never-never	the far-off outback
new Australian	recent immigrant
ocker	Australian male of crude manners
pokie	poker machine, fruit machine
pom, pommie	English person
property	farm
rort	rowdy party or scam
R.S.L.	Returned Servicemen's League
salties	saltwater crocodiles
semi-trailer	articulated truck
Sheila	female
she'll be right	it'll all be O.K.
shout	to buy a round of drinks
slab	24-pack of beer
smoko	work break
station	extensive farm
stingers	jellyfish
strides	pants
swag	gear or personal belongings
ta	thank you
tea	evening meal
thongs	flip-flops
tucker	food
uni	university
ute	pickup truck
Wet	rainy season
wowser	puritan, killjoy
yakka	work

The best food in town next to the river!

Media
Newspapers and periodicals

A glance inside a newsagent's (news seller's) will be enough to convince you that Australians are great readers. The array of publications includes national and regional daily broadsheets, lurid tabloids with screaming headlines, local newspapers, and countless magazines dealing with every conceivable interest.

The Australian was founded in 1964 by the controversial Rupert Murdoch to perform the role of a national general interest daily paper, supplementing the less popular *Australian Financial Review*. Regionally produced papers like the Melbourne *Age* and *Sydney Morning Herald* are considered superior by many readers, although visitors from abroad may find coverage of non-Australian news rather selective (check how well your

The Abbey Church at New Norcia, Western Australia

favorite home paper covers Australian affairs before judging them too harshly). Australian tabloids, like most such newspapers, are not of the highest standard. Most ethnic groups have dailies or weeklies in their own languages.

Television and radio Radio recalls newspapers in its divisions. The A.B.C. (Australian Broadcasting Corporation) has countrywide coverage and remains a bastion of high-mindedness, with excellent news coverage and magazine programs. In contrast are the numerous commercial stations, many of which run on a shoestring, broadcasting pop music, phone-in shows, traffic reports and similar time-fillers. In addition, there are a number of special interest and community radio stations.

Commercial television, as elsewhere in the world, suffers from a surfeit of advertising and a reliance on imported programs (though this may enable foreign visitors to catch up on their favorite soap). A.B.C. T.V. maintains high standards generally and S.B.S. (Special Broadcasting Service, not available over the whole country) is largely devoted to programs for ethnic minorities broadcast in their own languages.

Money matters

The Australian currency was decimalized in 1966, when sterling (pounds, shillings and pence) was replaced by dollars and cents (100¢ = $1). Coins come in 5¢, 10¢, 20¢, 50¢, $1 and $2 denominations, and there are $5, $10, $20, $50 and $100 notes. The $5, $10 and most $20 notes are made of polymer. You can take as much money as you want into and out of the country, although for amounts over A$5,000 you must complete a report form.

Changing money is rarely a problem, with plenty of exchange bureaus at places where tourists congregate, as well as at banks. Bank hours are usually 9:30–4 Monday to Thursday, and 9:30–5 on Friday. Traveler's checks made out in Australian dollars are likely to be dealt with more speedily. Credit cards are widely in use, but may not

Australia Day celebrations, Sydney

be particularly welcome in remote areas or in small shops.

National holidays

- **New Year's Day** — January 1
- **Australia Day** — January 26 (commemorates the landing of the First Fleet on January 26, 1788)
- **Labour Day** — Varies from state to state (commemorates achievement of the eight-hour day)
- **Good Friday**
- **Easter Monday**
- **Anzac Day** — April 25 (commemorates Gallipoli landings on April 25, 1915)
- **Queen's Birthday** — Second Monday in June
- **Christmas Day** — December 25
- **Boxing Day** — December 26 (December 28 in South Australia)

Opening hours

Museums and galleries Usually closed on Christmas Day, Good Friday and Anzac Day. Major institutions are usually open 10AM–5PM on weekdays and Saturdays, and 12PM–5PM on Sundays, although they may be closed on one day of the week. Many smaller museums open only on weekends or holidays, so the best advice is to check before you set out.

Offices Monday to Friday, 9AM–5PM.

Stores These are generally open 9AM–5PM (or 5:30PM) Monday to Friday and 9AM–4PM on Saturday, with late-night shopping on Thursday or Friday until 8PM or 9PM. Corner shops keep longer hours and also open on Sundays.

Pharmacies

Called both pharmacies and "chemists," these dispense a range of medicines and products that will probably be familiar to you. Many are open long hours, and you will find a 24-hour service in big cities. Prescriptions must be written by an Australian-registered doctor. Prices of pharmaceuticals are fairly high.

Places of worship

Most religions are represented in Australia, although outside the big cities only the major Christian denominations have places of worship. The Roman Catholic Church and the Anglican Church have roughly the same number of adherents; their cathedrals were once among the dominant buildings of city centers. The Uniting Church was formed in 1977 as a union of Methodists and Congregationalists. Islam was intro-

Fly fishing on London Lakes in Tasmania

duced by the Afghan camel drivers in the 19th century and there are now some two dozen mosques throughout the country. Synagogues are concentrated in the state capitals.

Police

Australia has both state and federal police, the latter (the A.F.P.) being responsible for the investigation of major crimes, intelligence work and antiterrorist activities, as well as for policing the Canberra area (A.C.T.).

The boys in blue are usually extremely helpful to visitors from abroad, but don't expect any special privileges if you break the law (see Driving tips on pages 257–8). In the unlikely event that you are arrested, you must give your name and address, but are then entitled to say nothing until you have contacted a friend or legal representative. In this situation, the best thing to do is to ask to be put in touch with your consul (see Embassies and consulates on pages 258–9).

Post offices

The offices of Australia Post are to be found in city centers, suburban areas and all over the country, often combined with a general store in smaller places. Larger offices have a wide range of services like fax and telex. Services are reasonably efficient.

Airmail letters can arrive in Great Britain or the U.S. after a few days, provided the correct rate has been paid and the letter or postcard is clearly addressed. A package sent by surface mail to Europe will undergo an interminable sea voyage. An alternative to paying the full airmail charge in this case is to send it Economy Air, which should ensure its arrival in the U.K. or U.S. after about two weeks. Post offices usually have a good range of stationery and packaging material for sale, and poste restante and telegram facilities are also available. Some mailboxes are of the traditional type but most (painted red with a white stripe) resemble trash bins.

Public transportation

The sprawl of low-density suburbs surrounding major cities is not conducive to the operation of an effective public transportation system, and Australians have become very dependent on cars for work, shopping and recreational trips. However, public transportation services based on bus, rail, tram (Melbourne), and ferry (Sydney), are surprisingly extensive, frequent and efficient, albeit a heavy drain on the public purse. Most systems offer special deals that are likely to be of interest to a tourist (day tickets covering the whole network, reduced fares for travel outside the rush hour and so on). Further details are given in the travel sections headed within each chapter. For long-distance transportation, see Domestic travel on pages 256–7.

Student and youth travel

There are relatively few official concessions in Australia for young visitors from abroad, but given the relative cheapness of the country this does not constitute a problem. Accommodation is provided by the countless hostels and backpackers' lodges. Membership in your national Youth Hostels Association may get you the occasional discount and also entitles you to use Australian youth hostels. Long-distance travel by bus is not expensive, and hitchhiking is easier than in many countries, although not entirely without danger. The noticeboards in lodges and hostels are an invaluable source of information on car-sharing and on what is available in terms of meals, excursions and entertainment.

Working vacations, once very popular, have become less feasible in harder economic times. **S.T.A. Travel**, a specialist in youth travel, may be able to help here, as well as with other travel arrangements; they have offices in the U.S. at 48 East 11th Street, New York, NY (tel: 212/477 7166) as well as in Australia.

Telephones

The public telephones of Telecom Australia are easy to find in most places. Long-distance calls can be made from telephone booths with the letters S.T.D. (Subscriber Trunk Dialling), and international calls can be made from booths designated I.S.D. (International Subscriber Dialling). Many machines take phone or credit cards. Local calls have no time limit, while interstate calls are relatively inexpensive given the distances involved. Cheap rates apply between 6PM and 8AM on weekdays, and between 6PM on Saturday and 8AM on Monday. Hotels frequently double the cost of a call made from your room.

To call an Australian number from overseas, dial the international access code, the country code for Australia (61), the local code (minus the initial 0), then finally the subscriber's number. To call an overseas number from Australia, dial the international access code (0011), the country code, the local code (minus its initial 0), then finally the subscriber's number. It is also worth working out the time disparity between home and Australia (see Time below).

Time

The enormous width of Australia has resulted in the creation of three time zones. Eastern Standard Time (E.S.T.) applies to New South Wales, A.C.T., Victoria, Tasmania and Queensland; Central Standard Time (C.S.T.) to South Australia and the Northern Territory; and Western Standard Time (W.S.T.) to Western Australia. C.S.T. is half an hour behind E.S.T., while W.S.T. is two hours behind. Daylight Savings Time is practiced in all states except Queensland, the N.T. and Western Australia, from October or November through March, when clocks are advanced one hour. Eastern Standard Time is 10 hours ahead of Greenwich Mean Time.

Paddling on Bondi Beach

TRAVEL FACTS

Tipping
Tipping is not widespread in Australia —for example, tips are not expected by taxi drivers, airport porters and hairdressers. Railway porters have set charges and hotel porters can be tipped at your discretion. Service charges are not normally added to restaurant bills; given good service you might leave a tip of 10 percent.

Tourist information
Australia supplies its visitors with an abundance of information from a variety of sources. The **Australian Tourist Commission** provides information on individual states and the country as a whole from its offices abroad (see below), while each state has its own Tourism Board with headquarters in the state capital, and offices in some other state capitals. Places of any size in Australia will have one or more information centers, with plenty of material on local attractions and reservation facilities for accommodations and excursions. The advice given may not always be impartial, however, since the center may have links with the services it recommends.

Other useful sources of information are motoring organizations, which give out free maps for members of allied organizations abroad, and the visitor centers or offices of the National Parks and Wildlife Service.
Australian Tourist Commission:
● **New Zealand**: Level 13, 44–48 Emily Place, Auckland 1 (tel: 09 379 9594).
● **U.K.**: 1st Floor, Gemini House, 10–18 Putney Hill, London SW15 6AA (tel: 0181-780 2227).
● **U.S.A.**: 100 Park Avenue, 25th Floor, New York, NY 10017 (tel: 212/687 6300); 2121 Avenue of the Stars, Suite 1200, Los Angeles, CA 90067 (tel: 310/552 1988).

Washrooms
Australian cities are exceptionally well provided with (usually clean) public lavatories. City maps often make a point of identifying their location.

Women
Australia is a reasonably safe place for women, and female travelers should encounter no special problems, although the more extreme manifestations of "ockerism" (see Language on page 259–61) may be irritating.

The Northern Territory Tourist Commission will provide information on sights of interest such as the Devils Marbles

HOTELS AND RESTAURANTS

HOTELS AND RESTAURANTS

ACCOMMODATIONS

The wide variety of accommodations available in Australia ranges from some of the world's finest and most luxurious hotels through motels, "units" (equipped apartments), "hotels" (which may be the most basic of inns), to backpackers' hostels with no pretensions whatsoever. You are rarely likely to have difficulty in finding somewhere to stay, although it's advisable to reserve in advance during the peak seasons (July through September and December through February). Prices compare very favorably with those in other devel-oped parts of the world, and discounts can often be obtained for longer stays or if you use hotels in a particular chain.

The following recommended hotels have been divided into three price categories:

- ● budget ($)
- ● moderate ($$)
- ● expensive ($$$)

SYDNEY

Cambridge Hotel ($$) 212 Riley Street, Surry Hills (tel: 02 9212 1111). This hotel is situated just to the south of the city center and lies within easy walking distance of Darling Harbour, the Entertainment Centre and Chinatown.

Chateau Sydney ($$) 14 Macleay Street, Potts Point (tel: 02 9358 2500). In the Kings Cross area, with a pool, good facilities and harbor views.

Grand Hotel ($) 30 Hunter Street (tel: 02 9232 3755). One of Sydney's oldest hotels, right in the city center.

Harbour Rocks Hotel ($$) 34 Harrington Street, The Rocks (tel: 02 9251 8944). This medium-sized hotel is situated in an excellent location.

Hereford Y.H.A. Lodge ($) 51 Hereford Street, Glebe (tel: 02 9660 5577). Excellent value accommodation just

to the west of Darling Harbour and city center.

Hotel Bondi ($) 178 Campbell Parade (tel: 02 9130 3271). Located on the famous beach.

Hotel Inter-Continental Sydney ($$$) 117 Macquarie Street (tel: 02 9230 0200). Partly housed in the authentically restored Treasury Buildings dating from 1851, the hotel occupies a landmark site on historic Macquarie Street in the very center of the city.

Hotel Nikko Darling Harbour ($$$) Corner Sussex and King streets (tel: 02 9299 1231). A glossy new five-star hotel overlooking Darling Harbour and close to the city center.

Hyatt Kingsgate ($$$) Kings Cross Road, Kings Cross (tel: 02 9356 1234). The deluxe standards of the Hyatt chain in the heart of Sydney's nightlife area.

Manly Beach Resort ($) 6 Carlton Street, Manly (tel: 02 9977 4188). This hotel is a short distance from all the attractions of Manly and its popular beach.

Manly Pacific Parkroyal ($$$) 55 North Steyne, Manly (tel: 02 9977 7666). This Pacific Parkroyal hotel has a beachfront location in Sydney's own seaside resort of Manly, which lies only a short and enthralling ferry trip away from the city center.

Mercantile Hotel ($$) 25 George Street (tel: 02 9247 3570). Small, atmospheric pub in a central location.

Oakford Executive Apartments ($$) 10 Wylde Street, Potts Point (tel: 02 9358 4544). Comfortable self-contained apartments with water views in the Kings Cross area.

The Observatory Hotel ($$$) 89–113 Kent Street (tel: 02 9256 2222). This is one of Sydney's newest and most luxurious boutique hotels, and is situated close to The Rocks area.

Old Sydney Parkroyal ($$$) 55 George Street (tel: 02 9252 0524). Right in the middle of The Rocks, this luxurious and charming hotel has

a main section that once served as a warehouse and stables.

Park Hyatt Sydney ($$$) 7 Hickson Road, The Rocks (tel: 02 9241 1234). Winding itself elegantly around the edge of the harbor, this hotel could not be better located.

Peppers Double Bay ($$$) 22 Knox Street, Double Bay (tel: 02 9363 0100). This upscale boutique-style hotel is located in one of the city's most colorful and exclusive inner suburbs.

Ravesi's Hotel ($$) Corner of Campbell Parade and Hall Street, Bondi Beach (tel: 02 9365 4422). Small and interesting boutique-style hotel overlooking world-famous Bondi Beach. The restaurant is excellent.

The Regent of Sydney ($$$) 199 George Street (tel: 02 9238 0000). Situated near The Rocks, The Regent has terrific views of the harbor and city.

Sebel Town House ($$$) 23 Elizabeth Bay Road, Elizabeth Bay (tel: 02 9358 3244). Not far from Kings Cross, this intimate hotel is where the rich and famous stay when visiting Sydney, and is a member of the Leading Hotels of the World group.

Sheraton Motor Hotel ($$) 40 Macleay Street, Potts Point (tel: 02 9358 1955). Convenient to transportation and shops, located in a pleasant street near Kings Cross.

Sydney Hilton ($$$) 259 Pitt Street (tel: 02 9266 0610). Recently emerged from a lavish refurbishment program, the Hilton was one of the first high-rise buildings in the city center and is close to all the central attractions.

Sydney Travellers Rest Hotel ($/$$) 37 Ultimo Road, Haymarket (tel: 02 9281 5555). Better than average budget accommodations near Darling Harbour and Chinatown.

Thelellen Beach Inn ($) 2 Campbell Parade, Bondi Beach (tel: 02 9130 5333). Recapture the atmosphere of the shore as it was during the 1930s in this refurbished hotel, which is located on the beachfront at Bondi.

Victoria Court ($$) 122 Victoria Street, Potts Point (tel: 02 9357 3200). This delightful Victorian-style guesthouse is located in a leafy street near Kings Cross.

Wynyard Travelodge ($$$) 7–9 York Street (tel: 02 9299 3000). Aimed at business travelers, this Travelodge is conveniently close to Circular Quay, Wynyard bus station and the city's business area.

CANBERRA (A.C.T.)

Embassy Motel ($$) Hopetoun Circuit, Deakin (tel: 06 281 1322). Located in the city's diplomatic district.

Hyatt Hotel Canberra ($$$) Commonwealth Avenue, Yarralumla (tel: 06 270 1234). Canberra's best hotel. The service is excellent and the facilities comprehensive in this restored 1920s art deco building.

Lakeside Hotel ($$/$$$) London Circuit, Canberra City (tel: 06 247 6244). Close to central attractions and with great views.

Macquarie Private Hotel ($) 18 National Circuit, Barton (tel: 06 273 2325). Situated in a peaceful suburb within walking distance of Parliament House.

Olims Canberra Hotel ($$) Corner Ainslie and Limestone avenues, Braddon (tel: 06 248 5511). Good quality accommodation at a reasonable price, and located close to the city center.

Tall Trees Motel ($$) 21 Stephen Street, Ainslie (tel: 06 247 9200). This motel is but a short distance from the city center in a quiet and attractively landscaped setting.

NEW SOUTH WALES
Blue Mountains

Blue Mountains Guesthouse ($$) 46–50 Portland Avenue, Medlow Bath (tel: 047 88 1122). This charming guesthouse dates from the 1890s and lies within easy reach of the major attractions of the mountains.

Fairmont Resort ($$$) 1 Sublime Point Road, Leura (tel: 047 82 5222). Excellent accommodations as well as good recreation facilities are available in this modern resort. There are also some wonderful clifftop views.

Hydro Majestic Hotel ($$$) Great Western Highway, Medlow Bath (tel: 047 88 1002). This famous confection of art nouveau and art deco overlooks the Megalong Valley from its wonderful 200-acre grounds.

Jenolan Caves House ($$$) Jenolan Caves (tel: 063 59 3304). A splendidly rambling and comfortable 19th-century survivor in Tudor style from the great days of mountain lodge vacations.

Lilianfels Blue Mountains ($$$) Lilianfels Avenue, Echo Point, Katoomba (tel: 047 80 1200). The most exclusive place to stay in the Blue Mountains. The original 1890s home now houses an award-winning restaurant.

Victoria and Albert Guesthouse ($$) 19 Station Street, Mount Victoria (tel: 047 87 1241). Established in 1914, this charming boutique-style hotel is located in the historic village of Mount Victoria.

Hunter Valley

Peppers Guest House ($$/$$$) Ekerts Road, Pokolbin (tel: 049 98 7596). Most attractively located among the vineyards, colonial-style Peppers consistently receives awards for its comfort, facilities, hospitality and, not least, for the food in its Chez Pok restaurant.

Pokolbin Village Resort ($$) Broke Road, Pokolbin (tel: 049 98 7670). The Pokolbin is centrally located within the Hunter Valley, and the resort offers its guests a choice of either suite-style accommodations or self-contained villas.

Southern Highlands

Berida Manor ($$$) 6 David Street, Bowral (tel: 048 61 1177). English-style manor house accommodations, set in attractive gardens. Antique furnishings and fine dining complete the picture.

Mildenhall Guesthouse ($$) 10 Anzac Parade, Bundanoon (tel: 048 83 6643). In an intimate garden setting, this is an attractively restored guesthouse built in the 1920s on the fringe of Morton National Park. There is a dining room for guests.

Milton Park Country House Hotel ($$$) Hordern's Road, Bowral (tel: 048 61 1522). Glorying in its reputation as one of the best places to stay in Australia, this prestigious country hotel is set in splendid grounds and has the full range of modern facilities as well as fine dining.

Resort Hotel Bowral Heritage Park ($$) 9 Kangaloon Road, Bowral (tel: 048 61 4833). This award-winning hotel offers a full range of resort facilities, including large gardens, tennis, croquet, golf and billiards.

VICTORIA
Melbourne

Albany Motor Inn ($) Corner Toorak Road and Millswyn Street, South Yarra (tel: 03 9866 4485). Offers budget-priced accommodations in the normally more expensive South Yarra area of the city.

All Seasons Crossley ($$/$$$) 51 Little Bourke Street (tel: 03 9639 1639). Modern "boutique" hotel with excellent range of facilities.

Banks Hotel ($$/$$$) Corner Flinders Lane and Spencer Street (tel: 03 9629 4111). Located in the heart of the financial district, Banks Hotel prides itself on catering to the discerning visitor.

269

HOTELS AND RESTAURANTS

Batmans Hill Hotel ($$) 66 Spencer Street (tel: 03 9614 6344). Located opposite Spencer Street Station behind a fully restored historic façade.

Chateau Melbourne Hotel ($$) 131 Lonsdale Street (tel: 03 9663 3161). A centrally located hotel that offers good service and facilities at reasonable rates.

City Park Motel ($/$$) 308–10 Kingsway, South Melbourne (tel: 03 9699 9811). Reasonably priced accommodations, close to the city's Botanic Gardens and the colorful St. Kilda area.

Georgian Court Guest House ($) 21–5 George Street, East Melbourne (tel: 03 9419 6353). This guesthouse is located in the exclusive and attractive area of East Melbourne, and lies within easy walking distance of the city center.

Grand Hyatt Melbourne ($$$) 123 Collins Street (tel: 03 9657 1234). Probably the most luxurious hotel in the heart of the city, the Hyatt offers a full range of leisure and dining facilities.

Kingsgate Private Hotel ($) 131 King Street (tel: 03 9629 3049). Offering extremely good value accommodation in the city center, the Kingsgate Hotel also has a restaurant, a coffee shop and a bar.

Le Meridien Melbourne at Rialto ($$$) 495 Collins Street (tel: 03 9620 9111). Splendidly Gothic late 19th-century hotel with all the usual comforts.

Oakford Gordon Place ($$/$$$) 24 Little Bourke Street (tel: 03 9663 2888). Situated between Parliament and Chinatown, the Oakford's luxuriously appointed apartments (there are even books on the shelves!) open onto a vine-clad interior courtyard with a huge palm tree. The historic building the hotel occupies has a deli, a bar and Rose's Restaurant, and literally buzzes with big city excitement.

Oakford The Park ($$) 631 Punt Road, South Yarra (tel: 03 9820 8544). One of a number of "Oakford" buildings of excellent serviced apartments that can be rented at locations scattered around the city.

Old Melbourne Hotel ($$) 5 Flemington Road, North Melbourne (tel: 03 9329 9344). Has a flagstone courtyard around which are grouped three restaurants and a couple of bars.

Olembia Private Hotel ($) 96 Barkly Street, St. Kilda (tel: 03 9537 1412). Somewhat along the lines of a European pension, this pleasant and relaxed establishment is located in the characterful bayside suburb of St. Kilda.

Parkroyal on St. Kilda Road ($$/$$$) 562 St. Kilda Road, St. Kilda (tel: 03 9529 8888). An elegant boutique-style hotel with large rooms and excellent service. Located a short tram ride from the city enter, this Parkroyal can be found in one of Melbourne's most interesting inner suburbs.

Rockman's Regency Hotel ($$$) Corner Exhibition and Lonsdale streets (tel: 03 9662 3900). Melbourne's most luxurious boutique hotel is close to the city center. There are excellent facilities and the hotel is home to some of the city's most upmarket bars and restaurants.

St. Kilda Road Travelodge ($$) Corner St. Kilda Road and Park Street (tel: 03 9699 4833). Opposite the Botanic Gardens and close to the Arts Centre, this 230-room hotel represents good value in a prime location.

Sheraton Hotel ($$/$$$) 13 Spring Street (tel: 03 9650 5000). A reliable city center hotel, the Sheraton overlooks the Treasury Gardens.

South Yarra Hill Suites ($$/$$$) 14 Murphy Street, South Yarra (tel: 03 9868 8222). These serviced one to three bedroom apartments are situated in exclusive South Yarra. They come complete with fully

equipped kitchens and spacious living rooms.

Townhouse Hotel ($) 701 Swanston Street, Carlton (tel: 03 9347 7811), and **Lygon Lodge Carlton** ($) 220 Lygon Street, Carlton (tel: 03 9663 6633) are two high-standard motels in the inner suburb of Carlton.

Victoria Hotel ($$) 215 Little Collins Street (tel: 03 9653 0441). This comfortable turn-of-the-century hotel is located in the city center and has become a Melbourne institution.

The Windsor ($$$) 103 Spring Street (tel: 03 9653 0653). This grand old-fashioned hotel has been splendidly restored and furnished with antiques. It has an unbeatable location opposite Parliament and has been classified by the National Trust.

Great Ocean Road

Caledonian Inn ($) Corner Bank and James streets, Port Fairy (tel: 055 68 1044). With its bar and seafood lounge, the Caledonian Inn claims to be the oldest continuously licensed hotel in Victoria. However, no such claim is made for the motel section.

The Cumberland Lorne ($$$) 150 Mountjoy Parade, Lorne (tel: 052 89 2400). A recently completed luxury apartment resort in the center of this well-established seaside resort.

Erskine House ($$) 136 Mountjoy Parade, Lorne (tel: 052 89 1209). Rudyard Kipling stayed in this venerable hotel, situated among immaculately maintained gardens.

Seacombe House Motor Inn ($$) 22 Sackville Street, Port Fairy (tel: 055 68 1082). One of the older buildings in this delightful old harbor town, Seacombe House has been classified by the National Trust. The Inn, however, consists of modern motel units.

Northeast Victoria

Eucalpyt Ridge ($$$) 564 Skyline Road, Eildon (tel: 057 74 2033). An upscale

ACCOMMODATIONS

mountain lodge with views of Lake Eildon. Luxurious suites and fine dining are complemented by 250 acres of bushland and a national park located nearby.

Mount Buffalo Chalet ($$) Mount Buffalo National Park (tel: 057 55 1500). A splendidly old-fashioned Alpine-style establishment situated in the exhilarating surroundings of this mountain national park.

Rose Cottage ($$) 42 Camp Street, Beechworth (tel: 057 28 1069). Bed and breakfast style accommodations in a charming old cottage that is full of atmosphere.

Snowbird Lodge ($$) Alpine Highway, Hotham Heights (tel: 057 59 3503). Providing an excellent base for summer walking and winter skiing, this inn is located in the Alpine National Park and has wonderful views from its bar.

Tanswells Commercial Hotel ($) 50 Ford Street, Beechworth (tel: 057 28 1480). In the middle of this perfectly preserved goldfields town, the 19th-century Tanswells has fine iron-work and is authentically furnished. The building has been National Trust-classified.

Trackers Mountain Lodge ($$/$$$) Schuss Street, Falls Creek (tel: 057 58 3346). Luxurious accommodations in the heart of one of Australia's most popular ski resorts. The location is also perfect for a summer walking, horse-riding or fishing vacation.

SOUTH AUSTRALIA
Adelaide
Adelaide's Bed And Breakfast ($$) 239 Franklin Street (tel: 08 8231 3124). Cozy rooms situated in a historic sandstone building dating from the 1870s, centrally located in the City Square.

Apartments on the Park ($$) 274 South Terrace (tel: 08 8232 0555). Self-contained units at the southern end of town. The apartments are ideal for families or small groups.

Barron Townhouse ($$) Corner Hindley and Morphett streets (tel: 08 8211 8255). Conveniently central apartments.

Earl of Zetland Hotel ($) Corner Gawler Place and Flinders Street (tel: 08 8223 5500). Comfortable old-fashioned hotel in a central location.

Festival Lodge Motel ($$) 140 North Terrace (tel: 08 8212 7877). Reasonably priced motel-style accommodation in Adelaide's most famous street.

Grosvenor Hotel ($$) 125 North Terrace (tel: 08 8231 2961). More or less opposite the Hyatt, this is where up country farmers and their families would stay when in town. Rooms are available at a variety of rates.

Hindley Parkroyal ($$) 65 Hindley Street (tel: 08 8231 5552). A good-quality hotel with a pool, spa and restaurant, on Adelaide's main restaurant and nightlife street.

Hilton International (Adelaide) ($$$) 233 Victoria Square (tel: 08 8217 0711). The usual good standards of the Hilton group, this time right in the heart of the city.

Hyatt Regency Adelaide ($$$) North Terrace (tel: 08 8231 1234). Decorated with stunning works of art inside and out, the Hyatt is the city's most sumptuous hotel, centrally located near major attractions.

The Mansions Apartments ($$) 21 Pulteney Street (tel: 08 8232 0033). Well located self-contained apartments in an interesting old building.

North Adelaide Heritage Apartments ($$) (tel: 08 8272 1355). Self-contained apartments in a variety of North Adelaide locations.

Ramada Grand Hotel ($$$) Moseley Square, Glenelg (tel: 08 8376 1222). The best hotel in Adelaide's most famous beach suburb—a short and pleasant tram ride from the city center.

Richmond Hotel on The Mall ($$) 128 Rundle Mall (tel: 08 8223 4044). Central business district apartments.

Terrace Inter-Continental Adelaide ($$$) 150 North Terrace (tel: 08 8217 7552). Adelaide's most elegant hotel offers good views, excellent service and tastefully decorated rooms and suites.

Adelaide Hills
Hahndorf Inn Motor Lodge ($/$$) 35 Main Street, Hahndorf (tel: 08 8388 1000). This inn offers reasonably priced motel-style accommodations in the heart of the Hills' most picturesque town.

Mount Lofty House ($$$) 74 Summit Road, Crafers (tel: 08 8339 6777). Luxury country house living, South Australian style. The hotel is located just below the summit of Mount Lofty in the Adelaide Hills only a short drive from the city itself. There is also a gourmet restaurant.

Thorngrove Country Manor ($$$) 2 Glenside Lane, Stirling (tel: 08 8339 6748). Thorngrove lies just 20 minutes from the city center, but is another world of European-style country grandeur. This elegant hotel features gardens, European antiques and large suites.

Barossa Valley
Blickinstal Hillside ($$) Rifle Range Road, Tanunda (tel: 085 63 2716). With magnificent views over the Barossa, this bed and breakfast establishment has a German name meaning "valley view."

Collingrove Homestead ($$$) Eden Valley Road, Angaston (tel: 085 64 2061). Stay comfortably in the servants' quarters of this fine National Trust property on the edge of the Barossa, once the home of one of Australia's greatest landowning families. Dinner is available by arrangement.

271

HOTELS AND RESTAURANTS

The Hermitage of Marananga ($$$) Corner Seppeltsfield and Stonewell roads, Marananga (tel: 085 62 2722). These colonial-style buildings rising out of the Barossa vineyards offer superior bed and breakfast. Gourmet dining is also offered. (see page 279).
Tanunda Hotel ($) 51 Murray Street, Tanunda (tel: 085 63 2030). Budget accommodations in the often expensive Barossa Valley area.

WESTERN AUSTRALIA
Perth

Airways City Hotel ($$) 195 Adelaide Terrace (tel: 09 323 7799). This provides an affordable alternative to the nearby Sheraton.
Baileys Parkside Motel ($) 150 Bennett Street (tel: 09 325 3788). These budget-priced self-contained units are centrally located: family units and suites are available.
Burswood Resort Casino ($$$) Great Eastern Highway, Rivervale (tel: 09 362 7777). On the far bank of the Swan River from the city center, Burswood is a luxury resort with its own golf course. It is claimed that the casino itself is the largest in the southern hemisphere.
Carlton Hotel ($) 248 Hay Street East (tel: 09 325 2092). Possibly the friend-liest pub in town. The price includes your morning paper.
Chateau Commodore Hotel ($$) 417 Hay Street (tel: 09 325 0461). Good quality accommodations at a reasonable price. The hotel has a swimming pool and restaurant and is just a short walk from the city's central business district.
City Waters Lodge ($/$$) 118 Terrace Road (tel: 09 325 1566). This lodge offers self-contained apartments on the Swan River foreshore.
Cottesloe Beach Hotel ($/$$) 104 Marine Parade, Cottesloe (tel: 09 383 1100). Just 15 minutes drive from the city, this beachside

hotel provides good-value accomodation, as well as bars and a café.
Hyatt Regency Perth ($$$) 99 Adelaide Terrace, East Perth (tel: 09 225 1234). One of the city's best hotels, the Hyatt Regency is located just to the east of the city center and overlooks the Swan River.
Metro Inn Apartments ($) 22 Nile Street, East Perth (tel: 09 325 1866). Budget self-contained apartments and hotel rooms, close to the city center and near the river.
Miss Maud Swedish Hotel ($$) 97 Murray Street (tel: 09 325 3900). Scandinavian chic in city center location. Miss Maud also provides good and reasonably priced eating.
Parkroyal Perth ($$$) 54 Terrace Road (tel: 09 325 3811). The Parkroyal offers luxury accommodations in the heart of the city, yet with good views of the Swan River. This is one of the best addresses at which to stay in Perth.
Parmelia Hilton ($$$) 14 Mill Street (tel: 09 322 3622). One of the most individual of all the hotels in the Hilton chain, the Parmelia is located right in Perth's city center.
Radisson Observation City Hotel ($$$) The Esplanade, Scarborough (tel: 09 245 1000). A luxurious five-star resort on the boardwalk at Scarborough beach, just a 15-minute drive from the city center.
The Royal Hotel ($) Corner Wellington and William streets (tel: 09 481 1000). A renovated pub-style hotel in the city center with both self-contained and shared facility rooms.
Sheraton Perth Hotel ($$$) 207 Adelaide Terrace (tel: 09 325 0501). Sheraton comforts and conveniences on one of Perth's main arteries.
Sullivans Hotel ($$) 166 Mounts Bay Road (tel: 09 321 8022). A small, friendly hotel that is located at the edge of Kings Park. Some

rooms have views of the river.

Fremantle

Bakery 11 ($/$$) 11 Little Howard Street (tel: 09 335 7531). A renovated bakery complex, dating from 1896. This bed and breakfast style hotel offers comfort and charm.
Esplanade Hotel ($$$) Corner of Marine Terrace and Essex Street (tel: 09 430 4000). This international standard hotel is situated in the heart of historic Fremantle. Rooms, studios and suites are available, and the hotel also has excellent recreation and dining facilities.

Kalgoorlie–Boulder

Hannan's View Motel ($$) 430 Hannan Street, Kalgoorlie (tel: 090 91 3333). Recommended central motel.
Quality Plaza ($$) 45 Egan Street, Kalgoorlie (tel: 090 21 4544). Claimed to be the finest hotel in town, and certainly true as far as comfort and facilities are concerned. Reasonably close to center (unlike most Kalgoorlie motels).
York Hotel ($/$$) 259 Hannan Street, Kalgoorlie (tel: 090 21 2337). This is a splendid hotel from the early days of the century, with an authentic feel of the gold-rush days including darkly furnished rooms and balcony bathrooms. The restaurant will serve you chops and steak for breakfast—a real gold-miner's feast!

Other historic hotels in Kalgoorlie/Boulder include the **Exchange** on Hannan Street (tel: 090 21 2833) and the **Palace**, also on Hannan Street (tel: 090 21 2788).

NORTHERN TERRITORY
Darwin

Beaufort Darwin ($$$) The Esplanade (tel: 08 8982 9911). Housed in an intriguing pink and blue post-modern complex in an enviable position on Darwin's Esplanade, the luxury

Beaufort is one of the more striking additions to the city's post-Tracy skyline. There are also excellent restaurants here, including the **Siam** (fine Thai cuisine) and sophisticated **Siggi's** (international).

Capricornia Motel ($) 44 East Point Road, Fannie Bay (tel: 08 8981 4055). Comfortable and well priced units, situated just out of the town center. The motel has a restaurant and a swimming pool.

Cherry Blossom Motel ($) 108 The Esplanade (tel: 08 8981 6734). This motel provides acceptable accommodations in an excellent Esplanade location that is convenient for the city center.

City Gardens Apartments ($$) 93 Woods Street (tel: 08 8941 2888). Centrally located complex that offers apartments and family units, as well as a swimming pool and barbecue area.

Darwin Travelodge ($$/$$$) 122 The Esplanade (tel: 08 8981 5388). A good quality modern hotel on Darwin's waterfront.

Diamond Beach Hotel Casino ($$$) Gilruth Avenue, The Gardens (tel: 08 8946 2666). Deluxe hotel that is part of Darwin's casino complex. Located on the beach, just out of the city center.

Novotel Atrium Hotel Darwin ($$/$$$) Corner Peel Street and The Esplanade (tel: 08 8941 0755). This medium sized modern hotel has good facilities and service. Rooms vary from standard to deluxe suites and the hotel has a great boardwalk position.

Plaza Hotel Darwin ($$$) 32 Mitchell Street (tel: 08 8982 0000). The tallest building in Darwin, the Plaza has a cool and spacious atrium that provides some welcome relief when Darwin's heat and humidity start to become too much for any weary sightseers.

Poinciana Inn ($$) Corner Mitchell and McLachlan streets (tel: 08 8981 8111). Good-value single to family rooms, just a five-minute walk from the city center.

Alice Springs
Alice Springs Pacific Resort ($$/$$$) 34 Stott Terrace (tel: 08 8952 6699). Attractive resort-style accommodation with family, standard and deluxe categories. The resort has a restaurant, swimming pool and barbecue area.

Alice Tourist Apartments ($) Corner Gap Road and Gnoilya Street (tel: 08 8952 2788). Two-bedroom apartments at a very reasonable price. The small complex is just out of town and provides a pool and full cooking facilities.

Diplomat Motor Inn ($$) Corner Gregory Terrace and Hartley Street (tel: 08 8952 8977). In tasteful two-tone pink, very superior motel-style accommodations laid out on two levels in the heart of town. Executive suites with spa baths are also available.

Frontier Oasis Alice Springs ($$) 10 Gap Road (tel: 08 8952 1444). Well located motel-style accommodations with good facilities, including a pool and gardens.

Lasseters Hotel Casino ($$/$$$) 93 Barrett Drive (tel: 08 8952 5066). This is one of the town's most upscale hotels, and is part of the Alice Springs casino development. The hotel offers both rooms and suites.

Melanka Backpackers Resort ($) 94 Todd Street (tel: 08 8952 2233). Possibly the best range of inexpensive accommodations in central Australia, from basic rooms to motel-style accommodations with own bathroom and so on. There is a licensed restaurant and two pools, and the lodge lies in a central location.

Plaza Hotel Alice Springs ($$$) Barrett Drive (tel: 08 8952 8000). Provides resort-type luxury at the foot of the stark MacDonnell Ranges, just a short distance to the south of town.

Ayers Rock
All accommodations and most other facilities at Ayers Rock are provided and managed outside the National Park at Ayers Rock Resort (formerly Yulara). You can stay in luxury at the superbly landscaped **Sails in the Desert** (tel: 08 8956 2200), in comfort at both the **Desert Gardens** (tel: 08 8956 2100) and the somewhat plainer but very affordable **Outback Pioneer Lodge** (tel: 08 8956 2170). Backpackers and campers are also welcome. There are restaurants in each of the hotels, all of approximately the same quality and in the same price range.

QUEENSLAND
Brisbane
Albert Park Inn Hotel ($$) 551 Wickham Terrace, Spring Hill (tel: 07 3831 3111). A comfortable hotel located near Albert Park, a short walk from the city center. The pool and terrace overlook the park and the hotel has full à la carte dining.

Bellevue Hotel ($/$$) 103 George Street (tel: 07 3221 6044). This well-priced central city hotel offers a pool and restaurant, and is close to the South Bank Parklands.

Coronation Motel ($) 205 Coronation Drive, Milton (tel: 07 3369 9955). Budget-priced motel rooms situated a short distance from the city center. The motel isn't anything special, but it does offer good value accommodations.

Gateway Hotel ($$) 85–7 North Quay (tel: 07 3236 3300). Located close to the city center, the Gateway Hotel overlooks the river and South Bank parklands. This comfortable hotel features some excellent facilities, including bars, restaurants and a pool.

Gazebo Hotel ($$) 345 Wickham Terrace (tel: 07 3831 6177). The most prominent among the cluster of hotels on the leafy heights overlooking the city center (which is

273

HOTELS AND RESTAURANTS

within easy walking distance).

The Heritage ($$$) Corner Margaret and Edward streets (tel: 07 3221 1999). A luxurious city center hotel that makes the best of its location near the waterside and the famous Botanic Gardens.

Kirribilli Apartments ($$) 150 Oxlade Drive, New Farm (tel: 07 3358 5622). These serviced apartments are located on the Brisbane River, and lie just minutes from the city by car or ferry. Both one- and two-bedroom apartments are available.

Metro Inn Tower Mill ($$) 239 Wickham Terrace (tel: 07 3832 1421). Overlooking the city from high on Wickham Terrace, this comfortable hotel offers balconies, a cocktail bar and 24-hour room service.

Powerhouse Hotel ($$/$$$) Corner Kingsford Smith Drive and Hunt Street, Hamilton (tel: 07 3862 1800). This elegant boutique-style hotel is conveniently close to the airport, yet only a short drive from the city. It has good facilities, including an excellent restaurant and bar.

Ryan's on The River ($$) 269 Main Street, Kangaroo Point (tel: 07 3391 1011). This lodge offers fine views of the city center from the far bank of the Brisbane River (there is a ferry link to the city). Rooms are moderately priced.

Sheraton Brisbane Hotel and Towers ($$$) 249 Turbot Street (tel: 07 3835 3535). All the luxury of a Sheraton in the heart of the city.

Sunshine Coast

Hyatt Regency Coolum ($$$) Warran Road, Coolum Beach (tel: 074 46 1234). A self-contained and extremely luxurious resort with a wide variety of types of accommodations as well as an extraordinary range of sports and recreational facilities. Located between Mount Coolum National Park and the glorious sands of the Sunshine Coast. Among the places to eat,

Petrie's Restaurant is a regular award-winner. Bargains and special offers are available.

Netanya Noosa Resort ($$$) 75 Hastings Street, Noosa Heads (tel: 074 47 4722). A delightful resort located right on the boardwalk. All suites have a balcony and kitchenette, and the hotel offers a licensed restaurant and cocktail bar.

Novotel Twin Waters Resort ($$$) Ocean Drive, Mudjimba Beach (tel: 074 48 8000). Another exclusive resort on the Sunshine Coast, Twin Waters has a wide range of facilities and is located near the mouth of the Maroochy River.

Sheraton Noosa Resort ($$$) Hastings Street, Noosa Heads (tel: 074 49 4888). Up-scale accommodations in a well designed, low-rise, resort complex. Rooms are spacious and provide spas and kitchenettes.

Sun Lagoon ($$) Quamby Place, Noosa Sound (tel: 074 47 4833). This waterfront resort is on the Noosa River and provides fully equipped self-contained apartments that can accomodate up to six people.

Noosa has a good variety of accommodations, not in brash high-rises like the Gold Coast but mostly in pleasing modern buildings of a more human scale. Details can be obtained from: **Accom Noosa,** Hastings Street, Noosa Heads, P.O. Box 694, Noosa, Qld 4567 (tel: 074 47 3444).

Gold Coast and Hinterland

Conrad Jupiters ($$$) Broadbeach Island (tel: 07 5592 1133). With its 600-plus rooms and 24-hour casino, this is one of the Gold Coast's prime places to see and be seen.

Diamonds Resort ($$) 19 Orchid Avenue, Surfers Paradise (tel: 07 5570 1011). Diamonds is situated in the heart of Surfers Paradise and just a block back from the beach. Rooms, apartments and suites are

all available at a reasonable price.

Sheraton Mirage ($$$) Sea World Drive, Main Beach (tel: 07 5591 1488). Proving that not everything on the Gold Coast is the last word in brashness, the Sheraton is a tasteful and luxurious low-rise complex of buildings with impeccable landscaping. The famous eat at the prestigious Horizons Restaurant.

In the green hills beyond the coast:

Binna Burra Mountain Lodge ($$) Beechmont, via Nerang (tel: 07 5533 3622). This is an excellent alternative to O'Reilly's (see below).

O'Reilly's Rainforest Guesthouse ($$) Lamington National Park, via Canungra (tel: 07 5544 0644). Still run by a pioneer family, O'Reilly's has been welcoming people into the mountains for over 80 years. The price of your accommodations includes meals and activities.

St. Bernard's ($) Alpine Terrace, Tamborine Mountain (tel: 07 5545 1177). Kookaburras make their usual racket in the rain forest around this rambling old hotel near the top of Mount Tamborine.

Springbrook Mountain English Manor ($$) Springbrook Road, Springbrook (tel: 07 5533 5344). Rural hotel with lots of the atmosphere of the "Old Country" as well as fine food.

Cairns and the Far North

Cairns Colonial Club Resort ($$) 18–26 Cannon Street, Manunda, Cairns (tel: 070 53 5111). A popular resort-style complex with extensive gardens, the Colonial Club is located a short drive from the center of town. Features include tennis courts, swimming pool and two restaurants.

Club Tropical Resort ($$$) Corner Wharf and Macrossan streets, Port Douglas (tel: 070 99 5885). Club Tropical offers total luxury—it is expensive, but it's also the most exotic and upscale resort in the area.

Coconut Beach Rainforest Resort ($$$) Cape Tribulation (tel: 070 98 0033). This unique resort is well integrated into its wonderful rain forest and tropical beach surroundings.

Coconut Grove Motel ($) 58 Macrossan Street, Port Douglas (tel: 070 99 5124). Pleasant motel in lush tropical surroundings, and with a restaurant that prepares excellent fresh food while you cool off with an expertly mixed cocktail at the bar.

Daintree Cape Tribulation Heritage Lodge ($$) Turpentine Road, Cooper Creek, via Mossman (tel: 070 98 9138). Stylish modern units designed to fit into their rain forest surroundings.

Garrick House ($$) 11–13 Garrick Street, Port Douglas (tel: 070 99 5322). High-standard apartment units with all amenities in a quiet street in delightful Port Douglas.

Mercure Hotel Harbourside ($$) 209 The Esplanade, Cairns (tel: 070 51 8999). This impeccable but rather anonymous modern hotel is located along The Esplanade, and is within easy walk of the center of Cairns.

The Outrigger ($$) Corner Florence and Abbott streets, Cairns (tel: 070 51 6188). This modern interpretation of traditional north Queensland architecture can be found just back from the waterfront in the center of Cairns.

Radisson Plaza at the Pier ($$$) Pierpoint Road, Cairns (tel: 070 31 1411). The Radisson offers luxury living atop the lively new Pier Marketplace on the Cairns waterfront.

Reef House ($$$) 99 Williams Esplanade, Palm Cove (tel: 070 55 3633). Situated on one of the beaches north of Cairns, this is a tropical-style resort with the best facilities and a high reputation.

Tradewinds Esplanade Hotel ($$) 137 The Esplanade, Cairns (tel: 070 52 1111). An attractive and centrally located hotel with views of Trinity Bay, gardens or the swimming pool.

TASMANIA
Hobart
Balmoral Motor Inn ($) 511 Brooker Highway, Glenorchy (tel: 03 6272 5833). Budget-priced motel units: a few minutes out of town, but good value.

Battery Point Guest House ($$) "Mandalay," 7 McGregor Street (tel: 03 6224 2111). Just up the steps from Salamanca Place are the attractively converted coach house and stables of "Mandalay."

Crabtree House ($$) Crabtree Road, 4¼ miles north of Huonville (tel: 03 6266 4227). An easy drive from Hobart down the Huon Highway amid fine countryside is this colonial residence, beautifully furnished, providing bed and breakfast and a sumptuous dinner.

Hadley's Hotel ($$) 34 Murray Street (tel: 03 6223 4355). Good value accommodations in a central location. The hotel has two bars and a licensed restaurant.

Hobart Pacific Motor Inn ($$) Kirby Court, West Hobart (tel: 03 6234 6733). The inn offers comfortable, reasonably priced accommodations but the best feature is its location—just a few minutes from the center with excellent views over the city.

Lenna of Hobart ($$/$$$) 20 Runnymede Street, Battery Point (tel: 03 6232 3900). This is a Victorian villa with a modern extension and overlooks the Derwent River.

The Lodge on Elizabeth ($$) 249 Elizabeth Street (tel: 03 6231 3830). At the top end of town, but within walking distance of the center is the oldest residential building in Hobart, tastefully

converted. Your courteous hosts serve pre-dinner drinks.

Marquis of Hastings ($) 209 Brisbane Street, West Hobart (tel: 03 6234 3541). This is a somewhat forbidding 1960s red-brick building, but the accommodations represent good value.

Regent Park Apartments ($$) 17–23 Regent Street, Sandy Bay (tel: 03 6223 3200). Located near the casino, these well-appointed self-catering apartments are ideal for small groups and for families.

Salamanca Inn ($$$) 10 Gladstone Street (tel: 03 6223 3300). Integrated with unusual sensitivity among the old warehouses of Salamanca Place, the Salamanca is a luxury apartment hotel.

Tantallon Lodge ($$) 8 Mona Street (tel: 03 6224 1724) and **Barton Cottage** ($$) 72 Hampden Road (tel: 03 6224 1606) are well-established bed and breakfast villas that are conveniently located in Battery Point.

Wrest Point Hotel Casino ($$$) 410 Sandy Bay Road, Sandy Bay (tel: 03 6225 0112). The casino's hotel provides some of the best accommodations in Hobart, in an excellent riverside location. As one would expect, there are good dining and entertainment facilities.

Cradle Mountain
Accommodations for visitors to the national park range from the chic cabins (log fires) of **Cradle Mountain Lodge** (P.O. Box 153 Sheffield, tel: 004 92 1303) to a campground and bunkhouses. Further into the park are the **Waldheim Huts** ($$) giving wilderness living with some home comforts. The handsome wooden lodge has bars and an excellent restaurant. Possums and maybe a Tasmanian devil or two are likely to join you by the balcony after dinner.

275

Launceston

Adina Place Motel Apartments ($$) 50 York Street (tel: 003 31 6866). Fully serviced self-contained apartments just a few minutes from the city center.

Ashton Gate Guest House ($) 32 High Street (tel: 003 31 6180). This elegantly restored Victorian home is a short walk from the city center and overlooks St. George's Square Park.

Colonial Motor Inn ($$) Corner George and Elizabeth streets (tel: 003 31 6588). Once an old school, this building has been modernized and accommodations added, to say nothing of the Quill and Cane restaurant.

Country Club Casino ($$$) Country Club Avenue, Prospect Vale (tel: 003 35 5777). Although situated some distance outside Launceston, this pricey international standard resort and casino is a great place to stay. Facilities include an 18-hole golf course, horse-riding and fishing.

Kilmarnock House ($$) 66 Elphin Road (tel: 003 34 1514). With National Trust classification, this splendid large villa has been carefully refurbished and redecorated to evoke the atmosphere of the time (one night in 1904) when it was patronized by the Prince of Wales.

Novotel Launceston ($$) 29 Cameron Street (tel: 003 34 3434). All the services and comforts of a modern luxury hotel that has made some effort to fit in gracefully with its town center surroundings. Call first to check for any special offers that may be available.

Old Bakery Inn ($$) 270 York Street (tel: 003 31 7900). This well-restored old inn is a member of Historic Hotels of Australia and offers accommodations along traditional lines.

Tamar River Villas ($$) 23 Elouera Street, Riverside (tel: 003 27 1022). This standard but well-priced motel offers comfortable accommodations with views of the river.

RESTAURANTS

Eating out is relatively inexpensive in Australia, with a wide choice of ethnic cuisines and generally excellent ingredients. Costs can be further trimmed if you B.Y.O.—bring your own (wine or other liquor), which is allowed by many establishments. The "counter meals" served in many pubs are usually excellent value, and most places where tourists congregate have a reasonable variety of take-out outlets.

The following recommended restaurants have been divided into three price categories:

- budget ($)
- moderate ($$)
- expensive ($$$)

SYDNEY

Arun Thai ($$) 13/39 Elizabeth Bay Road, Elizabeth Bay (tel: 02 9357 7414). One of Sydney's most reliable Thai restaurants with a pleasant outdoor dining area. It is conveniently situated close to the many hotels of the Kings Cross area.

Balkan Seafood ($$) 215 Oxford Street, Darlinghurst (tel: 02 9331 7670). Excellent seafood at very reasonable prices, in a lively atmosphere on trendy Oxford Street.

Bayswater Brasserie ($$/$$$) 32 Bayswater Road, Kings Cross (tel: 02 9357 2177). The best and most stylish brasserie in town. A three-course meal tends toward the expensive, but there are cheaper alternatives.

Borobodur ($) 123–125 Glebe Point Road, Glebe (tel: 02 9660 5611). Good value and friendly service are provided in this B.Y.O. restaurant on the way out to trend-setting Paddington.

Choys Jin Jiang ($$$) 2nd floor, Queen Victoria Building, George Street (tel: 02 9261 3388). Impeccable food is served in refined surroundings in the lavishly refurbished Victorian shopping gallery.

Doyle's On the Beach ($$$) 11 Marine Parade, Watsons Bay (tel: 02 9337 2007). Classic "fish and chips" are served in huge quantities to up to 700 enthusiastic diners in this, one of the world's most famous fish restaurants. In its splendid location near South Head, there are great views of the harbor. There is also another branch of Doyle's at Circular Quay West (tel: 02 9252 3400).

Golden Harbour ($$) 31 Dixon Street (tel: 02 9211 5160). Among the wealth of inexpensive Chinese eateries that can be found in Chinatown, the Golden Harbour was identified by *The Sydney Morning Herald* as serving the very best value in *yum cha* (also known as *dim sum*).

Harbour Restaurant ($$$) Sydney Opera House, Bennelong Point (tel: 02 9250 7577). This is the best of the Opera House's 4 food and drink outlets, with excellent food (particularly seafood) served with wonderful 180° views out over the harbor.

Imperial Harbourside ($$$) 15 Circular Quay West (tel: 02 9247 7073). One of Sydney's very best Chinese restaurants, the Imperial has a sensational location opposite the Opera House.

Jordons Seafood Restaurant ($$) Harbourside, Darling Harbour (tel: 02 9281 3711). One of the best places to eat at Darling Harbour. Good seafood and an excellent atmosphere with views of the water.

Kable's ($$$) The Regent, 199 George Street (tel: 02 9238 0000). Attentive service and a wide ranging wine list complement the stylish cooking of Kable's, one of the best hotel restaurants in the city.

Kamogawa ($$$) Corn Exchange Building, corner Sussex and Market streets,

Darling Harbour (tel: 02 9299 5533). A newcomer, the Kamogawa has already established a reputation equal or superior to the Suntory (see below).

Kim-Van ($$) 147 Glebe Point Road, Glebe (tel: 02 9660 5252). Serves what is possibly the finest Vietnamese cuisine to be had in the city.

Laurie's ($/$$) Corner Victoria and Burton streets, Darlinghurst (tel: 02 9360 4915). A wonderful, great-value vegetarian eatery situated in the Kings Cross region. B.Y.O. and no-smoking area.

Malaya ($$) 761 George Street (tel: 02 9211 0946). This old-established restaurant, which has an attractive decor, offers good Malaysian food such as *satay* and *sambal* at reasonable prices.

Nelson Bistro ($$) The Nelson Hotel, 232 Oxford Street, Bondi Junction (tel: 02 9389 1442). Some of Sydney's best-value modern Australian cuisine in the back of a traditional Aussie pub.

Palace Hotel ($$) 122 Flinders Street, Darlinghurst (tel: 02 9361 5170). Innovative food created in a designer pub setting.

Ravesi's ($$/$$$) Corner Campbell Parade and Hall Street, Bondi Beach (tel: 02 9365 4422). Another great brasserie, this restaurant can be found in the boutique-style Ravesi's Hotel overlooking Bondi Beach.

Rossini's Rosticceria ($) Shop W5, Circular Quay (tel: 02 9247 8026). There are harbor views to accompany Rossini's swiftly served and tasty food and drink. There is also a branch at 395 George Street, between King and Market streets, (tel: 02 9299 7202).

Suntory ($$$) 529 Kent Street (tel: 02 9267 2900). Something of a Sydney institution, Suntory offers exquisite Japanese food in elegant surroundings.

Sydney Tower Restaurant ($$$) Sydney Tower, Centrepoint (tel: 02 9233 3722). There is an unsurpassable panorama over the city and harbor from this revolving restaurant perched more than 980 feet above ground level. Fortunately, the food's not bad either.

Taylor's ($$$) 203–5 Albion Street, Surry Hills (tel: 02 9361 5100). Mouthwatering north Italian food served in the charming setting of two converted Georgian cottages.

Thai Flora ($) 46 Hall Street, Bondi Beach (tel: 02 9130 2751). Bangkok comes to Bondi Beach. Although fairly basic, this restaurant serves great food at even better prices and is a local favorite.

Thai Orchid ($) 628 Crown Street, Surry Hills (tel: 02 9698 2097). One of the places that made Thai cuisine fashionable.

Tre Scalini ($$) 174 Liverpool Street, East Sydney (tel: 02 9331 4358). Simple and good food, especially fish. A lunchtime favorite.

Twenty-One Espresso ($$) 21 Knox Street, Double Bay (tel: 02 9327 2616). Memories of a mostly vanished Central Europe live on among the cream cakes.

CANBERRA (A.C.T.)

Cavalier Restaurant ($/$$) Red Hill Lookout, Red Hill (tel: 06 273 1808). Modern international cuisine is on offer here. In the downstairs café, there is the bonus of spectacular lake and city views.

Fringe Benefits Brasserie ($$) 54 Marcus Clarke Street, City (tel: 06 247 4042). Fringe Benefits has been described by Sydney-siders as the nearest thing the capital has to a trendy Sydney brasserie.

The Lobby ($$) King George Terrace, Parkes (tel: 06 273 1563). Contemporary Australian cuisine is served in an attractive garden setting near the old Parliament House.

The Oak Room ($$$) Hyatt Hotel Canberra, Commonwealth Avenue, Yarralumla (tel: 270 1234). The Oak Room provides an elegant setting for equally refined food.

Vivaldi's ($$) Australian National University, Campus Arts Centre, University Avenue, Acton (tel: 06 257 2718). This restaurant is usually full of locals, which can't be a bad sign. It serves generous portions and offers BYO.

NEW SOUTH WALES
Blue Mountains

Cleopatra ($$$) 4 Cleopatra Street, Blackheath (tel: 047 87 8456). Marvelous French cooking in one of the best restaurants in N.S.W.

Lurline Cottage Swiss Restaurant and Tea Rooms ($$) 132 Lurline Street, Katoomba (tel: 047 82 2281). Swiss and other specialties in a cross between an Australian weatherboard cottage and a mountain chalet.

The Paragon ($$) 65 Katoomba Street, Katoomba (tel: 047 82 2928). A National Trust-classified café, similar to the Hydro Majestic Hotel in style, The Paragon is worth visiting for its own sake as well as for its delicious chocolates.

Table Manners ($$) 54 Waratah Street, Katoomba (tel: 047 82 4465). Quality modern Australian food with great service. The desserts are wonderful.

VICTORIA
Melbourne

Caffe Grossi ($$) 199 Toorak Road, South Yarra (tel: 03 9827 6076). A popular Italian restaurant with great food and good service.

Colonial Tramcar Restaurant ($$$) (tel: 03 9696 4000). Dine on Australian fare while traveling Melbourne's streets in a beautifully renovated old tram car.

Fanny's ($$$) 243 Lonsdale Street (tel: 03 9663 3017). This Melbourne institution serves award-winning

277

French food in elegant surroundings.

Geppetto ($) 78a Wellington Parade, East Melbourne (tel: 03 9417 4691). A quiet café and inexpensive Italian restaurant.

Granny's Place ($$) 44 Spencer Street (tel: 03 9629 5255). Australian-style meals, including "Bush Tucker," are served in this city-center restaurant.

The Great Australian Bite ($$) 18 Molesworth Street, North Melbourne (tel: 03 9329 9068). Housed in an 1860s building, and serving fine Australian food with a French influence.

The Last Aussie Fishcaf ($) 256 Park Street, South Melbourne (tel: 03 9699 1900). This light-hearted "fish and chip" shop has a 1950s theme.

Malaysian Delight ($) 1335 Burke Road, East Kew (tel: 03 9817 2459). Everything the name promises at a reasonable price.

Maria Trattoria ($) 122 Peel Street, North Melbourne (tel: 03 9329 9016). A firm favorite with the academic crowd from the nearby university.

Mietta's ($$$) 7 Alfred Place (tel: 03 9654 2366). Rarified atmosphere of a fine old mansion with wonderful wines and food for elite eaters.

Mount Lebanon Restaurant ($$) 177 Toorak Road, South Yarra (tel: 03 9826 9080). The best Lebanese food in town at good prices. Entertainment includes live music and belly dancers. The restaurant is licensed and offers B.Y.O.

The Pavilion ($$$) 40 Jacka Boulevard, St. Kilda (tel: 03 9534 8221). Great seafood is served both inside and outside a splendidly restored bathing pavilion overlooking the bay.

Rogalsky's ($$$) 440 Clarendon Street, South Melbourne (tel: 03 9690 1977). An army cook finally able to realize his full culinary potential, Tony R. runs one of the city's most sensational French restaurants.

Stephanie's ($$$) 405 Tooronga Road, Hawthorn East (tel: 03 9822 8944). Consistently the critics' favorite since the 1970s, and a source of culinary wisdom, Stephanie Alexander runs one of Australia's top restaurants in a series of elegant dining rooms in a venerable Victorian mansion.

Sukhothai ($) 234 Johnston Street, Fitzroy (tel: 03 9419 4040). Good Thai cooking is dished up at very reasonable prices. Salads and curries are a specialty and there is a large vegetarian selection. The restaurant offers B.Y.O.

Suntory ($$/$$$) 74 Queens Road (tel: 03 9525 1231). Fine Japanese food and service in traditional oriental garden surroundings.

Thy Thy ($) First floor, 142 Victoria Street, Richmond (tel: 03 9429 1104). Excellent and very inexpensive Vietnamese food. It is also worth trying **Thy Thy** 116 Victoria Street, Richmond (tel: 03 9428 5914).

Turkish Palace ($) 831 Sydney Road, Brunswick (tel: 03 9386 3462). Mouthwatering delicacies are served here.

SOUTH AUSTRALIA
Adelaide

Adelaide Casino Pullman Restaurant ($$) North Terrace (tel: 08 8218 4273). Adelaide's casino houses this surprisingly reasonable buffet-style restaurant. The menu includes salads, pastas and a wide variety of hot dishes.

Alphütte ($$/$$$) 242 Pulteney Street (tel: 08 8223 4717). "The Antipodean home of rösti" (delicious Swiss roast potatoes) is a phrase that fails to describe adequately this Adelaide institution. Swiss professionalism guarantees excellent, albeit predictable food.

Bangkok ($$) 217 Rundle Street (tel: 08 8223 5406). Adelaide's longest established Thai restaurant offers authentic cooking at very reasonable prices. It is conveniently located in the city center.

Café Violetta ($$) 199 Hutt Street (tel: 08 8232 3655). This city café provides vegetarian food, Italian style. The prices are average and there is an excellent wine selection available.

Caffe 48 ($) 48 Unley Road, Unley (tel: 08 8272 2989). Soups, diverse main courses, salads and a variety of interesting desserts can be had in this friendly restaurant in Unley—just a short distance away from the city center.

Chloe's ($$/$$$) 36 College Road, Kent Town (tel: 08 8362 2574). In a splendidly restored Victorian villa with veranda and antique furnishings, elegant but friendly gourmet food is served.

Earl of Aberdeen ($$) 316 Pulteney Street (tel: 08 8223 6433). This stylish old pub has an excellent restaurant—you can enjoy steaks and even sample kangaroo here.

Fishcaf ($$) 100 Flinders Street (tel: 08 8232 3660). A good-value fish restaurant in superior surroundings.

Jolleys Boathouse ($$$) Jolleys Lane (tel: 08 8223 2891). This refurbished old boathouse is right on the River Torrens and serves modern Australian food. Great views.

Mona Lisa's Bistro ($$) 160 Hutt Street (tel: 08 8223 3733). This bistro describes itself as "strongly Mediterranean influenced." It is housed in a heritage-listed former general store.

Nediz Tu ($$) 170 Hutt Street (tel: 08 8223 2618). Smart but not pretentious, this relaxed restaurant is run by an Anglo-Chinese couple.

Old Parliament House ($) North Terrace (tel: 08 8211 8361). Tucked away beside the venerable Old Parliament Building, this restaurant is a charmingly intimate place.

Paul's Seafood Restaurant ($$) 79 Gouger Street (tel: 08 8231 9778). The dishes served here are basic, but reportedly the "best fried fish in Australia." There are generous helpings of whatever you fancy—garfish, whiting, snapper.

Adelaide Hills
Petaluma's Bridgewater Mill ($$) Mount Barker Road, Bridgewater (tel: 08 8339 3422). This lovely old flour mill is part of the Petaluma winery and serves the best food and wines in the Hills area.

Barossa Valley
The Hermitage of Marananga ($$/$$$) Corner Seppeltofield and Stonewell roads, Marananga (tel: 085 62 2722). This highly acclaimed Barossa Valley hotel and restaurant offers breakfast, lunch and dinner.

WESTERN AUSTRALIA
Perth
Café Piccante ($$) Corner Hill and Hay streets (tel: 09 221 1339). This Mediterranean-style eatery serves pasta, seafood, steaks, coffee and cakes in both indoor and garden areas.
Canton Restaurant ($$) 532 Hay Street (tel: 09 325 8865). One of Perth's best and longest running Chinese restaurants. The Canton is licensed and offers B.Y.O.
Dusit Thai ($$) 233 James Street, Northbridge (tel: 09 328 7647). This popular Northbridge establishment serves excellent, authentic Thai cuisine.
Fraser's ($$) Kings Park (tel: 09 481 7100). Fine western Australian produce provides the flavor at this Kings Park eatery. There are wonderful city and river views.
Gershwin's ($$$) 99 Adelaide Terrace (tel: 09 225 1274). You'll find good international cuisine in this upscale restaurant located in the city's Hyatt Regency hotel.
The Loose Box Restaurant ($$$) 6825 Great Eastern Highway, Mundaring (tel: 09 295 1787). This restaurant has one of the best reputations in all of Western Australia, and is well worth the half-hour drive out of

Perth along the highway into the Darling Ranges.
Mamma Maria's ($) Corner Aberdeen and Lake streets, Northbridge (tel: 09 328 4532). Both cheap and highly cheerful, Mamma Maria's is a Perth institution *all'Italiana*.
Matilda Bay Restaurant ($$$) 3 Hackett Drive, Crawley (tel: 09 386 5425). Excellent seafood specialties are served in a relaxed setting by the Swan River among the houses of the prosperous citizens of Perth's western suburbs.
The Oyster Bar ($$) 20 Roe Street, Northbridge (tel: 09 328 7888). Described as "Perth's leading seafood restaurant," this friendly, family-run concern has just moved into spacious and stylish new premises among its numerous competitors. It provides good, cheap food in Perth's trendsetting Northbridge area.
Perugino ($$) 77 Outram Street, West Perth (tel: 09 321 5420). A fully licensed restaurant serving fine Italian cuisine.
River Room ($$$) 207 Adelaide Terrace (tel: 09 325 0501). Excellent international cooking and elegant surroundings in this Sheraton Perth dining room.
Vino Vino ($$) 157 James Street, Northbridge (tel: 09 328 5403). Tasty, traditonal Italian food served with style. Wines include Italian as well as Western Australian vintages. Meals are half-price every Monday.

Fremantle
Pier 21 Marina Restaurant ($$) 3 John Street, North Fremantle (tel: 09 336 2222). Good seafood (selected daily from the fish markets) and meat dishes are served with great views of the Swan River.
Pricklers Café ($$) Corner Douro Road and South Terrace, Fremantle (tel: 09 336 2194). Western Australia's favorite "bush tucker" restaurant. Sample buffalo, prawns and

kangaroo, cooked in an innovative style.
Spinnakers ($$/$$$) Esplanade Hotel, corner Marine Terrace and Essex Street (tel: 09 430 4000). Excellent seafood but not just seafood, imaginatively prepared and presented. At the same address is the much more affordable **Atrium**.

Kalgoorlie–Boulder
Margarita's Mexican ($) 6 Maritana Street (tel: 090 21 7235). This restaurant makes a good attempt at promoting the merits of another far-away cuisine.
Top End Thai ($$) 71 Hannan Street (tel: 090 21 4286). Located in the same building as a skimpie bar, but much more refined, is this excellent Thai restaurant.

NORTHERN TERRITORY
Darwin
Christos on the Wharf ($$) Stokes Hill Wharf (tel: 08 8981 8658). In a unique wharfside location, this restaurant is deservedly popular for its seafood.
Corellas Restaurant ($) The Atrium Hotel, corner The Esplanade and Peel Street (tel: 08 8941 0755). Inexpensive soups, salads and buffet meals are dished up in a tropical garden setting. Open daily to 10PM.
Genghis Khan Mongolian Barbecue Restaurant ($$$) 44 East Point Road, Fannie Bay (tel: 08 8981 3883). As well as steaks derived from more conventional creatures, you may be able to taste crocodile, kangaroo and buffalo.
Jessie's ($$) Parap Hotel, 15 Parap Road, Parap (tel: 08 8981 2191). Excellent steaks and other satisfying fare—served up just outside town.
The Magic Wok ($$) 48 Cavenagh Street (tel: 08 8981 3332). Wok-cooked meals that include such exotic ingredients as buffalo, crocodile, deer and camel. More everyday seafood and vegetables are also available.

279

HOTELS AND RESTAURANTS

Raymond's ($$) 15 Cavanagh Street (tel: 08 8981 2909). Locals come here for an Italianate treat. Good ingr-edients are used in well prepared and presented dishes.

Rock Oyster ($$) 110 Mitchell Street (tel: 08 8981 3472). This long-running establishment claims to be Darwin's best seafood restaurant.

Rooftop Restaurant ($$$) Darwin Frontier Hotel, Buffalo Court (tel: 08 8981 5333). International cuisine is served in this restaurant, with its fine views of Darwin's skyline and harbor.

Siam ($$) The Esplanade (tel: 08 8941 2555). Thai cooking, including steamboats, in this Beaufort hotel restaurant.

Alice Springs
Alice Springs Bush Restaurant ($$) P.O. Box 1820, Alice Springs (tel: 08 8952 9355). Lies 18 miles from Alice Springs. Under the ownership of the same Territorian family that runs Bojangle's (see below), this is a replica of an Outback stock camp offering a "total Outback experience," including a bush walk, entertainment, and serving substantial quantities of typical Australian fare such as beef, billy tea, bread pudding and spotted dog.

Bojangle's Bush Bistro ($$) 80 Todd Street (tel: 08 8952 2873). Buffalo and camel feature on the menu of this cheerful establishment with its long bar and live entertainment.

Miss Daisy ($$) Diplomat Motor Inn, corner of Gregory Terrace and Hartley Street (tel: 08 8952 8977). Gourmet aspirations are catered to in the sophisticated surroundings of this excellent restaurant.

Overlanders Steakhouse ($$) 72 Hartley Street (tel: 08 8952 2159). Rough cast walls, low timber ceilings and swagman's impedimenta together with huge portions of stockman's tucker create an agreeable Outback atmosphere.

Ristorante Puccini ($$/$$$) Undoolya Road (tel: 08 8953 0935). A serious rival to Miss Daisy (see above).

Ayers Rock
See hotel listings on page 273.

QUEENSLAND
Brisbane
Bellevue Hotel Restaurant ($) 103 George Street (tel: 07 3221 6044). Good value international-style food is served at the Bellevue, with both set menus and à la carte dining.

City Gardens Café ($/$$) Brisbane Botanic Gardens (tel: 07 3229 1554). A delightful surprise in the lush setting of the city's botanical gardens, this cottage with a terrace serves delicious snacks to restore your sightseeing energy. Full meals are available too, until 9:30PM.

Coronation Seafood Restaurant ($$$) 205 Coronation Drive, Milton (tel: 07 3369 9955). The Coronation enjoys a high reputation for serving the best seafood in town—no mean feat!

Emperor's Palace ($$) Chinatown Mall, Fortitude Valley (tel: 07 3252 3368). This is one of the more pretentious of the many eateries that characterize Brisbane's diminutive Chinatown.

Il Centro ($$$) 1 Eagle Street Pier (tel: 07 3221 6090). Modern Italian food is served in this popular, elegant riverside restaurant.

Jean Pierre's ($$) 485 Boundary Street, Spring Hill (tel: 07 3839 9831). An award-winning establishment boasting five-star cuisine at very reasonable three-star prices.

La Grange ($$) 153 Elizabeth Street (tel: 07 3221 5590). French provincial cooking is served in this city center restaurant.

Lotus Room ($$) Corner Elizabeth and Edward streets (tel: 07 3221 8546). The service is both fast and efficient in this popular Chinese eatery.

Michael's Riverside Restaurant ($$$) Riverside Centre, 123 Eagle Street (tel: 07 3832 5522). Italian and international cuisine are available in two dining rooms, both of which have excellent views over the river.

Mount Coot-tha Summit Restaurant ($$/$$$) Sir Samuel Griffith Drive, Mount Coot-tha (tel: 07 3369 9922). Good food and stunning views over the city and out to Moreton Bay are available from this mountaintop restaurant, within the city boundary.

Oshin Japanese Restaurant ($$) 1st floor, Koala House, Corner Adelaide and Creek streets (tel: 07 3229 0410). Serves Japanese fare, including traditional dishes such as *yakiniku* and many others.

Piccolino's ($) 19 Nash Street, Rosalie (tel: 07 3368 1601). Brisbane's western suburbs (Rosalie, Paddington, Red Hill) have a number of stylish and inexpensive places to eat, much in favor with the younger set. Italian Piccolino's is a good example of such a restaurant.

Pier Nine ($$/$$$) Corner Creek and Eagle streets (tel: 07 3229 2194). Here, riverside views and menus reflect the availability of delicious seafood.

Siggi's at The Port Office ($$$) Corner Edward and Margaret streets (tel: 07 3221 4555). *The* place to meet and celebrate in Brisbane, Siggi's is part of the Heritage Hotel.

Sunshine Coast
Lindoni's Ristorante ($$) Hastings Street, Noosa Heads (tel: 074 47 5111). Highly recommended Italian food.

Pavilions ($$$) Netanya Noosa, 75 Hastings Street, Noosa Heads (tel: 074 47 4722). Gourmet restaurant with well-earned country-wide reputation for excellent food and service.

Touche Restaurant ($$$) Bay Village, Hastings Street, Noosa Heads (tel: 074 47 2222). Serves fine food with international accents.

Gold Coast and Hinterland

Great Wall ($$$)
Marina Mirage, Seaworld Drive, Main Beach (tel: 07 5591 0898). Some of the best Chinese food in Australia served in elegant surroundings.

Oskar's on the Beach ($$$)
Marine Parade, Coolangatta (tel: 07 5536 4621). On Coolangatta Beach just on the border with New South Wales, Oskar's is famous for its refined and delicious food. This reputation is well deserved, for it has been voted one of the world's top ten restaurants.

Cairns and the Far North

Barnacle Bills ($$) 65 The Esplanade (tel: 070 51 2241). On the Esplanade in Cairns, this is a popular seafront seafood eating emporium whose fame has spread to the shores of the Inland Sea, and an evening spent here is an essential part of any tourist's stay in Cairns.

Marina Connection ($)
Marina Mirage, Port Douglas (tel: 070 99 5258). Food here is served both indoors and outside near the jetty for the Barrier Reef wave piercers.

McCrossan's ($$$)
Sheraton Mirage, Davidson Street, Port Douglas (tel: 070 99 5888). Part of the opulent resort set back discreetly from the palm-lined highway leading into Port Douglas, McCrossan's produces fine food that is also presented in a most elegant way.

Tawny's ($$/$$$) Marlin Parade (tel: 070 51 1722). Overlooking Cairns' Trinity Inlet, this is a relatively old-established and sophisticated restaurant, with a welcoming ambience in which to enjoy such delicious specialties as fresh mud crab. The cost of the dishes ranges from moderate to expensive.

TASMANIA
Hobart

Alexander's ($$$) 20 Runnymede Street, Battery Point (tel: 03 6232 3900). This excellent, award-winning restaurant serves seafood and international cuisine in the elegant surroundings of the Victorian Lenna of Hobart hotel.

Asian Restaurant ($$$)
Wrest Point Hotel Casino, 410 Sandy Bay Road (tel: 03 6225 0112). Serving dishes that are far above the usual standard of Chinese and other Asian food, this restaurant is presided over by a particularly genial host. Reserve early for seats if you wish to have a view of the Derwent.

Ball & Chain Grill ($$) 87 Salamanca Place (tel: 03 6223 2655). Charcoal-grilled steaks, poultry and seafood are dished out at affordable prices. There is also an outdoor courtyard area in summer.

Dear Friends ($$$) 8 Brooke Street (tel: 03 6223 2646). Considered by many to be Hobart's finest restaurant, this award-winning establishment produces international fare and the very best service.

Drunken Admiral Restaurant ($$) 17–19 Hunter Street (tel: 03 6234 1903). Well established in one of Victoria Dock's old warehouses and decorated with maritime memorabilia, this popular restaurant naturally specializes in seafood.

Little Bali ($) 84a Harrington Street (tel: 03 6234 3426). This eatery serves limited range, value for money Indonesian food, and also has a take-out on the premises if you fancy eating al fresco.

Mures Lower Deck ($)
Victoria Dock (tel: 03 6231 2121). Long lines form next to the fishmonger's counter for top value seafood to eat here, on the quayside beyond, or to take out.

Mures Upper Deck ($$)
Victoria Dock (tel: 03 6231 2121). From its glazed second floor pavilion between Victoria and Constitution Docks, Mures serves the bounty of the sea with great flair. Reservations advised.

The Point Revolving Restaurant (same address and telephone number as Asian Restaurant – see above). Fresh Tasmanian ingredients are carefully prepared and served while you sit and watch the view revolve.

Sisco's ($$$) 121 Macquarie Street (tel: 03 6223 2059). Reputedly one of the best Spanish restaurants in Australia.

Cradle Mountain

See hotel listing on page 275.

Launceston

The Gorge Restaurant ($$)
Cliff Grounds (tel: 003 31 3330). Fine Tasmanian produce and wines in a superb location, overlooking Launceston's famous gorge and its surrounding gardens.

Novotel Launceston ($$/$$$) See the hotel listing (page 276) for the address and telephone number for bookings.
The restaurant and bars of this hotel have affordable light meals as well as "themed" specialties in the evening.

Royal Oak Hotel ($$) 14 Brisbane Street (tel: 003 31 5346). Bistro-style meals and a good wine selection are available in this centrally located hotel dating from 1851.

Shrimps ($$) 72 George Street (tel: 003 34 0584). This popular establishment, located in a National Trust classified building in the town center, serves excellent seafood—mussels, oysters, Atlantic salmon, sea trout.

Squires ($) 70 Brisbane Street (tel: 003 34 1466). Just down the arcade opening off this central street, Squires serves delicious local seafood and game dishes.

Woofies ($$) Macquarie House, Civic Square (tel: 003 34 0695). In another historic building in the heart of town, this restaurant has a good choice of attractively priced dishes.

Index

283

INDEX

INDEX